AMERICAN COACH

AMERICAN COACH

The Triumph and Tragedy of Notre Dame Legend FRANK LEAHY

IVAN MAISEL

GRAND CENTRAL

New York Boston

Cover design by Greg Mollica
Cover photograph by INP photo, Library of Congress, Prints & Photographs Division

Grand Central Publishing
Hachette Book Group
1290 Avenue of the Americas, New York, NY 10104
grandcentralpublishing.com
@grandcentralpub

First Edition: September 2025

Grand Central Publishing is a division of Hachette Book Group, Inc. The Grand Central Publishing name and logo is a registered trademark of Hachette Book Group, Inc.

The publisher is not responsible for websites (or their content) that are not owned by the publisher.

Grand Central Publishing books may be purchased in bulk for business, educational, or promotional use. For information, please contact your local bookseller or the Hachette Book Group Special Markets Department at special.markets@hbgusa.com.

Library of Congress Cataloging-in-Publication Data has been applied for.

ISBN: 9780306835780 (hardcover), 9780306835803 (ebook)

Printed in the United States of America

LSC-C

Printing 3, 2025

To Freida Gutlow Maisel (1928–2023)
Business Pioneer
Strict Grammarian
Woman of Valor
Thanks, Mom.

CONTENTS

AMERICAN COACH

CHAPTER ONE

A NAME IN A RECORD BOOK

THEY CAME FROM NEAR AND FAR TO THE GLEAMING NEW ATHLETIC & Convocation Center at Notre Dame to honor the football coach they once called The Master.

The calendar said that Frank Leahy was sixty years old on that last night of January 1969. One look at Leahy would have labeled the calendar a fabulist. He still stood erect, five foot eleven, and his waistline barely had wavered from those postwar days when he strode the Fighting Irish sideline, an American celebrity at the peak of his command. But the crevasses in Leahy's face, the ruddy cheeks, and the thinning gray hair indicated the ravages taken by time and leukemia.

Once he had radiated a fiery mettle fueled by his desperate need for success. In many ways, Leahy personified the American Dream narrative that served as the backbone of national culture for most of the twentieth century. He had come from nothing. He had worked hard, gone to church, used football to go to college, married the right girl, climbed the coaching ladder, all at a furious pace. He was a head coach at thirty, the Notre Dame head coach at thirty-two, a national champion as a player and a coach.

As a player, he took motivation from the doubts of a hometown friend who told Leahy that he would never make it at Notre Dame. As a coach, the more Leahy won, the more pressure he applied to himself to match public demand. Leahy drove his players hard, and in return they played so fiercely that his Fighting Irish teams lived with accusations of dirty play. They fought hard because Leahy demanded it. He tried so hard to live up to the Notre Dame legacy of success that losing devastated him. At the end, winning did, too.

When he played, his drive cost him his health. His body could not withstand what he put it through. Leahy won a job as a starting tackle in the preseason of his junior year, yet the number of games he actually started in his Notre Dame career could be counted on one hand. When he coached, his drive cost him his health again, which in turn cost him his coaching career at the age of forty-five, cost him the one job he ever really wanted.

Fifteen years to the day after Leahy and Notre Dame parted ways, he wore a red blazer, a crisp white shirt, and what in his later years had become his trademark bow tie. Leahy long ago had given up wearing a traditional necktie. So many times in a restaurant, a fan had interrupted Leahy's meal. The coach, ever polite, would stand in greeting and drag the bottom of his necktie through his soup.

More than a thousand guests came to the dinner at twenty dollars a plate, back when that was a good portion of a daily wage in South Bend. A short story in *The South Bend Tribune* announcing the dinner elliptically explained that it would not be stag. "Inviting the ladies represents a policy departure from most affairs of this sort," the newspaper said.

They came, men and women but mostly men, to honor Leahy and to benefit him (those blood transfusions weren't cheap), to remind him and surely themselves of who he had been, what he had meant to them.

And they wanted to remind others, namely the men who for more than a decade had refused to vote Leahy into the College Football Hall of Fame.

No coach in the last forty years had been more singularly identified with his university than Leahy had been with Notre Dame. He loved the campus, loved the statue of Our Lady (English translation of Notre Dame) atop the Golden Dome, loved it from the day he first laid eyes on it as an eighteen-year-old freshman in the winter of 1927. Like so many Catholic boys in small towns and big cities across America, Leahy, a shy innocent from the South Dakota prairie, had dreamed of playing for the great Knute Rockne. Unlike nearly all of those boys, not only did Leahy play for Rockne, but when a knee injury ended his career, he became his coach's protégé. Rockne saw not only the hunger in Leahy but a keen mind for the game. The coach arranged for his protégé to become an assistant coach at Georgetown. Three months later, Rockne would be gone, perishing in a plane crash on a Kansas farm.

Leahy spent one season at Georgetown before moving to Michigan State and then to Fordham, where he attracted acclaim for developing the offensive front forever known as the Seven Blocks of Granite. One of those blocks, a squat Italian with a quick temper named Vince Lombardi, became a coach, too.

In the winter of 1939, at the age of thirty, Leahy became head coach at Boston College, where he took a commuter school that consisted of four buildings (none of them dorms) and in two seasons went 20-2, including an 11-0 record in 1940 that concluded with a 19–13 upset of mighty Tennessee in the Sugar Bowl.

But Notre Dame came calling, literally the same day that Leahy signed a five-year extension with the Eagles. Eleven days later, Leahy left Boston College and that new contract behind. This was Notre Dame, his school, the school that had taken in a poor boy and made him a man.

Rockne, by dint of his success and a personality born for marketing, had put Notre Dame on the American cultural map. Rockne fomented the image of a small Catholic university in a remote Midwestern town as the premier college football program in the nation. It is easy now, with the benefit of hindsight, to see Notre Dame as a monolithic power in college football for most of the twentieth century. But in January 1941, you could make the case that Notre Dame's success during Rockne's thirteen seasons belonged to the coach, not the school. In the ten seasons after Rockne's death, Notre Dame neither went undefeated nor won a national championship. Two head coaches tried and failed to maintain the Fighting Irish at the level to which Rockne had taken them.

If Notre Dame had not hired Leahy—and the decision didn't happen until Santa Clara head coach Buck Shaw took himself out of consideration; his wife, Marge, said that she would rather live in a tent in California than a castle in Indiana—who can say Rockne's greatness would have been handed down? California dominated the years before Rockne peaked, Minnesota the years after his death, and both have rarely been heard from again. A school changes. The sport changes.

But Leahy returned to his alma mater, bristling with energy, and made Notre Dame Notre Dame again, not only restoring Fighting Irish football to its pedestal but transferring the imprimatur of winning from Rockne to the university. Only two years into his tenure, a fellow coach declared that Leahy belonged in the same breath as Rockne.

Pittsburgh coach Clark Shaughnessy came to South Bend to speak in 1943, days after Leahy won his first national championship. "I was a contemporary of Knute Rockne and was proud of my friendship with him," Shaughnessy said. "There never was a man like Rock for his all-around influence on football. Now I'm going to close by saying that Frank Leahy is his old coach's peer, and future events will bear me out."

They did. When Leahy retired from Notre Dame after the 1953 season, he had the second-best record in the history of the game (107-13-9, .864), second only to Rockne.

Rockne went undefeated five times in thirteen seasons at Notre Dame.

Leahy did so six times in only eleven seasons.

In the seventy-one seasons since Leahy's retirement, the Irish have finished the regular season undefeated only five more times.

Leahy also won four Associated Press national championships (an award that the AP didn't give in Rockne's time).

Red Grange, the Galloping Ghost who became an American icon during the Roaring Twenties as an All-American back at Illinois, became an analyst in the early days of college football telecasts, which also happened to be the prime of Leahy's championship run at Notre Dame. In that era Grange called Leahy "the greatest college football coach who ever lived. He's greater than Knute Rockne ever thought of being and I'm not knocking old Rock... They complain and say that he [Leahy] teaches dirty football and all that silly talk. The reason they complain is that Leahy is superior and he wins. They steer clear of Notre Dame for one reason: Frank Leahy. They don't want to get beat."

As Leahy made the Irish dominant again, he made himself into an American colossus, one of the best-known sports figures in a postwar nation craving a return to normalcy. In the years after World War II, major American sports consisted of Major League Baseball and college football. The New York Yankees and Notre Dame became synonymous with greatness, interchangeable icons, loved by their faithful and hated by every other fan in America. From 1946 through 1953, the Yankees won six World Series and Notre Dame won three national championships. The Fighting Irish didn't lose a game from 1946 to 1949, then handed the baton to the Yankees, who didn't lose a World Series from 1949 to 1953.

Daring to compare one to the other, one New York columnist described the Fighting Irish's annual game against Army in Yankee Stadium as "the top annual sports event in the country's greatest city." Again, this is in an era when the Yankees made the World Series almost every October. During this postwar run, Leahy made the cover of *Time* magazine, celebrity real estate typically reserved for political leaders and authors. "In the old culture," essayist Lance Morrow wrote, appearing on the cover of *Time* served as "a secular version of being beatified by the Catholic Church." If you read the pages of *Time* and of *Life*, the picture-laden newsweekly also published by Time, Inc., you would have thought that Notre Dame was the only American university with a football team.

Leahy succeeded just as the GI Bill poured billions into American higher education, and just as postwar anti-Catholicism surged. Catholics across the country clung to the Fighting Irish as a ticket to assimilation. Nuns lit candles for football success. As a significant portion of American life centered on universities, Leahy cemented Notre Dame's stature as not only the most prominent Catholic university but a symbol of athletic greatness. Author Mark S. Massa pegged the high-water mark of American Catholic self-confidence, cultural influence, and optimism to the decade after World War II, when Bishop Fulton J. Sheen captivated television viewers and Notre Dame football captivated everyone else.

Leahy's successes bolstered the university so that it could take advantage of its football renown to transform into the premier Catholic institution of American higher learning. In theory, it's not impossible for football dominance to exist on the same campus as academic prowess. In reality, when Notre Dame football toppled off its pedestal in 1950, losing eight games over three seasons, no one had to look far to find the culprit. Father Theodore Hesburgh, then the university vice president, was as confident as he was dynamic. Hesburgh wanted to shift Notre Dame's focus toward academia. "Father Ted" capitalized on Leahy's football success even as he stunted it. He used the spotlight that shone on the university because of football even as he reined in Leahy. Hesburgh wanted to illustrate to the coach (and the world at large) which was the dog and which was the tail.

The friction between two ambitious men who envisioned Notre Dame from opposite poles put neither man in a favorable light. Leahy, as his team tumbled from four consecutive undefeated seasons to a 4-4-1 record in 1950, never fully trusted Hesburgh again. Hesburgh, as driven in his dream as Leahy had been in his, became as successful in making Notre Dame a world-class university as Leahy had been in restoring Notre Dame football to greatness. Hesburgh ascended to the presidency of Notre Dame in 1952, a job he would hold for thirty-five years. In later life Hesburgh felt remorse about his relationship with Leahy. He would give voice to that remorse at the dinner honoring the former coach at the new Athletic & Convocation Center.

"You battled a lot of odds," the priest, looking down the dais, said to Leahy, "including me."

That dinner took place three weeks after the College Football Hall of Fame announced its newest coach. No one could quibble with the choice of former Oklahoma head coach Bud Wilkinson, who won three national championships and lost only twenty-nine games in seventeen seasons with the Sooners. Yet even Wilkinson went 0-2 against Leahy, who, in failing health, again would have to wait for one more January.

Year after year, the Honors Court, the committee made up largely of former coaches entrusted with selecting former players and coaches for the Hall, met to consider Leahy and passed him over. It wasn't just that the Honors Court selected men with poorer coaching records—after all, the only better record belonged to Rockne. It was that the Honors Court selected coaches who barely won more than they lost, and in one case (Tuss McLaughry, 1962) lost more than he won. They selected coaches whom Leahy defeated regularly until they refused to play Notre Dame any longer. The American Football Coaches Association never gave Leahy its highest honor, the Amos Alonzo Stagg Award.

The fact was, in case it needs to be spelled out, Leahy didn't have many friends in what is referred to as the coaching fraternity. "He lost only 11 games in 11 years against competition Rockne never dreamed of," wrote Jim Murray, the iconic columnist at the *Los Angeles Times*. "He did it in such a charming way there wasn't a football coach in the country who wouldn't have cheerfully bought him a drink—of arsenic." Leahy's celebrity did not alter the introvert inside, and when he spoke, he did so with an off-putting formality. His diction was the envy of every high school speech teacher, and he used vocabulary as if getting paid by the syllable. Leahy came off as unctuous, especially when he professed a public pessimism that sounded more like condescension. Any coach who scouted Notre Dame understood the level of talent that Leahy recruited. Yet he would predict three losses a season (or, before one undefeated season, seven), and often he believed his own pessimism.

When Leahy went to coaching clinics and conventions, he didn't close the hotel bar with the other coaches. He rarely had more than a social drink (save for one desperately unhappy period after coaching) and didn't smoke. And it wasn't just that Leahy beat the other coaches every fall. It was the way he did it. The saying was that Rockne beat you and after the game threw his arm across your shoulder and made you laugh and, gee, what a great guy. Even when Leahy lifted his foot off the accelerator, his teams still dominated. "They not only beat you," said a coach of the day, Pappy Waldorf, "but ruin your team for the next weekend."

Waldorf went 0-4 against Leahy. He was elected to the Hall of Fame in 1966.

Leahy had a few champions. The ABC broadcaster Chris Schenkel, an Indiana native, pushed for his election. The testimonial dinner had been the brainchild of Bob McBride, who returned from a German POW camp to resume his playing career for Leahy, and then became his most devoted assistant. McBride would recall how every single invitee to the dinner, no matter his celebrity, insisted on paying his own way. Some 150 former players returned to campus that night to pay tribute, men in middle age who loved Leahy for the reasons they once hated him. As demanding as he had been, Leahy was never a dictator, just haunted by perfection.

The coach's four Heisman Trophy winners—five if you count Paul Hornung, whom Leahy signed but never coached on the varsity—lined up alongside him on the dais for a photo. Players from his two seasons at Boston College came, too, including George Kerr, who graduated from the interior line to the priesthood.

The Massachusetts House of Representatives, in awarding Leahy an official citation presented at the dinner, proclaimed: "[I]n recognition of his masterful coaching ability and supreme contribution to the youth of America, Coach Leahy richly deserves to be enrolled in Football's Hall of Fame."

Telegrams poured in from Leahy's friends, men whose fame he had once matched, from former President Dwight Eisenhower (less than two months before his death) to Governor Ronald Reagan of California to Supreme Court Associate Justice Byron White, from entertainer Bing Crosby to Cardinal Richard Cushing of Boston to Chicago Mayor Richard J. Daley. Wintry weather limited retired Army coach Earl "Red" Blaik, Leahy's greatest rival in the 1940s, to a wire. In five games against Notre Dame, Blaik's Black Knights scored a total of seven points, that touchdown coming in the third quarter of the fifth game, when Army trailed, 20–0.

"The reason Red didn't show up," Johnny Lujack, the 1947 Heisman winner and Leahy's greatest player, said in his remarks, "was he thought he'd be shut out again tonight."

There were jokes, of course, but many more tributes. "It was not only a privilege to play for you," Lujack said to Leahy, "but also a great thrill just to have known you."

Sid Luckman, the former Chicago Bears quarterback whom coach George Halas dispatched to South Bend in 1942 to teach Leahy the T formation, recalled the twenty-hour days the two of them put in together. Leahy, Luckman said, flipped the relationship. "From the bottom of my heart I say that I never learned as much football as I did from Coach Leahy during that time. He exacted the best and last ounce from his men. In turn he gave his best."

Ara Parseghian, then the current Notre Dame head coach who had restored the Irish to the greatness they had not known since Leahy's departure, said, "My offseason duties take me into every part of this country on speaking engagements and at every gathering I address, after current and routine topics are disposed of, there always surfaces the recitation and discussions of the great deeds of Frank Leahy."

Former Georgia coach Wally Butts, Leahy's closest friend in the game, called him "the greatest of them all. And he belongs in the Hall of Fame." Yet that endorsement paled before the one that came from the Notre Dame president, the official who had ushered Leahy out the door those fifteen years earlier.

Hesburgh recalled to Leahy how he coached with "chin out and a glint in your eye, instilled dedication, drive, discipline, and character in your players so that while they may have groused some at the time, there developed in them a great pride that will remain in them forever."

Hesburgh, who knew how to deliver a homily, said, "If Leahy isn't named to the Hall, the whole idea seems to be useless . . . Frank Leahy, you are long overdue in Football's Hall of Fame!"

The cheer that arose from the floor and bounced off the walls of the Convocation Center woke up the echoes of cheers for Leahy's teams long before.

Soon the guest of honor stood to speak. That very day, the Associated Press reported, some five hundred North Vietnamese troops attacked an American base forty-three miles northwest of the South Vietnamese capital of Saigon. Leahy, as he often did in his paid speaking gigs, railed against the Communist menace to American society. But soon he turned to the reason that the Convocation Center had filled on this twenty-nine-degree night. Leahy paraphrased Apollo 8 astronaut Jim Lovell, who had just become one of the first three men to orbit the moon and then spoken to a joint session of the US Congress. "Have I really been there? It's so hard to believe," Leahy said.*

* Lovell told that joint session of the US Congress, "I stepped out of the house a few days later and looked up at the moon and I could scarcely believe that I was there."

He began to employ his trademark flowery language in his round, lyrical tone.

"My thoughts often go back to this place," Leahy said, "to coming here to play for Rockne, to the day I was told I would be coming back to the campus to direct the gridiron forces of my alma mater.

"I never thought anything this nice would happen to me. But let me tell you this, with all the sincerity that I can command, that none of this would be possible if it weren't for the truly wonderful players and assistant coaches that it was my great fortune to work with here on the campus of Our Lady."

Leahy regularly exhorted his players to "pay the price." He certainly did. The stress of meeting the standard of success of Notre Dame fans and of Leahy himself extracted a costly toll on his health and on his family. The married father of eight, who put his wife and family in a palatial home thirty minutes from campus, spent football seasons sleeping on a cot in the campus firehouse. He spent the other nine months of the year coaching and tending to the celebrity side of his life. Leahy traveled to numerous coaching clinics per year, more interested in learning than in teaching. He made speeches to Notre Dame clubs across America and to plenty of other clubs as well.

"Dad belonged to the world," his son Fred once said, "and Mom had eight kids."

Even in the 1950s, when the word "housewife" was a description and not an epithet, the marriage of Frank and Florence Leahy felt the strain of his absence, a strain manifested in her alcoholism and his stress-induced illnesses. Several times over the course of his adult life, Leahy suffered from what was labeled "nervous exhaustion" or a "nervous breakdown." The American Dream had a dark side, the side that authors such as F. Scott Fitzgerald and Arthur Miller had revealed. Frank Leahy, who tried and succeeded more than millions of others to live his life in superlatives, paid a price for success. Turns out that Leahy was human.

By the 1953 season, Leahy's health problems became so severe that he collapsed in the locker room at halftime of the Georgia Tech game. A campus priest summoned from the stands administered Leahy the last rites of the Catholic Church. He had suffered an attack of pancreatitis, exacerbated by stress. Leahy recovered well enough to finish out the season, coaching the Irish to a 9-0-1 record and No. 2 ranking. But he was cooked and he knew it.

Today, as intercollegiate athletics undergoes its most wrenching changes in generations, Notre Dame stands among a handful of schools—Stanford, Northwestern, Virginia, Duke—that continue to represent the beau ideal of universities that strive to achieve academic and athletic success. If Notre Dame sacrificed Leahy on the altar of academia, it's way past time to recognize his success anew.

Amid all the hosannas he received from the writers who had covered his greatest successes, one columnist paused. Furman Bisher of *The Atlanta Constitution* would go on to become a legendary figure in sports journalism, a man who wrote for six decades. At that time, he was a thirty-five-year-old columnist just beginning to make a name for himself. "Any football coach who can survive 13 years with an average of one defeat per season is threatening immortality," Bisher wrote. "Rockne was already an immortal, anyway, but the tragic way in which he died ballooned his stature.

"It may or may not come to Leahy. That may depend on how he conducts himself from here on out... [I]t seems incredible that he should be walking out on the biggest job in his field. But when the agony begins to kill, it's time to go. It won't be known for awhile yet if he has won the immortality he worked for so fiercely."

Leahy lived for twenty years after retirement from Notre Dame, a period in which he found that the agony came from within, not from football. His battle with stress prevented him from accepting other coaching jobs. He made a lot of money and lost nearly as much, proving that as a businessman, he was nothing more than a former football coach. Leahy died in 1973, slipped away at age sixty-five, and the fame and celebrity that once dictated his life did not survive his demise.

Today, Rockne remains a touchstone of the university campus. The outsized personality of Lou Holtz continues to hover over Notre Dame football a generation after his resignation as head coach. Leahy's players, the men who tried to keep his legacy alive, are gone, too. Leahy, seven decades after his resignation and five decades after his death, has become a name in a record book. But if there had been no Leahy, there's no guarantee there would be the Notre Dame football that college football fans continue to love—and hate. Leahy left an enormous impression on the Notre Dame campus. He came so far. He would not fail.

CHAPTER TWO

VOW ON THE SPOT

THE DETAILS OF FRANK LEAHY'S CHILDHOOD HAVE ONE FOOT IN AN earlier America, the Wild West of John Ford's films, of Zane Grey's fiction. Leahy grew up on the prairie, with enough cowboy in him that as an adolescent he drove horses and worked as a cowhand. But he also fell in love with sports, a love that would marry with his fierce drive to succeed. Given the life that would unfold before him, it's easy to surmise that Leahy's drive to succeed dominated that marriage, overwhelmed the football side of him, and brought him fame and wealth as it wrecked his health. Lost in that dark view is Leahy's sincere desire to live a proper life according to the tenets of his Catholic Church and of society. Life is rarely black-and-white.

Francis William Leahy was born on August 27, 1908, in O'Neill, Nebraska, a first-generation American. It may be redundant to say that his ancestors endured great hardship to establish a life in the pioneer days of the nineteenth century. Life on the unsettled Canadian and American prairies did not allow much in the way of comfort.

Great-grandfather Patrick Leahy, a laborer from the southern coast of Ireland, came to Canada on the ship *Fortitude* in 1825. Land in Upper Canada was plentiful, and in the years after the War of 1812, it seemed like a good idea to the Brits to get more able-bodied subjects of King George IV over to Canada, just in case those upstart Americans got any ideas about crossing the border and starting another skirmish.

Patrick's youngest son, Michael, immigrated south to Iowa farmland with his wife, Bridget, and their family in 1869. Francis Patrick, the fourth of what would eventually be ten children, was five years old. In 1883, the Leahy clan moved to another farm, 375 miles west, near Wisner, Nebraska. Francis, known as Frank, would marry Mary Kane, whose family had moved to Nebraska from Scranton, Pennsylvania, and they got a piece of farmland of their own.

Francis and Mary named their first two boys Eugene (Gene) and John (Jack). They didn't name a son after Frank until Boy Number Three and even then gave him a different middle name. Francis William Leahy, the sixth of eight children, also would be known as Frank. His younger sister Margaret remembered the family calling him Bud as a child to differentiate him from his father (the nickname appears nowhere else in family memoirs or the volume of profiles written about Coach Frank Leahy). The different middle name didn't cause the emotional gulf between father and son, but it certainly characterized it.

"I never got much in the way of academic or career achievement from my father," Francis William said. "He was a huge giant of a man, perfectly constructed, and I'm convinced he had the mental potential of a genius. People used to come in his cream station and bet him that he couldn't define a certain word in Webster's Dictionary—a standing bet he had with everyone in town—and I never heard anyone stump him."

In a world where men often settled disputes themselves, the elder Frank looked for disputes to settle. He became known for his wrestling. His best friend was the heavyweight champion wrestler Martin (Farmer) Burns. The elder Frank Leahy was one of the few, if not the only, men to defeat Burns in the stick-pull, which is about what it sounds like. Two competitors face each other on the floor, legs outstretched so that the soles of their shoes meet. They grab the same heavy stick, (say, a pick handle) and they commence pulling until one of them is off-balance or loses his grip.

"When I was sixteen," Tom Leahy, the youngest of the four Leahy boys, said, "I thought I was a pretty good wrestler and I took on my father, who was sixty-eight. He threw me before I knew the match had started."

If the elder Leahy was itching for a fight, maybe it was to vent his frustration. Twice he washed out as a farmer. After the first time in Nebraska, he spent some time running a tavern. Then he moved to Roundup, Montana, and sent for Mary and the children. "How she ever made the trip with the six of us and retained her sanity will always be the eighth wonder of the world to me, for Frank was a baby in her arms," recalled Gene, who was twelve at the time.

The elder Frank found that the Montana altitude didn't agree with him. He entered a government lottery distributing prairie land in southwestern South Dakota and won the chance to homestead again. After a year in Montana, the family moved to the new town of Lamro, South Dakota, in the dead of winter. They found a foot of snow and a severe winter on the southwest South Dakota prairie. The Leahys spent that winter in a tent with a wooden floor and walls but a canvas roof.

The land in South Dakota proved to be more conducive to ranching than to farming. Gene recalled the winter weakening their cattle so badly that they couldn't climb out of the creek on their own. He would help his dad back the wagon up to the creek, wrap a chain around an animal's horns, and pull him out.

"One day, one of them was down near our barn," Gene said, "and Frank, then but two years old, walked out to where the critter was and tried to get on its back, when we discovered it all and got him away from there. The critter was too weak to harm him or he might have been killed."

As a toddler and a young boy, Frank Leahy fully engaged the curiosity God gives children. When Gene taught him how to hammer a nail, Frank proceeded to do so into everything in the house that didn't move. One Sunday morning, when his parents went to church, Frank went into the family barn and found some matches. Wonder what happens when you light one?* He lit the hay on fire, and within minutes the fire consumed a team of mules, four sets of harnesses, the granary, some furniture, the barn, and nearly young Frank as well. The neighbors reported seeing him run out just before the roof collapsed. As the story was told and retold throughout Frank's childhood, it never stopped embarrassing him. Finally, as his mother, Mary, told the tale again, from the next room Frank piped up.

"Mom, if you will forget about that barn, I'll build you a new one someday."

She never spoke of it within his earshot again.

The Leahys moved up the road from Lamro to the next town over, also new, called Winner. By then the elder Frank Leahy had given up farming for good and began a freight business. He served the local taverns by delivering them full kegs of beer and hauling out the empty ones. He would barter with farmers along his route.

"My dad would buy cream and eggs and cowhides from the neighboring farmers, and in exchange would sell them such things as flour, wheat and grain. I well remember Dad rousing me out of bed at six o'clock in the morning to help lift flour sacks," Frank said.

Young Frank got his first job on a neighbor's farm at age six, making a dollar a day, and by the time he grew big enough to be effective,

---

* How old Frank Leahy was when he burned down the barn is lost to history. Gene remembered him being a toddler. Margaret remembered him being seven.

he made five dollars per day as a cowhand. As a boy, he often said his goal was to grow up to be a millionaire. Not that he didn't enjoy what money could buy. Gene recalled giving Frank twenty-five cents to spend at a carnival that came to Winner. Frank disappeared into the crowd. When the Leahys decided to leave, Frank was nowhere to be seen. He had spent his entire quarter on tickets to ride the carousel, and there he stayed, in circular bliss, until Gene found him.

Frank showed his maturity early. As a ten-year-old, he saw one of his friends struggling to keep his head above water in a pond and coolly swam out to save him. About that time, Frank* and a friend got a job to take a dozen horses 150 miles west-northwest to Washabaugh County. The boys got about halfway there when they lost the horses. They found them in a local livery stable, where they reclaimed them, but not without having to confront the woman who had the horses put there after they tore up her garden. The woman insisted that the boys pay for the damages, which took every dollar they had. They had no money or food as they drove the horses for two more days to deliver them. Frank stayed in Washabaugh County for the rest of the summer, working jobs for a buck a day, before returning home awash in homesickness.

In his teens, he worked as a clerk for his dad, as a soda jerk at the Morosco sweet shop, and as a clerk at the Outlaw Trading Post in Winner that served the Rosebud reservation. He learned to speak enough Lakota to transact business with the Sioux in their language.

Frank proved to be a dutiful son but what looking after he got from a male in the family came from Gene. All the Leahy boys proved to be talented wrestlers and boxers; Gene proved to be a skilled baseball and football player as well. He went to Creighton University, the Jesuit school in Omaha, where he played both sports. He took great pride in the letter sweater he won there, until Frank discovered it and began playing football in it, stretching it so much as to make it unwearable.

---

* Arch Ward, the first Leahy biographer, claimed that Leahy was ten; writer Francis Wallace wrote that Leahy was sixteen.

Gene forgave him, because he realized the remarkable innate gifts his little brother had for athletics.

"He was ever anxious to learn," Gene said, "so I spent a lot of time with him, trying to teach him the technique of passing, punting, and football in general, and also baseball. He was a great student, and never had to be told anything more than once. Of all the kids I ever tried to teach, he learned the quickest and retained what he learned."

Years later, Knute Rockne would say almost the same thing.

Frank was big for his age, and, if not clumsy, then not very agile. He came to Gene one day, nearly in tears, bemoaning how nearly every kid in school could outrun him, and what could he do about it. Nearly a century earlier, *Fortitude* had brought Leahy's ancestors to a new life, and Gene decided the same attribute would fill in the gaps left by Leahy's inability to run.

"Don't mind that, Frank," Gene said. "Courage will take you where speed don't dare tread, and these same kids who are outrunning you now will be reading about you someday."

Frank had courage, all right. He told the story many times that when he got home from school, his father would ask him, "Did you get into a fight today?" When Frank said no, his father would warn him, "Don't come home tomorrow without having one." The elder Frank Leahy usually said that to get a rise out of his wife, who did not like fighting. The Leahy boys didn't go looking for a fight, but they took on any fight that came their way. Gene was a big, graceful athlete, and Frank became the most storied, but the four brothers agreed that Jack, who weighed but 165 pounds, was the fiercest, toughest fighter among them. Frank might have voted for his older sister Eileen, whom Gene described as "a wildcat in a scrap." She and Frank once fought each other in the ring, where her uppercut split his nose wide open.

Nonetheless, it was Frank who their father believed had the size and skills to develop into a boxing champion. Frank had a lot more interest in football. "He was a brilliant person," Frank said of his father, "but I could never derive anything from him in the way of encouragement to do anything but become a fighter. I was never totally convinced it was the right road for me and as time went on I became more and more obsessed with football, much to my father's dismay."

In eighth grade, Frank weighed upward of 185 pounds, enough size to attract the attention of the football coach at Winner High. He got a uniform, but he rarely got a spot on the field. So Leahy hatched a plan. Jack Crowley, a young man new to Winner, was sweet on one of Leahy's sisters. He also refereed Winner High's football games. Frank badgered Crowley to eject one of the Winner players from a game so that Frank could play. Crowley did so more than once, Leahy recalled, which allowed him to learn the game as he played it. When the local power, Gregory High, defeated Winner, 108–0, Leahy remembered Winner's one kickoff, to start the second half. "I thought my job was to go down the field and, instead of tackling the ball-carrier, block one of their interferers," Leahy said. "I thought this wonderful. I fell down and someone fell over me. I thought, 'Gee, this is great. We're really picking up here. I got my man.' But he didn't have the ball."

Frank played whatever was in season for Winner High, and, at the direction of his father, he continued to box. When Frank came home with his letter sweater for football and moved right into basketball, his father mocked him. "What do they give you for that? A kimono?" The elder Frank saw to it that his boys had a heavy bag on which to work out, and he continued to harbor the dream that Frank would become a professional fighter. The elder Leahy, now about sixty years old, suffered from arthritis sufficiently that he no longer conquered anyone who dared challenge him. A big man came into town from north of Winner and set out for the elder Leahy, who got the worst of it, at least until young Frank got home from school. Dad enlisted his son to finish the fight, and off they went in search of the man. He would regret agreeing to fight this boy. Young Frank ended the fight in two punches.

All of which encouraged his father, who, at one point, according to Margaret, came home one day and announced that he had signed Frank up for a professional fight back in O'Neill. Mrs. Leahy had heard enough. She intended for Frank to graduate from college. She knew he might have the talent to get a football scholarship, and she knew that a pro fight would cost Frank his amateur standing. She warned her husband that if he went through with this scheme, "I'll disgrace you by climbing into the ring to stop it."

Mr. Leahy backed down—sort of. On July 4, 1924, in an open-air arena in an O'Neill lumberyard, the Knights of Columbus put on an athletic program. In the next-to-last fight of the night, a local blacksmith named George Blaha, known as Silent because he was deaf, fought a young unknown named Frank Kane. That would be Frank Leahy, eight weeks shy of his sixteenth birthday; Kane, remember, was his mother's maiden name. The way Leahy told the story, his father got him the fight and Frank made a hundred dollars. The pseudonym, in place to protect his amateur standing, didn't exactly fool anyone. The homemade kelly green trunks that Leahy wore, a gift from the mother of a friend, sported the initials FWL.

"As soon as the bell rang I came out to meet this behemoth—he must have weighed 210 pounds—and as soon as we began I knew this was going to be a long afternoon," Leahy said.

Blaha knocked him down five times in the first round, knocking out a tooth to boot. Leahy said he didn't remember the first round, coming to only when he sat in his corner afterward. Leahy rallied a bit, and then unexpectedly was declared the winner in the third round because Blaha continued, after repeated warnings, to punch low. The referee, Hugh Coyne, a friend of Leahy's father, held up the hand of "Frank Kane" and announced, "Leahy wins on a foul!"

"I was a pro at that moment whether I liked it or not," Leahy said.

More than three decades later, Coyne remembered Leahy more than holding his own against the older fighter. Whatever happened, that fight served Leahy well. A look in the mirror the next morning—one eye swollen shut, lips puffy, cheeks scratched—convinced him to give up his father's boxing dream. More important, the realization that he had sagged during the fight because he wasn't in shape galvanized him throughout his coaching career to make sure that he had the better-conditioned team.

"Perhaps my reputation as a hard taskmaster stems from that fight with Silent Blaha," Leahy said. "I don't know. I only know—as I painfully knew for the first time that next morning—that a man can't expect himself to excel on the playing field without first excelling on the practice field."

Leahy continued to box, more as a means for conditioning than as an end unto itself. He sparred with Ace Hudkins, a noted welterweight known as "The Nebraska Wildcat" who in 1929 lost a world title bout on points. But Leahy dedicated himself to football. His father resented his choice, and Frank resented his father. Frank didn't understand how his father could be so smart and not use his intellect for anything more than freighting or selling eggs. Leahy wasn't much for introspection, but looking back at his life, he said, "I suppose that resentment along with the prospect of playing football was one of the forces behind my determination to get to Notre Dame."

Leahy became enamored with Notre Dame the way every American Catholic schoolboy did. Notre Dame served as a beacon of hope and pride for a population discriminated against in American society. But Leahy had the good fortune to land on the radar of two of Rockne's former players. First, the fortunes of Winner High reversed over the course of Frank's high school career, thanks to a new coach hired before Leahy's senior season. Earl Walsh, a former player for Rockne at Notre Dame, led Winner to a 10-0 record and a sectional championship. Leahy played fullback, called the signals, and captained the team. He captained the basketball and baseball teams, too. Walsh wrote a letter to Rockne to tell him about Leahy and his backfield mate, Clayton Balfany.

The other former Irish player, Tommy Mills, had coached Gene Leahy at Creighton. Mills had left the head coaching job at Creighton to work for Rockne. Gene Leahy wrote his old coach about Frank, and Rockne, who now had two letters about Leahy, offered scholarships to him and to Balfany.

Frank never wavered in his desire to go to Notre Dame, perhaps because Gene encouraged him to reach for his dream. Gene had had a chance to go to Notre Dame, too, but had chosen Creighton instead. He liked his time at Creighton, graduating from pharmacy school. He turned down jobs with drug companies to make a life in the Omaha area. He became a pharmacist in Rushville, Nebraska, where he played town baseball in the summer and hunted in the fall, got married, raised a family. But he understood the difference between playing for Creighton and playing for Rockne and the Fighting Irish. That became critical for Frank's future, because their mother didn't want her boy going to far-off Indiana for college, Rockne or no Rockne.

"I have a million dollars' worth of writeups while playing with Creighton, but who ever heard of me outside of Council Bluffs?" Gene recounted in his memoir. "I would rather Frank be a fifth-string waterboy under Rockne than a star player anywhere else." Gene told his mother that if Frank went to Notre Dame, Gene would fund him. But if she sent Frank somewhere else, not only would Gene not fund him, but Gene would never come home to South Dakota again.

"Most certainly Mother is well pleased that Frank attended Notre Dame," Gene understated.

Mary Leahy may have been thinking of her boy's well-being and her maternal love. Leahy didn't set out to prove himself at Notre Dame because of what his mother said. He went to prove his friend Clayton Balfany wrong.

One man's small talk becomes another's manifesto. Maybe Balfany expressed self-doubt hoping for encouragement. But that's not what happened. On the day that the Class of 1925 graduated from Winner High, Balfany told Leahy that he had decided not to go to Notre Dame. He had decided to stay home, to attend college in South Dakota. He wanted to play where he knew he would make the team, and possibly even excel.

"Then he looked me straight in the eye and told me I was crazy and not just a little dumb for thinking I could play football for Notre

Dame," Leahy said. "'Frank,' he said, in effect, 'You'll never make the team and you'll never be any good on the field, because you're too slow and too small. They'll probably laugh you out of the clubhouse when you show up for tryouts.'"

As Leahy recounted the story decades later, he remained irritated. In fact, he said the comment pretty much ended their friendship. But he acknowledged that he owed Balfany a great debt.

"I know that Balfany was right—I was too small, and I was too slow, especially for a halfback, which is the position I wanted to play and had played at Winner High School," Leahy said. "But he said it with such sincerity, and with such an attitude of defeatism, that I remember vowing on the spot that if I never did another thing for the rest of my life, by God I was going to play football for the Notre Dame varsity!"

That whatever-it-takes attitude is the reason that Frank didn't blink when Gene suggested coming down to Rushville for what we now call a gap year. Go to a better high school, play another year, get bigger, stronger, and faster, and pitch and play outfield on the town baseball team, too. Frank told Gene to find him a job that involved hard labor. Gene hooked Frank up with a local teamster, hauling rock, gravel, or whatever needed hauling. The first day, Frank stopped in Gene's drugstore for a drink of water.

"Gene, I know damned well I am going to college now, if this is the other alternative," Frank said.

Gene accelerated his introverted little brother's ascension into adulthood. He took him on a camping trip to Yellowstone National Park. He taught him how to hunt birds. Frank became an outstanding pitcher for the Rushville town team. Gene's friends took Frank in, even as they teased him to the point of embarrassment. One of them, Logan Musser, watched Frank fall down while chasing a fly ball and teased him about it for a long time. When Logan saw his niece Frances at a dance with Frank, he said, "Frances, don't ever marry that clumsy Irishman. He'll fall down on the way to the altar." Frank did not like being teased.

That fall, Leahy enrolled at Central High School in Omaha, and with the help of coach Pep Schmidt, got one job in the school cafeteria and another as a dance hall bouncer. That turned out to be kismet. Leahy's fellow bouncer was Jack Crowley, the football official who threw Winner players out of the game in order for Leahy to play (alas, the romancing of Leahy's sister didn't last). In the early going, plenty of patrons took Leahy on because he looked so young for a bouncer. Word got around fast not to mess with him.

At Central High, Schmidt moved Leahy to tackle, and the switch suited both him and the team, at least until word from Winner filtered south that Leahy had graduated from high school and had no more football eligibility. His Central career came to an abrupt halt. Leahy stayed in Nebraska, training for the fall of 1926, at least until Notre Dame informed him that the school would not have a scholarship for him until the spring quarter of 1927. That may be the earliest recorded incidence of "grayshirting" in college football history.

When the Notre Dame team train came through Omaha in December 1926 on the way home from the Irish's first-ever game at USC, Gene and Frank went to the station to meet them. Tommy Mills grabbed Frank and introduced him to his future teammates. It would be the biggest thrill in Frank Leahy's life for exactly two months. Frank caught the train in Rushville in February to go to Notre Dame. As he said his goodbyes, Logan Musser spotted him from across the street and gave him a going-away needle.

"Oh, Frank," Musser yelled. "Don't forget to get off the train in South Bend."

CHAPTER THREE

A CERTAIN COURAGE

LEAHY ONCE SAID THAT LIFE BEGAN FOR HIM ON THE FIRST DAY HE set foot on the campus of the University of Notre Dame—February 2, 1927, according to his transcript. He was eighteen years old and had just weathered a train trip in the dead of winter. He bundled up for the ride because he sat too far from the train car's pot-bellied stove to receive any warmth, as apt a metaphor as any for a shy incoming freshman who wanted to conquer his self-doubt and prove himself to the best football coach in the nation.

In Leahy's back pocket was a wallet, a high school graduation gift from the Larsons, his next-door neighbors in Winner. In the wallet was nineteen dollars, every cent Leahy had in the world.

Upon arrival in South Bend, Leahy waited in vain for a promised ride from Tommy Mills, who had gotten the date of arrival wrong and never showed up. After the passing of a good chunk of the evening, Leahy treated himself to a thirty-five-cent cab ride from the train station, an extravagance that Leahy would never forget because it would be the last money he spent for weeks. Hours later he discovered that his wallet and that nineteen-dollar bankroll had vanished.

There would be another memory from his arrival that stuck with Leahy for the rest of his life—the first time he laid eyes on the Golden Dome. It was winter, it was gray, it was a landscape of snow and ice, and it was everything Leahy hoped it would be. He felt a connection to his core, the Irish Catholic core that had rendered him an outsider in the America of his youth. Indiana, the home of the rebirth of the Ku Klux Klan in the 1920s, may have liked Catholics even less than did South Dakota or Nebraska. Indiana Governor Ed Jackson was a KKK member. But this small campus in the northwest corner of the state nonetheless served as a beacon and a haven for Catholic boys across the nation. In 1924, just three years earlier, some five hundred Notre Dame students disrupted a KKK parade in South Bend and prevented the organization from establishing a toehold in the city.

Leahy never forgot the pride he felt as he gazed upon the Dome and the ivy that covered what few campus buildings that existed. He dedicated himself to living a life that illustrated that "being Catholic was not wrong in America."

Life came at him fast—a dorm assignment to Carroll Hall, where his ten-foot-by-fifteen-foot space was partitioned by bedsheets; a dedicated desk and eating table in Carroll Hall; and a walk across campus to meet Mills and get practice gear. As he stood in the gymnasium talking to Mills, the head coach of the Fighting Irish strode out of his office. Mills waved Rockne over and introduced one of the most famous men in America to the introvert from South Dakota.

"Oh yes!" Rockne began. "It's Leahy, of course. Heard much about you from Earl Walsh. Hear you play football pretty well. They tell me you don't run as well as you hit people. Don't worry about speed. No trouble there. Speed isn't everything. You can play for Notre Dame if you want to hit people and win football games."

Rockne, whose genius resided as much in how he read people as it did in Xs and Os, began pumping up one more freshman desperately searching for his bearings.

"Feel scared as hell, don't you, Frank?" the coach began. "It's got to be tough. You'll get over that lost feeling in a couple of days. I did. Oh, God, did I feel like there wasn't a friend in the world! There are a lot of other fellows who feel just the same way. In a couple of weeks, when the snow's off the ground and Tommy here has you out on the field with the other freshmen, you'll think you never left South Dakota. If you need to talk to me in the meantime, I'll be around. I'm not one of those coaches who hides in the office. Four years from now when you're a senior, you'll see freshmen like yourself and you'll know how scared they feel. I never forgot."

Rockne eyeballed Leahy as he spoke. "You've got football players' legs, that's for sure."

Leahy might have floated back to Carroll Hall.

"If I was impressed with his name and his very presence," Leahy recalled late in life, "I was equally impressed with his warmth and smile. He was the kind of man who made you feel as if you'd known him for a long time."

LEAHY DID MAKE TWO QUICK FRIENDS WITH WHOM HE REMAINED CLOSE the rest of his life—Jack "Judge" Carberry, who from day one and forever more called him "Frankenstein," and Lawrence "Moon" Mullins. Carberry, of Ames, Iowa, had been told to keep an eye out for Leahy; Mullins was related to Earl Walsh. Mullins, a strapping fullback from Southern California who resembled Leahy, was the other freshman assigned to Leahy's eating table. By custom, Leahy and Mullins had to wait until the six upperclassmen at the table served themselves from the family-style meals. That first night, Bob Snell, the senior in charge of the table, tested Leahy and Mullins by giving them first dibs on the dessert, a bowl of strawberry ice cream meant to serve eight. Mullins took half, Leahy the other half, and they never received the privilege of going first again.

Leahy endured the doubts that every freshman football player has endured since the dawn of football time—the other players looked enormous, he was a long way from home, and two classes, Logic and Rhetoric, may as well have been taught in Greek for all he comprehended.

But Leahy had made it to Notre Dame from Winner. He thought of Gene's encouragement; he wasn't about to make Clayton Balfany's prophecy come true, and he kept at it.

"A man should always know there's someone out there who believes in him," Leahy said, looking back at his college days. "My brother Gene is a concrete example—I knew that he, down deep in his heart, was absolutely certain I'd get to the varsity at Notre Dame. If you know just one person truly believes in you, you're going to die before you'll let him down."

After spring practice began in March, Leahy decided to show he wouldn't quit. In those days long before the NCAA began to restrict practice time in the interest of player safety, Leahy tried to be the last man off the practice field. He had a lot of competition. Rockne, as a matter of principle, refused to cut any student who came for the team. Leahy recalled being one of about 250 players reporting for this eleven-man sport, and an inexperienced, nearly anonymous player at that.

"I got very lonesome very often, that spring," Leahy said.

As many players as there were, Rockne remembered every name and what position each one played. That made a big impression on Leahy, as did the opportunities that lay before him. A century ago, going to college was a privilege. In the late 1920s, less than 10 percent of people aged eighteen to twenty-four enrolled. Young people didn't look forward to college as a four-year party. Schools didn't cater to students with posh dorms and food courts. Leahy intended to do what he had to do to succeed. That included getting a job. He had no money coming in from home. After his wallet disappeared, he had no money, period.

Eugene "Scrapiron" Young, the senior who served as student employment foreman, had an office in the Brownson gym. One morning, two upperclassmen, Fred Miller and John McManmon, showed up with two young players in tow, one of them Leahy, to ask for work. Young told them to come back after classes. Leahy showed up first in Young's office. He described to Young his acquaintance with hard work from an early age. Young remembered Leahy for his lack of ego and his manner of speech: slow, careful, articulate, never a syllable swallowed.

Young put him and the other three to work performing tasks such as setting up and tearing down bleachers in the gym and lining the indoor and outdoor tracks. He paid Leahy forty cents an hour to do it. That's about $7.25 in modern dollars, and Leahy considered himself rich. He also began receiving a windfall because Studebaker, the auto manufacturer with headquarters in South Bend, began renting out the Brownson gym for their employees to use; Rockne charged Studebaker enough to provide well more than forty cents an hour to the four workers.

When Rockne found out that Miller had one of the jobs, he instructed Young to give Miller an alias for the work report filed with the university. Miller, who came from the Milwaukee family with the eponymous brewery, possessed an ebullient personality and a decided lack of entitlement. Rockne knew that if the campus priests found out a wealthy student had such a lucrative job, they would have instructed Rockne to take Miller off the payroll for someone in need.

More important, Scrapiron Young and Fred Miller began relationships with Leahy that would last for many years. In 1930, three years after Young graduated, Rockne hired him to become the Fighting Irish athletic trainer, a job he still held eleven years later when Leahy returned to campus as head coach. Miller would become Leahy's mentor, de facto older brother, assistant coach, business advisor, and, at the height of Leahy's fame, gatekeeper. Miller held all those roles in Leahy's life even as he transformed Miller Brewing Company from a regional brand to a national one. The combination of Leahy's introversion, his single-minded devotion to winning, and his celebrity made developing trustworthy friendships difficult. Miller made it his mission to be at Leahy's side whenever and for whatever he needed.

The gymnasium gig served Leahy as means to an end. He dedicated himself to making good grades and the obligation of daily Mass. He cut back on going to movies, cut back on whatever constituted a party on an all-male campus in the midst of Prohibition. Most of all, he focused on doing whatever he had to do to play football. In retrospect, it's easy to see in that focus the outline of the coach he would become. In the moment, he returned to Gene's home in Nebraska for the summer barely closer to his dream of playing for Rockne. But one semester in, the dream remained intact, even if he barely passed Rhetoric (70) and failed Logic (60). He made grades between 88 and 90 in three of his other four classes. Rockne had funneled Leahy into a major in physical education, and for four years he stayed afloat on that curriculum, even if he did go on academic probation twice in the 1927–28 school year.

Leahy spent the summer as a manual laborer at the Rushville train station, carrying hundred-pound sacks of dry goods such as sugar and rock salt from the depot to the town stores. In the afternoon he would practice and play baseball on the Rushville town team with Gene. He returned to Notre Dame in shape, with money, and presumably a new wallet in his pocket. Upon arrival, he was given a questionnaire to fill out for the athletic publicity office. For example:

Question: "Why did you come to Notre Dame?"
Answer: "On account of Knute Rockne."

The freshman team was a team in name only; Rockne scheduled no games for his first year players. They served as the scout team and daily practice fodder for the upperclassmen. There was a survival-of-the-fittest sense about the freshmen. With 250 players coming out for practice, if you couldn't take the punishment, there were always one or two or five others ready to take your place. Leahy played tackle on both sides of the line, both tortured and fueled by doubts of whether he would ever step on the actual playing field on an autumn Saturday. He never rose above second-string. He couldn't beat out a classmate named Art McManmon, the younger brother of Leahy's workmate John, who also happened to be the co-coach of the freshmen.

Many years later, after seeing freshmen step gingerly into his locker rooms for thirteen seasons, Leahy would marvel at those, like he did, who conquered their fears and inexperience and stuck their faces into the contact and learned they not only could survive but thrive.

"I'll never forget the day Coach Rockne called all the freshmen linemen over to tackle the varsity ballcarriers," Leahy recalled, "and I'm not at all ashamed to admit that when it came my turn to tackle the varsity player charging at me, I would have crawled under the ground and away from the scene had there been any possible way to do it. But I couldn't and I had to stay there and do the undesirable thing. I had to stay there and do the thing I was afraid to do—afraid physically, to a certain degree, afraid that I wouldn't be able to perform properly in the coaches' and players' eyes. Just plain frightened, and my knees were shaking and I was as scared as any human being could be. But it worked out, as it has so many millions of cases before and since, and as time wore on the fear subsided and a certain courage replaced it, a courage that enables a player to continue playing and to develop a certain excellence at the sport, knowing all the while that he can in fact do certain things that before he wasn't sure he was able to do."

Leahy called it one of the greatest lessons that football teaches.

One day at practice, Rockne wandered over to watch the freshmen. As he was about to return to the varsity, he said to the freshman coaches, John McManmon and John Wallace, "Why don't you try Leahy at center?"

Leahy felt seen, and he felt energized. If Rockne wanted him to try center, then by God he would try center. He went to trainer Pat Canny and badgered him for a football to take back to the dorm so he could practice. He cajoled his roommates, John Sullivan, and the

Kosky brothers, Ed and Frank, into lining up as a backfield. In the '20s, the handoff snap to the quarterback had yet to be invented. The center had to learn the correct pace and direction to deliver the ball to each of the four backs, sometimes after they had begun moving. Leahy so hounded the starting center, Tim Moynihan, for tips that eventually Leahy was told to leave him alone and just observe.

One night late in the season, Leahy went into the hallway at Carroll Hall and practiced long snaps to the punter. He launched the ball down the hall, well over the head of Sullivan, his intended "punter," and straight through a window at the end of the hallway. Leahy froze as Father Vincent Mooney, the priest in charge of Carroll Hall, arrived to find out what in blazes just happened. Mooney, to Leahy's good fortune, loved Rockne and loved the football team. He pretended to be mad, but with Leahy's promise to curtail his career as an indoor long snapper, dorm life moved on. With a new window.

Something happened off the field that gave Leahy not only a boost of flattery but a sense of belonging. Late in October of Leahy's first autumn on campus, without his knowledge or even his participation, a classmate nominated him as a candidate to be president of the freshman class. Throughout his long coaching career, Leahy would be criticized for being a politician; that is, always saying the "right" thing, never giving offense, etc. In his first fall at Notre Dame, he wasn't a politician at all. But he was an affable young man, good-looking, and he was a football player. He won the election, and the affirmation of his classmates did wonders for his feelings of isolation and homesickness.

Others noticed Leahy's leadership abilities. About the time that he was busy breaking windows, Notre Dame (5-0-1) went to Yankee Stadium in New York to play Army. In those days, the Academy filled its roster with players who came to West Point having already played for other universities; in 1927, that description applied to 62 percent of the Cadets. Army dominated the game, taking advantage of uncharacteristic mistakes by the Fighting Irish and the fast feet of Chris "Red" Cagle—one rushing touchdown, one receiving touchdown—to win, 18–0.

Notre Dame freshmen, being ineligible, didn't make the trip east. The next night, Leahy received a telegram in Carroll Hall from Canny, who told him that the team train arrived in South Bend at 5:45 a.m. Monday, and it would do the Fighting Irish a world of good if the student body awaited them. Leahy got going, and as the train pulled into South Bend, the band struck up the fight song and hundreds of students began waking up the echoes in that predawn hour. Leahy always said that was the moment he knew he belonged at Notre Dame.

Leahy found out that he could contribute on the field, too. In every spring, the coaching staff held skills competitions and awarded the winners with gold medals named for Frank E. Hering, who had played quarterback at the University of Chicago before attending law school at Notre Dame shortly before the turn of the century. Hering helped coach the Fighting Irish while enrolled. The coaches presented Hering Medals to players who, for example, displayed the most accurate passing, the longest punting, the fastest pulling by a guard, etc. In the spring of 1928, Leahy, who may have been participating in his second spring practice but had yet to be eligible for a varsity game, won the Hering Medal for center snaps. It served as tangible evidence, something he could take back to Rushville and hand to his brother Gene, that Leahy had a place in Notre Dame football. Long after he retired, Leahy described his Hering Medal as "one of my most prized possessions to this day, [so] you can well imagine what the award meant to me."

In practice on the last day before Easter vacation, Leahy got kicked in the eye during a scrimmage. He got stitched up and left on a hitchhiking trip to Ontario with the Kosky brothers and another classmate, quarterback Frank Carideo. On the trip home, they got caught in a cold spring rain; by the time Leahy got back to campus, he was so sick and his eye so troubled that he spent several days in the infirmary. He recovered in time to play in the spring game. Afterward, Rockne took time to praise Leahy in a way that indicated he saw something special in Leahy the young man as much as in Leahy the player.

"That Leahy was superlative," Rockne said. "There's a young man you can count on. Not the best football player around, but certainly one of the smartest. He'll be on the traveling squad next year. Be sure of that."

The writers may have been assured. Leahy was not. But first came the summer, when Leahy returned to Rushville and again depended on manual labor and baseball to remain in shape. He took a job crushing rocks for a contractor and pitched and played right field alongside Gene for the town team. Not only did they play towns like Hay Springs—Frank pitched Rushville to a 17–5 victory on July 3 and hit a home run in the holiday game the following day—but Leahy recalled playing a barnstorming team of Black players with a young pitcher named Satchel Paige. Perhaps he did, but in the summer of 1928, Paige was a second-year pitcher for the Birmingham Black Barons. Paige occasionally left the club during the season for lucrative side gigs, although a barnstorming tour through Nebraska hardly seems to qualify.

When the 1928 season began, Rockne had coached Notre Dame for ten seasons and lost only eight games. The Fighting Irish that season would lose half that many. A combination of key injuries and a lack of experienced depth hindered Notre Dame all season. Starting halfback John "Butch" Niemiec aggravated an old knee injury on the day before the opener, and the Irish had a surprisingly difficult time defeating Loyola (Maryland), winning 12–6.

Rockne even resorted to playing untested sophomores. Mullins moved into the starting lineup at fullback and showed signs of stardom. Leahy began the season as a third-string center, sometimes moving up to second-string. He played a few plays in that opener, an experience that filled him with pride for contributing to a Notre Dame victory.

The next week the Irish played at Wisconsin. Rockne took thirty-four players—three lineups and an extra quarterback—to an away game. Rockne wanted to reward the best performers in practice each week, so the travel roster wouldn't be posted until Thursday night. The list of players would be taped to the scale in the locker room. Rockne told Leahy of the decision in a backhanded way, asking him, "Ever eat a steak on a Pullman dining car, Frank?" But that didn't carry the emotional wallop of the list.

"With a squad of about 230 lads, the tension that mounted while waiting for the 34 names to be posted on the scales was almost unbearable," Leahy said late in life. "Of course, most of the fellows more or less knew who the first two teams would be, so it amounted to waiting to see whether you were selected for the remaining 12 out of 228 players." The thrill of seeing his name on that sheet of paper stayed with him for the rest of his life.

In midseason, after a couple of tackles suffered injuries, Rockne moved Leahy back to that position, where he backed up his buddy, team captain Fred Miller. It made an impression on Leahy that Rockne asked if he was interested in returning to tackle. He didn't order him to do it.

One of the few films that exists of Rockne coaching on the practice field shows the coach in a chair, to the left of the offensive backfield, his hands on his thighs. The quarterback calls the signals, the backs shift, and the center snaps the ball to the right halfback. Rockne zeroes in on one of the tackles.

"And you didn't get that man out here, Leahy. Get your head on the inside of him, Frank. Carry him out."

In another snippet, Rockne is standing behind the linemen, watching a play. "You *trail* on the line of scrimmage, Leahy, so he can't come through, and then go through to the secondary."

"Rock was fantastic on the practice field," Leahy said nearly four decades later. "He could be extremely complimentary. And ten seconds later, he'd be saying the most sarcastic, cutting words I had ever heard. Fortunately, he was a great psychologist. He knew exactly when to criticize and when to encourage."

Leahy remembered how Rockne dulled the sting of a coaching barb with natural wit. The coach loved the off-tackle run as a meat-and-potatoes portion of his playbook. Leahy, at right tackle, had to open a hole for Marchy Schwartz. Three times they ran the play in practice, and three times Schwartz failed to cross the line of scrimmage.

"Rockne called me over and let me have it," Leahy remembered. "He said, 'Leahy, I always knew you were a fine defensive tackle but I never knew how really fine a defensive tackle you were until just now. You've just succeeded in stopping three of our own plays while playing on offense."

The Irish had a 3-2 record as they prepared to play Penn State in Philadelphia (Franklin Field, the first American stadium with a second deck, had 78,000 seats; Beaver Stadium in State College had 30,000). On that road trip, Leahy heard Rockne's barbed tongue again. The Irish arrived in Philadelphia on Friday morning and went to the hotel. When the bus taking the team to Friday afternoon practice blew a tire, Leahy and Mullins went for a walk. They promptly got lost. When they finally found the hotel, they found their teammates milling about, waiting for them so that the team could leave on the bus for practice. Rockne let the two sophomores have it.

"Mullins, you have no excuse for this, because you were born and raised in a big city," the coach said. He turned to Leahy and said, "Leahy can be excused, though, because if you take the cow turds and horse manure away from him, he has no signposts."

Being a backup for Miller meant Leahy saw little playing time; Miller had no interest in leaving the field. The inactivity gnawed at Leahy, made him question whether he would prove Clayton Balfany wrong. His roommate, a free-spirited reserve end named Jonathan O'Brien, tried to buck up Leahy's spirits.

Leahy made the travel squad for the November 10 game at Yankee Stadium against undefeated Army before a crowd of 85,000 at the original Yankee Stadium. Leahy didn't play, but he had a front-row seat for one of the seminal moments in the history of Notre Dame football. He heard Rockne's Gipper speech, the pep talk–cum–magic spell that the coach cast on the Fighting Irish at halftime. The inspirational talk has taken on the mantle of legend, burnished by the 1940 film of Rockne's life that only occasionally stumbled into relaying the facts of Rockne's life. Whether Gipp actually made the speech to Rockne is an unanswerable question.

"There are many mangled facts about that afternoon," Leahy said late in life, but he assured that Rockne actually made the speech to the team. The fact is, Leahy loved Rockne and loved Notre Dame so much that he wasn't about to challenge the mythmakers. Contemporary and eyewitness accounts support the notion that Rockne's words inspired the Fighting Irish to "win one for the Gipper" and come from behind to defeat the Cadets, 12–6.

After a scoreless first half, Leahy recalled Rockne's speech reducing him to tears. He remembered looking around the locker room and seeing New York Mayor Jimmy Walker sobbing. Army scored first, but Notre Dame matched them late in the third quarter, with Jack Chevigny crossing the goal line and saying, "That's one for the Gipper." In the final two minutes of the fourth quarter, with the score tied, 6–6, the Irish faced a 3rd-and-26 at the Cadet 32. Rockne inserted O'Brien at left end. Niemiec watched as O'Brien loped downfield, put a move on Army star Chris Cagle, and got open. Niemiec put the ball right where O'Brien could get to it, and O'Brien caught the ball as he fell across the goal line. Leahy remained pretty sure that O'Brien gave himself the nickname One Play.

The good news is that the Irish won the stunning upset and created a legend that thrives nearly a century later. The bad news is they came home from Yankee Stadium emotionally spent. Notre Dame lost its last two games, to Carnegie Tech, 27–7, and at USC, 27–14. The 5-4 record would be Rockne's worst, and he vowed that the next season would be different. Leahy played a total of fifty minutes in 1928, ten minutes shy of the minimum necessary to earn a monogram. But he made a lasting impression on the head coach whom he revered. Gene Leahy used to tell the story that, at a postseason banquet, someone asked Rockne if, especially after a season like this one, he ever got tired of coaching.

"I'll relate an incident which happened in the Carnegie Tech game," Rockne said. "I sent a boy into that game, and we were taking a bad beating. This boy rushed into the game shouting, 'Come on fellows. We can lick them yet!' That, gentlemen, answers your question, or should, for how could a coach ever tire of the game, with boys like that to handle?"

Rockne didn't identify the player to the writers, but Gene claimed that everyone knew he meant Frank because Carnegie Tech was the first game in which Frank appeared, and he was the only Notre Dame player to make his debut in that game. That confirming evidence doesn't happen to be true. But the story illustrates Frank's indefatigable attitude, his love of competition, and his love of his school.

The 1928 *Notre Dame Football Review* profiled thirty-six players from the team. The last one profiled is left tackle Frank Leahy.

The magazine described how Leahy, surrendering roughly forty pounds to Carnegie Tech back John "Bull" Karcis, "sliced through and nailed Mr. Karcis at the line of scrimmage. Leahy is not an exceptionally large fellow. He looks much lighter than he really is but is always first to strike. He is fast and his charges are strong, his blocking good. Frank has done well in his sophomore year, and has every chance to go far along football's path of fame."

Leahy's version of progress may have been subtler but a lot more meaningful to him. By the end of his sophomore season he realized that the monogram winners began to ask him to dinner, hang out with him. He may not have played enough to earn a monogram, but his teammates believed he had the talent to be one of them. You couldn't wear it on a sweater, but you could carry it with you every day and have a very warm feeling.

CHAPTER FOUR

UNDER ROCK'S WING

THE 1929 NOTRE DAME FOOTBALL TEAM HAD A DAUNTING TASK. NOT only did the team have to rebound from an uncharacteristically mediocre season, but the schedule illustrated the nickname that the newspapers had applied: the Ramblers. As the long-hoped-for construction of a campus stadium came to fruition, Notre Dame would have to play all nine games away from home: four games on opposing campuses, three at Soldier Field in Chicago, and against Navy in Baltimore and Army at Yankee Stadium.

When preseason practice began, junior Frank Leahy realized his chief competition for the starting job at right tackle was Dick Donoghue, a six-foot-two, 220-pound giant for his day. Donoghue had one year, three inches, and thirty-seven pounds on Leahy. Donoghue didn't stand a chance.

"If I had any advantage at all over Dick," Leahy recalled, "it was speed and agility combined with the fiercest desire to make the first team [that] any football player ever had in the history of the game."

Actually, Donoghue was the outlier. Linemen weighing fewer than 200 pounds remained the norm in the late 1920s. The Fighting Irish starting interior line in 1928 averaged 187 pounds per man, with Fred Miller the heaviest of them at 200 even.

Leahy carried average size and, at best, average speed. But he knew his responsibilities and played with an internal fire fueled by ambition. In one regard, the next two years proved Clayton Balfany right. It wasn't that Leahy wasn't good enough to play at Notre Dame. He made the starting lineup. But he couldn't stay healthy. That might have been nothing more than bad luck, but the fact is, Leahy's body continually failed to withstand the comparatively padless battering of college football circa a century ago.

The deeper into preseason practice that the Irish went, the more it dawned on Leahy that he had begun to get the majority of the reps with the first team. The papers said he was banged up and didn't practice much. Yet when Rockne announced the starting lineup in the visiting locker room at Indiana for the opening game on October 5, he said, "Right tackle, Leahy." The starting right tackle filled with joy, pride, and determination.

But he didn't start, not technically, anyway. Rockne liked to deploy his second team, which he called his "shock troops," when the game began, a tactic he used to soften the competition physically and psychologically. Leahy still played forty-five minutes in the opener, a 14–0 victory over the Hoosiers. Jack Elder scored both touchdowns, the first by "following perfect interference on a 24-yard trip around right end," as *The South Bend Tribune* reported.

Notre Dame had a big test in week two, traveling to Baltimore to play Navy, a game big enough that it attracted two of the most prominent sportswriters in the nation, Grantland Rice and Westbrook Pegler, to Memorial Stadium. Rockne missed practice Tuesday because of his chronic struggle with phlebitis in his right leg. He managed to get to the Wednesday workout but his doctors urged him to save his strength for the long season, so he didn't make the trip; line coach Tom Lieb served as interim head coach.

When the train arrived in Baltimore on Friday morning, the team didn't go directly to its headquarters, the Gibson Island Club, an hour south of the city. The Irish instead took a bus to Brookland, just inside the Washington, DC, limits, to attend Mass and receive Communion. Brookland included the theology school for the Congregation of Holy Cross, where John Cavanaugh studied to become a priest. John's brother Frank, a priest at Notre Dame, had written to tell him to look out for Leahy. John had taken a circuitous route to the seminary. He had left home as a teenager and gone to work in a Ford plant. He eventually made his way to Notre Dame as a secretary, where he convinced the priests to allow him to enroll. He graduated and fell in love, got engaged to be married, then renounced his engagement so that he could enter the priesthood.

John Cavanaugh and Frank Leahy spent at least a half hour together, the start of a long friendship whose cement truly set the next day, when Notre Dame came from behind with a late touchdown to beat Navy, 14–7. Rockne may not have made the trip but his presence loomed over the team. Before the game, he called a phone in an alcove off the locker room, where he spoke to each of his regulars one by one, discussing Xs, Os, strategy, and pumping them up as only he could.

Late in the game, Leahy sprinted the width of the field on defense to track down a Midshipman back on a sweep. Leahy didn't quite get there, but he leaped at the ballcarrier as he reached the line of scrimmage to try to hold him to no gain. As Leahy grabbed the running back with his left arm, Elder crashed into both of them. When the three of them went down, Leahy's elbow got slammed out of joint. He had to be helped off the field and into the locker room. He received an injection to ward off the pain and was loaded into an ambulance. As he lay in the vehicle, Leahy heard a knock on the window. It was his new friend John Cavanaugh, who had left the stands to find him and try to comfort him. Leahy never forgot the gesture.

The ambulance delivered Leahy to a hospital, where his elbow was set and a cast placed on the arm. Two games into his starting career, Leahy got knocked out of the lineup. He was, he would later say, "terribly discouraged." Four games later, he tried to come back against Drake—he went in for Donoghue in midgame—and didn't last long. The elbow hadn't healed sufficiently. He knew it. But Leahy refused to stay off the field.

Rockne wasn't much better off than Leahy. He had been confined to home since the week of the fourth game of the season. Two and a half weeks later, he insisted on coming to the Tuesday practice before the USC game. Rockne arrived in an ambulance and coached from a wheelchair. On Thursday night, after practice, Leahy went to Rockne's home and explained to him that he simply had to play on Saturday. His brother Gene, his brother Jack, and other family members were coming to Chicago to see him play.

Rockne demurred. The doctors didn't want Leahy to play, did they? Leahy insisted his arm was fine.

"Raise it above your head," Rockne asked.

Leahy raised his right arm, the uninjured one, high above his head and waved it at his coach. Rockne stared at him for a long time, and then told him he would play against the Trojans. Leahy never knew whether his head coach understood the ruse that Leahy had pulled. As Leahy aged and became a head coach himself, he had an idea. Some two decades later, columnist Red Smith asked Leahy, "Do you consider it ethical to deceive your coach about an injury? Suppose one of your lads tried that today."

Leahy grinned. "I've always suspected that Rock knew when we were telling a bit of a fib," he said.

Leahy not only played in the USC game, he started it. Rockne, who attended the game against the advice of his doctors, announced that his shock troops would start the game. But when the game began he sent the first-team linemen onto the field for the opening kickoff. Leahy didn't make it to the second half, but he played in front of his family as Notre Dame held on to win, 13–12.

He played again the following week against Northwestern and started the season finale against Army in the frigid weather of Yankee Stadium on the last Saturday of the season. Five weeks after the stock market crashed on Black Friday, the papers delivered daily stories of gloom and collapse. But somebody still had money. Scalpers got fifty dollars per ticket (nearly $900 in today's dollars) even as temperatures barely climbed into double digits. Given the wind that swept through the stadium, the wind chill would have hovered around zero if wind chill had been invented.

A dousing rain turned the field into an icy, muddy mess. To fight it, Rockne ordered sneakers for his players. When they didn't arrive in time, the Ramblers sharpened their cleats in the locker room in an attempt to gain traction. The cleats didn't make any difference to Leahy's recuperating elbow; the cast he wore on his left elbow cracked when it hit the Yankee Stadium tundra. He played enough plays to learn that Army played a physical brand of football. After the game, which Notre Dame won 7–0, Leahy stood in the lobby of the McAlpin Hotel waiting for an elevator. Illinois coach Bob Zuppke approached him (the Illini had finished their season the previous Saturday). Zuppke didn't know who the young man was, but Zuppke didn't care. He could carry on a conversation with a potted plant.

Zuppke said he thought that the Fighting Irish had been lucky. When Leahy suggested that maybe Notre Dame had been the better team, Zuppke asked him if he had seen the game. Without heeding the answer, Zuppke then explained in precise, condescending detail exactly why his young listener didn't have any idea of what had happened on the field. When the old coach finished, Leahy said he would like the answer to one question. He opened his mouth and pointed to a newly created vacancy.

"Tell me, Mr. Zuppke," Leahy said, "which Army player knocked a tooth from my mouth on the second play of the game?"

Zuppke wasn't struck speechless very often.

On the Wednesday after the season, Notre Dame released the list of thirty players who would receive a letter. Leahy was the last of the six tackles listed. He was initiated into the Monogram Club on Sunday morning, December 15, though he did not receive his letter sweater for a couple of weeks. The *Notre Dame Football Review* for the 1929 season described Leahy as "the original tough luck boy of the Notre Dame squad, if ever there was one." The writer captured the desire that hurled Leahy forward, sometimes against the concrete wall of reality. The capsule called Leahy "too light almost for a tackle" but that he had showed enough talent to reach the starting lineup. The injuries "would have discouraged most men, but not Frank. He always came back for more and was in there at the end of the season fighting as hard as at the beginning, handicapped almost overwhelmingly, but battling his heaviest opponents to a standstill."

With the start of the new semester after the first of the year, Leahy could experience a campus life more like the other boys, his friends in Carroll Hall and across campus who didn't play football. He awoke at six a.m., with Mass and Communion at six thirty a.m. A quick breakfast, followed by classes until early afternoon, when he would report to the gym. Leahy worked as a member of the crew that performed the bidding of the equipment man, Jack McAlister. Leahy would sweep the basketball court, line the track, do whatever McAlister asked him to do and several things he didn't. He worked so much that McAlister urged him to clock out and try to be a college student: go downtown, see a movie, etc. It wasn't until Leahy returned to campus more than a decade later as head coach that Leahy thought to explain to McAlister that as a student he never went downtown because he didn't have money to spend on a movie.

Leahy's empty pockets did not alter his opinion of his college. For one thing, in these early days of the Great Depression, a lot of his classmates had empty pockets. For another, he radiated his love of Notre Dame. At a dinner one night hosted by a campus friend, the host asked Leahy's fellow lineman Jack Cannon to provide his description of the ideal Notre Dame Man. "I do not have to leave this room to offer you my conception of the perfect Notre Dame Man," Cannon said, "for in Frank Leahy we have that man."

The summer before senior year, Leahy chose to go to Chicago with a group of his friends, most of them football players, to work in a Waukegan plant covering pipe with asbestos for seventy-five dollars per week (this was five years before the first diagnosis that connected asbestos to lung disease). Hughie Mulligan, the business agent for the Asbestos Workers Union in Chicago, always had summer jobs for Notre Dame football players. Judge Carberry, one of Leahy's closest pals, got to Chicago a couple of days in advance and went to the most popular restaurant in Waukegan. He made a deal with the owner, another Notre Dame fan. Carberry would steer his buddies to take their meals there every day; in exchange, the owner allowed Carberry to eat free.

"Frank could never figure out why I always ordered the best, even for our box lunches," Carberry said. "Then I made a mistake. I told him about my deal with the owner. He went back to the same place the following summer and talked himself into the deal as my partner."

The dawning of senior year and the 1930 season promised a bountiful reward for Leahy. His body had fully healed, he had a starting job on the best team in the nation—not only did Notre Dame return six starters, but the five new ones had plenty of experience as members of the shock troops—and the Ramblers would have to ramble no longer. The brand-new Notre Dame Stadium awaited them. The stadium had 54,000 seats and cost $750,000 to construct. It would be ready for the season opener against Southern Methodist University on October 4.

What happened in Leahy's senior year would have a profound effect on his adult life. He never played a down, he started down the road of becoming a coach, and he lost the father figure who made the start of that coaching career possible. Either the career-ending injury or the death of Rockne in a plane crash alone would have delivered an emotional blow that would incapacitate most twenty-one-year-olds. That Leahy endured both in a six-month period tested his fortitude and his will to go forward in pursuit of his dreams.

In Leahy's time, sportswriters gilded the story of his relationship with Rockne, lathering it in schmaltz. With the benefit of hindsight they looked back and found the clues that foretold why the protégé matched the success of the mentor. The backbone of hagiography, of course, is predicting the already-known outcome. Just such a treacly anecdote began appearing in national magazines and New York papers in which Rockne is quoted posthumously lauding the football acumen of Leahy, in real time an oft-injured lineman whose career starts could be counted on one hand.

In October 1941, as Leahy began his first season as head coach of his alma mater, Tim Cohane wrote a profile of him for *The Saturday Evening Post*. Cohane had been the PR man for Fordham football at Fordham when Leahy served as an assistant coach there in the '30s. They remained friends for years; Cohane wrote Leahy's first-person piece after he left Notre Dame in 1954 for *Look* magazine. In the *Saturday Evening Post* profile, Cohane told the story of a friend of Rockne, a businessman from Chicago named Jack McCarthy, who visited the coach at the Kahler Hotel in Rochester, Minnesota, when Rockne took Leahy to the Mayo Clinic after the 1930 season.

"This day, Rock said to me: 'I want you to walk down to the hospital with me and meet a boy I have brought here from Notre Dame to receive treatment for a bad knee. His name is Frankie Leahy and the reason I want you to meet him is that someday he will be recognized as the greatest football coach of all time, unless I am badly mistaken.'

"At the hospital we talked for a few minutes with young Leahy, a blond kid, who seemed to be enjoying his stay in bed. On the way back to the hotel I said to Rockne: 'What is so exceptional about him?'

"He replied: 'Well, I'll tell you. That kid has the greatest football brain I have ever come in contact with. He is just simply a genius when it comes to planning ways and means of getting that ball across the goal line and smothering the play of the opponents. You wouldn't sense his genius unless you saw him on a football field, but you can take it from me, he is a superstrategist already.' "

After the war, the anecdote began appearing in stories written by the New York writers, a happenstance that coincides with Notre Dame's hiring of Charlie Callahan as sports publicity director in 1945. Callahan's ability to pitch favorable stories into print and massage unfavorable ones out of existence basically created the job category of sports information director. He could deftly apply the blarney when and where he deemed necessary.

Allison Danzig, a well-regarded college football historian who wrote for *The New York Times*, mentioned one version of the story in a cover story on Leahy for the third-ever issue of *Sport* magazine, in November 1946. Danzig told his readers that Rockne, speaking to his friend Jack McCarthy of Evanston, Illinois, said of Leahy, "That kid is a genius when it comes to getting the ball across the goal line and smothering the play of opponents."

Wilbur Wood spelled it out in *The New York Sun* during the 1948 season, quoting Rockne: "[H]e has the keenest football mind I ever have come in contact with. Remember his name, because some day he is going to be the greatest of all football coaches." The next year, Harold Weissman wrote a similar anecdote in the *New York Mirror*, in which Rockne, again speaking to McCarthy, said: "His name is Frankie Leahy, and unless I'm badly mistaken someday he will be recognized as the greatest coach of all time."

The truth of the matter never needed the schmaltz. Rockne did see something in Leahy, who worshipped Rockne before he met him and continued to hold him in the highest esteem after he got to know him. Leahy called Rockne the father figure he never had. Rockne showed an interest in Leahy that Leahy's father never showed. Rockne encouraged Frank in pursuit of the sport that the elder Leahy barely acknowledged. It was Rockne's special gift to find ways to motivate young men. It was Rockne's special gift to motivate, period. His biographer Francis Wallace, who worked for him as a student and as a graduate, described the coach as having "an intuitive knowledge of human behavior."

Rockne began grooming Leahy in earnest during his senior year.

The coach had a captive audience. Leahy's playing career ended in a scrimmage during practice on Wednesday, October 1. He injured the cartilage in his right knee. Here again, during Leahy's coaching career, the story went that Rockne ended the last practice of the week on Thursday, then called the team back for one more play, a run around the right side by Marchy Schwartz. That was Leahy's side of the line, and that's the play when Leahy went down. *The South Bend Tribune* begs to differ. The Thursday paper had a headline, "Leahy Suffers Recurrence of Old Leg Injury," and mentions nothing of the last-play soap opera. The *Tribune* also quoted Rockne saying that Leahy would be back in a few days. The Friday paper said Leahy would be out at least two weeks. The truth proved more dire. He never played college football again.

Leahy sunk into what now might be diagnosed as depression. Rockne encouraged Leahy to come to every practice and every game home and away, not as a spectator, but to pay attention. That would be easy; Leahy had never not paid attention on the football field. That would be his strength even as his knee continued to fail him. Rockne must have wanted to nurture the future coach but he couldn't help but see how devastated Leahy was. Cohane recalled seeing Leahy limping around the practice field as "a quiet, pathetic figure."

But those practices proved to be the beginning of his life's work.

"The 1930 season was almost the entire basis of the football knowledge that later carried me to success as a coach," Leahy said. "Whereas a coach who is a former player usually is an expert at his particular position and has a knowledge of the fundamentals of the ten other spots, plus the defense, I had the chance to rove the field, listening in and working with the line coach, the backfield coach, the defensive coach, the end coaches, the punting coaches, the head coach himself, etc. I could gather knowledge as a senior that rarely presents itself to one so young, especially one who aspired to coaching position in later life."

The year before, Leahy had camouflaged his injured elbow and talked his way into returning to the playing field. This injury couldn't be hidden. The knee continued to lock, and the physical therapy he underwent did little to improve his mobility. When he tried to take on the blocking machines, he could not hide the limp. Cohane, forty years later, recalled Rockne watching Leahy.

"That's Frankie Leahy," Rockne said to the writers at practice. "He would have been our left tackle. The poor guy has a torn cartilage and he's washed up. But he won't admit it. He still thinks he can get ready for the Army game. Look at him."

One day at practice, after taking on the blocking machine, Leahy informed Rockne he was physically ready to return to the field. Rockne called his bluff.

"Let's see you sprint 20 yards," the coach said.

Leahy made it a few steps and fell. As he walked away, Rockne said, "You've got more guts than brains."

Rockne put Leahy in charge of the B-team, which had two scheduled games. He encouraged Leahy's replacement at tackle, Al Culver, to seek out Leahy for advice, a gesture that revivified the injured player's self-esteem. "I was so flattered I almost cried," Leahy said. "I could not believe the great Rockne had so much trust in me. What's more I gained confidence because I saw Culver taking my advice."

Meanwhile, the 1930 team may have been Rockne's best. After defeating SMU by a touchdown in the first game, the Fighting Irish won their next seven games by at least two touchdowns. They played their last two games away from home. Because the season-ending game would be played at the University of Southern California, in this era of train travel Army agreed to play Notre Dame's penultimate game in Chicago instead of New York. Schwartz skittered 54 yards atop an ice-slicked field to break a scoreless tie in the fourth quarter, and Notre Dame escaped with a 7–6 victory when Army missed an extra point in the final minutes. The following week, Rockne pulled a fast one to camouflage the changes that injuries forced him to make in the backfield. When the team disembarked from the train in Tucson for practice, Rockne had his backs switch jerseys and didn't give the new fullback, Bucky O'Connor, a single snap in front of the writers. At a banquet given for the two teams on Friday night, Rockne gave a master class in psychology. When he spoke to the assembled players and coaches, he apologized to USC for the state of his ailing team and asked the Trojans to go easy once they took a big lead the following day.

Final score: Notre Dame 27, USC 0.

Leahy's Class of 1931 closed out its career with a nineteen-game winning streak. They celebrated that night with a party at the home of Johnny "One Play" O'Brien, the hero of the 1928 Army victory and Leahy's roommate for three of his four years on campus. At one point during the festivities, Leahy got down on the floor with O'Brien's girlfriend, Leona Martin, to play tiddlywinks. Some movement caused Leahy's knee to lock and left him gasping in pain on the floor—from tiddlywinks. His teammates helped him up and back to the Ambassador Hotel, where he stayed in bed until the team boarded the train to return home. Leahy made it onto the train and parked himself with a magazine, when Rockne boarded and strode down the aisle. Rockne took note of Leahy's glum expression, grabbed his shoulder and said, "What's wrong with *you*? What are you looking so downhearted about, kid? We won, didn't we? Ten for ten, aren't we? National champs again, right?"

Leahy told him he had reinjured his knee again, and as Leahy described what happened, he could see the concern cloud Rockne's face. The coach listened intently and provided a solution—Rockne had scheduled a trip to the Mayo Clinic to battle the phlebitis in his legs, and Leahy would come with him and get his knee fixed. Rockne told him they would leave for Rochester, Minnesota, in two weeks, don't worry about it, and continued on to his compartment.

Leahy didn't take the offer seriously. The coach had too much on his mind. Surely he wouldn't remember the offer. Two weeks later, on the day that classes ended, team manager Danny Halpin appeared at the door of Leahy's room in Carroll Hall and told him to be at the South Bend train station packed and ready to go at 8:15 that night. Years later, a man who had traveled incessantly for at least twenty-five years remembered every detail.

They stayed in the Kahler Hotel for four nights until their hospital stay would begin. Leahy, still intimidated by Rockne's magnetism, tried to remain in the background as Rockne dealt with well-wishers and friends. The coach would have none of it. "I admire you and I think you have a great career ahead of you," Rockne told his twenty-two-year-old roommate. "Someday you may make them forget old Rock. You're my friend and I hope I'm yours. How about looking at things the way they really are? You and I are just a couple of broken-down football folks up here trying to get fixed up. How's that sound?"

For four days in the hotel and throughout the two weeks or so at Mayo, Leahy talked football with his coach. During that trip, Leahy said, he recalled Rockne bragging on him. He didn't bring up McCarthy, Rockne's suburban Chicago friend, but Minnesota coach Fritz Crisler, who had traveled the eighty-five miles south to see his pal Rockne. Crisler would go on to become Leahy's nemesis at Michigan and on the NCAA Football Rules Committee.

"Know what I told him?" Rockne said to Leahy. "I said, 'I've got this kid with me who's going to make a great coach someday, Fritz. His name is Frank Leahy and right now he knows as much about line play as any assistant I ever had and you know I've had some fine ones.' How does that strike you, Frank?"

Rockne the salesman was determined to sell Leahy on his own future. Leahy claimed in later life that he played Rockne, that he emphasized his concern over his knee in order to win Rockne's sympathies and induce the coach to help him find a job. If so, his ploy remains an island of affected behavior in a sea of self-doubt. Over two weeks, both men underwent treatment—surgery, in Leahy's case—and convalesced in the same hospital room, Rockne's idea again. They talked football, from broad concepts to specific play calls in the USC game that ended the season. Leahy would write down questions as they came to him and when the opening presented himself—and with Rockne, there was always time to talk—Leahy would fire away. He had had enough of a taste of coaching that fall to expand his horizon. He no longer thought merely of going back to Winner to coach. Someday, he thought, with hard work he could become line coach for Rockne himself.

On this particular day, Leahy poured out his angst over whether his injury-curtailed career would pave the road to a coaching life. Rockne responded by handing him a sheaf of seven letters from other head coaches, asking that Rockne recommend an assistant coach for hire. Rockne had been a head coach only thirteen seasons, but the rest of college football teemed with former Rockne players as head coaches.

"If you're worried about a coaching job," Rockne said, "just help yourself."

The letter on top had been written from Georgetown by Tommy Mills, the same Tommy Mills who had coached Frank's brother Gene at Creighton and been Frank's freshman coach at Notre Dame. Leahy later said he never looked at the other letters.

He had a job, one of seven Notre Dame players Rockne steered into jobs as college assistants for the 1931 season. Now he had to graduate. Leahy returned to South Bend on crutches, which precluded him from performing the student teaching he needed for his diploma. Even though he would advance from crutches to a cane, Leahy would have to stay for the summer session. He didn't take any class that would be too strenuous. Two of the four classes were in the speech curriculum. Leahy learned the hard way that he had to face the consequence of being a Notre Dame football player: celebrity. Civic groups came with offers to speak, a prospect that mortified him. Not for nothing did his teammates refer to him as the Silent Nebraskan.* He finally accepted an offer from a Knights of Columbus group in Chicago because several teammates would be speaking as well. He thought he would gain courage from seeing them perform. When he stood in front of the group, Catholic laymen who made up as friendly an audience that Leahy

* Gene also wrote that in Frank's junior year, assistant coach Jack Chevigny mentioned to Rockne that Leahy had made a speech at a pep rally. "How I would like to hear that," Rockne said, laughing, "I can't get a word out of him on the field." Leahy's account of his talk in Chicago raises skepticism regarding him speaking at a pep rally a year earlier.

might ever draw, he hemmed and hawed and managed to sputter his gratitude for the invitation before sitting down.

The humiliation compelled him to enroll in the speech classes. They served him so well that when he returned as head coach, he urged his players and assistants to take public speaking classes, too.

The last Tuesday in March began like a typical early spring day in South Bend—warmer (mid-40s) if not warm, overcast if not rainy. In early afternoon, Leahy stretched out on his bed in his Carroll Hall room. He heard a commotion, thought he heard someone in the hallway say that Rockne had died in a plane crash. Leahy limped his way outside to join the swarm of students and try to find out what happened. When told of the news reports, he refused to believe them. First, how could that happen? Second, if anyone could escape such a predicament, it would be Rockne.

He chastised some students kneeling in prayer, as if by doing so they had given up hope. Finally, a priest walked out onto the porch of Sorin Hall to inform everyone that Rockne had died. The priest asked that everyone return to their campus chapels to pray, but few of the young men moved. It's hard to move when you've been hit with a two-by-four.

Leahy took the news as hard as anyone—harder, perhaps, after his disappointment over not being among the players selected to be the six active pallbearers. Given his physical state, it's understandable that he was not chosen to help carry a casket. Nor did he serve as one of the players who served as honor guards, staying with the body at the Rockne home in two-hour shifts for the twenty hours prior to the transport of the casket to the funeral. Leahy attended the service on that Holy Saturday, the day before Easter, sitting with his teammates among 1,400 mourners admitted to the Basilica of the Sacred Heart on campus by invitation only. After Rockne's body had been laid to rest, Leahy tried to pick up the pieces of his life and continue forward without the father figure he only recently had gotten to know.

"It was years," he said, "before I was really the same."

Leahy would graduate in August 1931 with a degree in physical education. He had played a little, been hurt a lot, and his grade-point average of 77.87 skirted over the minimum of 77 that Notre Dame required of its football players. He graduated the epitome of a run-of-the-mill football player. The next time he returned to Notre Dame, he signed a contract to have Rockne's job.

CHAPTER FIVE

SEVEN BLOCKS, TWO JOBS—AND FLOSS

Frank Leahy agreed to coach at Georgetown for the subprincely annual sum of $1,200, which is why when he left South Bend after graduation he didn't head east to the campus in Washington, DC. He went west to Chicago to rejoin his buddies working the asbestos gig for Hughie Mulligan (and that sweetheart lunch deal at the restaurant). Leahy, after being in South Bend for most of the summer, missed his friends. But he also wanted the money—in the three remaining weeks of his summer, he would be paid at triple the rate of his Georgetown salary.

Once Leahy reported to Georgetown, he delighted in the responsibility that Mills gave him. Leahy coached the linemen, coached them so well in an otherwise mediocre season that at least one opposing coach took notice. On October 24, the Hoyas (2-1-1), who hadn't scored in their last two games, traveled to play at Michigan State (3-1). The Spartans were coached by Jim Crowley, one of the Four Horsemen made famous by Grantland Rice at Notre Dame seven years earlier.

The Hoyas didn't score in this game, either. They lost 6–0, on the scoreboard, at least. What Georgetown lacked in talent, the Hoyas more than made up for in fight. They beat up their hosts, shut down flashy Michigan State halfback "Battering" Bob Monnett, and, surely not a coincidence, got called for 12 penalties for 120 yards. *The Lansing State Journal* described Georgetown as the roughest team Michigan State played in years, presaging the charges of "dirty football" made against Leahy's players at Notre Dame. On the other hand, Michigan State suited up only twenty-seven players in 1931; Crowley stopped scrimmaging in practice to keep his players healthy. The lack of depth made them more susceptible to the physical brand of football that the Hoyas played.

That Michigan State went 5-3-1 with such a small roster certified the twenty-nine-year-old Crowley's coaching credentials. He wasn't merely a star-turned-figurehead. After the season, Iowa fans clamored for Crowley to fill their vacant head coaching position. He came to Iowa City but soon pulled his name from consideration and refocused on Michigan State. In the spring of 1932, Crowley traveled to Chicago and sought out Leahy. At that time, assistant coaching jobs did not extend over the entire calendar year; Leahy had returned from Washington and taken a job as a salesman for the Garvey Printing Company.

Crowley took Leahy to Joe Dugan's, the saloon where sports people hung out. Over the course of the evening, Crowley probed Leahy's interest in coming to Michigan State, then invited him up to campus. He told Leahy that the Jesuits at Georgetown had begun to sour on football, and he ought to consider leaving before the program diminished. Salesmanship, yes; prognostication, no. Georgetown didn't drop big-time football until after World War II, when many Catholic universities did so rather than begin funding athletic scholarships.

Leahy appreciated the attention. It validated the fulfillment he had received in his first year out of school. Looking back, Leahy said, "By now I began to feel like a permanent part of the world of sports. I knew I was secure in the coaching profession and that I was doing exactly what I wanted to do with my life. I knew I would never be head coach at Winner High School. I knew that I would do more than that with my life."

Crowley invited Leahy to come to East Lansing and see what an improvement Michigan State would be. When Crowley offered the job, he nearly doubled Leahy's coaching salary, to $2,200. Leahy said, "I signed even before I could send my resignation to Georgetown," an interesting admission given what would happen nine years later when Notre Dame pried him loose from Boston College. Crowley also directed Leahy toward a summer job as a counselor at Camp St. George, a Catholic boys' camp in Wisconsin, where Leahy worked for three summers. Combining the income from sales, coaching, and the camp, Leahy's income rose as the Great Depression continued to worsen. In 1932, the average salary of a single man with no family was $2,005. Leahy didn't feel comfortable, much less wealthy; he felt compelled to find a job and make more money. He had worked since childhood. He didn't possess the gene for not working.

Michigan State went 7-1 in 1932, losing 26–0 to a Michigan team that allowed only two opponents to score as it went 8-0. It's hard to say how good the Spartans really were—among their opponents were Alma, Grinnell, Illinois Wesleyan, and South Dakota. But Michigan State did win consecutive road games, upsetting undefeated Fordham, 19–13, at the Polo Grounds, and a week later, winning at Syracuse, 27–13. Leahy's line made a star of the same "Battering" Bob Monnett that his Georgetown defenders had shut down the previous season. On the first play from scrimmage against Fordham, Monnett burst through right tackle and raced 80 yards down the sideline for a touchdown. The Spartans' winning touchdown in the fourth quarter also came thanks to a perfectly blocked play. Abe Eliowitz threw a crossfield lateral to Bernard McNutt, who went untouched as he ran 62 yards for the score.

The Fordham head coach, Major Frank Cavanaugh, in the last year of his contract, spent much of that season in ill health. Rumors that he would not return hung over the team most of the season, so it came as no surprise when he resigned the week before Christmas (Cavanaugh lived only a few more months). At the NCAA Convention in New York the following week, Fordham tried to hire Louisiana State University coach Biff Jones. When he said no, Jack Coffey, the graduate manager (nowadays known as the athletic director), kept thinking about the way that Michigan State had played against Fordham, and he went after Crowley. New York money often wins—Fordham offered Crowley a salary of $11,000, an increase of $3,000 over his Michigan State salary, and that was that. The press release on January 4, 1933, announced that Crowley would bring his top assistant, Glen "Judge" Carberry, captain of the 1922 Notre Dame team and Jack's brother.

The release did not mention assistant coach Frank Leahy coming to the Bronx. Leahy held off Crowley in order to pursue replacing him at Michigan State. You could call it unbridled ambition, but Leahy hadn't gone entirely delusional. It was not unheard of for a twenty-four-year-old, two years out of college, to get a head coaching job at a major program, especially if he had played for Rockne. One of Leahy's Notre Dame classmates, Frank Carideo, had been hired the year before by Missouri.

On the other hand, Leahy's ambition blinded him from a reading of the situation. He bounded in to see Dr. Robert S. Shaw, the president of Michigan State, and nominated himself for the job. Shaw, Leahy said some four decades later, "looked for all the world like a man who had lost the powers of speech." He never heard a word from Shaw and if Leahy ever heard from anyone else on campus, he didn't share. Pretty soon, the silence informed Leahy he better take Crowley up on his offer to come to Fordham. Michigan State hired Charlie Bachman, who had just resigned from Florida. He would coach the Spartans for thirteen seasons.

One of Crowley's assistants, Miles Casteel, chose to stay behind in

East Lansing. Leahy suggested to Crowley that he hire Earl Walsh, Leahy's high school coach and a former Notre Dame player. Crowley did just that, and not only did Walsh, Carberry, and Leahy coach together, they rented a three-bedroom apartment in the Bronx together.

It wasn't as if Leahy had no experience with big-city life. He had spent part of two summers living in Chicago. But just as he had been separated from his wallet as soon as he arrived on the Notre Dame campus six years earlier, Leahy got taken for a ride again. He stayed in the twelve-story Grand Concourse Hotel, a short walk from Yankee Stadium. He walked into the coffee shop, ordered a cup, and gave the waiter a twenty-dollar bill. He returned after some time with change for a two-dollar bill.

"By sundown, I was something less of a rube," Leahy said.

If a school hired a head coach with a Notre Dame background, then the school received the box offense developed by the great Rockne himself. It was no small transition from the single-wing scheme that Cavanaugh had coached to the Notre Dame box, with its shifts and dependence on timing. There's a reason that Crowley, a Notre Dame man, brought with him three Notre Dame men as assistants. Crowley was a celebrity, a salesman, a coach who relished the spotlight, all important attributes in the New York City of the 1930s. He brought other stars of the day—boxer Jack Dempsey, singer Kate Smith, dancer Bill "Bojangles" Robinson, Giants head coach Steve Owen—to practice or the pregame locker room to motivate his team. Crowley, known as Sleepy Jim for his heavy-lidded eyes, had an easy disposition and a wit so dry it could cure meat. He used humor to communicate—in later years he became sought after as a toastmaster—and possessed a keen sense of how to prepare a team to reach its emotional peak on the field. His longtime publicity man at Fordham, Tim Cohane, recalled how when Crowley took over the team, he told the Rams' two best players, left halfback and team captain Ed Danelski and center Johnny Dell Isola, "You fellows will never play for me. You're not fast enough."

Both players took offense but said little, at least at the outset. But

Dell Isola wasn't one to keep his mouth shut. He struck back with the sharp tongue of a New Yorker.

"Is it all right if we draw uniforms?" he snapped at his new coach.

Crowley broke into a grin. "That is what I wanted to hear you say."

Crowley coached as he had run for Rockne. He had been known as the best open-field runner, a guy who could make adjustments on the fly and make it look effortless. Anyone with that kind of natural skill is not a grindstone guy. Crowley let his coaches coach. He delegated, and he didn't work twenty hours a day. There is no question that Leahy matured as a coach as rapidly as he did because at age twenty-four he was given responsibility for line play on both sides of the ball. But Leahy had gotten that opportunity because he was a grindstone guy. No other coach worked longer, harder hours than Leahy.

Crowley would be the last coach that Leahy ever worked for; when Leahy left after six seasons, early in 1939, he went to Boston College as its head coach. In a press release, Crowley once praised Leahy's skill as an advance scout. (Before swapping game film became ubiquitous, teams sent at least one coach to watch the next opponent. Rockne famously skipped a game against Carnegie Tech in 1926 in order to scout USC and the Irish lost, 19–0). The problem, Crowley added, was that same skill came in handy on the sideline. If Leahy went on the road, he took with him his ability to recognize an opponent's weakness and capitalize on it.

From 1933 until Crowley resigned following the 1941 season, Crowley led the Rams to the fourth-best record in major college football (56-13-7, .783), trailing only Minnesota, Alabama, and Tennessee. Not for nothing, but Fordham defeated Alabama, 2–0, in Crowley's first season, and beat Tennessee, 13–12, in his second.

Leahy settled into his routine. He obtained a job in Manhattan selling billboard space for an advertising firm. He would awaken, take the subway south, work until he needed to leave for practice, then commute back to Fordham. His bachelor existence with Carberry and Walsh began to come to a halt in the spring of 1934 when a friend from the Notre Dame Class of '33, John Abbatemarco, convinced Leahy to come to a classic Italian Sunday afternoon dinner at his parents' home in the Flatbush section of Brooklyn. And oh, by the way, John's girlfriend had a girl that John wanted Leahy to meet for a date that night.

The twenty-five-year-old Leahy didn't make time for women. He never had. Leahy had the rugged good looks of a classic Irishman. While he never made himself the life of the party, he could turn on the charm when he deemed it necessary, such as in his second career as a salesman. When Leahy first laid eyes on Florence Reilly of Brooklyn, he quickly decided that he could make time for this woman. She had strawberry-blond hair and a warm face made warmer by a delightful smile. She had more lace-curtain Irish in her than did her date—Florence's father ran a furniture business in Brooklyn. One of her classmates at Erasmus Hall High, Al Davis, grew up to be the longtime owner of the Oakland/Los Angeles/now Las Vegas Raiders. Davis once told one of the Leahy children, "Your old man, the best thing about him was your mom."

Frank enjoyed the evening—they went to a movie and came back and played cards—but he didn't call Florence for a couple of weeks. Ghosted, in the modern parlance. He didn't think a football coach with a side hustle as a salesman had the goods to date someone like Florence. But he also couldn't stop thinking about her. With another prod from Abbatemarco, Frank asked Florence out again, and so it began. That summer, Frank wrote often from Camp St. George to Brooklyn, and between the letters and the separation, by the time he returned from Wisconsin for the 1934 football season, Frank and Floss, as he called her, had fallen in love.

Floss had two older sisters, and the tradition of the day demanded that she wait until they married before she did. Elinor had just gotten married, and the next oldest wanted to, so their predicament could have been worse. But Frank Leahy already had shown in his twenty-six years that once he set his mind upon a goal, he would stop at nothing to achieve it. They got engaged on February 14, 1935, her twenty-second birthday (Floss's middle name: Valentine) and quietly got hitched by Father Joseph Scanlan at Our Lady of Refuge in Brooklyn on July 4. So quietly, in fact, that they didn't tell Floss's family until the summer ended and the football season stood on their doorstep.

"I was so in love with him," Floss said, "I would have done anything he said."

Frank always considered the task of informing Sandford Reilly that his daughter had been married for several weeks one of the toughest he ever undertook. But they didn't have a choice. Floss was pregnant.

"Were you married in church, son?" Mr. Reilly asked.

Leahy had the right answer, and shortly thereafter Mr. and Mrs. Leahy moved into her parents' house for what turned out to be a year. Frank Jr. was born on April 28, 1936, nine months and three weeks after his parents wed, if you're keeping score at home. When the new father came to the hospital after hours to see the baby, a nurse told him no. He snuck up the back stairs.

Crowley's first two teams went 6-2 and 5-3, respectively, good records considering the difficulty of implementing the Notre Dame system with players not recruited to play it. Beginning in 1935, Fordham became a perennial threat to win the national championship. The Rams' strength during Leahy's six seasons came on defense, and thanks to a catchy nickname promoted by Cohane, Leahy's linemen received the most credit.

Because Leahy wasn't much older than his players, and because of those injuries that had kept him off the field, Leahy didn't have a lot of football miles on him. In those days, an assistant coach taught by example. He got down in a stance and fired out at the player in front of them. Leahy delivered his coaching not only with a chalkboard, but with a forearm, a shoulder, and precise footwork.

"I was young in those days," Leahy said. "I had a philosophy that the best way to test a man was with your fists… I think I had the edge because my father had made all of his sons very skilled, technical boxers."

The first player with whom Leahy formed a bond was an undersized guard with an oversized motor named Joe McArdle. Leahy became so enamored with McArdle that their relationship extended long past Fordham. He served as an assistant coach on twelve of Leahy's thirteen staffs (McArdle entered the service during World War II one year before Leahy). The following season, 1934, brought to the starting lineup an undersized tackle from New Jersey named Vince Lombardi.

"Lombardi was just another player, physically," Leahy recalled. "He was 5-10 and 180 pounds. But he was very dedicated and an extraordinary fighter. Mentally, he never missed a play despite a horrible temper. He was a leader and he would most certainly have been elected team captain except that he had decked about half of his teammates."

Center Alex Wojciechowicz made the varsity a year after Lombardi. It's no coincidence that 1935 is the first year that Crowley returned the Rams to national prominence. Wojciechowicz excelled on both sides of the ball, making the All-America team in 1936 and 1937. Leahy worked with Wojciechowicz as tirelessly as with any other player. On one memorable afternoon, Leahy lined up against his center in the same blocking drill, over and over, trying to teach Wojciechowicz the proper sequence of attack. Leahy, the older of the two, must have had a touch more patience. "Wojie," tired of being corrected, frustrated with not performing well, or all of the above, landed his arm and elbow squarely on his coach's jaw, cutting Leahy's lip and loosening a tooth. Wojie may have been mortified, but not for long. Leahy turned his head, spat out the tooth, and continued the drill. Wojie would be among the first of many of Leahy's players who named a son for him.

The Rams didn't threaten many teams with their offense, but they didn't let anyone's offense threaten them, either. The impenetrability of the Leahy-coached line led Cohane to resurrect a nickname used on the Fordham line several years earlier—the Seven Blocks of Granite. This time, it not only stuck, it became legend.

Two of the blocks of granite, Wojciechowicz and Ed Franco, are members of the College Football Hall of Fame. Three of the blocks—Wojciechowicz, Franco, and Nat Pierce—made the 1936 All-East team. John Druze joined McArdle as an assistant on Leahy's staff for the head coach's entire career, save for one year during the war. From 1935 to 1937, Fordham shut out thirteen opponents and had a record of 18-2-5. They might have won more had they not played Pittsburgh. Three times the Rams played the Panthers; three times neither team scored. Cohane coined the phrase "Much ado about nothing to nothing," which never gets old.

Pittsburgh finished with a better record than Fordham in each of the three seasons, including 1937, when the Panthers (9-0-1) won the AP national championship. The Rams (7-0-1) finished third.

The year before, Fordham appeared to be a shoo-in for the Rose Bowl. The Bronx campus sits on what long has been known as Rose Hill. "From Rose Hill to the Rose Bowl" is as catchy as the Seven Blocks of Granite and might be remembered as readily had the Rams not tripped up at the end of the season. Fordham, with a record of 5-0-1—the tie being scoreless tie number two against Pitt—had risen to No. 3 in the AP poll. In the next-to-last week of the season, a mediocre Georgia team came to the Polo Grounds. Before the game the Fordham band played "California, Here We Come." After the 7–7 tie, the band changed its tune. A 7–6 upset loss to New York University five days later on Thanksgiving removed any doubt.

It was right about this time that the Leahys heard from an old friend—John Cavanaugh, now Father John Cavanaugh, now a vice president at Notre Dame. Cavanaugh had come to New York on business, contacted Leahy and came up to Fordham to watch practice. Afterward, Leahy brought him home to have a drink. There, Father Cavanaugh spoke as he played with Frank Jr., telling Leahy that he wanted to see him coach to see if someday he might be able to handle coaching Notre Dame. Leahy dismissed the idea out of hand and said that Cavanaugh didn't bring it up again until Notre Dame contacted Leahy to hire him.

Leahy was a family man now; in fact, after his father died at age seventy-two in 1935, his mother eventually moved east to live with them. Leahy responded to the responsibility as successful men of his day responded—by burying himself in his career. He left the advertising business and talked himself into a job at U.S. Rubber Company, which had created a rubber-soled canvas shoe for children that the company dubbed Keds. Leahy saw an opportunity to combine his two business interests. Keds sneakers, with their lighter weight and the rubber sole, would be ideal for basketball. In the offseason, he traveled the country on U.S. Rubber's dime to market the shoe to college athletic departments and to attend football coaching clinics. He dedicated himself to the shoe business as thoroughly as he did to coaching, at one point taking a class in practipedics, a study of foot comfort popularized by a controversial Indiana doctor named William M. Scholl. Yes, that Dr. Scholl.

Leahy could sell shoes. He liked the business. He still loved football, loved the game so much that he went back to Notre Dame and played in the Old-Timers Game in March 1937. All but one of his line mates returned as well, perhaps compelled by the death a month earlier of Johnny O'Brien. "One Play" had died in a car crash.

The sport continued to mesmerize Leahy. The shoe business had made him more comfortable speaking before groups, and his reputation among coaches had begun to grow to where Leahy began to speak at coaching clinics as well as learn from others.

Perhaps the sudden death of Leahy's college roommate made the young coach reassess his career. Perhaps it was his native impatience. But as Leahy moved into his late twenties, and still had not become a head coach, he began to consider setting aside coaching as a dream that did not mesh with the real world. He certainly took the shoe business as seriously as he did coaching. Leahy went out on a summer tour of campuses for Keds in 1937 that took him from Daytona Beach to

Springfield, Massachusetts, to the Texas Panhandle, driving himself so hard that by the time he arrived in Chicago, he had to lay up in bed in the Auditorium Hotel. It wouldn't be the last time he pushed himself to exhaustion.

CROWLEY, SIX YEARS LEAHY'S ELDER, SENSED HIS ASSISTANT'S RESTlessness and counseled patience. But what did Crowley know? He had become a head coach at twenty-seven, and here Leahy was turning twenty-nine, with another baby on the way.

Crowley got through to Leahy eventually, and it proved beneficial for both, because the 1937 Fordham team nearly won the national championship.

The Rams went 7-0-1, the lone blip being scoreless tie number three against Pitt, which finished No. 1 because the Panthers played two more games and went 9-0-1. Pitt pulled itself out of bowl contention—the players who had gone to the Rose Bowl the year before didn't want to go back—so it looked as if Fordham would be selected. In those days, the West Coast team selected its opponent. California chose to play Alabama instead of Fordham. The Crimson Tide had played in four Rose Bowls, belonged to a conference, and, word was, could be had this season (Cal won, 13–0). The snub devastated Crowley. Wojciechowicz and Franco not only repeated as All-Americans but Wojciechowicz finished fourth in the Heisman Trophy voting. Leahy's reputation as a line coach began to waft down from Rose Hill. When someone told Pitt head coach Jock Sutherland, a taciturn Scot, that Leahy ought to be considered for a head coaching job, Sutherland said, "Maybe if they can get him, we'll be able to beat Fordham."

Years later, stories came out that Purdue, which went 2-2-1 against Fordham during Leahy's five years there, tried to hire Leahy as a head coach. There are no contemporary newspaper stories about Purdue pursuing Leahy; when Purdue made a change at head coach in 1938 because Noble Kizer had fallen ill, the school promoted interim coach

Mal Elward. In the late 1940s, in a life story of Leahy, Notre Dame sports publicity man Charlie Callahan wrote that after the 1937 season, Purdue tried to hire him as an assistant, which would make sense given Kizer's illness and Elward's promotion. Leahy, who had just been turned down for a raise by Fordham—he hoped for $500—let his bosses know he had a chance to leave. He got a raise of $2,000. Perhaps that tamped down his wanderlust for another year.

Between coaching and selling Keds, Leahy worked a twelve-hour day. He paid the nickel subway fare in the Bronx to get to Manhattan, then walked to the U.S. Rubber office by eight thirty a.m. Four hours later, he ducked out, grabbed lunch and took the subway back north. He walked nine blocks to Fordham, dressed for practice, and went out and did his hands-on work with his linemen for a couple of hours. After practice, Crowley and his three assistants played handball. Only then would Leahy walk twelve blocks to the apartment he and Floss had on 196th Street. He got home about seven thirty p.m. to his wife and two children, Susan having arrived on April 5, 1938.

The 1938 Fordham team may have been Leahy's best work. The Rams, despite losing the two All-Americans on the line, shut out seven of their nine opponents. They finished 6-1-2, losing only to Pitt and its All-American back, Marshall Goldberg, 24–13. Purdue, the other team to score against Fordham, managed a 6–6 tie.

At the end of every college football season, Ruppert's Brewery, the institution in the Yorkville section of the Upper East Side in Manhattan, held a party to which it invited coaches, graduate managers, and the writers who covered them. In 1938, Boston College graduate manager John Curley and Father Patrick Collins of Boston College made the trip down to New York for the event. Curley had stopped in New York on Saturday, October 22, the afternoon following BC's 26–26 tie with Temple in Philadelphia, and attended Fordham's 26–0 rout of Oregon. Curley and Father Collins spent a good chunk of time chatting with Leahy; if they did so with a purpose, it escaped Leahy.

Curley first met Leahy back in the fall of 1931, when the Georgetown assistant came to scout Boston College. He recalled meeting him on a few more such trips in the intervening years. "I always felt Leahy did the best job of scouting us," Curley said. "We could tell by the way the team he helped coach played against us."

Georgetown beat BC that year, 20–2. From 1933 to 1935, Fordham beat BC handily. When Gil Dobie arrived to take over the Eagles in 1936, the Rams came off the Eagles' schedule. Problem solved.

Dobie had spent a long career winning games and losing support. "Gloomy Gil" had a knack for not getting along with his bosses. After the 1938 season, in which the Eagles came into their season-ending game against archrival Holy Cross with a 6-0-2 record and left with a 29–7 loss, the sixty-year-old Dobie issued a statement that read, "I will not be a candidate for reappointment." He never coached again.

Over the next five weeks, more than a hundred candidates applied to Boston College for the job. Curley pared the list of applicants down to six, among them stalwarts at other Catholic institutions such as Clipper Smith at Villanova and Gus Dorais at Detroit, as well as the outstanding former Eagle tackle, Warren McGuirk, the coach at Malden (Massachusetts) High. But Curley didn't love any of them and decided to take another look around and make sure he hadn't missed anyone. In late January 1939, Curley picked up the phone and called Frank Leahy.

CHAPTER SIX

YOUNG, SCRAPPY, TOUGH, BRILLIANT

In December 1938, it came to light that Stamford High, a perennial Connecticut prep football power, owed a large debt to a sporting goods store. This being nine years into the Great Depression, large debts were not unknown. But the school board was embarrassed and urged Stamford High coach Mike Boyle to raise the necessary funds by playing a game against the high school from the next town over, Norwalk.

The game would attract ticket buyers because Norwalk High had stopped playing Stamford back in 1925 after enduring a 60–0 beating. Norwalk agreed to play Stamford but not before extracting a promise from Boyle not to run up the score. When the first team scored, Boyle would have to send in his second team, and so forth, until he got to the fourth team. The fourth team would have to keep playing. There was no fifth team.

Judge Paul Connery, active in Democratic politics in Norwalk, had a son on the Norwalk High team. Connery, a Fordham grad, also had a friend on the Fordham football staff, Frank Leahy. Connery introduced Leahy to Norwalk High coach Ike Kern, just two years out of Colgate, and the two dedicated football men hit it off. Leahy helped Kern with the team before the season, and when Fordham didn't get a bowl invitation—again—Leahy returned to Norwalk to help the team prepare for the big game. The headline in *The Norwalk Hour* two days before kickoff read, "Coach Leahy of Fordham Assists Norwalk High Grid Squad."

In modern times, a college coach assisting a high school team would bring the wrath of the NCAA down upon his head. It represents about seventy-three different kinds of recruiting violations. But the NCAA had few national rules of any sort in 1938; in fact, the NCAA didn't adopt national recruiting regulations for another two decades. Conferences performed the governing in those days, and Fordham didn't belong to a conference. Leahy broke no rules, save the unwritten one about turning off his football brain once the Rams' season ended. His decision to coach more football at Norwalk High explains why he couldn't become a fulltime shoe salesman more clearly than he ever did.

Before the game, five hundred Stamford High students paraded through downtown to City Hall, singing songs and cheering. Stamford (6-2), ranked third in the state, came into the game as a heavy favorite. Its two losses came to the teams ranked above it. On the day of the game, an *Hour* reporter wrote of twelfth-ranked Norwalk (7-1-2), "While it is too much to expect Norwalk to win, it is felt that the locals will give Stamford a real good battle. The consensus of opinion is that Stamford is two or three touchdowns better than Norwalk and a defeat by that margin will not be discouraging."

The writer, fortunately for him, did not add a byline to the piece.

And no mention of Stamford's fourth team seeing the field made it into the game stories.

For decades afterward, mention of the 1938 Norwalk High team made the residents of a New England town pause and put their hands over their hearts. Norwalk stunned Stamford, winning 20–14. Norwalk's star player, back Mickey Connolly, rushed 29 times for 87 yards and two touchdowns, but his 47-yard punt return for a touchdown in the second half made the difference.

With the victory, Norwalk got invited to play a local all-star team in Jacksonville, Florida, in the first week of January, on one condition—that quarterback Rudy Costa, who was Black, not make the trip. The team didn't want to go without him, but Rudy spoke to his teammates and convinced them to make the trip. If Leahy voiced an objection to the discrimination, he did so quietly. In all likelihood, given the tenor of the times and his ambition, he kept his mouth shut.

At a December 28 team banquet attended by four hundred people, Connolly presented Leahy with a "fine wristwatch" on behalf of the team for his help, according to the *Hour*, one of the few recorded instances of a prospect paying a college coach, rather than vice versa.

For the Jacksonville game, Leahy helped Kern install a five-man defensive line. The next day, at least five thousand fans jammed the train station to cheer on the team as it headed south. Leahy made the trip with the team. On Monday, January 2, in the pregame locker room, Coach Kern read a wire to the team from Costa, urging them on to victory. As the two teams warmed up, a Norwalk player heard from a Jacksonville player that his coaches knew all about the five-man line. Leahy and Kern quickly shifted the defense to a seven-man line in the first half, then used the five-man line in the second. Norwalk came from behind to win, 14–7, but didn't seal the victory until the last play, when that five-man line stopped Jacksonville at the Norwalk 1-yard line. When the team returned home the following night, it was greeted by thousands of fans who paraded with the team from the station to City Hall, where bands played and fireworks lit up the winter sky.

A couple of years later, Leahy estimated he had stopped in Jacksonville and watched the game film of Norwalk's victory fifteen times. It would be Leahy's last game before he became a head coach.

At some point in January, Jack Curley at Boston College called Cornell head coach Carl Snavely to pick his brain about replacing Dobie. Snavely urged Curley to take a look at that bright young man at Fordham, Frank Leahy. Snavely had met Leahy on the coaching clinic circuit. In the first week of February, Curley called Leahy at his home in the Bronx one night and asked him if he would be interested in coaching at Boston College. Leahy, ever polite, explained to Curley that he wouldn't leave Fordham for another assistant coaching job. No, no, Curley told him. We want you to be our head coach. Curley asked Leahy to take the early train to Boston the following morning. In those long ago days when cash was king, Leahy literally had to break the bank—Frank Jr.'s piggy bank—to make the trip. Dad had no money on him. Before he left, Floss ran to the store and bought Leahy a new pair of shoes and a scarf, and he took the rest of the change with him to buy the train ticket.

When Leahy arrived at South Station, he found Curley and Father Collins, whom he had met in New York, and two other university priests, Father Francis Low and Father Francis J. Coyne, waiting for him. They went to the Kenmore Hotel to discuss the job.

As 1939 began, Boston College served as a commuter school for the substantial Catholic community in and around Boston. The school, founded in 1863 to serve the 130,000 Irish immigrants who settled in Boston in the fifteen years before the Civil War, served as an island of educational refuge for a citizenry striving to rise above the station of laborer or domestic. The school's financial condition reflected that of its 2,654 students. BC had no endowment, no foundation funding its mission. It paid its operating expenses with tuition fees. Campus consisted of four buildings, none of them dorms. Most of the students were the first in their families to attend college. Guard Frank Galvin, for instance, lived in Framingham. He would walk a mile to catch a bus to

Longwood, then hitchhike the two miles to campus. After classes and practice, he reversed the itinerary, got home at nine p.m., had dinner—and then worked in his father's store for two hours.

After Curley and the priests quizzed Leahy about his football philosophy, all Leahy wanted to know was if they had enough money to pay him, three assistants, and have money left over for recruiting. After that discussion, Father Low abruptly stood, grabbed his coat and hat, and declared, "As far as I am concerned, this is the man for the job."

When Leahy got the invitation to interview in Boston, he had been unable to speak to Crowley, his Fordham boss. He spoke to Jack Coffey, the Fordham graduate manager, and he spoke to Tom Young, his boss at U.S. Rubber. Coffey congratulated him and urged him to ask questions; Young told him he could work out of the company's office in Boston. When Leahy returned to Fordham, he had the offer in his pocket, figuratively if not literally. Courtesy, if nothing else, dictated he speak with Crowley. Leahy went to see his boss and found himself having to defend the opportunity to become a head coach. Crowley urged him to get more seasoning, told him that if he took the job before he was ready and failed, he would be washed up before he got to thirty-five. That was what happened to Frank Carideo, Leahy's Notre Dame classmate, who became a head coach at Missouri at twenty-four, won two games in three seasons, and was fired at twenty-six.

Leahy was no Carideo. He had been an assistant coach for eight years, and Crowley himself had praised Leahy not only for his teaching but for his scouting. Leahy had become a regular on the coaching clinic circuit, and had represented Crowley often at the weekly in-season luncheon meetings of the Football Writers Association of America chapter in New York. Leahy couldn't help but think that Crowley wanted what was best for Crowley. He told his boss that as long as BC met his demands, he would take the job.

Within the week, Leahy returned to Boston to hold an introductory press conference. This time, Frank Jr.'s bank was safe. BC arranged for a prepaid ticket.

Leahy did not like crowds, and, at that point in his professional career, he preferred to avoid attention. That wouldn't seem to be a problem in Boston—one paper referred to him in the headline as "Unknown." Still, Joe McArdle, who played guard for Leahy at Fordham and had gone into the insurance business in the Boston area, played a hunch that Leahy would not put himself in the hustle and bustle of South Street Station.

"I guessed that he would get off at the Back Bay Station instead," McArdle said, "so I met the train and sure enough, he got off. I took him to BC and asked him for a job." McArdle didn't leave Leahy's staff until Leahy left coaching. McArdle then returned to the insurance business.

In addition to McArdle, Leahy hired Johnny Druze, one of his Seven Blocks of Granite, who after one year of the NFL had gone into business in Manhattan, and a young assistant from Texas Tech named Ed McKeever. Leahy had done a clinic in west Texas and hit it off with McKeever, who informed him that he had started out at Notre Dame when Leahy was an upperclassman. McKeever didn't stay in South Bend, but he remembered Leahy. In addition, so that the staff would have some built-in connection to the players and to campus, Leahy kept on an assistant from Dobie's staff, Ted Galligan.

The coaches met in the Bronx and began mapping out their plans for spring football. In mid-March, Leahy, Floss, their two children, and the three assistants packed up Leahy's car and began to drive to Boston. After they crossed into Massachusetts, they ran smack into a late-season blizzard that added three hours to the drive.

He may have never been a head coach but Leahy had watched Crowley work a room. Unlike Dobie, his crotchety predecessor, Leahy wanted to make a good impression. He learned the writers' first names and used them. He asked about their families. He bonded quickly with the young publicity man at BC. Billy Sullivan had been the speaker when his Class of 1937 graduated. Sullivan spent six weeks writing and committing to memory a speech that named all 284 graduates—in verse. The next year, he talked the Jesuits into creating a PR position for him. The priests expressed skepticism about promoting the university, at least until Sullivan pointed out that Harvard had an entire department dedicated to protecting the university's image.

Two days after he arrived, Leahy spoke to the student body. He gave them the same sort of ultimatum he would give the players among them. Leahy warned the students—not just his team but the students—against apathy. It would not be tolerated. He told them not merely that they were welcome at practice but that he expected them to attend.

When Leahy met with the team, the assistant coaches handed each player a sheet of paper with a literal list of dos and don'ts.

Dos:

1. Refer to coaches as "Coach."
2. Trot to and from the field.
3. Go to work at once after arriving on the field.
4. Strive constantly for improvement.
5. Work under pressure.
6. You're on the field only so many hours a week, so utilize all of your time.
7. Watch your diet and get proper rest.
8. When teams line up, run to your positions.
9. Develop the urge to excel.
10. Give the game all you have on each play.
11. Practice makes perfect, so get what you give.
12. Remember: This is the time to make that first team.

Don'ts

1. Don't report late for practice.
2. No insubordination.
3. No dirty play will be tolerated.
4. Slugging is cowardly.
5. No alibis.
6. No loafing.

7. Don't play easy just because you are playing against friends.
8. Don't develop the habit of hitting easy.
9. Cut down on griping. A certain amount is justifiable, because it is unhealthy when there is no complaining.
10. Best boys on first team.

The rules emphasize hustle and respect, two pillars in the young head coach's life. He never stopped working, and he planned to hold his players to the same high standard to which he held himself. He also believed in institutions—the Catholic Church, the game of football. It would be another generation before kids questioned authority as a matter of course. There would be no questioning authority on Leahy's team. "Coach" is a title. Football is a calling. You honor it by doing your best every single minute of practice.

"He was young, scrappy, tough, brilliant," said Mike Holovak, a freshman on his first team. "He surrounded himself with winners. Every assistant coach was great. Every player was forced to drive himself to the limit of his potential. If you failed, then Leahy was there to say something caustic." Holovak said Leahy reminded him of a drill sergeant. "Once he had a big tackle blocking. The tackle flattened [his] man, but Leahy was unhappy. The man lay on the ground and Leahy called the squad around.

" 'Lads, look at this man. Hardly touched. Hardly blocked. He wasn't even knocked down with basic tactics. Poor blocking, Poor tactics. Now I want this stopped. To win you must put the man down to stay. You must hit, hit, hit. Hit hard. Hit hard. I won't stand for anymore of this gentle play.' "

Leahy said to the boy on the ground, "Okay, lad. Get up."

"The kid stayed down," Holovak said. "His leg was broken."

Holovak may have been among the reasons that Leahy and Crowley had little regard for each other. Both remain heroic figures in the Notre Dame canon, and all fans' first reaction is to believe their gods get along. They are men, not gods. While Crowley and Leahy never expressed outward animosity, each of them spoke almost dismissively of the other.

If the seeds of their discontent were not planted when Crowley didn't show his enthusiasm for Leahy's head coaching opportunity, they almost certainly took root in the first weeks of Leahy's tenure at Boston College. The dispute centered on recruiting, where disputes among coaches have centered for as long as there have been recruits. Coaches have always paid lip service to the idea that if they change jobs, it is bad form to go after the as-yet-unsigned recruits they tried to lure to School A, to tell them to forget everything they told them and instead come to School B. Lip service to an idea is cheap. In reality, coaches do what they feel they must to win. Crowley believed that Leahy steered a few Fordham recruits to follow him to Boston College. Leahy believed he did not cross a line.

Billy Connolly, the star of the Norwalk team that Leahy helped coach, decided to attend Boston College over Fordham. Another disputed recruit, Holovak, came down on the side of Leahy. The New Jersey back, who went on to a distinguished playing and coaching career in college and pro football, said that when Leahy recruited him and his Seton Hall Prep teammate Joe Repko to Fordham, he promised nothing, and asked only if they wanted to play for him.

"I can't speak for anyone but myself," Holovak said. "Leahy never specifically mentioned the school."

Holovak told Leahy he didn't want to play for Fordham. Two weeks later, Leahy went to visit Holovak and Repko and asked them to play at Boston College. They agreed. The next time Leahy saw Crowley, his former boss said to him, "You've been busy, haven't you?"

As for the recruiting itself, Holovak said that Leahy promised him nothing. In reality, he said, playing for Leahy "provided nothing but a scholarship, some books, and a hard time. Some coaches talk about character building, but Leahy was a practitioner of it."

Crowley left Fordham after the 1941 season and never returned to college football. But nearly three decades later, he and Leahy continued to take shots at each other. Crowley once told broadcaster Lindsey Nelson that he thought Leahy had been a brilliant head coach but not particularly good as an assistant. Leahy told his biographer Wells Twombly that he liked Crowley personally, calling him a "wonderfully kind, sentimental man." But Leahy believed that Crowley succeeded because of his "young, vigorous assistants" and Leahy chafed at how Crowley took all the credit. He said Crowley taught the backs well, and that was about it. "I would like to say that I learned a lot from Crowley, but I did not," Leahy said. ". . . [A]s a head coach, he left a lot to be desired."

His experience with Crowley appears to have planted the seed of Leahy's insistence throughout his career of deflecting credit to his assistants. Leahy did so as a matter of reflex, driving writers to distraction with what they deemed false modesty. They came to praise his genius, not that of his underlings.

But Leahy knew that his success depended on the work of his assistants, and he always remembered what it felt like to have a fierce ambition go unrecognized by his boss. In December 1949, only days after Leahy had coached Notre Dame to its third national championship in four seasons and fourth in his seven years on campus, Leahy appeared as a guest star on CBS's *The Jack Benny Show*, the most popular radio broadcast in the country. The original script called for Leahy to say that the credit for the Fighting Irish's ongoing thirty-eight-game unbeaten streak should go to the players. On the producer's copy of the script, written in pencil above "players" is "and the assistant coaches." Only Leahy could have deemed it important enough to ask for the change.

Leahy made a lot of changes wherever he went. As hard as practice may have been, he made sure it ended in time for the team to shower and eat a meal together, no small thing at a commuter school. After the meal, the team met for more instruction before Leahy released them to go home.

Leahy didn't move his family to Boston right away. He bunked with Druze and McKeever in a rooming house. Druze was the only one who had a car. As far as Leahy was concerned, Druze was the only one who had a closet. Druze liked nice clothes. Leahy never made time for the haberdasher. He would borrow a shirt here, a tie there, "and never return it," Druze said. "It got to be a habit."

The coaches spent the spring installing Rockne's Notre Dame box system. Leahy tweaked it a little, adding more movement in the line. In August, Leahy stopped in Omaha to visit family before he attended a coaching clinic in Iowa.

"Frankly, I'm anxious to get this head coach nervousness out of my system with a game or two," Leahy said. Switching to Rockne's system "will slow us this year, but we may pull a surprise or two."

Leahy and Floss settled into a home at 820 Chestnut Street in Waban, not far from campus. The night before Leahy's first game as head coach, Sullivan stopped by the house and found his head coach vomiting from nerves. The Eagles would be playing Lebanon Valley, for God's sake, a small Pennsylvania college. Leahy would coach BC for only two seasons, but it's difficult to capture the size of the effect they had on his life. He came to Boston to take over a program that had no national profile and directed it to twenty wins in twenty-two games. He arrived as a relatively unknown assistant who had promise and left to take the biggest job in college football. He began an introvert and ended a celebrity. But he also came face-to-face with racial bigotry and responded in a way that he would live to regret.

The Eagles won that opener, 45–0. Their first touchdown came on a 17-yard run off tackle by sophomore Lou Montgomery of Brockton. Montgomery stood only five foot eight and weighed only 150 pounds, but his speed and quickness fit snugly into Leahy's Notre Dame offense. Montgomery was Black, the only Black member of the team. Like Jackie Robinson in baseball a few years later, Montgomery checked every box. Not only was he fleet of foot, but Montgomery had been team captain at Brockton High. The Massachusetts sportswriters voted him the most outstanding performer in the state. Schools that already had Black athletes, like Ohio State (Jesse Owens) and UCLA (Jackie Robinson), recruited Montgomery, but he wanted to stay home.

Montgomery played well again the following week in a 20–6 victory over St. Joseph's in the first-ever night game at Alumni Field. Yet Leahy benched him for the third game. It had nothing to do with his play. Boston College had scheduled Florida, and in the contract between the schools, Boston College had agreed to exclude any Black players from the game. The Eagles had only one. Some northern schools didn't want to play southern schools for that reason. But Leahy wanted to upgrade his schedule, and Boston College, because of its size and, yes, its pedigree, had trouble getting local games. Harvard wouldn't deign to play BC.

Florida and Auburn not only were willing to play, they would come to Boston to do so, albeit with one important condition. Taking Montgomery off the field did not go over well in the Eagle locker room. Some of Montgomery's teammates discussed boycotting the game or waiting until Saturday to say, "If he doesn't play, we don't play." But Montgomery dissuaded them from going through with it. Leahy didn't like losing Montgomery, but he didn't put up a fight. Besides, he didn't think it would matter. He told the Eagles before the game that they would win. He was wrong.

Whether it was overconfidence, not having Montgomery, the five-man defensive front that Florida sprung on Boston College—not nine months after Leahy had used one for Norwalk High in Jacksonville—or all of the above, Boston College lost to a mediocre Florida team, 7–0. Leahy never again predicted that his team would win a game, not even in the privacy of his locker room. His trademark public pessimism, which at times made him sound condescending, other times silly, and still other times divorced from reality, had its roots in the loss to the Gators.

Leahy went home and used Floss as the audience for berating himself. He decried how he could have put all the work he had put in since February and not have his team prepared to play.

"That defeat was my fault," Leahy said, the anger building. "I do not enjoy losing football games. There is no reason for it. No reason!"

Floss said what reasonable people would say. "Frank, it's not possible to win every game."

She had known her husband for only four years.

"Where is that written, Floss?" Leahy lashed out. "In the Bible?"

Auburn came to Fenway Park three weeks after Florida. Not only did Leahy hold Montgomery out of that game, but he played him very little the week before, against St. Anselm's, in order to give the backs who would play against Auburn more reps. Six games into the season, Montgomery had missed half of them because of the policies of Boston College's opponents.

BC came back from a 7–0 deficit to defeat Auburn, 13–7, and won its final four games as well. Not only did the Eagles adapt quickly and efficiently to the Notre Dame schemes, they won games in the fourth quarter. In addition to Auburn, they scored two touchdowns in a cold drizzle in the fourth quarter to beat archrival Holy Cross, 14–0. The Crusaders had been 7-1. More important, Leahy said years later that he didn't really understand the emotional depth of playing an archrival. At Notre Dame, he said, everyone wants to beat you every week, not to mention that the annual games with USC hadn't had time to develop the appropriate emotion of a rivalry before Leahy graduated in 1930.

Boston College finished 9-1 and—waited. The five bowl games had to make their decisions. In the meantime, Leahy busied himself recruiting. It looked like a cinch. The father of a star at nearby Lowell (Massachusetts) High worked at Sullivan Printers, as in the uncles of Leahy's right-hand man, Bill Sullivan. The firm did all of Boston College's printing work. The Sullivans threatened the father, saying that if he wanted to remain employed his son would sign with Boston College. But the son had his heart set on playing for Lou Little at Columbia. He wanted to be in New York. Jack Kerouac signed with Columbia, though Leahy continued to pursue him right up until he enrolled the following fall.

The Sullivans did fire Jack's father, Leo. And for what? It turned out that Kerouac had trouble with authority; Little quickly soured on him. He didn't last long on the team. He decided to pursue writing instead.

REPUTATION ALWAYS HAS MEANT SOMETHING IN COLLEGE FOOTBALL. If you have been good in previous years, the public, the writers, and the bowl reps think you will be good again. That held even more true in the days before television. As good as the Eagles had been in 1939, they came out of nowhere, and the loss to Florida, which finished 5-5-1, stuck to Boston College like gum on its shoe. The Orange Bowl even took two-loss Georgia Tech, which had beaten Florida by two touchdowns late in the season.

But nine days after the Holy Cross game, Boston College received an invitation from the Cotton Bowl, the four-year-old game in Dallas. The Cotton Bowl discussed inviting Duquesne but with some gentle urging from Boston College decided that two Catholic schools from the northeast might not sell tickets. Instead, the Cotton Bowl invited Clemson, from South Carolina, the third Southern team on the Eagles' schedule. That made Montgomery a target again. You could ask why Boston College would accept an invitation that the school should know would exclude any player, much less one of its stars. If you did, the answer would be money and exposure. The Cotton Bowl offered $15,000, which would pay for the trip and leave something in the bank.

"Boston College currently needs football gate receipts more than a lot of other colleges and on that basis can defend what would otherwise be an untenable position," Victor O. Jones wrote in *The Boston Globe.* Nearly fifty years later, Montgomery would say, "I understood myself that money was the big reason. They didn't want to lose the money, and they had made headway and were going to the top."

The week after the invitation, Curtis Sanford, the founder of the Cotton Bowl, said, "In view of the general attitude toward Negroes in Texas, it was advisable that Montgomery refrain from playing. We conferred with Boston College officials and Montgomery will come to Texas with the team but not play." Two days later, Montgomery told the Boston papers that no, he wouldn't go to Texas to not play.

Some schools had taken a stand for their Black athletes. Wisconsin, for instance, had withdrawn from a track meet at Missouri against the Tigers and Notre Dame earlier that year rather than leave a Black hurdler home. The year before, the University of California, Santa Barbara, had canceled a football game with the Texas College of Mines.

The Pittsburgh Courier, the leading Black newspaper in the nation, reported that Leahy had pushed for Montgomery to play. If Leahy pushed, he didn't get much support from the Boston College priests, who said publicly they made the decision in Montgomery's interest. If Leahy considered Montgomery's participation a priority, that would have been news to Montgomery, who said he didn't hear from Leahy until after the decision had been made.

Montgomery believed that the Eagles would win without him. He sent the team a wire before the game. "Expect you fellows to take this one for BC, Coach Leahy, and for me. Shall be with you in spirit while listening to the game in Philadelphia. Good luck and keep smilin'—Lou."

For all of his success as a rookie coach, Leahy had to learn plenty by doing. He had neither played nor coached in a bowl game in his career, and the decisions he made in the run-up to the Cotton Bowl created more obstacles than they solved. Exhausted at the conclusion of the season, he chose to prepare the team at home instead of going to Dallas two weeks early. But the snows came with a vengeance that December, forcing practice indoors. Leahy tried to install ten new plays, which muddled things further. A scheduled practice in St. Louis on the way to Dallas also got moved indoors (to a horse arena) because of snow. The team arrived in Dallas on December 28 to unseasonably warm, humid weather; Leahy had been told it would be cold in Dallas, and never thought about it again. But the same players who had pulled out three games in the fourth quarter that season were no longer in condition for that kind of sweating.

The temperature dropped nearly nineteen degrees on New Year's

Day—a high of forty-nine—but it quickly became apparent that Boston College had not prepared properly for Clemson. Their timing was off, which is not unusual in bowl games after a layoff of a month or more. But it cost the Eagles dearly. Three starters left the game with injuries. Trailing 6–3 in the fourth quarter, Boston College drove inside the Clemson 10 but failed to convert. Leahy chose not to attempt a tying field goal, and halfback Charley O'Rourke threw incompletions on third and fourth down.

When the Eagles stepped off the train back home in Boston, they found a reception not typically afforded losing teams. A sea of two thousand fans greeted them, including Mayor Maurice Tobin and, more important, Lou Montgomery. Leahy didn't shrink away from the player he had left behind. "Louis," he said, "if they had let us bring you along we wouldn't have lost."

Most of the Eagles returned for 1940. Leahy converted third-string fullback Joe Zabilski into a starting guard. It wouldn't be the last time that Leahy shopped his closet for players. He also didn't have to worry about the interest on campus or among the local fans. The spring Old-Timers Game, in which the team played a team of former Eagles, drew ten thousand fans to Alumni Field. One of them, Tulane head coach Red Dawson, introduced himself to Leahy after the game. Boston College had agreed to play at Tulane on September 28, 1940. The Green Wave had played in the Sugar Bowl—its home field—to end the previous season. Leahy leapt at the opportunity, then fretted the rest of the offseason about playing that good of an opponent that early in the season. It would be Tulane's opener. But Leahy adroitly scheduled a game against Centre (Kentucky) College for the previous Saturday.

Given his success, and the nimble fingers and salesmanship of Bill Sullivan, Leahy had begun "writing" a syndicated weekly column during the season. He and Sullivan split the proceeds fifty-fifty. It was coachspeak at its finest, and it would be a shock if Leahy ever took the time to read the columns. But eighteen months into their relationship, Sullivan had Leahy's thinking down cold: "Our worrying department was working overtime as we contemplated the 1940 season. Everyone expected so much and we were worrying that we might fail to satisfy the fans' desire. We had a group of players who had already traveled the gridiron glory road and we feared that they might not be set up for another journey up the tempestuous trail to national competition."

Boston College trounced Centre in the opener, 40–0, with Montgomery swinging around end for a 37-yard touchdown run in the second quarter. Billy Sullivan highlighted the run in the game story he wrote for the *New Orleans Item-Tribune* without mentioning that Montgomery (a) was Black and (b) wouldn't be playing against Tulane six days hence.

Montgomery made the trip to New Orleans with his team but never with the hope that he would play. Tulane came into the game a prohibitive favorite (9–5 odds) and looked to be the dominant team right up until play began. The veteran Eagle linemen dominated the line of scrimmage. Tulane's talented backs never had a chance. The Boston College defense forced seven turnovers. The offense scored two quick touchdowns, stretched the lead to 27–0 by the third quarter, then coasted home. The game became so one-sided that Leahy used only nine plays—he didn't want to tip off future opponents to the rest of the playbook. Tulane scored a touchdown in the waning seconds of the game to avoid the shutout.

The day after the game, as the train carrying the Eagles home made its way north—Leahy and Curley stopped in Auburn for a brief visit with Tigers coach Jack Meagher, another Notre Dame man—Floss Leahy gave birth to the couple's third child. This is how big the win over Tulane was: They named her Florence, after her mom, and at the suggestion of Frank's mother, Mary, they gave her the middle name Victoria, to commemorate what the newspapermen called the biggest victory in Boston College history.

That title held up for six weeks.

History does not recall the Georgetown–Boston College game as vividly as another played on November 16, 1940: the "Fifth

Down" game. No. 2 Cornell defeated Dartmouth, 7–3, only to forfeit the victory after game film revealed that the officials mistakenly gave Cornell an extra down, which it used to score the winning touchdown with six seconds to play. But in the days leading up to the November 16 game, and for some time afterward, the Eagles' 19–18 victory over the Hoyas enthralled the sport, from fans to writers to the coaches and players who participated in it.

No. 8 Boston College (7-0) may have had the higher ranking, but No. 9 Georgetown brought the more formidable record to Fenway Park. The Hoyas had a twenty-three-game unbeaten streak dating to the last game of the 1937 season. During the week of the game, Georgetown coach Jack Hagerty showed that he didn't belong to the Frank Leahy School of Poor-Mouthing. He said that his team had thought of only one opponent all season—Boston College. He said a lot more than that.

"I think we'll beat them, and if Georgetown gets off on the right foot, it may not be close," Hagerty said. ". . . I don't believe we fully realize how good Georgetown is. The boys themselves don't know. I don't know because they haven't been extended."

The game proved once and for all that, for all the talent that Leahy had developed up front—linemen George Kerr, Chet Gladchuk, Gene Goodreault are in the College Football Hall of Fame—senior back Charley O'Rourke, all six feet, 158 pounds of him, played a different level of football than the other twenty-one players on the field.

At his size, O'Rourke always dealt with being underestimated. Dobie, Leahy's predecessor, didn't play O'Rourke in the first two games of his sophomore year. In the third, he came off the bench to lead Boston College to a 9–6 defeat of Detroit. After the game, Detroit coach Gus Dorais said he would trade any five of his players for O'Rourke. That quote never made it in front of Leahy. Shortly after his hiring, Leahy took the train up to Boston to attend the "B" banquet—when lettermen got their letters. The man who booked non-baseball events into Fenway Park, Bill McCarthy, introduced himself to Leahy on the train and began telling him about the team, especially the six-foot-two, 180-pound single-wing back named Charley O'Rourke. That night at the banquet, Leahy learned that the skinny, unprepossessing waiter at his table was his offensive leader. That marked the end of further football conversations Leahy might have with McCarthy.

In lieu of size, O'Rourke possessed an abundance of speed, quickness, brains, and an accurate passing arm, a rarity in those days. The forward pass had been legalized in 1906 but coaches still viewed it as if it might walk away with the family silver. The Hoyas limited the Eagles to 121 rushing yards, less than half their average of 258.1 yards per game. But O'Rourke completed 14 of 23 passes for 209 yards and the winning touchdown. He also played all sixty minutes.

The cold autumn rain had driven the Eagles indoors to practice that week. The skies cleared for the game, but it remained damp, dreary, and the temperature never rose above the mid-forties. O'Rourke needed all of his tools to defeat the Hoyas, who scored 10 points in the first five minutes of the game. The Eagles didn't pull ahead for good until O'Rourke threw that touchdown pass to back Monk Maznicki to take a 19–16 lead in the third quarter. But the play that highlighted O'Rourke's talent came in the last two minutes. Boston College had the ball on its 9-yard line and needed to punt. O'Rourke, standing in the end zone, took the snap and began sprinting horizontally in the end zone. When he didn't hear the thump of a punt, Holovak turned around and thought he must have missed a block.

As the seconds ticked away, O'Rourke's strategy became clear: He had no intention of leaving the end zone. He was running time off the clock. "Breaking away from the antiquated tradition of running forward, Mr. O'Rourke ran from side to side, like a burglar studying the wall of a house," wrote the celebrated columnist John Lardner.

After the eternity of twenty-five seconds had elapsed, O'Rourke, finally cornered, stepped out of the end zone. The safety cut Boston College's lead to 19–18, but O'Rourke got to punt from the 20, and the Hoyas had insufficient time to do anything about their deficit.

Leahy didn't tell O'Rourke to run the clock down and take the safety. But he did stress to his players that they learn the rule book. A year earlier, in that difficult game against archrival Holy Cross, O'Rourke foolishly tried to return a punt from his own end zone. Leahy didn't tell Goodreault to tackle his teammate. But Goodreault tackled O'Rourke before the Crusaders got to him, which meant a touchback and possession for Boston College on the 20-yard line instead of a safety for Holy Cross.

"The Leahy Rules: There's always something that can be done," Holovak remembered.

Across town, the Boston University Terriers, following their 50–0 rout of Springfield College, sat in their locker room in their dirty uniforms rather than shower so that they could hear the end of BC–Georgetown game. In the Fenway stands sat twenty-three-year-old John F. Kennedy, a recent Harvard graduate. Speaking in February 1953 to the BC Varsity Club, the newly elected senator from Massachusetts described the BC–Georgetown game as the greatest ever played.

The lords of the press box came away with their gobs smacked. Bob Considine of the New York *Daily Mirror* called it "the best and hardest played game of football I ever saw." Grantland Rice, as only he could do, elevated the game to mythic status with one sentence. "I not only saw football played, I heard it."

Henry Super of UPI turned his attention to Leahy, "a modest fellow who has been one of the great football teachers for years—only the world never heard of him. He has the highest-scoring team in the nation and the best compliment that can be paid to him is that many professional scouts have said the team could be lifted bodily from the collegiate ranks and do pretty well in the pay-for-play game."

Boston College closed the regular season with victories over Auburn (33-7, again without Montgomery) and Holy Cross (7-0), and then accepted a bid to play unbeaten Tennessee in the Sugar Bowl. A year earlier, the Sugar Bowl had shied away from BC because of its loss to Florida. The seeds that Leahy planted with the rout of Tulane in New Orleans at the beginning of the season bore wonderful fruit. Amid the excitement over the undefeated season and Sugar Bowl, *Boston Globe* columnist Victor O. Jones speculated about what might happen if Notre Dame decided to push coach Elmer Layden to become solely athletic director.

"Since Rockne's death, the South Benders have never really found a man to fill his shoes," Jones wrote. "The teams have been good and the coaching has been fine. But none of Knute's successors has possessed that certain subtle thing, the 'Rockne touch.' That's a pretty vague term, but it embraces such imponderables as showmanship, color, and personality. Leahy seems to have it."

In the second week of December, Curley, university president Father William J. Murphy, Father Maurice V. Dullea, Mayor Tobin, and Bill Sullivan accompanied Leahy to New York to accept the Lambert Trophy, awarded to the best team in the East, at a dinner at Toots Shor's Restaurant on West 51st Street. The sports world had anointed Toots's place as the unofficial clubhouse of American sports. Athletes, entertainers, and sportswriters mingled under the watchful eye of Shor, whose voice was as big as his heart. Crowley, Leahy's old Fordham boss, attended the dinner (sirloin, peas and carrots, minute potatoes, and "football ice cream"), as did Columbia head coach Lou Little and Leahy's former pupil, Vince Lombardi, an assistant high school coach in New Jersey. The trophy presentation, scheduled for eleven p.m., would be broadcast across the nation by CBS Radio.

In November, the school had denied a newspaper story that Leahy would get a five-year deal. But everyone, especially Curley, Leahy's boss, understood that the school needed to take care of its coach. In the celebratory atmosphere of the Lambert Trophy dinner, Curley gave the attendees the good news about the future of his school's football program: "Frank Leahy's going to stay at Boston College until his hair is white."

The Boston College group stayed at Toots's place until it was time to leave for the two a.m. train back to Boston. The party had not begun to slow down. The restaurant was just a few blocks from the train station, but Leahy began making his way to the door a half hour before he normally would have. That's how many well-wishers stood between him and the door.

In two seasons, Leahy had lifted Boston College to the edge of national power. The AP poll voters didn't quite fully believe in the Eagles. Four teams finished the regular season undefeated, and in the final poll (in those days, the AP didn't poll its voters after the bowls), Boston College ranked fifth. The school just wasn't that well known outside of New England. Sullivan wrote a story for the *New Orleans Item-Tribune* on December 15 about Boston College, describing it as "the Oxford of America." Sullivan was nothing if not a salesman.

Three days later, Leahy embarked on another train ride, this time with the entire team in tow. The coach having learned his lesson the previous year, Boston College left for the Sugar Bowl two weeks before the game. This year, the traveling party included Montgomery, but he was not on the thirty-three-man roster. At the sendoff party at South Street Station, the crowd chanted, "Speech! Speech!" Montgomery, with tears in his eyes, managed to get out, "I hope the fellows win."

Instead of staying in the hotel with the team, Montgomery would be the guest of Olympic gold medalist Ralph Metcalfe. No one held any illusion that he would suit up (a) in New Orleans against a team from (b) Tennessee. Blacks and whites lived more closely together in New Orleans than they did in almost any other Southern city but not out loud. The power structure remained the power structure, and Boston College again accepted the rules as it found them.

Leahy wanted to change the status quo in college football. No one at Boston College held any interest in changing it in society. Decades later, the Eagles had remorse in abundance.

"It's embarrassing to talk about it now," Father Dullea said four decades later. "But the [Sugar Bowl] committee made it clear that a Negro would not be allowed to play." He pointed out that at that time the United States Army remained segregated, and added, "One of our [officials] was afraid someone would shoot at Lou from the stands if we even let him on the sidelines with us." Holovak, Montgomery's backfield mate, said, "There can never be an excuse for it . . . This was in 1941. January 1. A whole world was going to war. And we quit on a big battle. We—as players—should have refused to play. Lou went on to become a great man in his own way. Maybe we all learned a lesson. I did. As the years went on I learned it more and more. Never quit on anything."

The Black press raised hell, shouting into the void per usual. Wendell Smith, among the most prominent Black sportswriters, castigated the school and Montgomery himself. "Pity of it all is that dark-skinned Lou was 'sold down the river' by an institution supposedly dedicated to the principles and teachings of Christ," Smith said. ". . . The fact that Lou Montgomery permitted himself to be segregated against and insulted and embarrassed is also regretful." He added that "Apparently, he had no self-respect or pride. Perhaps he did not realize it, but as he suffered, the entire Negro race suffered."

The Sugar Bowl did publish the Boston College team photo in its official history in 1946, a decade before it desegregated. Montgomery is in the photo and identified, but there is no mention of his absence from the game. Montgomery made it into the Sugar Bowl stadium for the 1941 Sugar Bowl—he worked in the press box helping out the statistician for the Boston College radio team.

Nearly fifty years later, Montgomery no longer took one for the team. He regretted not standing up for himself. "If I had to do it over again, I don't think I'd have gone to Boston College," he said.

The Eagles bivouacked at St. Stanislaus High in Bay St. Louis, Mississippi, sixty miles northeast of New Orleans, where Leahy conducted two practices a day and put his players on a spartan diet. Oh, they had steaks at dinner, but the other meals served consisted of salad at lunch and corn flakes at breakfast.

"We had nightmares about 'em," O'Rourke recalled. "We had a real hard scrimmage going three days before the game. The pressure's on, we're going at it pretty good, and it was all as serious as a Supreme Court decision. Right in the middle of a play big Chet Gladchuk, our center, stood up and yelled something in Polish to Mike Holovak, our fullback. Mike laughed, and right away Leahy stopped practice. He was sort of shocked, I think.

" 'Chester! Now, Chester, what was that you just said to Mike?'

"Chet looked at him sheepishly and said, 'Aw, Coach, it really wasn't anything.'

"But Leahy persisted. 'Now, now, lad, it had to be something to make Mike laugh, especially at a serious time like this.'

" 'What I told Mike in Polish, Coach, is that he was having such a good practice you were going to let him have an extra bowl of corn flakes.' "

Leahy joined in the uproarious laughter. And then everyone got back to work. "We had one helluva good practice that day," Holovak said.

Tennessee practiced in Gulfport, Mississippi, twenty miles farther from New Orleans than Bay St. Louis. Major Robert R. Neyland, the taciturn head coach of the Volunteers, wrote in his notebook, "Team looked too good 3 days before game. When favorite, or inclined to be overconfident, we must *make* team look bad Wednesday and Thursday."

The week of the game, Neyland called his Vols "the best team I ever had," which was saying something, given that Tennessee had won thirty-two consecutive regular-season games dating to 1937 and won a national championship in 1938. The Eagles and the Vols brought the two most prolific offenses in the game to New Orleans. Boston College led the nation in scoring with 320 points, one more than Tennessee. Yet with its history, its winning streak, and the fact that Tennessee had bigger players and more of them, the Vols came into the Sugar Bowl as favorites. Leahy believed in conditioning. His team had worn down Georgetown. His teams won games in the fourth quarter. He believed Tennessee would get tired of chasing O'Rourke. Two days before the game, Leahy had his team play a live scrimmage, the starters against the backups running Tennessee's single-wing offense. "Our team succeeded in stopping everything except one of Neyland's bread-and-butter plays," Leahy said. "...It was a fake pass run inside the end. During our final scrimmage it averaged 7 yards per try against our first line." Once Leahy considered the possibility of O'Rourke running in open field, he put the play in Boston College's playbook. Leahy named it "Shift Right, Tennessee Special" and on the next day, New Year's Eve, during a practice in a high school gym, the Eagles walked through the play while wearing sneakers and street clothes.

There could never be enough preparation, of course. When the team left Bay St. Louis for New Orleans for the game, Leahy had McArdle drive him in a car. The weather may have been warm and thick with humidity, but Leahy wore an overcoat. He sunk his head down, not saying a word, his mind working furiously as he considered all the things that can and would go wrong. McArdle, trying to break the tension, turned on the car radio. As the music played, Leahy glared at him. "Just what the hell do you think you're celebrating?"

McArdle turned off the radio.

When Boston College ran onto the Sugar Bowl field, they saw 68,486 spectators looking at them, by far the largest crowd that any BC team had ever played before. The Eagles began the game as if they had a case of stage fright. As Georgetown had earlier in the season, Tennessee dominated the early portion of the game, going directly over the right side of the Boston College line play after play to score the game's opening touchdown. It may have been too easy. The Vols played the rest of the half as if they believed they could flip a switch and dominate. They took the 7–0 lead into the halftime locker room.

Halftime speeches are usually a figment of the imagination of the screenwriter or the mythmaker. There are two versions of what Leahy said to the Eagles at the half, and each version supports the version of Leahy the writer intended to build. Dave Egan of the *Boston Record* pushed in his chips on Leahy-as-genius in a column on February 16, 1941, the day after Leahy took the Notre Dame job. In Egan's version,

Leahy taunted his players, who already looked as if they had been through it. The warm weather had done in the Eagles in Dallas the year before. O'Rourke said the first half in New Orleans felt like summer.

"The heroes!" Leahy sneered. "The worthy representatives of New England! They who have not learned how to lose! The heroes are bums!

"I am not going back to Boston with this kind of a team. You're going to take that ride alone."

Leahy walked out of the locker room, away from the stunned faces of his players, and McKeever ran the rest of the halftime meeting.

In another version promulgated in 1948 by Leahy's longtime PR man at Notre Dame, Charlie Callahan, Leahy sounded like a cinematic update of Knute Rockne. "Lads, all New England is listening to this game. The people back home who couldn't make the trip are blocking and tackling with you. Do not let these people down. Do not let New England down. Think how you are going to feel the rest of your lives. You have only thirty minutes... remember that, only thirty minutes to win the ball game. Now, go out and win it."

The smart money is on the first version.

The Eagles got themselves back into the game by blocking a Tennessee punt—the first one a Neyland team had suffered since 1933—and recovering it at the Tennessee 17. They quickly scored a game-tying touchdown that stunned the Vols.

"After that," remembered Ray Graves, the Tennessee center and captain, "they were a different ball club and we were sort of in a trance."

Tennessee struck back with a touchdown but failed to convert the extra point. Boston College did the same. With six minutes to play, the Eagles began possession on their 20-yard line. From a 3rd-and-10 at the Boston College 30, O'Rourke completed passes of 20, 19, and 7 yards to take Boston College to the Tennessee 24. The Vols called time and made a personnel shift, putting an extra man in the secondary to defend the pass. Back Henry Toczylowski, who called the plays, responded by calling the Tennessee Special. He had tried the play in the first half, but the Eagles had lost yardage. Now that Boston College had thrown five consecutive passes and threatened to score with the game on the line, Toczylowski thought the time had come to call it again.

O'Rourke caught the snap and took one step back, and the Vol defensive end bit, dropping back. O'Rourke faked a pass, to give his three backs time to get in front of him to block. Holovak and Toczylowski moved the end to the outside, O'Rourke cut inside them, and he was gone. Neyland got beat by his own play. O'Rourke intercepted a pass to seal the 19–13 victory. The New Orleans cops tried to prevent the Eagle fans from taking down one set of goalposts, then surrendered.

"Can you imagine," Graves told Marty Mulé for a history of the Sugar Bowl, "I missed O'Rourke twice and Frank Leahy has never thanked me for helping him to get to South Bend."

At midfield, Neyland shook Leahy's hand and complimented him on the team's execution of the Tennessee Special. Tom Siler, the longtime columnist in Knoxville, maintained that until the day Neyland died, twenty-one years later, he never got over that Sugar Bowl loss.

The locker room had a much different vibe after the game than it did at the half. Gladchuk grabbed O'Rourke and planted a kiss on his cheek. When Leahy addressed his team, he told them he hadn't made an idle threat at halftime. He wasn't returning to Boston with them. He was taking Floss to Florida on vacation.

Leahy didn't know he had coached his last bowl game. He spent the rest of his coaching career toeing the Notre Dame company line about the unnecessity of bowl games. But he spent the rest of his life with a deep regard for the team that won the 1941 Sugar Bowl.

"The longer I coached the more I appreciated the dedication, determination, and devotion of those lads at Boston College in 1940," Leahy said. "They were a squad of truly remarkable character. Charles [O'Rourke] had a simply fantastic desire not to lose."

Like his three linemen and Holovak, his fullback, Charley O'Rourke would be selected for the College Football Hall of Fame. That makes five members of the Eagle starting eleven so honored, as well as their head coach, an astounding accomplishment at a commuter school with little national track record. In twenty-three months, Leahy had transformed from "Unknown" to elite. He was thirty-two years old, with a 20-2 record, an undefeated season, and an asterisk, albeit of Boston College's own making, on the two losses.

"The kid coach is now a titan," wrote Bill Cunningham in *The Boston Post*.

In the same two seasons, Notre Dame had gone 14-4. While that record is very good, the Irish had in each season gone 2-2 after October. Ten seasons had passed since Rockne had died. The Irish had yet to return to what their fans considered their rightful place atop the sport.

The BC Alumni Special train pulled out of New Orleans on January 2 with 250 coaches, players, and alums aboard, very few of whom had slept. The players may have been Sugar Bowl champions but they were still unsophisticated boys. A number of them got into a midnight craps game on the train and got taken for every cent they had. Someone went and awoke Arthur "Izzy" Siegel, the columnist for the *Boston Traveler*. Siegel, in his pajamas, got into the game, and won all the money back. The next morning, he went through the dining car and handed the winnings back to the players.

When the train pulled into South Street Station on January 4, the team found ten thousand fans waiting for them, so many people that no one could physically leave the train. Fire engines had to be summoned to extricate them. On that same Saturday, a writer for *The Atlanta Constitution* named Jack Terry, who had covered the Sugar Bowl, wrote, "It is the private opinion of more than one football observer that Frank Leahy, who has enjoyed unusual success at Boston College in his two seasons, will be the next head coach at Notre Dame."

Stories, especially with nothing more than opinion or repeated gossip, didn't go viral in 1941. Terry's story didn't generate the media frenzy that the same story would today. In fact, very little was said for a month. But Terry heard a drumbeat and wrote about it. Five weeks later, the drumbeat became a full-on recital.

CHAPTER SEVEN

A DREAM REALIZED, MESSILY

A BIOGRAPHER MUST BE CAREFUL ABOUT USING OMNISCIENCE TO STEER the direction of the story. Knowing the outcome can cheat the reader's understanding of how events unfolded in real time. Ike didn't know the Allies would succeed on D-Day. John, Paul, and George didn't know that bringing in Ringo would transform the four of them into icons.

At only thirty-two years of age, Leahy had become the hottest name in coaching. In recent months, he had turned down several feelers, if not outright offers, for other head coaching jobs. But of course Leahy would leave Boston College to take the Notre Dame job if offered. Notre Dame was his alma mater. It was still a campus where success in football mattered. It was Notre Dame. And it was Leahy, a young man with unbridled ambition. Given his devotion to his alma mater, given his maniacal drive to succeed, what was the power of his word, his barely dry signature on a five-year contract? The only people who ever failed to understand that fact worked or cheered for Boston College.

First, though, the job had to become available. Elmer Layden, one of the Four Horsemen immortalized by Grantland Rice, had just completed his seventh season as the Fighting Irish head coach. They had been very good but not great under Layden, every season leaving at least one task undone. Take the 1935 season, when his Irish delivered one of the great comebacks in the history of the game, spotting Ohio State a 13–0 lead in Columbus before scoring three fourth-quarter touchdowns to win, 18–13. In 1950, the Associated Press named that one the college football game of the half-century. The defeat of the Buckeyes made Notre Dame 6-0, yet the Irish followed up with a loss to Northwestern and a tie with Army. And there were the November fades of the most recent two seasons. Layden's buoyant personality had benefited his alma mater—he wooed and wooed Michigan athletic director Fielding Yost, a noted Rockne antagonist, until Yost finally agreed to put the Irish back on the Wolverines' schedule in 1942. Layden also instituted more rigorous academic standards than the football program used under Rockne.

After Leahy left Boston College, he allowed publicly that he had been contacted about the Notre Dame job in January, after Boston College's upset victory in the Sugar Bowl. However strong the "feeler" that Leahy received, it didn't convince him that there would be imminent change at his alma mater.

On January 17, 1941, the National Football League changed the title of its CEO position from president to commissioner. The team owners decided not to give the job to the league's current president, Carl Storck. A subset of owners sounded out Arch Ward, the sports editor of the *Chicago Tribune*, about his interest in the job. Ward always had been more interested in brokering power than in journalism. He created the baseball All-Star Game and the annual college football All-Star Game, in which a team of graduating collegians played the NFL champion, and promoted both games without hesitation in the pages of the *Trib*.

More to the point, Ward never attempted to hide his devotion to

Notre Dame, his alma mater. The university appointed Ward chair of the Chicago branch of the Notre Dame Foundation. He often spoke at Friday night pep rallies. When Ward told the NFL owners no, they asked him to travel to South Bend and probe Layden about his interest in becoming commissioner. Ward had heard the grumbling about Layden at Notre Dame. In the season just concluded, Michigan back Tom Harmon had won the Heisman Trophy. Harmon grew up in Gary, Indiana, about an hour from the Notre Dame campus. Somehow, Layden lost the recruiting battle. Harmon became a legend in Ann Arbor.

Layden never said that Notre Dame pushed him out. But he had lived with goldfish-bowl scrutiny for a long while. He returned to Chicago with Ward. Francis Wallace, a sportswriter and Notre Dame alum who knew the university as well as anyone (he wrote three books about Notre Dame and served as president of the alumni association), described Layden's departure in retrospect as "an unusual step to take, unless gently urged." The NFL announced the hiring of Layden on the evening of February 3. The news broke in Boston around seven p.m.

One hour earlier, Leahy had signed a five-year extension with Boston College.

On the way home from his two-week, post-bowl vacation in Florida, Leahy stopped in Atlanta to speak to the second annual stag dinner of the Atlanta Touchdown Club. The speaking roster included coaches Bill Alexander of Georgia Tech, Wally Butts of Georgia, Pooley Hubert of Virginia Military Institute, and Frank Thomas of Alabama. Leahy glided into the Ansley Hotel on the acclaim of the Eagles' victories over SEC champion Tennessee, as well as two other SEC schools, Tulane and Auburn. Those wins carried a lot of weight in a ballroom of five hundred men in Atlanta. "Any coach in this room could have done as well as I with the kind of players we had at Boston College," Leahy said. "We had some lads who could have made any team any year. It was remarkable that we had so many good men on such a small squad."

Leahy informed his listeners that the SEC schools (and everyone else) could strike back in the fall.

"We lost 16 by graduation and I know some of these Southern teams whom we were fortunate enough to beat will be gunning for us next year," Leahy said. "In fact, I'm getting my alibis ready."

Leahy's humility and charm captivated the room, according to Dr. Louie D. Newton, the pastor of Druid Hills Baptist Church, one of Atlanta's most influential congregations. The pastor compared the speech of the Boston College coach who came south favorably with a revered speech made a half-century earlier by an Atlantan in Boston. It was revered in Atlanta, anyway. *Constitution* publisher Henry Grady, speaking at Faneuil Hall in 1889, urged the US Congress not to pass a bill that would provide for federal intervention in elections in which Black citizens were denied the vote. The speech, entitled "The Race Problem," achieved mythological status in Atlanta because the bill died in the US Senate, bathing Grady in posthumous glory. Ten days after his oratory, Grady died of pneumonia. Comparing Leahy to Grady meant that the Yankee coach made some kind of an impression. Leahy had begun to grow comfortable in the spotlight. It was about to get a lot brighter.

Back at Boston College, Curley and Leahy needed several weeks to create a contract they both liked. After the season, Leahy had an offer from the Detroit Lions for $200,000 over ten seasons, a salary nearly double what Boston College paid him. It would be the first of several runs that NFL teams made at him over the next fifteen years or so. He turned the Lions down more quickly than he would the others.

Boston College had first presented Leahy with a five-year deal in December. But he balked at signing it until the school coughed up more money for his assistants. Curley sent him a new contract in mid-January, and Leahy sat on it for three weeks. On the evening of Wednesday, February 3, Curley asked Leahy to sign the contract, and Leahy agreed.

What unfolded from that request through the next eleven days would be disputed by the two parties almost from the moment it happened. Leahy insisted publicly that during negotiations Boston College—specifically, Curley—had given him an out clause should Notre Dame ever offer him its head coaching job. Leahy said so in his initial interview with Notre Dame, he said so to the writers in Boston, he said so at his introductory news conference at Notre Dame, he said so over and over again for the rest of his life. The story appeared in Arch Ward's 1944 book, *Frank Leahy and the Fighting Irish*. It appeared in the sixty-three-page biography of Leahy written by Notre Dame publicity man Charlie Callahan in 1948. It appeared in his official biography by Wells Twombly, published in 1974, the year after Leahy died. Boston College insisted, albeit less publicly, that it never granted Leahy such an escape, orally, contractually, scribbled on a cocktail napkin, or in any other way, shape, or form.

Leahy's version is that when he signed the contract, he told Curley, "I'm in no hurry to leave Boston College, I've told you that. There's only one other job I'd take and that would be...well, aaaaahhh...it would be at Notre Dame. Naturally, I would want to go there. But I am not at all sure the job ever would be offered to me, Jack. I think you can understand my position in the matter." Ward wrote that Curley, without prompting from Leahy and in the presence of Billy Sullivan and Ed McKeever, said, "Thanks a lot, Frank. If Notre Dame should ever ask you to go back, we'll be very happy to release you." That version of events would allow for Leahy to have received a feeler from Notre Dame. But at the moment he signed the deal, he didn't know the Notre Dame job had come open.

Leahy's memory at the end of his life faltered. He sets the scene as if he and Sullivan are in a hurry to leave for his speech in Atlanta, which had happened two and a half weeks earlier. In fact, after Leahy signed the contract, he and Curley traveled separately to Haverhill, Massachusetts, to attend a 1,500-person testimonial dinner for hometown All-American lineman Gene Goodreault. Curley had no intention of announcing the agreement that night. He wanted to wait six days and unveil it to the Boston College faithful at the Varsity Club "B" banquet at the Statler Hotel. But the news of Layden's departure went public, and the wire-service guys and the beat writers somehow phoned the dinner venue and asked to get Curley on the line. He put in a phone call to Father Murphy, the university president, and got the go-ahead to announce the agreement that night. Only then did he talk to the writers.

Curley ran Boston College athletics as the quintessential congenial Irishman, always ready with a smile and a story. He liked people and wanted to be liked. He was not a martinet. "When the question was asked that if Leahy wanted to go to Notre Dame, would I stop him, I said, 'How could I?' " Curley said. But Curley added that he had no worry that Leahy would leave because Leahy had signed the contract. If Curley had given Leahy permission to leave, why would he say he had no worry? When Leahy arrived at the dinner to speak, he told the writers in attendance he had no comment about Notre Dame.

The story combining Leahy's signing and Layden's resignation ran above the fold on page one of *The Boston Globe* the next day. Because of the contract, *The South Bend Tribune* felt the same way as Curley, ruling Leahy out of consideration as a replacement for Layden.

Given the priests presiding over the Notre Dame hiring, there could be little doubt that Leahy would be vetted as a candidate. Father J. Hugh O'Donnell, who had been university president for just a matter of months, put the coaching search in the hands of Leahy's friend Father John Cavanaugh, the university vice president. Cavanaugh had written congratulatory letters to Leahy on November 29—the day before Boston College closed out its undefeated regular season with a victory over Holy Cross—and again on January 3, in the wake of the upset of Tennessee. "Certainly as much as I was pulling for you I had hardly hoped for such a victory," Cavanaugh said. Whether he had an ulterior motive in writing the letters isn't known. But what's interesting is that Leahy responded to Cavanaugh's January 3 letter on February 4, the day the newspapers trumpeted Layden's resignation.

"I wish you could have seen the Boston College vs. Tennessee contest," Leahy wrote. "Our team displayed a marvelous fighting spirit from start to finish. Their demonstration of courage and will to win will always serve as a real inspiration to me. Our plays surely won the fancy of those who were fortunate enough to wittness [sic] the Sugar Bowl game.

"Here's hoping Father I will have the opportunity to visit with you in the not too distant future."

Uh-huh.

Exactly how much say Cavanaugh had over whom Notre Dame would hire is hard to pinpoint, except to say that Leahy wasn't Notre Dame's only choice. The writers who named candidates included Joe Boland, Layden's top assistant; Buck Shaw, the coach at Santa Clara; Arthur "Dutch" Bergman, who had taken Catholic University to two bowl games; and Leahy. Boland, as the in-house candidate in a house that prized loyalty, had enough prominence as a candidate that *Time* magazine sent a photographer to South Bend to photograph him and his family. But another Layden assistant, Chet Grant, told the priests to hire Leahy. Bergman appeared to be the people's choice. The university administration received more endorsements of him than it did any other candidate. The Notre Dame Club in Washington sent an endorsement. So did a Minnesota congressman who had a Notre Dame law degree. And on Monday, February 8, Father Hugh O'Donnell received a telegram from Washington that read:

I AM INDEED PLEASED TO JOIN WITH FRIENDS AND ADMIRERS OF ARTHUR DUTCH BERGMAN IN RECOMMENDING HIM TO YOU FOR CONSIDERATION IN CONNECTION WITH ATHLETIC COACH VACANCY. KIND REGARDS=

J EDGAR HOOVER.

All the coaching candidates had the prerequisite Rockne pedigree. But the priests in charge didn't look any farther than Shaw and Leahy. Contemporary accounts said that Shaw turned the job down before Notre Dame hired Leahy. In his autobiography, Leahy maintained that he had been the first choice. This much is known: Father John Cavanaugh intended to keep the coaching search private and resorted to Hitchcockian-style spycraft in doing so. He made his first run at Shaw, traveling to northern California, where he called Shaw and identified himself as Jimmy Egan. Shaw apologized and said he didn't know a Jimmy Egan.

"Now, Buck," Father Cavanaugh said, "are you sure you don't remember a Jimmy Egan with whom you visited in the St. Francis Hotel back in 1923?"

"John! What are you doing out here?"

Father Cavanaugh arranged all this cloak-and-dagger because he knew the optics of Notre Dame poaching a newly signed coach from another Catholic college would embarrass the university. Not that he allowed the risk of embarrassment to stop him from actually going through with it. Father Cavanaugh took a train to Salinas and stepped off into a driving rainstorm to find Shaw waiting for him in a car. Shaw drove, parked on a side street, and they sat in the car for an hour, talking above the rain noise about the coaching job.

On the opposite coast, at Father Cavanaugh's direction, one of Leahy's Notre Dame classmates, Eddie Dunigan, called the coach at home. It was the morning after the Goodreault dinner.

Dunigan told him that the good fathers wanted to talk to him about replacing Layden as head coach and athletic director. According to Leahy, Dunigan told him that he ranked first among the candidates. He asked Leahy to meet him in Albany and check into the DeWitt Clinton Hotel under an assumed name. Leahy had the B banquet that night, and would return to Norwalk on the following night, February 10, to speak at a dinner honoring Mickey Connolly, one of his first Boston College recruits. He planned to go to Albany from there.

At the Norwalk dinner, Leahy displayed the aptitude that college coaches have displayed from the dawn of time to preach the verities of a team publicly while looking for a better job privately. Every player on the undefeated Boston College team, Leahy said, eschewed individual acclaim and "was striving for team success and team progress. Each was part of an organization far greater and bigger than they were individually." When he left the dinner, Leahy had a car service waiting for him to drive him to Albany. He arrived around four a.m. to see a story in the local paper from the *Los Angeles Herald-Express* that Notre Dame had hired Shaw. Leahy proceeded to the hotel anyway, where he registered under the name "Leary" and crashed for a few hours. At nine a.m. he met Cavanaugh's brother, Frank, who not only was also a Notre Dame priest but had been a rector in Leahy's dorm during his sophomore year. Father Frank and Leahy peppered each other with questions. Leahy wanted to bring his assistants with him from Boston College, and only one of them had attended Notre Dame. This would go against precedent and tradition, which Notre Dame never took lightly.

Father Frank, identifying Leahy as "Frank O'Flaherty" for any nosy telephone operators or hotel clerks, put Leahy on the phone with Father John out in California. They made a lot of progress toward an agreement. Father John assured Leahy that he could hire the assistants he wanted, regardless of their alma mater. But Father John wanted assurance that Leahy could leave Boston College despite his new contract.

Shaw bowed out of consideration, his wife publicly proclaiming her preference to camp out in northern California rather than become the First Lady of northern Indiana. Leahy had become the guy. On the following day, February 12, Leahy returned home, called Curley, told him he didn't feel well and asked him to come by his house.

Curley said the subject of Leahy's departure didn't come up between them until that visit to Leahy's house, nine days after Leahy said it did. According to Curley, the coach asked him that, if he received an offer, would Curley release him from the newly signed contract. Curley said he would but that it wasn't his decision to make. Leahy would have to obtain the release from Father Murphy, the president. Two days passed, with Notre Dame drumming its fingers and Leahy getting antsier and antsier. It was about this time that a letter from the Notre Dame president, Father O'Donnell, arrived at Boston College asking for permission that Notre Dame already had granted itself.

Finally, Leahy forced the issue. He rented a suite at the Kenmore Hotel and invited the Boston writers and radio correspondents. When everyone assembled, he phoned Curley and told him he planned to announce his departure for Notre Dame after he came out and picked up the release. Could Curley have it ready?

Boston College had it waiting for him. Leahy could fulfill his dream and become head football coach, as well as athletic director, at Notre Dame. Leahy returned to the Kenmore to meet with the Boston writers.

"I deeply regret leaving Boston College, but I consider it my duty to return to Notre Dame," he said. "Every Notre Dame man would welcome a chance to go back as head coach, for it is the greatest honor that can come to any of us... Boston College has treated me so well that I never would have considered any other college. But it is like going home for me to return to Notre Dame." Leahy concluded the quick presser and rushed to South Street Station, where he barely made the seven p.m. train, Niagara number 29, to head to South Bend.

At Notre Dame, Father O'Donnell sent a telegram to boosters and the Chicago writers, which read, in toto, "FRANK LEAHY, CLASS OF THIRTY-ONE, SUCCEEDS ELMER LAYDEN. REGARDS. HUGH O'DONNELL" Then he sent a telegram to the Springfield, Massachusetts, train station to intercept Leahy. "PRESIDENT OF YOUR ALMA MATER IS VERY HAPPY AND ASSURES YOU OF CORDIAL WELCOME TOMORROW. I KNOW THE BLESSED MOTHER WILL GUIDE AND PROTECT YOU IN YOUR NEW WORK."

In his statement, Father O'Donnell tried to smooth over the feathers Notre Dame ruffled in Chestnut Hill: "Mr. Leahy leaves Boston College with regret, but with the best wishes of his friends there, and I am grateful for the sympathetic cooperation given us by that splendid institution of learning. We welcome the return of a loyal son and wish him Godspeed in his new position."

O'Donnell supported the work his second-in-command, Father John, had done to procure Leahy, even if Cavanaugh didn't exactly play by the rules. Curley, on the opposite side of the transaction, also said the right things. Per his nature, he said for public consumption, "Leahy has been a grand fellow. BC appreciates his work. I don't think any college in the country would stand in the way of a coach's returning to his alma mater." Privately, he said, the resentment lingered at BC over how Notre Dame and Leahy did it.

"When Coach Leahy went to Notre Dame, Dad went with him," said Billy Sullivan's son Pat. "They never forgave Leahy for leaving. They never forgave my dad, either. Not even the Jesuits, who are supposed to do that."

When Father Murphy told assistant coach Joe McArdle of his sorrow over their leaving, McArdle said, "Father, what would you do if you could go to another area and become a cardinal-archbishop? That's what they are offering Frank."

In that sense, McArdle is correct. Most of us would figure out a way to take our dream job when it is dangled in front of us. But McArdle's analogy came with a dash of salt. Boston College didn't like to think of itself as a rung below any Catholic college or university. That included Father Dullea, the priest newly in charge of Boston College athletics, who never absolved Leahy or Notre Dame for their perfidy. He objected to Leahy creating an out clause out of thin air. But Leahy was a coach, a layman, not a priest. Father Dullea saved his real ire for Notre Dame's failure to ask permission to contact Leahy or even just give Boston College a heads-up until the deal was pretty much done. Notre Dame offended his definition of honor. Priests don't act that way, especially toward other priests.

Shortly after Leahy left, Father Dullea handwrote a nearly four-page memo laying out the events as he knew them. He wrote it for public consumption, or perhaps for history; he never released the memo. Cooler heads likely prevailed, and it wasn't difficult to have a head cooler than Dullea's. As we shall see, he held the whole transaction against Leahy and Notre Dame for years to come. The memo is among the papers he donated to the university archives.

"Neither the trustees, who authorized the signing, nor the Reverend President, who approved, nor the faculty director of athletics nor the graduate manager stated before, during, or after the signing that a release would be given in the event of Mr. Leahy's desiring to coach at any other college," Dullea wrote. "Mr. Leahy's letter of February 14 requesting his release from his contract is on file at the college. In this letter no mention is made of such an understanding."

He followed up in April with a three-page, single-spaced letter to the Very Reverend Albert F. Cousineau, head of the Congregation of Holy Cross—Notre Dame's order of Catholicism—asking that something be done. Cousineau forwarded it to Father O'Donnell at Notre Dame, who replied with a four-page, single-spaced explanation from Father John Cavanaugh. "Confidentially," O'Donnell wrote to Cousineau, "the authorities at Boston College have assumed the attitude of a 'martyr' during the entire affair, for reasons best known to themselves."

Cousineau, rather than get involved, wrote Dullea a nice cover letter and included Cavanaugh's response, which only angered Father Dullea more. Cavanaugh wrote, "If I had any offense to urge against the authorities at Boston College, I do not think I would take it to the press or to their Father General in Rome. If I had an offense involving athletics, I would go directly to Father Dullea, confident that in him, a priest, I would find a fair hearing." Perhaps so, but when Father Cavanaugh wanted to hire Dullea's coach, Cavanaugh failed to go directly to him.

Dullea responded with a *five*-page, single-spaced letter to Father Cousineau. "Your men have Leahy. Let them keep him. We have no desire to have him back," Dullea said. And there he let it die.

A writer in Boston sympathetic to Leahy pointed out that if he had waited one more day to sign his new contract, or if Layden had resigned one day earlier, Leahy never would have put himself in an ethical pickle. But Leahy signed the new contract when he signed it. And he ran over it when he needed to run over it in the same way that he taught his players to play: This is the mission and nothing is going to stand in the way of completing it.

When the news hit the morning papers, Father O'Donnell began receiving congratulatory telegrams, including one from one of Layden's fellow Four Horsemen, Wisconsin head coach Harry Stuhldreher, as well as from Arch Ward ("I AM SURE YOU CHOSE WISELY.").

Leahy arrived in South Bend on the afternoon of February 15. He always remembered the hour that he set foot on the Notre Dame campus again—3:15 p.m. He went to Father O'Donnell's office and signed his contract. When he and Father O'Donnell walked out, Elmer Layden was standing there for a ceremonial, if accidental, handing over of the whistle.

"Athletically speaking, this is the happiest day of my life," Leahy said at a press conference. "It is a dream come true. All real Notre Dame men regard the appointment as the highest honor they could get."

Just about every real Notre Dame man who had been a teammate of Leahy at Notre Dame sent him a telegram saying something to the effect that they knew he would get the job someday, except for fullback Joe Savoldi. He wired, "I didn't think you had it, kid."

Joe Diereckx, the Notre Dame Stadium caretaker, took in Leahy's return to campus and called his wife. "Mary," he said, "he looks like another Knute Rockne."

Leahy tried to cut off that discussion. He said it couldn't happen. "There will never be another Rockne," Leahy said. "The day of the undefeated team is over."

The first half of that sentiment can be debated. Leahy needed only one season to prove the second half wrong.

CHAPTER EIGHT

NO ONE WILL EVER OUTGAME THESE BOYS

One way of not being Rockne was not coaching like Rockne, a tall order at a university that also served as a shrine to its former coach. Leahy had the requisite Rockne pedigree, but he intended to make changes that neither Hunk Anderson nor Elmer Layden, Rockne's immediate successors, had the interest—or stomach—to make.

Leahy started on the day after he signed his contract, his first full day at Notre Dame. Leahy got word to the football team to report to equipment manager Jack McAllister, get gear and return to the field house in full uniform at three p.m. This was mid-February, four weeks before Leahy scheduled the official start of spring practice. "Leahy believed spring practice should begin in December and last until August," said Joe Doyle, who covered Notre Dame football for decades for *The South Bend Tribune*.

Leahy learned quickly that he had to set McAllister straight. McAllister had held the job when Leahy played, and he ruled the equipment room as his fiefdom. If he liked you, he called you "Pissant." If he called you by your last name, watch out. McAllister performed his own hazing of the freshmen. He would dole out clean socks and jocks, but he handed out woolen green jerseys to freshmen that got more uncomfortable the wetter they got. Then he would give them the wrong size shoes on purpose. Whether Leahy remembered the hazing or learned of it anew upon his return, he quickly let McAllister know that he should treat freshmen as he did everyone else on the team.

Then there was scrimmaging in the old field house, which took a strong stomach. One half of the field house held a basketball court. The football team worked out on the other half, which had a packed dirt floor. A local farmer would come to campus with his horses, plow, disc, and harrow to loosen the dirt. When the horses answered the call to nature, the farmer didn't hesitate to plow the manure into the dirt. Scrapiron Young, the forever trainer at Notre Dame, kept a supply of tetanus shots on hand for any player who suffered a wound that broke the skin.

A practice field dusted with manure didn't faze Leahy. After all, he had an indoor 100-yard field, a luxury he didn't enjoy at Boston College, not to mention that his return continued to stir his emotions. "Just think," he recalled. "Many a time I've raked the pebbles and scraps of papers out of this place."

In his small office, Leahy paid homage to Rockne. A photographic portrait of Rockne hung on the wall behind Leahy's right shoulder as he sat at the desk in a chair that had been used by Rockne. Leahy hung a framed poem about Rockne as well as photos of Rockne's three best teams. Showcasing Rockne was Leahy's way of putting the Rock's imprimatur on Leahy's arrival. Leahy didn't do so to stroke his own ego. Six weeks after his hiring, Leahy's office door still read, "E.F. Layden."

During that month of "secret" practices, when the team worked outside, Leahy and his assistants would watch from atop the scoreboard on the north end of the stadium. That is, when Leahy was in town. With Floss planning to remain in Boston until the end of summer, not to mention his continued affiliation with U.S. Rubber and its Keds brand, Leahy didn't come to South Bend to stay until early March. On March 11, the night before spring practice began, Leahy spoke to the South Bend Elks Club annual Father-Son Banquet. He brought along his assistants, who weren't difficult to round up. Leahy shared a suite of rooms at the Hotel Oliver with McArdle and Druze. McKeever, married with twins, rented a two-bedroom furnished apartment five blocks from campus.

"At the end of next season our mark of effort will be 100 percent," Leahy told some three hundred in attendance. "Our mark of achievement we do not know."

Leahy scheduled the opening session of spring practice for three p.m. the following day. At a noon meeting with the team, Leahy told them that, weather permitting—and it snowed that day—practice would be held on Cartier Field. During the lunch hour, Leahy spoke to nearly the entire student body at a rally at the field house that included the band and the cheerleaders.

"Men of Notre Dame," Leahy began, "today is a momentous occasion for all of us." He spoke extemporaneously, and at length, during which he used his oddly formal manner of speaking to reveal to his new constituents his courtliness, humility, and determination.

On his time as a student: "No one ever accused us of being too nifty on our feet on that football field but when Adler and Livingston [a local haberdasher] came out to try to relieve us of some money which we owed them, we were just as elusive as Steve Juzwik [an Irish halfback]. We always managed to give the aforementioned clothiers the shadow and then we quickly took it away. The thought often came to us that if we had been as clever in avoiding people on the field of play as off it, we might have been another Red Grange instead of a plain, old-fashioned tackle."

On their role as students in his football program: “You men of Notre Dame will be the twelfth man on our team, as you have been in the past. Our success is in large measure dependent upon your efforts… With the best twelfth man on our side, we will try to field eleven others who will compare favorably with those who wear the colors of the colleges on our schedule. Please do not expect too much. There are many factors which militate against undue success. We always have a hard schedule here at Notre Dame. All teams are good today and every team which faces Notre Dame is shooting its best at us in an effort to upset the Irish.”

A call to arms: “All of us pulling together can assure continued athletic happiness. Notre Dame has thrown us a flaming torch. We reach for it eagerly and we hold it highly and proudly. Yet we need help from the faculty, the student body, and the players. And, above all we call upon Our Lady to guide our steps along the paths of goodness and truth, for these are the roads to genuine happiness.”

At three p.m., Leahy walked out of his office and discovered his team milling about the field house instead of on the practice field as instructed. He called Paul Lillis, as team captain, into his office and demanded an explanation.

“Coach, you said ‘weather permitting.’ Look outside,” Lillis said.

“But Paul,” Leahy replied, “it isn’t raining or snowing now. We will go out. So get the lads ready.”

The assistants eyeballed the players and ordered anyone wearing a lot of tape or bandages to remain in the field house until the writers and photographers left. This was supposed to be the first practice of the spring. Leahy didn’t want any questions about how his players got hurt if they hadn’t been practicing.

Leahy went out on the snow-covered practice field in sweats. His assistants showed up in mackinaws. “My coaching staff,” Leahy told the writers and newsreel men, lined up four and five deep on the sideline, “they believe in warmth. See what nice jackets they have on?” From the next day forward, the assistants wore sweats.

Jerry Nason, *The Boston Globe* writer who came to report on Leahy's first on-field work to the fans that Leahy left behind, called him "the most photographed man in America today." Nason might not have been far from the truth. The national interest in the new Notre Dame coach rose to Hollywood-like celebrity. In response to the deluge of mail, before the end of March Leahy had seven stenographers sending out more than two hundred letters a day. Some of the interest was competitive. Using film to scout opposing teams had not yet become customary. At one point during spring ball, Leahy got wind that opposing coaches had ordered copies of the Sugar Bowl game film from Paramount (which had shown it at theaters in New England to capitalize on Boston College's victory) to look for clues as to what Leahy might do at Notre Dame. Leahy made an emergency trip to New York to plead with Paramount executives not to fill the orders or sell the film to anyone, even coaching clinics. Paramount acquiesced.

Every new head coach sets his new rules. Every team subject to those new rules tests them. The Irish players found out quickly Leahy did not look the other way. In the first week of practice, Leahy heard a veteran guard curse aloud. Leahy kicked him off—not the field; Leahy kicked him off the team. Another guard tried to get McArdle's attention by calling, "Hey, Joe!" This violated the head coach's protocol about showing respect. He came running from two fields away and sent the player to practice with the B-team. The player didn't return to the varsity until 1942.

Leahy made a more significant change by shrinking the size of the roster. Rockne's policy, followed by Anderson and Layden as well, had been to open up the football team to any student who wanted to play. If two hundred players came out for a sport in which eleven play at a time, so be it. Leahy put an end to keeping around those he identified as "young, spindly-legged lads." He thought every 150-pound kid on campus would fancy himself a Midwestern Charley O'Rourke.

Leahy intended to limit the roster to fifty-five men, and the shock waves at changing Rockne's unwritten rule extended from campus to the diners and barber shops where the "downtown coaches" held court. If Rockne, Anderson, and Layden had a soft spot for every boy who wanted to say he played Notre Dame football, fine. Leahy saw it as an unwieldy distraction. He also knew that cutting the roster would focus the intent of his lads during practice in a way that no meeting or pep talk ever would accomplish. "No one wanted to get cut or lose his scholarship, so it turned into a bloodbath," Jack Barry, a senior end from Chicago, said. "I survived and I wasn't very big. There were brawls everywhere and I got into a few of them myself."

The Irish players also learned the difference between Layden's warmth and avuncularity and Leahy's desire for perfection. Leahy approached Lillis, poked his finger into the player's belly, and said, "You're pretty soft for a Notre Dame football captain, aren't you, Mr. Lillis? You don't keep yourself in very good condition in the offseason, do you?" Lillis slimmed from 225 pounds to 210. Tackle Walt Ziemba dropped 35 pounds to 225, still larger than most linemen of the day, and his improved quickness allowed Leahy to move Ziemba to play center.

Leahy believed in neither tackling dummies nor mechanized teaching aids. He wanted, as modern coaches say, a hat on a hat: halfbacks blocking ends, guards working against ends and backs, tackles on tackles. Leahy believed blocking a heavy bag to be a waste of time. No one would face a heavy bag in a game. The pounding day after day, week after week, wore on the players, as Leahy desired. At one point, the players asked Lillis to go into Leahy's office and tell him if he didn't ease up on practice, most of them would quit. It's hard to believe Lillis was smart enough to be captain and not smart enough to turn down his teammates outright. Leahy told Lillis to go back and tell them that practice had not started to get difficult.

"It taught us one of Coach Leahy's biggest lessons," lineman Bob McBride said. "He had a great fear of allowing an athlete to give less than his potential. He wanted above all to teach people to go all out in order to be a winner."

For all the changes that Leahy wanted to make, he treaded lightly when it came to the offense. The Irish still used the Notre Dame box, Rockne's version of the single wing. A lot of coaches continued to use it, perhaps because a lot of coaches had played for Rockne. That said, Stanford had gone from 1-7-1 in 1939 to 10-0 and a Rose Bowl victory in 1940 because new coach Clark Shaughnessy had installed the T formation. Leahy's insatiable appetite for football knowledge put the T on his radar. He only had four returning starters, so the team had a relatively blank slate. He worked a few T-formation plays into the Irish playbook. But at some level he understood he couldn't change everything all at once. He did try to tell the fans at the outset of spring practice that his team would do what the players did best.

"At Boston College we tried 'goofy stuff,'" he said. "Quick opening plays, long passes and short passes. At Boston College we were fortunate in having a fine passer and runner in Charley O'Rourke. If we come up with a good passer here next fall, we'll really open up. We gambled at Boston College and we'll gamble here, if we have a chance."

Leahy shifted the positions of several players, emphasizing speed at all positions. In Juzwik and Dippy Evans, he had a nucleus of speed in the backfield but none on the line. Not only did a much trimmer Ziemba move to center, but senior fullback Bernie Crimmins shifted to guard. Just to make sure that Crimmins committed to the move, in late summer Leahy stopped in Crimmins's hometown of Louisville en route to a coaching clinic and explained the position change to Crimmins, his mother, and his brothers. Leahy could sell. "He had everybody convinced that pulling at guard, leading the interference, was just being a blocking back," Crimmins said. It isn't. After Leahy spoke with the family, he took Crimmins to a neighborhood park and went over pulling moves and other footwork. Crimmins became an All-American and would be elected to the College Football Hall of Fame.

Leahy's emphasis on efficiency focused on every detail. He eliminated the old method of the team getting into formation and then having the quarterback yelling out a series of signals. Leahy had the quarterback deliver the play call in the huddle. Once the players got into position, the quarterback would yell "hike" to initiate a shift; after one second, he would then deliver the signal for the snap.

One day that spring, Leahy invited the thirty-year-old basketball coach of South Bend Central High to observe practice. During the first week of drills, Central, ranked second in the state, got upset by one point in the quarterfinals of the Indiana High School Basketball Tournament.

"I thought my basketball practices were well-organized and efficient," John Wooden marveled. "After observing Coach Leahy's practice, I realized more work was needed. There was not one minute wasted. Even the transitions from drill to drill were done with no wasted second."

Leahy inspired Wooden to begin spending his mornings writing down on index cards the plans for his team's afternoon workouts down to the minute, a habit he maintained throughout winning ten NCAA men's basketball championships at UCLA. Wooden believed in a lot of the same precepts as Leahy—not only organization, but superior conditioning; not merely teach on the chalkboard, but teach physically. For Wooden, that meant literally walking his players where he wanted them on the court. For Leahy, as ever, that meant his assistants, who ranged in age from twenty-seven to thirty-one, demonstrating to their players the moves they wanted them to learn.

On Wednesday, April 9, the Wednesday of Holy Week, spring vacation began for the student body, if not for the football team. Leahy sought and received approval from Father John Cavanaugh for the team to remain on campus for practice through Holy Saturday. On Good Friday, two days later, when the team came in from its second practice of the day, a holiday and a holy day, McBride sat at his locker, sweat and blood dripping to the floor. Neither McBride nor fellow lineman Lou Rymkus showed any inclination, not to mention physical ability, to rise, disrobe, and get to the showers. Rymkus turned to McBride and said, "Man, now I know exactly how Christ felt 1,941 years ago today."

After the team worked out twice more on Holy Saturday, Leahy turned them loose on spring break all the way until . . . Tuesday. Spring ball continued until late May, and woe be unto the man who tried to interrupt. The Notre Dame track and field team had a meet against Michigan, and coach Bill Mahoney went to see Leahy to make sure that a player on both teams would be available. Not only did Leahy not release the player, but when Mahoney didn't take no for an answer, Leahy came around his desk after him.

Midway through spring practice, the rancor Leahy left behind at Boston College ensnared him again. A freshman lineman named Gil Bouley didn't report for the Eagles' spring practice and told friends he intended to transfer to Notre Dame. The Boston papers turned it into an issue. About the time it built into a fever pitch, Leahy sent a telegram to every Boston paper that read, "You may rest assured that Gilbert Bouley, or any other Boston College student, will never participate in athletics at Notre Dame, because of the strict policy in vogue here." He didn't sign it, "Head Coach Frank Leahy," but "Frank Leahy, Director of Athletics."

After spring practice, Leahy dived into the other duties of offseason coaches. He barnstormed from coast to coast, beating the drum for Notre Dame, raising money for the school and recruiting players for himself. He made a trip to Daytona Beach, where he gave a talk railing at the softness of the modern American boy. "Boys aren't proud of their physical prowess anymore—or envious over the ability of one of their mates to knock them over on a football field. When they get knocked down or fall down they don't get up any more boiling with indignation. No, they get up and look for the bench to be called out, and their thought is, 'Well, I didn't get hurt so bad that I can't go to the dance tonight.'"

Leahy didn't think that about just "the American boy." He thought his players soft, too. Juzwik got his hand stepped on in practice that spring and suffered a broken finger. He thought he had won the golden ticket out of those grueling sessions.

"But Stephen," Leahy said, "you don't run on your hands. We can keep you out of physical contact until we can get a cast on your hand, but you will run."

A trip to Pittsburgh in late June provides a more typical example of Leahy's travels. He and Father John Cavanaugh began a whirlwind day by stepping off the train and going to morning Mass at St. Mary of Mercy Church downtown. They visited the seriously ill mother of acclaimed boxer Billy Conn, who the previous week had nearly upset heavyweight champion Joe Louis. They spoke that night to the first annual Notre Dame Scholarship Fund dinner sponsored by the local Notre Dame club, which presented the university a check for $2,500. Some five hundred people attended at the Hotel Schenley in un-air-conditioned swelter. Leahy took off his suit jacket before speaking.

"Our team may prove a disappointment to some," Leahy said. "We had a good spring training season. We are almost bound to lose a few games. Our type of play won't vary much from standard Notre Dame teams except that we're going to take chances—a team has to gamble at times. Our team has plenty of speed and the greatest lack is forward passing."

Leahy may have been playing possum there. Given his proclivity for worry, maybe not. But during the spring he had found a sophomore halfback who had some ability to throw. In a story in *The South Bend Tribune* right after the first scrimmage in late March, Jack Ledden mentioned a 30-yard completion thrown "by a sophomore left half-back, Bertelli."

Under Layden, in the Notre Dame box offense, Angelo Bertelli had been buried on the depth chart beneath a number of faster backs. As a fourth-string left halfback on the freshman team, he would watch the varsity practice and count four more left halfbacks returning the following year. He didn't want to return home to Springfield, Massachusetts, for Christmas, where everyone thought he would play for the Irish as a sophomore in 1941.

Leahy had tried to recruit Bertelli to play at nearby Boston College.

But Bertelli had his heart set on Notre Dame. When Ed McKeever traveled to visit him at home, Bertelli slipped out.

"I'd heard that McKeever was a smooth talker and I was afraid he would talk me into going to BC," Bertelli said a half century later. "I figured the best way to get to Notre Dame was to avoid McKeever, so I ducked out." Bertelli hid in a movie theater, where he took in a double feature—and two cartoons—leaving McKeever at his home with his Italian immigrant mother, who spoke little English.

So of course it was McKeever who worked with Bertelli on his passing skills throughout the spring and summer of 1941. McKeever taught Bertelli to snap the throw with his wrist, comparing it to a catcher trying to pick off a runner, and the speed and accuracy of Bertelli's throws improved immensely.

Leahy liked Bertelli's potential as a passer but wondered if the halfback had the necessary speed and toughness as a runner. One day in practice, Leahy watched Bertelli run a nice sweep. The coach asked to see it again. Bertelli turned the corner again. Those two sweeps convinced him to keep Bertelli on the team.

"Wouldn't that have been something if we had cut a Heisman Trophy winner?" McArdle mused.

In late July, Leahy went out to Hollywood and guest starred on the NBC Radio show *Kraft Music Hall*, hosted by Bing Crosby. His appearance had been the idea of Don Ameche, the cinematic star who also happened to be a huge Fighting Irish fan. Leahy became pals with Ameche and with the host himself.

Father Cavanaugh wired Leahy to tell him he had sat with Father O'Donnell and they enjoyed listening to the show. Leahy responded with a handwritten letter on stationery from the Rice Hotel in Houston, where he had gone for a coaching clinic. The coach got a taste of his new life as national celebrity and left Hollywood starstruck.

"Working with Crosby and Ameche was most enjoyable," Leahy wrote. "The big Hollywood stars are genuine people. Crosby, [Bob] Hope, and Ameche are just perfect in every respect. Had dinner in the latter's home and had a very interesting time. There was a lot of conversation about N.D. and Elmer, which I shall discuss with you later. I surely do like Don and his wife. Everyone in Hollywood is very N.D. conscious. What rabid fans they are.

"Judge Carberry [Leahy's Notre Dame teammate Jack] introduced me to innumerable directors and stars, all of whom were just grand. The Ameches and [producer] Mark Hellenger were asking all about you."

While in Southern California, Leahy attended the funeral of USC head coach Howard Jones, whose unexpected death from a heart attack at age fifty-five stunned the entire football world, including Leahy. Not two months earlier, Jones had stopped in South Bend to pick up a new Studebaker at the auto plant not far from campus. Leahy had had lunch with him and Father Cavanaugh and invited Jones to practice.

"Much to my surprise," Leahy wrote the priest about the funeral, "the church was only about 2/3 full. Life is surely funny."

No detail was too small to escape Leahy. He stretched the starting times of two-a-day practices to six thirty a.m. and four thirty p.m., in order to give his players more time to rest in the interim. He asked the administration to adjust the campus jobs that his players held. In the spring, the football players had worked in dining halls as dishwashers or waiters. By the fall, all non-freshmen served as hall prefects, distributing mail and doing "chapel check" in the morning. Leahy asked that the freshmen be assigned to the dining halls, but only as "dish stackers" and that they work three days a week, one hour a day, rather than in random twenty-minute shifts.

"It was extremely important to Coach Leahy that we do our jobs the best way possible," McBride said. "I can guarantee you that if a person fell down on any job that he was supposed to be doing for Notre Dame he was quickly straightened out by Coach. Mediocrity was not a part of him. He would not allow it to be part of you, and he wouldn't allow it to represent Notre Dame. I have never seen any human being have the depth of loyalty to an institution or organization that Frank Leahy had to Notre Dame. He made everybody who played for him feel the same."

Leahy had attempted to tamp down expectations from the moment he arrived. What would become known as Leahy's natural pessimism, and then as his faux poor-mouthing, had basis in hard-eyed analysis coming into the 1941 season. Leahy and his coaches could see they didn't have as much talent as they had the previous year. McArdle remembered Lillis asking him at practice one day, "Coach, how badly do you think we could beat your Boston College team of last year?" McArdle wanted to tell him the truth, that BC would have won in a rout. Instead, he dissembled with something about the game going either way.

As the season opener against Arizona approached, Leahy's bosses adopted his approach. Anytime Cavanaugh sent a letter to anyone who had contacted him to praise Leahy, Cavanaugh replied with variations of this: "I know he will give an excellent account of his stewardship. I warn you, however, not to expect the impossible of him the first year."

The national writers bought into Leahy's pessimism. "He must grapple with the specter that generates from knowing that there is no possible way that he can top his unbeaten 1940 record at Boston College," Bob Considine wrote in *The Washington Post*. Bill Cunningham wrote in *The Boston Post* that Leahy had too much to do to overcome Layden's reluctance to uncouple the team from all things Rockne. "Memories can't block and tackle and run," he said.

Those memories went away fast. The Irish shot out of the gate to defeat Arizona in the opener, 38–7, and followed it up with a methodical 19–6 defeat of Indiana. In week three, Notre Dame went to Atlanta where Leahy installed a four-man defensive front to clamp down on Georgia Tech's sweeps and passing game. Notre Dame won that one, 20–0, limiting the Yellow Jackets to 91 yards of total offense. Through three games, Bertelli had completed 22 of 35 passes for 331 yards—this in an era when a passer who completed more than half his attempts drew gawks and gasps.

The AP rankings debuted for the season with 3-0 Notre Dame at No. 8, a reflection of the Irish's light schedule and perhaps some residual skepticism among the voters. One writer who believed in Leahy moved the coach from the sports page to the national stage that week. Cohane's five-page spread on the coach appeared in *The Saturday Evening Post*. The headline, designed to warm the heart of every subway alum: "Rockne Picked Him." Cohane laid out Leahy's life story, his bond with Rockne, and quoted Crowley as the proud mentor. What could go wrong?

Notre Dame went to Carnegie Tech, the Pittsburgh school with an academic bent that had begun to de-emphasize football. Only three years earlier, the Tartans had finished in the top ten. But they would win only one game in 1941 and score but 37 points over eight games. Leahy took measures in his game plan to account for Carnegie Tech's weaknesses. He told quarterback Harry Wright, who called the plays, not to pass the ball unless Leahy sent it in (in that era, unlike now, players wielded the authority to call plays) and limited the running game to five plays.*

Leahy's largesse may have made his team relax. Carnegie Tech may have been fired up to play Notre Dame—a weekly hazard for the Irish. Sloppy, rainy conditions contributed to five Notre Dame turnovers. Whatever happened, Notre Dame had a 2nd-and-goal inside the Tartan 2-yard line and failed to score. The Irish missed another 4th-and-1 deep in Carnegie Tech territory. Notre Dame gutted out a 16–0 victory, but the train home could have run on the steam coming off the Irish head coach.

In fact, Notre Dame had planned to spend the night at the William Penn Hotel in Pittsburgh and return home Sunday. Leahy had business manager Herb Jones change the team's itinerary while the players took their postgame showers. Jones explained that with so little time he might not be able to arrange for a meal.

"I could care less whether they eat or not," Leahy said. "We're going to get back to South Bend. The way they performed this afternoon,

* Wright had wanted to play for Leahy at Boston College, but the coach deemed him too small. Layden signed him. The first time that Leahy ran into him at Notre Dame, he said, "Y'know, lad, I'm glad I turned you down at Boston College."

they don't deserve to eat." Jones managed to arrange for food. The team arrived in LaPorte, Indiana, near South Bend at four thirty a.m. Sunday. Leahy sent the managers through the train to inform the players that practice would begin at six thirty a.m.

The team ran wind sprints, performed calisthenics, then lined up at the goal line and ran the fullback into the line for, depending upon whose memory is trusted, ninety minutes or two hours. In those days of players working on offense and defense, the first team remained on offense and the rest took turns on defense. When Leahy finally blew the whistle and gathered the team, he told them, "Look me in the eyes. If there is ever a time in the future that a Notre Dame football team would fail to make a yard, think of this."

Another subpar team, Illinois, came to Notre Dame Stadium. It would be the legendary coach Bob Zuppke's last season, and the Illini finished 2-6. Their worst loss of the season would be the 49–14 beating they took from the Irish. The first time that Notre Dame got to the Illinois 5, tackle Jim Brutz said in the huddle, "For God's sake, let's push them out of here and score. I don't want to go through that crazy drill again." The line nearly drove the Illini defensive front through the back of the end zone.

Notre Dame stood 5-0, but the AP voters ranked the Irish only No. 6, perhaps because of the weak schedule. Playing No. 14 Army (4-0) at Yankee Stadium would take care of that. Army, like Notre Dame, had an outstanding coach, Earl "Red" Blaik, in his first season at his alma mater. Destiny had plans for the two of them.

Nearly two inches of rain began Friday night and continued so steadily on game day, the first day of November, that Yankee Stadium couldn't absorb it all. Leahy, forever seeking an edge, had made a deal with DuPont for Notre Dame to become the first football team to wear pants made of the company's new synthetic fabric, nylon, which weighed half of what cotton pants weighed and wouldn't absorb rain that cotton did. Still, the nylon pants—gold, of course—proved no match for the mud, which seeped over shoetops and hindered the center's ability to deliver the ball. The mud became so ubiquitous that the Irish players put strips of adhesive tape on their helmets so that they could tell themselves from their opponents. The players said the wet infield sand lodged itself between pad and skin, leaving everyone chafed.

The rain also validated the coaching wisdom that you can't trust a passing offense in bad weather, which left Notre Dame, a heavy favorite, to depend on a running game that Leahy didn't find dependable. Army made five first downs, Notre Dame three, and the game ended in a 0–0 tie. Afterward, Leahy sounded almost upbeat. His team had not lost but the players responded in the postgame locker room as if they had. That's what their head coach wanted to see.

"I feel more confident about the Navy and Northwestern games than I did before the game," Leahy said. "... Because these boys don't want to lose. They don't want to tie. They want to win."

Maybe Leahy saw his team mature that day, or maybe the Irish heard the confidence their demanding coach publicly professed in them. In the next two weeks, Notre Dame went on the road and defeated No. 6 Navy, in Baltimore, 20–13, before edging No. 8 Northwestern in Evanston, 7–6. Against the Midshipmen, Bertelli completed passes to six different receivers and finished 12 of 18 for the "staggering" total of 232 yards, as Allison Danzig described in *The New York Times*. Leahy had a hot hand. Twice he sent in plays that scored touchdowns.

After the Northwestern victory, the AP voters moved Notre Dame up to No. 5, but Leahy, in the column that Bill Sullivan ghosted for him, refused to rank the Irish in the top ten. "We are a bit superstitious, and for this reason, we hesitate to include our own team among the finest in the country," the column said.

Only Southern California stood between Notre Dame and its first unbeaten season since 1930, Rockne's last team. Only the Trojans, who had struggled to a 2-5-1 under interim coach Sam Barry after the death of their coach, stood in the way of Leahy enjoying his second consecutive unbeaten season.

"We will lose the game tomorrow," Leahy told Dave Egan of the

Boston Record. They sat in the coach's small, bare office. He explained how little depth the Irish have, how tired his front-line players felt. This was a team that didn't push anyone around. By the end of the year, no back weighed as much as 180. Notre Dame won because of Bertelli's arm and because they didn't beat themselves. Leahy loved this team. "No one will ever outgame these boys," Leahy said. The Irish would lose, Leahy concluded, because they hadn't lost yet. It was their turn.

The fans didn't share Leahy's pessimism. They bought all 57,000 seats in Notre Dame Stadium for the first time ever. The university added 350 office chairs on the sidelines and sold those, too. South Bend was overrun with fans, including Ameche, who spoke at the Friday night pep rally. People slept in the dorm hallways. Leahy got a phone call in his office Friday from someone in the administrative office telling him that the university had to find beds for eight fans. He called the campus infirmary and spoke to a nun.

"Sister, this is Frank Leahy. I'm one of the football coaches here. Could you do me two favors?"

He didn't demand the nuns do his bidding because he was Frank Leahy. He called as "one of the football coaches."

"Sister," Leahy said, "I'd like three or four touchdown plays for tomorrow's game, and I'd like eight beds in the infirmary for friends of Notre Dame who can't find lodgings."

He got the beds. He didn't need the plays. Notre Dame defeated USC, 20–18, the victory margin created by making two extra points to the Trojans' none. As in the Navy game, twice Leahy sent plays into the huddle and the Irish scored. The postgame locker room overflowed with backslappers, writers, and photographers. Leahy worked the room, too, but with a different purpose in mind. He moved player to player, locker to locker, speaking with praise and gratitude.

The season may have concluded—Notre Dame again would have to explain, both to the major bowls and then to the public, that its stance against participating in the postseason had not changed—but Leahy couldn't shut down the fuel that drove him.

On Monday, Leahy spoke in Detroit to the Downtown Quarterback Club, and by Saturday, according to nationally syndicated gossip columnist Louella Parsons, he was in Palo Alto with his new pal Bing Crosby to take in the Big Game between Stanford and California.

While in California, Leahy learned that his head coaching colleagues, in the annual poll conducted by the *New York World-Telegram*, narrowly elected him Coach of the Year over Bernie Bierman of national champion Minnesota. The poll counted only first-place votes, which Leahy won, 58–54. Had they used a point system based on the 1-2-3 ballots, Bierman would have won. On December 19, as the country convulsed after the attack on Pearl Harbor, Leahy got around the wartime strains on train travel and went to New York to receive the award at a dinner at Mamma Leone's.

Then there is the story that Joe Doyle told when Leahy died. After the season, Leahy fulfilled a promise he had made to have dinner with Rev. Wendell Corcoran, the pastor at nearby St. Joseph's. Leahy got in the car with the priest and Ed McKeever and suggested they stop by the office and watch film of the USC game "for a few minutes."

"Nothing would intrigue me less," Father Corcoran said.

McKeever, knowing it futile to argue with Leahy, said, "If you insist."

"I must insist," Leahy said. "If you get satisfied, the opposition will kill you. They're making plans for next season. So must we."

Leahy had a plan for the next season. It would be a blockbuster.

CHAPTER NINE

THE GUINEA-PIG TEAM

Clark Shaughnessy helped install the T with the Chicago Bears before he went to Stanford and led the Wow Boys to that zero-to-hero undefeated season in 1940. Before winning the Rose Bowl, Shaughnessy returned to Chicago to help the Bears prepare for the NFL Championship Game. They beat the Washington Redskins, 73–0. He had a pretty good year.

"Like everything else, the modern T was a bright man taking something good and making it better—a great deal better," Leahy said nearly a quarter-century later. "In his own way, Shaughnessy's innovation was just as revolutionary as the forward pass more than 30 years before. With the forward pass, football had begun to grow up. With the modern T, football had really come of age."

When the NFL champion Bears defeated the College All-Stars in Chicago, 37–13, in the summer of 1941, Leahy and Father John Cavanaugh watched together in the stands at Soldier Field. Leahy wanted to see his Boston College stars, lineman Chet Gladchuk and quarterback Charley O'Rourke, play for the All-Stars (O'Rourke played in an All-Star backfield alongside Jackie Robinson of UCLA). Leahy wanted to see the Bears run the T. But most of all, he wanted Cavanaugh to see the Bears run the T. After witnessing Chicago quarterback Sid Luckman throw two touchdowns, and the Bears gain 464 yards of total offense, Leahy suggested to Cavanaugh that Notre Dame switch to the T. Cavanaugh gave his blessing.

Leahy made clear during his tenure at Notre Dame that no one but he made the big decisions concerning Fighting Irish football. What a priest serving as university vice president could contribute to a decision about switching offenses is about what Leahy could contribute to an ecclesiastical conference. But Leahy had yet to coach a game at Notre Dame, and he knew setting aside Rockne's offense for something newfangled would stir up all Irish fans, from the big donors to the downtown coaches to the subway alumni. Getting Cavanaugh's approval reeked of smart politics.

That said, with the first game four weeks away, Leahy had no intention of tossing aside all the spring practice work for a new offense. He incorporated some T-formation schemes in the playbook that first season. But once it ended, he didn't wait long to start installing the T for 1942. While on vacation with Floss on the Florida Panhandle in early January, Leahy wrote Father Cavanaugh a letter and hinted at the transition ahead.

"Am so anxious for our lads to start their training program," Leahy wrote. "We have so very much work ahead of us."

A few weeks after Leahy retired, he looked back and said, "When a man is young he will do things like that, taking unreasonable risks to accomplish something he thinks can be done."

Talking Xs and Os fed Leahy's soul, so he took refuge in the opportunity to study this new offense. He met with Hunk Anderson, one of his Notre Dame predecessors, now the Bears' line coach, in Detroit; Bears head coach George Halas in Chicago; and, for two weeks, with

Shaughnessy himself at the University of Maryland, which had lured him away from Stanford to become head coach. But the meeting that had the greatest impact on the team took place at the Commodore Hotel in New York, where Leahy met with Luckman, the Bears quarterback, to go over the intricacies of the T.* Intricacies, as in, Leahy and Luckman spent two hours going over the center snap to the quarterback. One thing that Leahy liked about the offense is how quickly the holes open compared to the single wing. He liked how, with the quarterback under center, the latter could quickly engage in the blocking scheme.

Back on campus, Leahy called Bertelli into his office to let him know how much work lay ahead. "You are the finest passer in the nation," Leahy said to the Heisman runner-up. "You are also about the slowest running tailback I have seen since I played the position at Winner High School many years ago."

Leahy explained to Bertelli that he would take a snap under center and drop back. Leahy explained that the new offense would allow for man-to-man blocking, that deception would be utilized more than force, saving wear and tear on the players. And that Bertelli would have to learn eighty to a hundred plays. Bertelli's one question: "I handle the ball on every play, right?"

It turned out that Bertelli had more to offer the new offense than the arm that the writers had nicknamed "The Springfield Rifle." "We practiced hours and hours and hours, every spare minute," Bertelli recalled. "Deception was the name of the game with the T." At the snap, backs went in all directions and the defense had to figure out which one had the ball and where he intended to go. The deception would help do the work that the blockers did in the single wing—move the defenders out of the way. Bertelli recalled how patient Leahy remained over the course of the spring.

Leahy would go over plays with the team on the field before they

---

* Some versions say that McArdle joined Leahy in the meeting; another says it was Druze.

practiced them. He once explained to Bertelli, "Angelo, when you get the ball from center, drop back five steps, and when the right foot hits the ground, you dig in and look straight down the field, and you'll see Robert Dove, our left end, will be running down the sidelines. He will make a fake toward the sidelines. When he plants his left foot to make the fake, you throw to a spot to his inside, knowing that he's coming over the middle. Hit him right in the eye with the ball."

"Which eye, Coach?" Bertelli asked. This was no smart ass. He wanted to know.

When spring practice began, Luckman came into South Bend and brought another quarterback from the Bears, Bob Snyder, who liked coaching well enough that he retired in order to remain at Notre Dame for the entire year as freshman coach rather than sit on the bench behind Luckman. Snyder wouldn't be the only new assistant. McArdle and Druze both enlisted in the US Navy. Leahy replaced them with two former Irish players, Ed "Moose" Krause and Wayne Millner.

The war permeated every segment of American life, but a private all-male college faced more than the typical shortages and worry. It may be no coincidence that Druze and McArdle chose the Navy. That branch of the service all but took over the campus in the early months of the war. The Navy ROTC unit expanded, a thousand midshipmen arrived for training in a program assigned to Notre Dame, and construction began on a drill hall. The university also accelerated the four-year path to receive an undergraduate degree.

All football coaches are controlling by nature. The sport demands mental and physical discipline. Leahy insisted on control, thrived on it, drove himself to illness worrying over every small detail. Now the war caused Leahy to lose some control of who would be on his roster and for how long. The NCAA responded to the loss of men on campuses by making freshmen eligible to play on the varsity. Leahy found himself trying to install a new offense with a locker room of inexperienced players. The joke went that Notre Dame was too big to stop and too young to draft. The war also affected recruiting. One recruit in particular soured relations between Leahy and Army head coach Red Blaik.

Recruiting had many years to go before it became a public fascination, almost a sport in its own right. In those days, an area alum would serve as a conduit for information for the coaching staff. In small-town western Pennsylvania, a service station operator named Henry Opperman held that role for Notre Dame. His initial entreaties concerning John Lujack of Connellsville didn't arouse much interest. High school stars who were five foot eleven, 170 pounds, didn't turn the head of a top college coach.

Opperman kept pestering Leahy and finally got him to agree to speak at the Connellsville High banquet. Leahy met Lujack, went to his home and met his parents. Leahy asked him to come to campus in the spring of 1942 for a tryout.

"Johnny didn't throw eight times in high school," Leahy said, "but when I saw him throw four times, I said to him, 'Young man, if you still wish to enroll at Notre Dame, you have a home for four years.' "

That's not the story they told in West Point. L'affaire Lujack became so important, especially once Lujack starred for Notre Dame against Army, that a biography of General Maxwell Taylor discussed it. Taylor didn't became superintendent of the Academy until after World War II, three years after Lujack's recruitment.

Lujack's memory is that he visited West Point, where he didn't get to meet Blaik, and the assistant coach he did meet seemed unimpressed with him. By Blaik's account, he wanted Lujack, and Lujack's mother wanted her son to attend the Academy. The local congressman, J. Buell Snyder, responded by arriving at the Connellsville High graduation ceremony and announcing that he had awarded Lujack an appointment to West Point. He also presented Lujack with a flag and a scroll. *The Connellsville Daily Courier*, as it exalted the honor as an incentive to local children to work hard, also described it as "an unsolicited appointment."

Within two weeks, Lujack had hightailed it out of Connellsville and gone to Chicago for a summer job arranged by Leahy. Blaik, and the officers who oversaw athletics at West Point, believed that any person, place, or football program that stood between a young boy and a service academy appointment during wartime did the country a disservice. They complained loudly enough that Father John Cavanaugh felt it necessary to take Leahy with him to West Point to meet with the Academy Athletic Council before the end of June.

Each side presented their version of events. A memo written for the council summarizing the affair stated that Leahy had deployed such subterfuge against the wishes of Lujack's parents, then whisked him away to Chicago without his mother knowing his whereabouts. Leahy "at first denied all knowledge of what had taken place, but when faced with evidence provided by the boy's mother, he had to admit that he was lying. Father Cavanaugh was deeply distressed, but the harm had already been done, and Notre Dame kept the boy."

The aroma of sour grapes permeates the memo. For one thing, Blaik was as vicious a competitor as Leahy. For another, in Lujack's version of his recruitment, he didn't discuss being torn about his decision, or fought over by the two coaches. He said the offer from Notre Dame made a dream come true. "I didn't think I was good enough to make a Notre Dame team," Lujack said. "I said to my parents and my brothers and sisters, 'If I can make the traveling squad at Notre Dame my junior or senior year, I will be happy and feel that I had a successful career.' "

A few weeks later, in late July, the author and alumnus Francis Wallace wrote Father Cavanaugh from Hollywood, California, a letter recounting a story he had been told about how Leahy attempted to recruit freshman halfback Johnny Strzykalski off the Marquette roster. It turned out to be a not atypical story about a young player, momentarily unhappy, who given the opportunity to actually transfer and leave his friends and familiar surroundings, decided things weren't so bad after all.

Marquette coach Tom Stidham got his nose out of joint, and Leahy wrote him a letter of explanation and apology. But that's not the point.

Cavanaugh responded to Wallace with a long letter spelling out how the transfer never could have happened per university policy, then explained Leahy in a way that revealed the depth of their relationship.

"I am confident that Frank Leahy, by nature, has a blind spot for anyone who tries to befriend him," Cavanaugh wrote. "But when Frank comes back to the campus, I am going to make it a point to talk to him very earnestly about this matter. Always there are a few who, in one way or another, would use Notre Dame and Leahy for their own mean end. And he must be on the lookout for such individuals, or he will do himself and the University harm, very much against his own will.

"You are right in saying that Frank is extremely eager when he gets his eye on a prospect. I, too, have heard unflattering rumors about his 'recruiting,' but in every case I have honestly tried to get to the facts, and there has never been anything unethical in his actions which I have been about to discover. Very confidentially, I feel that most of this talk comes from the fact that Frank wants good boys, that he is because of his coaching success and because of Notre Dame's appeal rather effective in getting such boys, and therefore, gets into the hair of other coaches. So long as he operates ethically, and so long as Notre Dame's policies remain ethical, I cannot see the justice of restraining him from interesting, ethically, good boys, rather than mediocre ones."

But between Lujack and Strzykalski, Cavanaugh had heard enough. He felt the need to meet with Leahy and remind him that Notre Dame would not cut corners in its athletic pursuits. Out of their August 3 meeting came a two-page memorandum that emphasized that Notre Dame athletics would seek victory only in accordance with university "policies, practices, and the principles of true sportsmanship. If defeat is suffered because of honest adherence to these controlling and motivating factors, then defeat must be considered glorious . . . Every laudable effort and form of ingenuity may be directed to victory but never at the expense of any canon of fair play."

The memo declared that the athletic department could not help a recruit find a summer job until his second semester on campus; that no recruit could stay in or be entertained in the home of anyone in the athletic department, and that nothing resembling a tryout could be given by anyone employed in Notre Dame athletics. The memo also stated that any prospect trying to decide between Notre Dame and either West Point or Annapolis must be encouraged to attend the service academy "because of the special respect . . . and because of our time-honored friendly relationship with these two national institutions."

How long Leahy adhered to those rules is difficult to say. There are numerous stories regarding tryouts throughout the postwar years. The rivalry with Army remained feverish, driven by two demanding coaches competing to run the best program in the nation. Leahy remained ruthlessly competitive, so much so that he made himself ill in the forthcoming season.

Progress with the T came slowly. Leahy gave his players a lot to digest and expected them to digest it.

"It was a shock to us," said Bob Dove, a senior end in 1942. "Leahy said we would have to work harder than ever and that we'd be beaten. He said that we would be the guinea-pig team and therefore would be loved and remembered at Notre Dame."

Actually, no one loves and remembers a guinea pig. In the annual game that marked the end of spring football, the Irish unveiled the T against a team of Notre Dame grads before four thousand fans, among them Halas, who took the train from Chicago to see how far along Leahy had brought the team. The answer: not very far. The Irish didn't score a point, although Leahy limited them to only a handful of plays. He needed them to be ready in September, not May.

The result did little to convert the skeptics, which is to say, every Irish fan. This wasn't just any offense that Leahy had thrown in the garbage. This was Rockne's offense. "I was accused of heresy for the switch," Leahy would say. He knew how much ground the team had to cover to play to his standard. He refused to stop. There was so much to do.

One discovery he made turned out to be of little help for the upcoming season. The lack of familiarity with the T meant that the freshmen had a chance to make an impression. When they reported to practice before the season, they were only one spring practice behind the rest of the team. In an early practice, one freshman back made tackle after tackle. McKeever said to him, "Son, what's your name?"

"Lujack," the freshman replied.

The run-up to the season didn't go well physically. Leahy had returned to Chicago to see the Bears play the College All-Stars in late August, this time, as an assistant coach to the legendary Bob Zuppke, who had retired the previous season from Illinois. But Leahy contracted a skin infection before the game and returned home. It would be another warning sign that he ignored.

When the players reported for preseason practice, Leahy quickly gave the team the same workload they had in the spring. He overdid it. "That football team had to learn a totally new offense," McBride, a junior guard, said. "There were an awful lot of new fundamentals that went along with being able to play it properly. I do believe that there were times when that ball club left their best games on the practice field and Coach Leahy agreed with this in later life."

Coaches have debated forever whether injuries result from overwork or bad luck. But in the run-up to the September 26 season opener at Wisconsin, the Irish suffered a rash of debilitating injuries in the backfield. Senior halfback Dippy Evans (only the registrar knew his first name was Leon) blew out a knee. Junior halfback Creighton Miller had a bad ankle. Sophomore fullback Gerry Cowhig suffered a nagging groin injury. Also, center Wally Ziemba had trouble with both knees. And Bertelli, the reigning Heisman Trophy runner-up, the engine that would make this new offense go, got on the wrong train.

The team spent the Friday night before the Wisconsin game in Chicago. At the central train station Saturday morning, Bertelli sat down to read a newspaper near a concession stand that blocked his view of the rest of the team. When the announcement came to board the Chicago, Milwaukee & St. Paul train on track 23, Bertelli missed it. The student manager in charge of the head count on the train miscounted. The train departed.

Soon another announcement was made for the "Notre Dame Special," the train chartered for the student body. Bertelli heard that one. He boarded, sat down with paper and continued to read. He noticed that he didn't see any of his teammates, but no alarm bell went off until the conductor asked him for his ticket. He replied that he was with the team.

"You're with the football team?" the conductor replied. "Son, your train pulled out about ten minutes ago."

Meanwhile, on the team train, Leahy called a quarterback meeting, and Bertelli didn't show up. When he asked, McKeever told him that Bertelli had missed the train but that they had sent messages to the other trains to figure out which one he had boarded.

Leahy didn't take the news well. He yelled, "Stop the train!" and lunged for the emergency cord. McKeever executed a textbook tackle to prevent Leahy from exacerbating the problem. Leahy, already a jumble of nerves over the debut of his offense, spent the rest of the train ride grumbling. When they arrived at Camp Randall Stadium, he stood outside the locker room and asked passing ticketholders if they had seen Bertelli. He asked the officials to delay the game. They declined. The team warmed up, returned to the locker room, and went back on the field for the start of the game, and still no Bertelli.

Shortly before kickoff, Bertelli arrived, sprinted into the locker room, and donned his gear. He appeared on the field at 1:55 p.m., five minutes short of kickoff. Judging by his performance, the morning left him nearly as rattled as his coach. In unseasonably cold weather—some parts of Wisconsin got six inches of snow that day—Notre Dame ran 83 plays to Wisconsin's 51. The Irish gained well over 200 yards of total offense. But the Irish lost four fumbles and Bertelli threw two interceptions. Notre Dame turned it over at the Wisconsin 3-yard line, the 13, and the 11, and lost the ball on downs at the Badger 18. A late Irish field goal fell short, and the first game of the T-formation era ended in a 7–7 tie.

With the benefit of hindsight, the game could be judged a good first effort. In the heat of the moment, in light of Bertelli's misadventure and the Irish's inability to get the ball into the end zone, Leahy left Madison crushed. The tie felt like a loss. In Wisconsin, they celebrated as if the Badgers had won. Harry Stuhldreher, the Badgers coach, held a party at his home Saturday night, where in the pile of congratulatory telegrams lay one from Governor Julius P. Heil.

Leahy's personal unbeaten streak extended to twenty-one games, but the tie mortified him. He responded with his natural instinct. He worked harder and worked his team harder, exactly what neither one needed. By Thursday, Leahy felt so worn down, he went home and got in bed. Leahy blamed it on a back injury he suffered while diving some years ago. He had suffered neck and back pain at stressful times at Boston College. Frank Graham, the *New York Journal-American* columnist, told a story that during the 1940 season, shortly after Floss gave birth to the Leahy's third child, Leahy felt so poorly he went home and got in bed. Graham came to Boston to cover a game and dropped by Leahy's house to see him. At the end of the visit, Floss escorted Graham to see the baby, and once they went down the hall, asked Graham if he might speak to her husband about easing up on the throttle. After all, the Eagles prepared to open the season against Centre.

"Florence wasn't exactly whispering, was speaking softly," Graham wrote. "Yet from Frank's room, we heard, 'I will thank you, Mrs. Leahy, to look after the baby and allow me to look after the football team.'"

Georgia Tech came to South Bend in week two for the second consecutive year and brought a much better team. A week after playing in cold weather, the Irish played in unseasonable eighty-degree heat. Leahy coached the game but his exhaustion forced him to frequently take a knee. The offense again sputtered the closer it got to the opposing end zone, and Georgia Tech, which would start the season 9-0, had the better of the game all afternoon, winning 13–6. When Leahy returned home, he told Floss that his neck and back hurt and returned straight to his bed. He hadn't lost a game at Notre Dame. He hadn't lost a game anywhere since the Cotton Bowl at the end of the 1939 season. His mind and body fought hard to reject the loss. That fight took a toll. Leahy didn't stay in bed long enough for bed rest to help, so he didn't get any better. When he had suffered neck and back pain at Boston College, a doctor prescribed that he lay on a wooden board and try to clear his mind. Looking back nearly fifty years later, with the perspective that age and experience provides, Angelo Bertelli said, "You would have thought he was going to die because he lost a game."

Well, yes.

By Thursday, forty-eight hours before Notre Dame would play Stanford, Leahy had returned to bed. Father O'Donnell and Father Cavanaugh called a meeting with Leahy that in modern parlance would be termed an intervention. With Floss and McKeever, his top assistant, there as well, the priests told—they did not ask—Leahy to go to the Mayo Clinic. On Friday evening, Father Cavanaugh and the assistant coaches drove Leahy to the train station. McKeever would run the team in his absence.

Leahy arrived in Rochester on Saturday, greeted by a telegram to St. Mary's Hospital from his team promising a win and telling him not to worry. Exhausted as he felt, Leahy could not turn off his anxieties. On each of the next three Saturdays, he took "tablets"—presumably sedatives—to calm his nerves before listening to his team's games on the radio. It especially wounded Leahy not to be at the Stanford game. Playing Stanford had been his idea. The story went that Leahy wanted to play at Stanford in the years that USC visited Notre Dame so that the team would be in California every season (a strategy to which Notre Dame returned in 1988 and maintains to present day).

Leahy also didn't get to see the lineup change he made that turned the team's fortunes. While convalescing, Leahy gained the perspective he needed to reassess why his new offense sputtered. He came to understand that Bertelli's native humility worked against the team; the quarterback refused to call his own number. Notre Dame didn't have that problem the previous season in the old offense because quarterback Harry Wright called the plays. The quarterback in that offense subsisted largely on blocking; when Leahy switched to the T, he moved Bertelli to quarterback, switched Wright to guard. Wright also had developed a reputation for dirty play and disrespecting officials, a reputation that would gain more credence as the season continued. First things first—Leahy had seen enough sputtering out of his offense to know that he needed Wright to call the plays again. Bertelli still would play quarterback, of course. Against Stanford, Bertelli completed 14 of 20 passes for 233 yards and four touchdowns, and Notre Dame coasted to a 27–0 victory.

Once he got to his room, Leahy heard only the late part of the game on the radio. The Rochester radio station didn't broadcast the Notre Dame game until after it carried the Minnesota game. The win proved to be such a tonic that Leahy told an AP reporter it almost made him forget about his back. Then Leahy coachsplained why the Gophers, who had an eighteen-game winning streak broken the previous week in a loss to Iowa Pre-Flight, had lost again. "When a team like Minnesota hasn't been beaten for two or three years," Leahy said, "it is likely to lose two or three games in a row once it is beaten. The winning streak is broken and it's hard to get the boys back, mentally. You check and see if that isn't nearly always true."

Maybe that theory applied to Leahy, who had two bad games and went into the hospital, but Notre Dame played inspired football. The Irish exacted such a physical toll on Stanford that six Indians got back on the westbound train with significant injuries, from a broken collarbone to a hip pointer to two cut lips; from a black eye to a gashed leg to an injured ankle. "Stanford players were surprised at the attitude of the Fighting Irish," Harry Borba wrote in the *San Francisco Examiner*. "They wouldn't talk to the Indians between plays. When one of the Stanfords remarked about it being a tough game, he was sneered at by Mr. Leahy's cohorts." Actually, in March 1943, Leahy canceled the return game at Stanford (and USC's November 20 visit to South

Bend), scheduled as the opener on September 25, because of wartime travel restrictions. At least that's the official version of events. In truth, the Stanford administration didn't appreciate the physical beating that the Indians took and directed that the football team have nothing to do with the Irish as long as Leahy coached them. Marchy Schwartz, Leahy's Notre Dame teammate who coached Stanford in 1942, was quoted a few years later, saying, "I have never seen anything like it. The faces of our boys were like raw hamburgers when they came off the field." That might have been a little hyperbolic, but Wright drew attention for what Moose Krause described as "ill will and muscle" between Wright and a Stanford tackle. In 1952, a decade later, Stanford coach Chuck Taylor wanted to resume the rivalry but athletic director Al Masters still held a grudge over the rough play. The rivalry didn't resume until 1963.

The team sent Leahy a signed game ball, which he kept at his bedside at the clinic. Leahy came under the care of Dr. A. J. Rogers, a gastro-intestinal specialist known for his bedside manner. Dr. Rogers became a friend and important figure in his patient's life. He diagnosed Leahy's back pain as spinal arthritis and sent him to the hospital's "hangman room." Leahy, while seated, would be put in a rig of ropes and pulleys that would apply pressure to his neck while a male nurse rotated his head. After this procedure, Leahy would go to the "heat room," where he would be given diathermic treatment while lying on his stomach with heavy sandbags placed on his back. The diathermic heat came via ultraviolet rays; Leahy's description pronounced "violet" as "violent."

When not receiving treatment, Leahy kept McKeever on the phone at length, going over practice and discussing scouting reports of the next two opponents, Iowa Pre-Flight and Illinois. He watched the game films, which McKeever rushed to Rochester, on a movie projector that Leahy borrowed from a local sportswriter. After one very long call to discuss what he had seen, Leahy called back to tell McKeever he had forgotten to mention one thing. That took another twenty-five minutes.

The players called Leahy from the middle of the campus rally Friday night, the eve of their game against Iowa Pre-Flight, one of the many military bases bulging with college and professional football players now that war had begun. The college head coaches who volunteered for service in that first year got assignments coaching those teams. Bernie Bierman, like Leahy at the outset of the season, hadn't lost a game since 1939, leading Minnesota to 8-0 records in the 1940 and 1941 seasons. Before the Notre Dame game, Bierman had coached the Iowa Pre-Flight Seahawks to a 4-0 record, including victories over his Gophers and Michigan. The Seahawks came into Notre Dame Stadium as an overwhelming favorite. Leahy expressed his anxiety to Cavanaugh in a roundabout way, telling him of a nurse, Sister William, who hovered over Leahy during his entire stay. Leahy called her a "champion" and told Cavanaugh in a letter, "She nearly dies every time N.D. is scored on. Looks like the good Sister will experience very little comfort this coming Sat."

A couple of hours before kickoff, Cavanaugh composed a typewritten letter to Leahy. "I have just talked to Ed McKeever and he tells me that the boys are in excellent mental condition and want to win the game," Cavanaugh wrote. "They have everything to win and nothing to lose, in the sense that hardly any sensible person can expect them to beat the Seahawks, and if they do, they will regain a tremendous amount of prestige."

Cavanaugh also tried to remind his football coach of the big picture. "After all, it is very difficult for you to think of your own health when you are so anxious to get back in the saddle, but a mistake now of returning to coaching too early might be an expensive one later on in your life. You will have plenty of football games to be worrying about in the years to come, so don't overestimate the importance of one or two now. Moreover, I think Floss and youngsters have a very sacred right to your health."

There's a chance that by the time Leahy received the letter, he had settled down long enough to think of the big picture. In the meantime, Notre Dame stunned Iowa Pre-Flight, 28–0, a result that stunned all of college football as well. McKeever left the field on the shoulders of his players. Notre Dame gained 432 yards of total offense, forced nine turnovers, and so dominated the game that McKeever emptied the bench in the second half. One fourth-stringer, John Peasenelli, hadn't played in the first three games, so he didn't bother putting on pads. When an assistant coach determined that Peasenelli was the only player on the bench who hadn't gotten into the game, he sent him in. Peasenelli ran the ball without pads—and gained 25 yards.*

"Against the Seahawks," Bertelli recalled, "the T was starting to take effect. We were throwing the ball and that opened up things for the run as well." Jim Costin, the *South Bend Tribune* sports editor, called the performance "the greatest afternoon of Notre Dame football I've ever seen" in thirty-three years of coverage.

Leahy agreed with Costin. The coach listened to the game in his room, Sister William at his side. On Sunday morning, in a letter to Cavanaugh, Leahy called it "Notre Dame's greatest football victory." Leahy sounded overjoyed right up until the very next paragraph, when he began listing the mistakes the team had made. After that he implored Cavanaugh to talk to the team about how good Illinois, the next opponent, would be, about how they needed to guard against self-satisfaction. But after he signed the letter, he did add, "Boy am I happy over yesterday's <u>win</u>."

Perhaps Leahy didn't trust the good father to deliver his message, because he wrote team captain George Murphy a seven-page letter utilizing warmth, pleading, and hyperbole to remind him that perfection remained the ultimate goal. "We must strive each day for improvement, otherwise decay sets in," Leahy wrote. "...Keep working hard George and ask all others not to let up for one minute."

Dr. Rogers gave Leahy two options—leave for the game at Illinois and return to the Mayo Clinic, or remain, take more treatment, and

* In a practice later that season, Peasenelli dropped back to return a punt and his teammates, who liked him, let him return it for a touchdown, trying to disguise their largesse with would-be tackles. Leahy did not find it at all amusing. After practice, every first-teamer had to run thirty-six laps around the field—about nine miles.

be discharged for good as early as Tuesday of the following week. The doctor also instructed Leahy to return to the clinic after the season. When Notre Dame came back to defeat the unbeaten No. 5 Illini 21–14, Leahy listened from his bed in Rochester.

The treatments relieved Leahy's back pain, but so did seventeen days away from the grind. After Dr. Rogers released him from the Mayo on Tuesday, Leahy took the train home, where Floss and Cavanaugh met him at the train station. The news stories referred to him suffering from spinal arthritis. That diagnosis didn't live very long after the patient returned to South Bend. Leahy discussed how he had overworked himself into "a good case of the miseries." Profiles of Leahy during the team's glory years after the war, written by prominent sportswriters of the day, bluntly described Leahy suffering a "breakdown" in 1942. There is no record of Leahy or the university trying to counter that description in real time. Even Walter Kennedy, who became the publicity man for Notre Dame football during the war (Bill Sullivan left to work for the Navy in Washington, DC), described Leahy as someone who "worried himself into Mayo Brothers' hospital."

Dr. Rogers, presumably with a straight face, advised Leahy to work half a day at the outset. The time away refreshed Leahy's outlook. He noted that, with Wisconsin and Georgia Tech a combined 9-0 against other opponents so far, maybe Notre Dame hadn't started out as badly as he thought.

Leahy made the trip to Cleveland for a grind-it-out 9–0 defeat of Navy, which the Irish followed with a 13–0 victory over Army at Yankee Stadium. Notre Dame, despite its imperfect 5-1-1 record, rose to No. 4 in the AP poll. Perhaps to a patient like Leahy there is no cure like winning, but he appeared to be doing a better job of managing the stress of being head coach of the Fighting Irish. Cavanaugh, writing to Sister William after the Army game, said, "I really believe that Frank is trying hard to take care of himself better than he did. As you say, he is extremely conscientious about discharging his duties to Notre Dame. This anxiety has caused him at least some disposition towards his present trouble. But in spite of everything that either Father O'Donnell or I can say to him to relieve his tenseness, he has kept at it. Really, however, during these last few days, I noticed a wholesome improvement."

Now came another test, both of the Notre Dame team and its coach's ability to handle stress, and not merely because Michigan ranked sixth in the nation. The Irish had not played a game against the Wolverines since 1909, largely because Fielding Yost, the Wolverines' legendary coach in the early part of the twentieth century, didn't like Catholics in general and Rockne in particular. Yost led the blackballing of Notre Dame by the Western Conference, as the Big Ten used to be known. In Yost's later years—he retired as Michigan athletic director in 1940—Elmer Layden used charm, flattery, and Army–Notre Dame football tickets for one of Yost's friends to convince Yost to soften his stance against Notre Dame. The schools agreed to play a home-and-home in 1942–43, and the sports media of the day provided appropriate coverage of a once-in-a-generation event.

Notre Dame made room for ten different radio play-by-play crews, three more than any American sporting event ever. The school cut off credential requests two months before the game. A record crowd of 57,011 filled Notre Dame Stadium (gas rationing because of the war didn't begin until December 1). The crowd included Bob Hope, whose film *Road to Morocco* hit the theaters that week, and Harry Kelly, the governor-elect of Michigan, who happened to be the president of the Notre Dame Alumni Association.

Leahy felt well enough to appear before five thousand fans at the field house for the Friday night pep rally for the first time since he had returned from the clinic. Leahy found a frenzied crowd, worked up by a torch-bearing march and a bonfire beforehand. He got carried away enough to predict a Notre Dame victory, a tactic he supposedly swore off three years earlier at Boston College. In fact, Leahy predicted that the Irish would run the table and defeat Northwestern, USC, and Great Lakes Naval Training Station as well.

At noon, two hours before kickoff, Leahy led the team to Rockne's graveside, otherwise known as checking every emotional box. It only worked for a half. The Irish, came out of halftime with a 14–13 lead and proceeded to give the game away in the first half of the third quarter. The Wolverines scored three touchdowns, two thanks to Irish turnovers, and cruised home to a 32–20 victory. Leahy coached thirty-nine games at two schools before he suffered a double-digit loss; it wouldn't happen again until 1950.

Yost, now retired, had a grand time at Notre Dame, watching the game from the press box sitting next to Layden. It would prove to be a short period of glasnost. Not all Western Conference teams fell in line behind Michigan when it came to resisting Notre Dame. Northwestern, which followed Michigan on the 1942 schedule, played Notre Dame for many years. Wildcats coach Pappy Waldorf and his boss, Tug Wilson, a future Big Ten commissioner, visited South Bend at Leahy's invitation in July 1942 and had a grand time. "I don't know when I have enjoyed more such a pleasant time of all-around good fellowship as we had with you and the rest of your gang," Waldorf wrote to Leahy. "Such things go farther than anything else I know to put athletic and personal relationships on the basis that they should be."

Such bonhomie did not extend to the Los Angeles Memorial Coliseum the following week (save for Leahy's invitation to nine-year-old Gary Crosby, son of Bing, to sit on the Notre Dame bench for the game). Newspapers describe Notre Dame's 13–0 victory over USC as a free-for-all masquerading as a football game. The officials ejected five players (three Irish, two Trojans), assessed 17 penalties, and still never got control of the game. As soon as the game ended, the benches emptied and a melee commenced near the USC bench, sparked when a Trojan player snatched the game ball away from Irish back Creighton Miller. Leahy closed his locker room to the press and went into the USC locker room to apologize "for any unsportsmanlike conduct" by his team. *Los Angeles Times* veteran Braven Dyer wrote that Notre Dame had utilized more illegal tactics than any team he had seen in more than twenty years of watching football. Notre Dame publicity man Joe Petritz, writing a game story for *The South Bend Tribune*, blamed the "fast whistle" of West Coast officials for the rough play.

USC coach Jeff Cravath stayed publicly quiet about the brawl. Too quiet, if you asked the Notre Dame administration, who noted that no one at USC attempted to defend the Irish when the *Times* and other Los Angeles newspapers lit into them. Years later, Cravath told a *Time* magazine correspondent that Notre Dame didn't play "that kind of football" under Layden or Rockne. He also said, not for attribution, "Yeah, he beat us 13–0. But the hell of it is that if he had just gone ahead and played football instead of coming up with that kind of stuff he could have beat us 35–0."

If Wright was the culprit, he lit a brush fire that smoldered for years afterward. Michigan coach Fritz Crisler and Tulane coach Henry Frnka also accused Notre Dame of dirty play and/or poor sportsmanship. The resulting bad press and other smudges on the alma mater that Leahy loved extracted quite a cost. America loves a winner, but it also loves to hate one, too. Victory may have been the foundation on which Leahy built his self-worth. For a child of the prairie who grew up dreaming of Notre Dame football, victory represented belonging. Success earned respect. It surely didn't occur to Leahy that those he defeated, from his fellow coaches to the multitudes of fans of the vanquished schools, might resent him. Stu Holcomb, who coached Purdue after the war, regarded the complaints about Leahy as self-serving. Holcomb didn't take it personally when his teams got pummeled by Leahy's teams. He didn't pull his team off Notre Dame's schedule. He rejected the idea that Purdue lost because Notre Dame played dirty football. He captured how Leahy offended his fellow coaches. "Frank was so technically superior that he made the rest of us, no matter how good we were, feel somehow inferior," Holcomb said. Leahy had more talent and coached it better.

In the long run, the dispute with USC died out; wartime travel restrictions prevented the rivals from playing again until 1946. Notre

Dame closed the season against Great Lakes Naval Training Station, a Chicago base, in a 13–13 tie. Leahy's first T-formation team finished 7-2-2, and less than two weeks later, Leahy returned to the Mayo Clinic. Soon after, Leahy took Floss and the three kids to Miami Beach for an extended vacation with the blessing of his bosses. Blessing or no, Cavanaugh wrote Leahy a long letter dated January 30 telling him that he must put an end to the dirty play. He didn't excoriate his coach. Cavanaugh described much of what he heard as rumor. He treaded so carefully that he tied up some sentences in knots. For instance: "Ed McKeever himself has investigated some of these rumors and is inclined to think that they are not without basis." But Cavanaugh pointed out the consistency of the rumors regarding Wright, that stories had made their way to Cavanaugh from USC, Northwestern, and Iowa Pre-Flight, and from Wright's own teammates, who didn't appreciate how Wright's play provoked opponents to resort to similar tactics against them. Team captain George Murphy described Wright as "a bad influence" but didn't do so until both the season and Wright's eligibility had ended.

"I know very well that you stand for strict observance of rules and for gentlemanly conduct both on the field and off the field," Cavanaugh said, "and I feel confident that you would not tolerate the presence on one of your teams of any man who is not motivated by the highest principles of sportsmanship."

Cavanaugh also urged upon Leahy the importance of performing the public relations tasks incumbent upon the head football coach of Notre Dame. Two years into his job, Leahy had begun to build walls around him out of a need for self-preservation. Coaches, even the extroverts, get into the game to coach, not to gladhand alumni and cater to the national press. Leahy's single-minded focus on winning made little room for such duties, and his illness during the 1942 season left a lot of them undone. Take the Friday night smokers, receptions at which officials from both schools gathered with the writers for drinks and/or dinner and a convivial we're-all-in-this-together vibe. Leahy not only didn't attend them, he didn't ensure that any of his assistants would go in his place. Their absence embarrassed Cavanaugh, who made sure that Leahy understood such events were not optional.

The letter went on for two and a half single-spaced pages, and apparently, Cavanaugh thought twice and didn't send it. Another letter, dated four days later, begins as the first one did, with the same chitchat regarding a bridge date with the McKeevers, then goes into a great deal less detail on the charges. Leahy didn't write a response for three weeks, toward the end of his extended vacation in Florida. He made several suggestions to improve his work as a Notre Dame representative, from a goodwill tour of several opponents to wining and dining the important sports editors and sportswriters to meeting with student leaders. As for the dirty play, he offered to show the USC game film to the Notre Dame Athletic Board. "They violated rules, not Notre Dame," Leahy wrote.

Then there were the "bird dogs," alumni (either real or subway) who served as the first line of recruiting for coaching staffs in that less sophisticated era. Bird dogs wanted to help, reveled in their connection to the program, enjoyed the locker-room access they had to the players they shepherded onto the team and to the coaches themselves. They wanted to feel important, and protocol dictated that coaches at least pretend to let the bird dogs know how vital they were to the program.

Bird dogs had been especially important at Notre Dame before Leahy arrived; Layden, constricted by university policy and budget, didn't leave campus to recruit. But Leahy did, and the more he and his staff traveled, the less they relied on the bird dogs. When the bird dogs wrote letters to Leahy or called into the office, they often didn't hear back. They spent less time in the locker room. Their complaints made their way onto Leahy's desk, too. He wrote Wallace and asked for advice. Wallace, who described Leahy as having "a large dead spot in human relations," replied with a letter telling the coach to answer his mail; say yes, no, or I don't know.

Leahy wrote back and thanked Wallace for the suggestion—three months later.

CHAPTER TEN

WARTIME

It would not be accurate to say Leahy vacationed in Florida for three months. Leahy was incapable of vacationing that long. But he did take Floss and the kids to Florida, and they didn't return to South Bend until the first week of March. Floss later joked that he bivouacked the family to the Miami area because Boston College played in the 1944 Orange Bowl. Well, it may have been a joke. Denny Myers, his successor with the Eagles, invited Leahy to speak to the team before it played Alabama. Leahy's inspirational skills paled before the strength of the Crimson Tide, which won, 37–21.

With every month, the American war engine ran faster and more powerfully. In the year-plus since the country went to war, military personnel increased fivefold, from 1.8 million to 9.2 million. The Notre Dame student body in general, and the football team in particular, reflected the drain on college-age men. The 1943 team included twenty-nine Marines, fourteen Navy apprentice seamen—and four future members of the College Football Hall of Fame. That Leahy managed to keep that level of talent on his team spoke to the university's standing with the Navy, and to Leahy's unquenchable desire to win.

As the father of three small children, Leahy remained exempt from the draft. Most of his players and many of his coaching colleagues didn't wait to be drafted; Leahy chose not to enlist. Attempting to strike a balance between patriotism and his livelihood, Leahy told George V. Kelly of the *Catholic News Service* that "Notre Dame, like all other leading educational institutions, stands ready to conform to any governmental requests regarding athletics." But he also explained that football served as a rare wartime luxury for the public, and that it funded not only the rest of Notre Dame athletics, but also the stipends that aided some eight hundred Irish students, most of them non-athletes.

When Leahy returned to campus for spring football, which began on March 9—delayed for one day by snow and ice, as well as Big Ten meetings that Leahy attended in Chicago—only forty-eight players reported, the fewest since Notre Dame began holding spring practice more than twenty years earlier. The only reason Notre Dame had that many is that the Big Ten declared freshmen eligible in 1943. Leahy had one back with varsity experience—Marine reserve Ed Krupa—and eleven freshmen. Bertelli, who enlisted in the Marine Corps but had yet to be called up, played baseball that spring.

"Coach Leahy and his staff spent most all of their time working with people they knew were going to come back," said McBride, an Army Reserve Corps enlistee. The players on the roster could be divided into three groups: in the service waiting to be called up, too young to be called up, or ineligible for military service. One of the stars of the team landed in Leahy's lap because the Army wouldn't take him. Halfback Creighton Miller made a career of vexing Leahy, over and over. Take the 1943 Navy game in Cleveland, where Miller promised a couple of teammates that if he scored a touchdown, he would run to the goal line and stop cold. Miller did so, only he got confused in the unfamiliar stadium and stopped on the 5-yard line. The ensuing collision knocked him over the goal line. After the Irish won, 33–6, Leahy marched Miller to the 5 and demanded that he never confuse it with the goal line again. "He made it a point to tell me, 'Our Lady is watching,'" Miller said.

Miller, the nephew of Don Miller, one of the Four Horsemen, and the son of Red Miller, another former Irish star, arrived at Notre Dame in Leahy's initial class of freshmen in 1941. Creighton and his brother Tom both played on the team. Their family paid for their tuition to save two scholarships for Leahy to use elsewhere. However, that diminished Leahy's power over them. He couldn't threaten them with the loss of a college education.

Creighton Miller suffered from high blood pressure, so much so that a doctor initially refused to pronounce him eligible to play. Leahy looked at the strapping young man and simply didn't believe the doctor. The coach asked Miller to come watch practice. Then he put a yellow "no-contact" jersey on him and had him play defense. "The next thing I know," Miller recalled, "I'm carrying the ball in non-contact drills…then running with the ball in live drills." Miller solved that problem. He took a handoff, threw the ball back over his head, and ran right out of the gate off of Cartier Field. He didn't show up for another practice the entire spring.

Miller eventually got the go-ahead to play in the summer of 1942, but he hadn't worked out in eight months, and when practice began in the fall, it showed. He would be so taxed that he would have to lie down. Leahy would gather the team around Miller and call him "Fluffduff," figuring shame would motivate him in a way that Leahy couldn't. Miller let Leahy's derision roll off his back.

By 1942, his sophomore season, Miller became a star in the T formation. Bertelli hit him in stride with a pass that Miller turned into a 48-yard touchdown pass in the 13–0 victory at USC. Miller joined the Army the following spring. He got sent to Fort Dix in New Jersey, where it took all of four days for an Army doctor to check his blood pressure.

"You're not going to get in the Army," the doctor said.

"I'm already in the Army," Miller said.

"Well, you're not going to be for long."

Miller spent six weeks in the base hospital waiting for his discharge. Only his return to campus with a 4-F designation helped convince Leahy that Miller wasn't trying to pull a fast one. During the summer, Leahy received a letter from a member of the Coast Guard, a subway alum inquiring about Miller. The coach replied in the stentorian language he adopted for formal discourse: "Right now we cannot state with any degree of accuracy whether or not he will be able to play in the fall. We sincerely hope that Creighton will be able to participate during the forthcoming campaign because he is a grand young man and an outstanding performer. Of course, his health is the first consideration of us all." Two weeks before the season, Miller's family physician wrote Leahy from Cleveland to endorse Miller's physical ability to play.

It was all so tentative. The lack of certainty concerning which players would be available and for how long gnawed on a coach who wanted every detail covered. Leahy mused aloud that if he didn't have someone on the roster capable of replacing Bertelli, he would change the offense. "I'm not going to use the T formation just because it looks pretty," he said. "Unless Lujack can make it go like Bertelli did, or pretty close to it, Notre Dame will kiss off the T and go back to Rockne football until we can groom the right kind of quarterback for the job."

Leahy turned out to have an advantage that stabilized the Notre Dame roster: the Navy's huge presence on campus. Of the 3,800 students enrolled in the fall of 1943, 3,100 were part of either the V-12 or the V-7 program. The programs on campus not only served as a vehicle for players to remain on campus, but they attracted players from other schools, not to mention that in the hierarchy of military training programs, V-12s were the Ivy League. Leahy may not have had a lot of players, and he may not have known how long he had them, but he had a lot of talent.

Bertelli turned out to be available when the season began but he didn't start the opening game. With the opener at Pitt, Leahy wanted to start Lujack, who grew up fifty-five miles southeast of the city, and have him play the opening drive before his people. The sophomore, in his first game of varsity eligibility, moved the Irish to the Pitt 4-yard line before his jitters overcame him. On two plays in a row, Lujack intended to hand off to Miller, only to turn the wrong way. On third down, Lujack settled down enough to get the play right, and Miller scored. Bertelli took over and led the Irish to a 41–0 victory. The following week produced more of the same, a 55–13 win over a depleted Georgia Tech team.

The consecutive routs led to Notre Dame being ranked No. 1 in the first poll of the season, just in time to play No. 2 Michigan. What happened on that transformative Saturday in Michigan Stadium (another four decades would pass before college football identified it as the Big House) changed the trajectory of the Notre Dame's season, Leahy's career, and the relationship between the two universities.

Midway through the first quarter, Creighton Miller burst through the line, put a move on Michigan back Don Lund that left him grasping air, and raced 66 yards for a touchdown. In the second quarter, with Notre Dame ahead, 7–6, Bertelli threw a 70-yard touchdown pass to a freshman back, Fred Earley. Miller followed with a 58-yard touchdown run that the officials waved off because of an Irish penalty. In the third quarter, Miller scored again on a short pass from Bertelli as Notre Dame turned the game into a rout. Leahy played his backups for most of the second half, a screwy half because the scoreboard clock malfunctioned, and the third quarter extended to twenty-three minutes. Leahy and Michigan coach Fritz Crisler met with the officials, who decided to play a seven-minute fourth quarter. Leahy emptied his bench—Miller finished with 159 yards on 10 carries—and the Irish cruised to a 35–12 victory. Michigan made the final score that close with a touchdown on the final play of the game.

Crisler, an institutionalist with a healthy ego, lived and coached by the rules and looked askance at anyone he thought did not. He may have been prejudiced against Catholics; surely he thought religion had nothing to do with football and resented that all of Catholicism, in his view, seemed to line up behind Notre Dame. Crisler also plain did not like Leahy. Crisler had something Leahy wanted—for Michigan to continue playing Notre Dame—and he withheld it.

In December, Leahy ran into Crisler at a football luncheon in Detroit and pointed out to him that the schools' two-game series had sold 140,000 tickets worth $500,000 in gate receipts. "Frank asked me if perhaps this wasn't the time to begin talking about playing again," Crisler said. "But we agreed that maybe we'd better wait until we know more about what football will be like in the next few years."

Crisler coached the Wolverines through 1947, served as university athletic director until 1968, and the schools didn't play again until 1978. Father Edmund Joyce, who oversaw athletics for thirty-five years, said, "I always felt it was a personal thing between Crisler and Leahy, but we're not going to hold it against the institution." Crisler urged the other Western Conference schools to join Michigan in a boycott. They did not. (After the 1943 season, Iowa eagerly made a four-year deal with Notre Dame to begin in 1945. Northwestern told Notre Dame in 1945 that it would not renew the contract that ended in 1948, but Notre Dame replaced Northwestern with Indiana, another Western Conference member.) Crisler, after he retired from coaching, also became chair of the NCAA Football Rules Committee, a job in which he bedeviled Leahy again.

All of which served to position Leahy as different/other/not accepted by one of the best-connected coaches in the game. When their paths crossed, Crisler remained civil. He just never got around to scheduling Notre Dame again, despite repeated entreaties from Leahy and his successor as athletic director, Moose Krause. Six months after replacing Crisler as athletic director, Don Canham made a handshake deal with Krause to play again. They have played thirty-three times since resuming the rivalry.

As the 1943 season went on, it became apparent that Michigan didn't lose badly because the Wolverines came out flat, had a bad day, the Irish played dirty, or some other excuse. Notre Dame dominated every opponent. The Irish beat the eight collegiate teams on their schedule by a minimum of 19 points and an average of 33. They beat five teams ranked in the top eight, four of them in the top three at the time of the game. It's impossible to say what contributed more to Notre Dame's success—their mastery, at long last, of the T formation or the relative weakness of their opponents. But the Irish remained No. 1 even as the Marines ordered Bertelli to report to Parris Island, South Carolina, for duty the week of Notre Dame's game against West Point. Bertelli had been magical all season, aided by Miller in the backfield and a dominant offensive line. George Ratterman, who played quarterback for the Irish after the war, said he enrolled at Notre Dame because he remembered how clean Bertelli's pants were—the defense rarely touched him.

In Bertelli's place came Lujack, the sophomore who had played a decent amount but had experienced nothing like starting against undefeated, No. 3 Army in front of 76,000 at sold-out Yankee Stadium. The bookmakers made Notre Dame a 13-point favorite even with the untested, and inwardly unnerved, Lujack. Notre Dame traveled to New York in two waves. The civilian players left campus on Thursday. The military men didn't leave until Friday night, arriving in New York on the morning of the two p.m. game. On the train ride, Lujack approached team publicity director Walter Kennedy. Lujack wanted to use Kennedy's room to shave. An odd request, but Kennedy said sure. Lujack asked if Kennedy had an electric razor. Kennedy answered that he did.

"Good," Lujack said. "I'm so nervous I'd cut myself if I used my own razor."*

In his later years, Leahy said that in his pep talk before the game, he

---

* Kennedy went on to become second president and first commissioner of the NBA. He would be succeeded for many years by Bill Sullivan's brother Frank. Sullivan became the founder of the New England Patriots. "I guess you could say I was always a pretty good recruiter," Leahy told Jerry Nason of *The Boston Globe* in 1965.

advised the team to thank God that Notre Dame had a brilliant strategist, great tactician, and unsurpassed leader at quarterback, at which point Lujack began looking around to see who it was.

In reality, Lujack played all sixty minutes, threw two touchdowns, and rushed for a third in a 26–0 rout of the Black Knights. Miller excelled on defense, at one point chasing down "Mr. Outside," Army's sprinter of a halfback Glenn Davis, from behind.

Leahy understood how good a team he had. He must have—he had no stress attacks, not even when Earley missed three extra points, providing for the oddity of a 25–6 victory at No. 8 Northwestern. The following week, against No. 2 Iowa Pre-Flight, Earley made the winning extra point late in the fourth quarter to give the Irish a 14–13 comeback victory. Before that game, Leahy fulfilled what had become an annual tradition—he took the team for a visit to Rockne's cemetery. On Friday afternoon, after the team knelt at the grave, Leahy said, "Lads, bow your heads and say a silent prayer to Rock that he will be with us tomorrow and help us defeat this great team."

After the game, the story circulated that Leahy had given the team a pep talk while at the cemetery. The story visibly angered Leahy, who sputtered that the only time he brought up Rockne occurred at halftime, when he told his players that his old coach had loved a fighting team, and that the time had come for them to prove that they could fight at a level that Rockne would appreciate. "The boys then went out and played thirty minutes of the greatest football anyone has ever seen and won out over what was probably the toughest team any Notre Dame team has ever seen," Leahy said.*

After the narrow defeat of Iowa Pre-Flight, fans began to bring up how this team might be better than the 1930 Irish, Rockne's last team

* The story also brings to mind the anecdote told over and over by Leahy's players through the years, although no one ever pinned down in what season it took place, if ever. Leahy took the team to visit Rockne's grave, and during the visit, a couple of players drifted over to the gravesite of former Irish basketball coach George Keogan. Leahy called out to them, "Lads, lads, we'll pray for Keogan during basketball season."

as a coach and Leahy's senior season. One team stood between Notre Dame and an undefeated season—Great Lakes Naval Training Station, a base of more than ninety thousand sailors north of Chicago. Notre Dame, in an effort to support the war effort and show its gratitude to the Navy, offered to move the Thanksgiving Day game from Comiskey Park, the home field of the White Sox, to the following Saturday and play it before 22,000 sailors at Ross Field on the base. It was no small gesture. The decision cost the university $50,000 in gate receipts.

Great Lakes featured former college stars like quarterback Paul Lach, a Duke All-American who played for the Chicago Cardinals, former Western Reserve lineman Paul Anderson, and former Notre Dame starting halfback Steve Juzwik. Two NFL linemen suited up as well. Playing four highly ranked opponents in as many weeks appeared to take its toll on the Irish, and yet, Leahy's emphasis on conditioning paid off. In the fourth quarter, the Irish drove 80 yards on 20 consecutive running plays to score a touchdown and go ahead, 14–12, with 1:05 to play. Leahy would have his second undefeated season in three years at Notre Dame.

And then, suddenly, he wouldn't.

With the clock ticking, Lach dropped back, looked for a receiver, and bought time by scrambling. As the defensive backfield moved up to corral him, Anderson, who had lined up at end, ran downfield past everyone. Lach spotted him and threw a 54-yard touchdown pass. The lightning bolt of a touchdown rendered Notre Dame radio play-by-play man Joe Boland unable to speak for precious seconds. The Irish had time for one play from scrimmage, a Lujack Hail Mary that Emil "Red" Sitko, his future teammate, intercepted. Final score: Great Lakes 19, Notre Dame 14.

Leahy ventured into the winning locker room after the game to offer congratulations. When he met Sitko, a Fort Wayne native who would have been playing for Notre Dame had there not been a war on, the player, groping for words, got out, "How are you, Coach?"

"Not too well, Emil," Leahy said. "My school lost today."

Sitko replied, "So did mine, Coach."

The perfectionist coach chose not to lash out at his players over the irredeemable mental lapse that cost them the game. Leahy decided that Notre Dame lost because it had been beaten, not because it had made too many mistakes. "You can feel proud of the way you played," he said in a somber locker room. "You happened to be beaten by one of the most splendidly executed plays I have ever seen. I have no criticism to make of you for this game."

At Parris Island, Lieutenant Angelo Bertelli sat in a Quonset hut with a handful of other Marines, including Ray Kaffel, an Irish teammate who had enlisted with him, listening as Notre Dame suffered a stunning loss. He began crying, perhaps because his team lost, perhaps because his team lost and he felt like he should have been there to help. A few minutes passed, and someone came to tell him to report to the orderly room for a telegram. Bertelli gathered himself, went to the orderly room, opened the telegram, and learned he had won the 1943 Heisman Trophy despite playing only half the season. "I was crying one moment," Bertelli said, "and then crying and laughing the next."

Leahy returned to the Palmer House, even then a venerable institution of a downtown Chicago hotel. The phone in his room rang. Dave Egan, the *Boston Record* columnist, called to find out what happened. The season over, the pressure over, Leahy became effusive in praise of his team. Yes, the defenders fell asleep on one play and cost the team an undefeated record. But Leahy preferred to dwell on the Irish touchdown drive that preceded it.

"No inch was an easy one," Leahy said. "Every foot was desperately fought for. Each yard was a battleground. But inch by inch and foot by foot and yard by yard, we got it down there. That's the story we told, for it took more than mechanical ability and more than the T formation to do that. It took character and it took guts, and I am even prouder of my lads now after one defeat then I was after their nine victories. They needed a touchdown so they marched 80 yards and got it. And then, all hell broke loose."

But, Leahy emphasized, everyone needed to place the game in context.

"There were 22,000 sailors who saw that game," Leahy said. "They were chosen because, in a matter of days, they will be leaving for action in the South Pacific. For some of them it will be the last athletic contest they ever will see, and in the face of that fact the loss of a football game is not important. And for all of them, both the men of Great Lakes and the men of the fleet in all parts of the world, it should have been an inspiration and a lesson. It should have shouted to them that no battle ever is lost until the last shot has been fired from the last gun of the last ship afloat."

Maybe that softened the sting of the upset for some, although Leahy did say he had heard from one disgruntled fan: His father-in-law lost an eighty-five-cent bet on the game. For history's sake, however, Leahy and Notre Dame would be spared the consequences of a last-minute loss in the last game of the season. The upset left the AP poll voters a mess to untangle. Three teams had one loss—Notre Dame, Iowa Pre-Flight, and Navy. The voters sided with the Irish, who not only had beaten the other two, but had set an NCAA record by rushing for 313.9 yards per game.

The national championship, a muted affair in those early days of the poll, had yet to enchant and enrage fans as it would in decades to come. News of the poll didn't even get the biggest headline on the sports page of *The South Bend Tribune*, which didn't bother to ask Leahy for a comment. Just as well, for the coach had a bigger issue to solve.

Two days after the Great Lakes loss, *The New York Times* reported that the military planned to draft three hundred thousand men in January. Earlier in November, Congress passed a law extending the eligible age for draftees to thirty-seven. While the law said it would put fathers at the end of the draft line, the need for manpower was such that the reprieve would be for two or three months. Local Selective Service Board number 113 in Middlesex County, Massachusetts, did not wait. The board notified Leahy, who had registered for the draft while at Boston College, that he had been reclassified as 1-A. His number had come up.

Notre Dame leaped into action, filing a request that the board reconsider. "The registrant has entire supervision of the intercollegiate athletic program, in which by far the larger number are Navy V-12 trainees," Father O'Donnell, the university president, wrote. ". . . The discontinuance of this registrant's services at the university would seriously disrupt the effectiveness of the educational services being rendered by the University in connection with the war effort."

The accompanying form listed that Leahy worked an average of seventy hours per week and made a weekly salary of $211 ($11,000 annually, although Notre Dame would increase his salary to $13,000 in January 1944). The university also requested Captain J. Richard Barry, the commander of Naval training programs on campus, to write a letter supporting Leahy's reclassification. He sent just the type of letter that the university wanted, perhaps because he signed a copy of a sample letter the university provided him.

As we saw in the Great Lakes game, Leahy had great respect for the military. His delay in joining the service didn't stem from any philosophical or moral stance. If it stemmed from anything, Leahy was a thirty-five-year-old married father of four (Jerry had been born shortly before the 1943 season) who suffered from stress illnesses and focused on winning football games. He didn't make himself available to the military until the military made it clear it would come for him. Not all major college football coaches enlisted, but a good number did, and the ones who enlisted raised an eyebrow at those who didn't, especially one as successful and prominent as Leahy. Dick Hanley, who had been the Northwestern coach from 1927 to 1934 and a member of the Marine Corps reserve, went active shortly after Pearl Harbor and helped create combat conditioning programs. Hanley may have risen to lieutenant colonel but had a drill sergeant's voice and a no-nonsense, aggressive manner. There was talk that Hanley made clear his feelings about coaches who could have been doing something for the war effort and did not. He was a black-and-white man, and Leahy had not joined in the service.

The USO reached out to Leahy in February and asked that he go on a goodwill tour of US military bases in the European theater in early March. Leahy readily agreed and left campus for New York on March 1 to prepare for the trip. He got briefings, took his inoculations, and was told he would leave by March 6. The Army asked him to bring a highlight film of the 1943 team, and when Leahy found that he couldn't get it delivered in time through civilian production houses, the Army produced the film itself. Leahy also brought along prepared remarks, presumably written by Kennedy, to introduce the film. "As you perhaps know, the American sportswriters were kind enough to choose Notre Dame in 1943 as the National Intercollegiate Football Champions. Naturally, our boys were made very happy by the high honor and the coaching staff, including myself, liked it too."

Leahy stressed that the players on his record-setting national championship team were "average young Americans like yourselves," that many of them took part in the V-12 program. Maybe part of him defended himself as he defended his players. "Many of the boys who appear in these films have already left Notre Dame; some of them are even now on active duty. The point I want to impress upon you is this, that they are not slackers but they are boys like yourselves whose one aim is to help win the war as quickly as possible."

The military delayed the trip, and Leahy waited out the delay in New York, chatting up servicemen with overseas ribbons about what they wanted to hear from visitors from home. When he introduced himself, nearly to a man they asked him what happened in the last minute of the Great Lakes game. "Wherever I go and whoever I meet, I'm asked that question," Leahy said with a laugh. After three weeks, the USO postponed the trip and Leahy returned home. But while in New York, and after talking it over with Father Cavanaugh, Leahy made the necessary arrangements to accept a commission in the Naval Reserves. It might be too crass to suggest that Leahy did so because he thought it would help him win football games. But Moose Krause pointed out to Leahy that he needed to go into the service for competitive reasons. For one, he would be coaching veterans after the war and would have a much better idea of how to handle them if he knew what they went through. For another, when that veteran in Leahy's locker room asked what he did during the war, Leahy would have a good answer.

Leahy entered the Navy on May 19, 1944, for what would become an eighteen-month stint, broken up by one two-week leave at home in January 1945. Ed McKeever took over as interim coach. Leahy began his service by traveling to Princeton University for an eight-week course on what awaited him as a naval lieutenant. By midsummer, Leahy had been assigned to Pearl Harbor under Admiral Charles Lockwood, the commander of the US submarine forces in the Pacific theater. Lockwood, a beloved man known to his seamen as "Uncle Charlie," would come to the dock as each ship under his command returned from the war. He made sure a band accompanied him and welcomed the seamen ashore by playing "Happy Days Are Here Again." Lockwood gave Leahy the task of creating and organizing athletic activities and recreation for the submarine crews, who would spend several weeks in tight quarters underwater. A submarine that dived below the surface and undertook "silent running" had to turn off air conditioning and ventilation. The ship became a steamy, foul environment, filled with stagnant air, sweat, and, as they described in the Navy at the time, the stench of the three Fs: feet, farts, and fannies. Were it not for the cooling effect of the Pacific waters, the onboard temperature would climb to one hundred degrees. The seamen became pale and spent. By the end of a six-week patrol, climbing a ladder aboard ship would leave them gasping, their legs rubbery.

When a sub returned to port in, say, Midway or Pearl Harbor, the seamen would go to rest camp to rejuvenate. That's where Leahy came in. The military didn't want Leahy and his celebrity ilk in harm's way. He didn't come anywhere near the front lines. "The closest I ever came to a battle in the Pacific was in talking once with a Jap prisoner," Leahy said. The most grievous injury he suffered was seasickness, which came quite easily to him.

Leahy's initial efforts to give the seamen some exercise fell flat. "The boys weren't interested until we found that the secret was competition," Leahy said. "When we began pitting the crew of one submarine against another, interest perked up immediately."

Leahy spent time at Pearl Harbor and at Midway, and hit Guam, Tarawa, Kwajalein, and Saipan as well. He had his trusty highlight film of the 1943 Irish, which he showed, and showed, and showed again. On a Marine post in Guam, he discovered in his audience Lieutenant Angelo Bertelli. Leahy tried to coax him up to the front of the room to help comment on the first half of the film, since he dominated it, but Bertelli was too shy for that. After the film, when the rest of the Marines began yelling for him to get up there, Bertelli went up alongside Leahy and answered questions for an hour.

"I took him to the officers' club for dinner and introduced him to twenty people who were sitting at another table," Bertelli said. "He finished eating and before he left he went back to each of these people, shook their hands, and remembered everyone's first name. We were all amazed."

As luck would have it, or more to the point, as only Leahy would have it, he ran into other Notre Dame players who happened to be in his Pacific neighborhood. He would tell all of them some version of the same story. He would tell Lujack that he had just seen Bob Livingstone, who wanted to make sure that after the war, Lujack returned to Notre Dame. When Leahy saw Livingstone, he would reverse the story. He also spent time searching out football players who might be in his Pacific neighborhood. Some no longer had eligibility, such as Irish left tackle Lou Rymkus, whom Leahy watched play for a Navy team in Pearl Harbor in early January 1945. Some didn't even know they were going to be Notre Dame players; Leahy became famous, and infamous, for recruiting while in uniform. Holy Cross All-American tackle George Connor, a Navy ensign, was minding his own business one day at Pearl Harbor when a command car pulled up. "Commander Leahy would like to see you at the Royal Hawaiian [Hotel]," Connor was told. Leahy pitched Notre Dame to Connor, a Chicago native who already had an interest in being closer to home because his father had taken ill and was unable to work. Leahy told Connor that if he came to Notre Dame, he'd not only make the All-America team again he'd win a national championship.

"It all came true," Connor said.

Not every player succumbed to Leahy's charms. Illinois halfback Julie Rykovich came to Notre Dame as part of the V-12 program. Leahy tried to lure him to come back to campus after the war. Rykovich told Leahy of his academic interest in agriculture, a subject not taught under the Golden Dome. Leahy promised Rykovich that not only would he have a private tutor, he would have the honor of becoming the first Notre Dame agricultural student. Rykovich must have anticipated the response of the Notre Dame priests to Leahy's academic scheme. He returned to Illinois and helped lead the Illini to the 1947 Rose Bowl.

Oregon coach Tex Oliver, also a lieutenant commander in the Navy, arrived at Midway one time and said, "I'm just looking for a few boys Leahy might have overlooked." Leahy gained a reputation for in-military recruiting that exceeds the size of his haul. Only a handful of players came to Notre Dame after the war that hadn't been there before.

While at Pearl Harbor, Leahy befriended Admiral Chester Nimitz, commander in chief of the US Pacific Fleet and Pacific Ocean Area, who taught him how to pitch horseshoes. Nimitz became so fond of Leahy that he sent him an autographed copy of the Japanese instrument of surrender signed aboard the USS *Missouri*. He also signed a photo of the two of them with an inscription calling Leahy "an old friend and shipmate of long standing."*

---

* When Notre Dame awarded Nimitz an honorary degree in 1946, Leahy challenged him to a rematch in horseshoes and beat him. "How do you expect me to beat you with all those priests praying for you?" Nimitz asked.

During his eighteen months in the Navy, Leahy spent enough time assigned to the naval program at St. Mary's in northern California that he sold the family's South Bend home and moved Floss and the four children to a home in Lafayette, near the St. Mary's campus. Though the Pacific war ended in August, Leahy didn't receive his discharge until November 15, 1945, in San Francisco. He soon found out he had not been forgotten. Leahy's old champion from the *Chicago Tribune*, sports editor Arch Ward, had founded a new professional football league, the All-America Football Conference. With the NFL's operations hindered by the war, and literally millions of men returning to civilian life, Ward recruited as team owners a group of wealthy businessmen across the country, one of them being Mickey McBride of Cleveland. Ward believed he could deliver Leahy to McBride as head coach. He arranged a meeting at which McBride was smitten with Leahy and offered him $35,000 a year for five years and 15 percent ownership of the team. Remember, Notre Dame had increased Leahy's salary from $11,000 to $13,000 the year before. When the meeting broke up, McBride had a handshake deal, figuratively and perhaps literally.

But McBride proved to be no match for the righteous indignation of Father Cavanaugh, who felt betrayed not only by Leahy but by Ward, who, remember, served as president of the Notre Dame Foundation in Chicago. Ward immediately began backpedaling, saying he acted only as an intermediary. Leahy met with Cavanaugh for four hours, and the meeting ended with Cavanaugh promising he would facilitate Leahy gaining more business opportunities from wealthy alumni. As they parted, Leahy, having been reminded of what Notre Dame meant to him by his close friend and boss, looked up at the Golden Dome and pledged to Cavanaugh that under his coaching Notre Dame would not lose a game for ten years. "I pledge that to Our Lady and to you, Father John," Leahy said.

The next morning, Leahy returned to Chicago and broke the news to Ward and McBride. "If this isn't enough money, how much is?" McBride asked.

Leahy explained that he would be happier at Notre Dame. When McBride asked for a recommendation for a coach, Leahy suggested Paul Brown, who had coached Ohio State to the 1942 national championship and now coached Great Lakes Naval Training Station. McBride hired Brown, who won all four AAFC championships before the league went kaput, then won three NFL championships. McBride gave Brown 5 percent of the team, which he sold to new owner Art Modell in 1961 for $500,000. It wouldn't be the last time that Leahy made a career decision that wasn't a good business decision.

Two days after his discharge in San Francisco, Leahy sat in the stands at Northwestern, watching Notre Dame win, 34–7, to raise its record to 6-1-1. Hugh Devore, who took over in 1945 after Ed McKeever took the head coaching job at Cornell, had recruited some talented freshmen, players such as halfback Terry Brennan from Milwaukee and quarterback Frank Tripucka from New Jersey. There may have been a war on, but in the heart of good Catholic boys, Notre Dame was still Notre Dame. When a recruiter from North Carolina came to the Tripucka home, Frank's mother told him, "He has his heart set on Notre Dame. Outside of his schoolbooks, the only books he reads are the Bible and *The Life of Knute Rockne*."

The team may have been mostly freshmen and 4-Fs, but only one team overmatched them, and Army had its pick of the best college football players eligible for military service. In the last game before Leahy received his discharge, the Black Knights beat the Irish 48–0, an improvement for the losers. Army won the year before, 59–0. Leahy endured that loss while on Midway, he said, "listening to the radio—and the goony birds."

The week after Northwestern, Leahy, still wearing his Navy uniform, went to New Orleans to see No. 5 Notre Dame score five touchdowns in the second half to beat Tulane, 32–6. Tripucka threw the last touchdown pass, a 21-yarder to John Agnone. After the game, Leahy went into the locker room, found Tripucka, and introduced himself. "He asked if he could sit down next to me," Tripucka said, "and then asked if we could talk after my shower. Frank Leahy! I zipped through the fastest shower I ever took."

Notre Dame closed out the season with a 39–7 loss to Great Lakes. It was the kind of loss that Leahy despised—the Bluejackets outscored the Irish 26–0 in the fourth quarter. In all likelihood, Leahy let it slide. That week, he signed a ten-year contract with the university. Some of the Notre Dame family wondered if Leahy should come back. With Devore in charge, there had been no concern about the tail wagging the dog. There had been little controversy. But Notre Dame still needed football. America needed football. After three-plus years of war and deprivation, the country wanted to resume its life.

He served his country, missing two football seasons. Now, Leahy had his team back, and he dived right into the workload. Leahy had to reassemble a roster and a coaching staff—he announced quickly that John Druze and Joe McArdle would return to his staff after their discharges. He had to come up with a schedule for the following season. He had to find a home in the South Bend area, nearly impossible in a housing shortage that spread nationwide. He had to figure out how to handle the returning veterans who would make up the bulk of the team. Paramount among Leahy's challenges: He had to figure out how to beat Army, Notre Dame's oldest rival. Coach Red Blaik, taking advantage of having his choice of the nation's military draftees, won the national championship in 1944 and 1945. That didn't gall Leahy nearly as much as the way Army defeated Notre Dame in the two seasons he was away. Leahy ordered up a sign reading "59–0 and 48–0" and had it hung in the Notre Dame locker room.

As the calendar turned to 1946, as the nation tried to return to whatever normalcy would be after the war, the renewal of the Army–Notre Dame rivalry shone like a lighthouse on a halcyon shore, promising the nation that this new normal would be better than the old. This was Army and Notre Dame, winners of the last three national championships, an annual rivalry so integral to American identity that GIs in Europe used the score of the 1944 game as a password in the Battle of the Bulge. As a college football game, the Notre Dame–Army game would dominate the season. As an American sporting event, the game would dominate the year. As a missed opportunity, the game would haunt both Leahy and Blaik for the rest of their lives.

CHAPTER ELEVEN

ARMY IS OUT THERE

LEAHY TOLD THE STORY THAT IN PREPARATION FOR THE 1946 SEASON he asked lineman Bob Livingstone how difficult war had been: seeing friends die, the deprivation, etc. Livingstone's answer covered no such topic. Listening to Army beat Notre Dame 59–0? Now *that* was tough.

Whether the anecdote is true or not, it speaks both to the primacy of the Army rivalry and, bigger picture, how the returning veterans didn't want to talk about what they had endured. They wanted to restart their lives. For some it was easier than others. The Germans captured Bob McBride during the Battle of the Bulge in December 1944. He spent most of the next four months marching hundreds of miles back and forth across Germany at the point of a rifle. In captivity, McBride's weight dropped from 215 pounds to 104. At a field hospital after his rescue, an American doctor asked McBride if he was any kin to the Bob McBride who played for Notre Dame.

"I am him," McBride said.

"Bullshit," the doctor replied.

As they discussed Notre Dame, the doctor, an alum, said, "You really are, aren't you." After an exam, he told McBride that he suffered from extreme malnutrition, beriberi, jaundice, dysentery, and diarrhea, and that he wouldn't have lasted two more weeks. When McBride reenrolled at Notre Dame in January 1946, he had gotten back to 190 pounds. Leahy wrote him a letter to welcome him back.

"We are unusually happy over your decision to return not just because you are an outstanding football player but mainly because of your ability to give Notre Dame the kind of representation she deserves off the field," Leahy said. "I can truthfully say that I have never had the privilege of coaching a finer young gentleman than yourself; therefore, it is only natural that we should look forward with much pleasure to having you on our team again..."

When Leahy talked about McBride in an interview, his eyes filled with tears. "If young McBride fails to get his man on any play in any game, I'll not berate him in the style of prewar coaching," Leahy said. "He told me all about his war career, and every time I see him out on the field—other boys back from the service, too—I wonder if we're not taking this football game too seriously." He composed himself, then said, "I guess I shouldn't act this way, but I was close to it myself over in the Pacific at Midway, Tarawa, Guam, and Saipan."

Was Leahy's sympathy performative? He already had said he got no closer to combat than speaking to a Japanese prisoner. Both could be true. Leahy felt deeply for McBride, and he knew how to tell a story.

In February, Leahy described at length to Franklin Lewis of *The Cleveland Press* the challenge of coaching young men who had been in the war. Leahy said he would try to treat his players as individuals, that he understood that after the regimentation of the military, they would balk at one-size-fits-all rules as civilians, even in the quasi-military life of a football team.

"They're used to being ordered around. They don't want that

anymore," Leahy said. "... Of course there will be limitations. But these fellows who have served in the Pacific and in Europe don't need to be led around by the hand. They've been through plenty. They cannot be driven to football practice. They cannot be impressed with the customary hoorah stuff. They're men, and I think they will appreciate leadership. Not mass routine.

"You just can't take a GI back onto a football squad and expect him to react exactly as an eighteen-year-old freshman will react to a certain type of direction. That's why I want to use a personal approach. In fact, I've used it already."

Leahy's toughest task may have been sorting through the talent. He knew he had a lot. In February, speaking to the Notre Dame Club of Buffalo, Leahy predicted that Army and Navy would continue to be in a class by themselves but the Irish will have improved sufficiently to force any opponent to "use its first team for at least forty-five minutes, including that game in New York." Leahy said this nine months before Notre Dame played Army. He already had an eye on That Game in New York.

In the case of back Phil Colella, Leahy donned kid gloves, and to no avail. Colella, while serving in the Navy, twice had ships shot out from under him. When he returned to campus in 1945, he played well for Hugh Devore, scoring a 75-yard touchdown on the opening snap against Illinois, a touchdown that would remain the only points scored in the game. But Colella no-showed for spring football, three times after telling Leahy that he would come out "tomorrow." Colella reported to the first fall practice, on August 26. Leahy welcomed him back and sent him to the equipment room for gear. Leahy never saw Colella again. That fall Colella made the Little All-America team—for St. Bonaventure.

Maybe Colella knew what awaited him on the practice field. Leahy had returning starters from a very good 1945 team. He had returning starters from the 1943 national championship team. He had returning starters from his first two Notre Dame teams. He had players in their early twenties, married men, war veterans, and eighteen-year-old freshmen whose talent overwhelmed their inexperience. To this day it may have been the greatest assemblage of talent in one locker room in the history of college football. Nine players went on to make All-America teams—and remember, this is in the era of one-platoon football, when only eleven players made an All-America team, not twenty-five, as is the case today. Six made All-Pro.

Take, for example, Art Donovan, the tackle who would go on to play twelve years in the NFL and be elected to the Pro Football Hall of Fame. Donovan had been a scholarship player on the 1942 team before joining the Marines. The coaches didn't deem him talented enough to give him a scholarship when he came back. Donovan went home to the Bronx, then enrolled at Boston College. Fullback Bob Hanlon, who won a monogram with the 1943 national champs, got hurt in practice and decided to transfer to Loras College. He played in the NFL. Art Statuto got so little playing time that he never earned a monogram. When he left Notre Dame, he played three years of professional football. Guard George Tobin, a monogram winner in 1942, a starter for Iowa Pre-Flight in 1943, played little in 1946. The following spring he went to see Leahy, told him that the New York Giants had offered him $5,000 to sign, and what should he do? Leahy told Tobin to take the offer. He could start for the Giants, and he wouldn't play much for the Irish in 1947. Tobin took the offer—and started for the Giants.

"What I remember is that we fought every day—fought to win a job and then to hold it," Jim Martin said. He was a six-foot-two, 204-pound, twenty-two-year-old freshman known as "Jungle Jim," a Marine who had won a Bronze Star in the Pacific. "You had guys like me and then you had the older service vets," Martin said. "And practice was tough on them. They'd had enough of war, of guys beating the hell out of each other, but that's what practice was every day, a war."

Leahy's hunger for football after two seasons away radiated off him. In April, Joe McArdle invited the football staff and a few friends, including the writer Tim Cohane, to his house for a dinner party.

Leahy arrived with a football. He had come up with a new way for the quarterback to hand the ball off to a running back. When everyone else went to the table to begin the meal, Leahy continued his demonstration. McArdle looked at Cohane and just shook his head.

Leahy had a thirty-foot tower built on the sideline of the practice field so that he could survey everyone. Forget two-a-days. Leahy held three practices a day. He would winnow out the talent by testing the will of men returning from the greatest test of will that they would ever face. "The toughest football games that I have ever played in were scrimmages in the late part of spring practice and scrimmages during the fall of that year," McBride said. He added that the team really bonded during those weeks. Maybe Leahy knew what he was doing.

And always, there was Army. The players developed a chant for the practice field:

59 and 48
This Is the Year
We Retaliate!

Leahy may not have known exactly what kind of team he had but he knew pretty quickly that the team would depend upon Johnny Lujack to lead it. The halfback returned from the service with another fifteen pounds, weighing 190, and still had the quickness and intuitiveness that helped him lead Notre Dame to the national championship three years earlier. Leahy said he wouldn't trade Lujack for any player in the country, which raised an eyebrow in West Point, where Doc Blanchard had won the 1945 Heisman and Glenn Davis lined up alongside him.

"That isn't the way I mean it," Leahy said. "What I'm driving at is that Johnny Lujack means more to Notre Dame than any other single back means to his team. And that includes Blanchard, Davis or name one to suit yourself. He can be the difference, if you get the idea. If ever a coach had a key that would unlock the door, I have it in that fellow."

In the summer, a film crew arrived to create a documentary about the Fighting Irish. Coaches were not supposed to attend summer practices, so Leahy, by then in his late thirties, wore a helmet in order to appear to be one of the players. Leon Hart, a freshman on the 1946 team, recalled Leahy at the blackboard that the coaches had on the field, players huddled around him, when a plane flew directly overhead. Leahy tilted his head away from the plane until it passed over. "We couldn't believe it—he actually thought there were spies in the plane that would report him for being on the field during movie time," Hart said.

A high green wooden fence surrounded Cartier Field, the practice area. Leahy controlled access by deploying student managers at every gate. Visitors wore a pass, the color denoting identity (writer, faculty, friend, etc.). Eddy Gilmore, who had been the AP correspondent in Moscow, once said, "It was easier to get into the Kremlin." When the university constructed a liberal arts building with a second floor that overlooked Cartier Field, Leahy became convinced it would be filled with spies. Somehow he received permission during football season to control access to the second floor.

A month or so before preseason work began, Father John J. Cavanaugh, Leahy's boss, friend, and confidant, succeeded Father Hugh O'Donnell as president of Notre Dame. Leahy surely viewed this as a positive development, and the respect and friendship between the two men appeared to deepen at the outset of Cavanaugh's administration. His replacement as executive vice president, Father John Murphy, would be in charge of athletics, but Leahy knew he had an ally in the top job. Before Cavanaugh settled into his office, Leahy fired off a long memo to Cavanaugh in which he decried having more than a hundred players returning from the war years who didn't have the requisite talent to play to Leahy's standard. The coach acknowledged that he understood the scarcity of good players during wartime. "Please believe me—I do not wish to say anything derogatory about Coach McKeever or Coach Devore, both of whom are held very highly in my esteem; but I am forced to admit they were not particularly careful in their selection of material." He added that Notre Dame didn't have enough equipment for more than a hundred or so players, then played the safety card. "There is no question in my mind that it would be an injustice to these boys were we to ask them to participate in football during the 1946 and 1947 seasons."

Leahy scraped off a little rust in mid-August when he coached the South team in the first-ever Ohio (high school) All-Star Game. Leahy, after working with his players for eight days, predicted the North would win by a touchdown or two. The South, naturally, jumped out to a 26–0 lead before winning, 26–21.

By the time preseason practice began in August, more players arrived with their military discharges. Of the fourteen guards who reported for practice, eleven had won Notre Dame monograms; for the ends, the numbers were twenty-one and eleven, respectively. Leahy had them up at six a.m., with three practices a day and a team meeting every practice day at twelve thirty p.m. in the Law Building auditorium. The meetings continued during the season as well. Leahy would diagram one or two plays, which the players would copy into the notebooks provided them. On Mondays, during game week, the players would hear a scouting report, one that typically exaggerated the height, weight, and skill of every opposing player. Leahy would talk football, and his players soon learned to supply his rote questions with rote answers (football, it would seem, is a game of repetition). As Jack Connor recalled, Leahy would begin a question, "What are the prerequisites..." for playing well, performing a specific task, etc., and the players would begin their answers, "The burning desire to..."

But Leahy also would talk about life, and the skills necessary to interact with others. His men may have been war veterans, but in the coach's mind they remained young and untaught. Leahy demanded that they look people in the eye and deliver a firm handshake. He soon installed into the meeting schedule a three-minute segment in which a player would stand before the team and give a talk on a salient subject. This lasted until one of the ex-Marines, guard Joe Signaigo, concluded his story with an off-color punch line. Everyone in the room roared with laughter save the head coach, who left immediately. Connor said no one ever knew whether Leahy left because of his own moral code or because he didn't want the players see him laughing. The players' public speaking came to a close. Their attempts to deflate Leahy did not. Leading the charge: Ziggy Czarobski, the effervescent lineman from Chicago.

On September 14, two weeks before the opener at Illinois, the first team scrimmaged the second team—and lost, 14–7. When the team met that night at the Law School auditorium, Leahy spoke from the podium in his stiff, polite manner. "I must apologize," he said. "I believed that you returning players had some idea how to play the game of football. After what I have seen this afternoon, I was obviously in error." Leahy announced that the team would review fundamentals, just what a group of beat-up young men wanted to do on a postgame Saturday night. Leahy reached into the podium and held up an object.

"For your edification, this object that I am holding between my hands is commonly known as a football," Leahy said.

Czarobski, sitting up front, waved his hand like a first grader who had to go to the bathroom.

"Zygmont," Leahy said, "do you have something you want to say?"

"Please," Czarobski said, "I am trying to take notes. Don't go so fast."

The tension among the players broke and seemed to flow directly into the head coach, whose face turned red. To his credit as a leader, Leahy let his anger go and smiled. He discussed with the team how far they had to go in order to represent Notre Dame, and afterward, he called Czarobski aside.

"Zygmont, it was good that you did that," Leahy said. "It was good for the whole team. It relieved the tension. Any time you can come up with something like that, don't hesitate to talk."

The Ziggy stories sound like the tales that New York baseball writers would tell in years to come about Yogi Berra or Casey Stengel, so funny they couldn't be true. Leahy told Czarobski to lose fifty pounds before practice started. Czarobski put himself through hell but when the deadline arrived, he had lost only forty-three. He rigged the scale to show that he had passed the test and then went to Leahy to tell him he was ready for his weigh-in. Leahy said, "No, Zygmont. I'll take your word for it." At the next weigh-in, every other player on the team learned he had lost eight pounds. Or when Leahy heard the shower running moments before practice, ducked his head in and saw Ziggy. When Leahy asked why he wasn't already on the field, Czarobski told him he wanted to shower now; the showers got too crowded after practice.

Leahy looked the other way when the vets, led by Czarobski, went on field trips. They might charter a bus and go out to Michigan City on the shore of Lake Michigan, or north to Edwardsburg, Michigan, just to let off steam. They made their way to Flytraps, a bar in nearby Elkhart, for weekly meetings of "The Muggers Club." Of the seventy-two players who made the team, forty-nine of them had served in the military during the war. After Czarobski finished his Notre Dame football career, Leahy let him know he knew about the field trips all along.

Leahy may have given them some room, but he continued to push these men harder than they wanted to be pushed. McArdle once asked Leahy what would happen if he pushed so hard that the players revolted. Leahy thought for a moment, then shook his fist and said, "They wouldn't dare!"

At several points over the next four years, these men, not boys, would push back. Take the late-season game in 1946 at Tulane, which the Irish won handily, 41–0. The players celebrated deep into the night in the French Quarter, stumbled into eight a.m. Mass, then enjoyed a champagne brunch. They boarded the train home and went straight to the club car. When Leahy walked through, the players started booing. Czarobski tried to introduce the girl sitting on his lap to his head coach. Leahy walked through the car and never said a word about it.

In the days leading up to the opener, Leahy predicted that Notre Dame would lose at least three games, to Illinois, Army, and USC.

But he fooled no one. Word of what Leahy had assembled made its way not only to the daily sports columnists across the country who stood as the media giants but to the general press as well. The editors at *Time* magazine, smack in the middle of Manhattan, felt the drumbeat. They worked for several weeks to put Leahy on the cover shortly after the season began. The owner/editor of *Time*, Henry Luce, paid little attention to sports. He was too intellectual, and the world had too much at stake, for him to devote time and space in his precious editorial pages to baseball or college football. For instance, the cover subjects on the issues following Leahy were playwright Eugene O'Neill and Pennsylvania Governor Edward Martin, about to win election to the US Senate. The cynic who saw the Leahy cover noted that Luce's wife, Congresswoman Clare Boothe Luce (R-Conn.), had converted to Catholicism earlier that year. The conversion of the congresswoman, annually among the most admired women in America, had been front-page news. Whatever the reason, for the next several years, with an occasional exception, *Time*'s coverage of college football mainly consisted of regular stories on Leahy's Irish.

In what had become *Time*'s fashion, this cover story touched upon only the peak of a mountain of reporting. *Time* correspondents filed reports concerning Leahy's entire life and coaching career, up to and including his late entry into military service. Boston correspondent David Zeitlin reported, "I did not do well on anecdotes, as there does not seem to be much laughter connected with his career."

Snarky comments by other coaches and administrators didn't make the piece. Dick Hyland, a star for Stanford in the 1920s who had become a sportswriter for the *Los Angeles Times*, held a dim view of Leahy's ethics. He had been offended by the rough play of the Irish against his alma mater and USC in 1942. As a Marine captain and colleague of former Northwestern coach Dick Hanley, he agreed with Hanley that Leahy should have been in the military before 1944. Hyland, when contacted by a *Time* correspondent, told him that if the magazine put Leahy on the cover, it "will be the laughingstock of football."

The story, splashed across five pages, attempted to straddle the line between lionizing Leahy and the wealth of talent at Notre Dame and discussing the ethical lapses of postwar college football.

The piece absolved Leahy of buying players while discussing what top stars at other schools supposedly received. The examination of Leahy's personality quirks assumed a bemused tone. "He is a natural-born fanatic. But, like most good fanatics, he is businesslike about it. At his work, he is crisp and indefatigable... With people, he works almost too hard at being pleasant. He breaks out the big smile, and begins using six-bit words (sample: 'I will endeavor to obliterate the defects'). Some people think he is unctuous; some think he is just right."

What Notre Dame fans thought of the story depended on their degree of religiosity. Two quotes attributed to Leahy had enough flippancy regarding churchly matters that they didn't go over well with the campus priests. One, regarding Leahy's assemblage of football talent, appeared below the illustration of Leahy on the cover: "Prayers work better when the players are big." And two, regarding the importance of Lujack to the team: Leahy said that if something happened to his quarterback, "I guess we could send a wire to the Pope."

In the days after publication, *Time* received seventeen "mostly cantankerous" letters, including one from Father Cavanaugh. The university president called the story "an injustice to an intelligent educator." However, the Letters Report to the editors continued, "[O]ne blurb from Notre Dame indicated that students thought the report on Leahy generally first-rate." Leahy, rather than accept responsibility for a witticism that landed with a thud to his bosses, held a grudge against *Time* for years afterward.

When the story hit the stands, Notre Dame already had sailed to a 2-0 record. The team had the good fortune of its first two opponents, Illinois and Pittsburgh, playing each other on the Saturday before the Irish's first game. Leahy and Moose Krause went to Pitt Stadium as scouts. In a radio interview at halftime of the game, which the Illini won, 33–7, Leahy said, "We will lose several games but we are strong enough to force any team we meet to use its first team for thirty minutes." That's down from the forty-five minutes he predicted in the spring.

That's not the only scouting the Notre Dame staff did. Leahy dispatched Jack Lavelle, a bon vivant who threatened three hundred pounds, to every Army game. Leahy took this step because, after the Lujack affair, he and Blaik had so little regard for each other that they refused to swap game films. Lavelle, who had played for Rockne a few years before Leahy, would file lengthy reports on Army each week.* If Leahy read them as they arrived, he never acknowledged as much to his players. He wanted the team focused on the next opponent.

Illinois featured back Buddy Young and Julie Rykovich, the former Notre Dame starter whom Leahy promised an agriculture degree, in the backfield. The Illini would go on to an 8-2 season, a Western Conference championship and a 45–14 rout of UCLA in the Rose Bowl, and yet they never had a chance in the opener. Notre Dame won, 26–6, Illinois throwing a 63-yard touchdown pass in the final thirty seconds to avert a shutout. It was only the second time the Illini crossed midfield. And so it went the first four weeks of the season—33–0 over Pitt, 49–6 over Purdue, 41–6 at No. 17 Iowa (three of the first four opponents belonged to the Western Conference; so much for Crisler's boycott). Leahy, never one to enjoy success, kept pushing his players. After the Pitt game, he complained to Jim Costin of *The South Bend Tribune* about player after player.

"Didn't anyone play well?" Costin asked.

"Yes," Leahy said. "Bob McBride." McBride, Leahy's favorite, had settled in as a third-team guard.

The competition to make the first two teams remained fierce for more than the obvious reason. Leahy only took thirty-six players on the travel squad. After the coaches set the first team and the second team,

---

* Four years later, when Lavelle scouted for Herman Hickman at Yale, he had learned to trim his reports significantly. Hickman sent Lavelle to scout Princeton playing Harvard. After the Tigers won, 63–26, Lavelle sent a report that said, in toto, "Cancel."

they held a two-hour scrimmage on Thursday to determine the remainder of the travel squad. The coaches chose this method of winnowing because they found it too difficult to differentiate among the wealth of talent. They banked on a few players coming out of the scrimmage too banged up to be available two days later. The players, many of whom had once been starters, competed in these gladiator sessions to salvage their egos.

The Irish churned toward the top of the AP poll but stopped at No. 2. Army had been No. 1 in every poll but one since the middle of the 1944 season. Actually, the Black Knights hadn't lost since the last game of 1943. Blaik's detractors carped that the coach had used the draft and the war to assemble an all-star team—several starters, including Blanchard, had begun their collegiate careers at other schools. Early in 1946, Blaik began receiving daily anonymous postcards, presumably from the Irish faithful, advising him that his team's reign atop college football would soon end, signing them SPATNC. That stood for the Society for the Prevention of Army's Third National Championship.

That was the nicer sniping. Others called the Army players slackers, derision that appalled not only the entire Academy but image-conscious officers at the Pentagon. As both teams mowed through their games in September and October, their meeting at Yankee Stadium on November 9 at one thirty p.m. captured the imagination of a country yearning to pour its energy into civilian life. In 1946, more than eighty million Americans—57 percent of the population—went to the movies every week. The film *The Best Years of Our Lives*, depicting the struggles of three returning servicemen to adjust to civilian life, struck an emotional note with audiences and critics and would be awarded seven Oscars. In New York, the Yankees, Giants, and Brooklyn Dodgers combined to draw more than 5.2 million fans, an increase of 2.3 million over the previous year.

The Yankees split the tickets evenly between the two schools. In an attempt to control the demand, Notre Dame limited alumni to four tickets. West Point sold only to graduates before 1932. The schools still sent back more than $1 million in unfilled orders. "If Yankee Stadium had a million seats," West Point athletic director Biff Jones said, "we would fill it for this game. I have never seen anything like it."

On the Saturday before the showdown, Notre Dame played Navy in Baltimore. Leahy arranged for a secret practice at Catholic University in Washington the day before the game. Some secret—at least 2,000 spectators greeted the team when it ran onto the practice field. "I don't permit the boys to talk about anything but Navy," Leahy said, "but I can't control their thinking, and if they're thinking too little about Navy and too much about Army, that's no good. It's a grand way to get yourself upset." The Irish maintained their focus well enough to win, 28–0. Among the nearly 64,000 in attendance were Blaik, his line coach, Herman Hickman, and a couple of seats away, Bob Hope. The comedian brought a radio and kept the coaches abreast of the Army–West Virginia game with teasingly comic reports that Blaik, a humorless man most days, called "almost sadistic." The Black Knights won, 19–0.

Red Smith, the columnist for the *New York Herald Tribune* who graduated from Notre Dame four years ahead of Leahy, rode with the Irish team on the train from Baltimore to South Bend. Given that Notre Dame had lost to Army the last two seasons by a combined 107–0, if he could beat Army and Blaik 108–0, would he?

"No," Leahy said. "It's not good for relations between the schools. If the first three Army teams were poisoned and we had a chance to pour it on, I wouldn't want to. I don't think Army poured it on our team intentionally last year, although maybe they did in 1944, because that was the first time they beat us in so many years. But sometimes you can't help running up the score. The game gets away from you and your substitutes may play better than the regulars."

On Monday, the estimable Grantland Rice wrote in his nationally syndicated column, "This is the week. It is the big week of sport. It is a bigger week than any World Series game. It is a bigger week than any Joe Louis fight. It is the week of the Army–ND game." Rice added that the nature of the rivalry combined with the ranking of the teams "and other elements involved" gave the game "an extra flare of color that no other single football game has known in the memory of this generation."

Writers descended on both Notre Dame and West Point, churning out copy to satiate the national desire for news about the game. In national elections on Tuesday, the Republicans flipped control of both the House and the Senate for the first time since 1932. And yet, "It's a cinch bet," Lyall Smith of the *Detroit Free Press* wrote that week, "that more words have been written about the pending game than were penned on the recent elections." Tuesday also was the day that Notre Dame players received their tickets for the upcoming game. McBride recalled a scalper flying out from New York City and offering $250 a ticket to the players.

Notre Dame students hung effigies of Army stars Blanchard and Davis outside Leahy's office. They hung bedsheets from windows with painted witticisms: "End the meat shortage; slaughter the Army mule!" When the players weren't using their "Retaliate!" chant, Leahy continued to remind them of what Army did to Notre Dame the previous two seasons. "Lads, we all know Army picked on our youngsters. What will happen on Saturday when they face men?"

Leahy held a dinner Tuesday night for the writers who had come to campus. In a private dining room at the Oliver Hotel downtown, one of the New York writers complimented Leahy on how well the group had been treated and said, look, you're among friends here, cut the politeness and the diction and the vocabulary and tell us what you really think about things. It won't leave the room.

Leahy seemed puzzled by the request. He didn't quite fathom that his behavior could be seen as an act.

"We want you gentlemen of the press to know that you are indeed welcome at the University of Notre Dame," Leahy answered. "We intend to continue to extend every courtesy on this visit to our campus and we most sincerely hope you will find it agreeable and profitable. If there is anything we may have forgotten to provide for your comfort or enlightenment, please let us know, lads."

The writer, convinced he was being had, said, "See what I mean?" and threw up his hands. The room burst into laughter, Leahy among them. But he didn't get the joke. He didn't understand how "lads" turned into a punch line. That's the term his father used.

"He seemed genuinely surprised that the writers should have had such an opinion of him," Francis Wallace said.

Many years later, Edgar Hayes, a longtime writer in Detroit, recalled Father Cavanaugh asking him why so many writers gave Leahy a hard time.

"They don't think he is sincere," Hayes said.

"Suppose he is?" Cavanaugh replied.

Leahy skipped the Wednesday press conference to get a filling replaced, and that wasn't even the worst thing that happened to him that day. He had vowed not to scrimmage much before the game to keep his players healthy. But on Wednesday afternoon, disaster struck. Lujack, the indispensable Irish player, leaped to defend a long pass intended for Hank Kosikowski, a reserve end. They came down in a heap and Lujack didn't get up right away. Leahy watched "with an expression close to horror" on his face, Smith wrote. The trainers determined that Lujack had suffered a high right ankle sprain. Lujack went into the training room, where trainer Hugh Burns stuck Lujack's injured joint under the cold water tap for a half hour. The trainers began alternating hot and cold compresses on his ankle and did so throughout the night. Lujack slept in the campus infirmary.

Leahy put the rest of the team through a light workout on Thursday morning before they boarded a four p.m. train headed east. At the Studebaker automobile plant across the street from the South Bend station, workers waving banners filled the windows. The team doctor, Joseph Caton, assured Leahy that Lujack would be able to play. "I never had a night like this in my life," Dr. Caton said. "Every man who ever graduated from Notre Dame had to talk to me personally about

Lujack's chances of playing against Army." As the train headed east, it passed platform after platform filled with nuns and schoolchildren cheering the Irish as they passed through. Leahy called together all the New York writers on the train and gave each of them two tickets to the game (journalistic ethics were different in those days), quite the swag for men who might not be making a hundred dollars a week.

At West Point, the Corps lit a bonfire on the practice field after the sound of taps on Thursday. General Maxwell Taylor, the Academy superintendent, might have been looking the other way at the breach of conduct.

Notre Dame decided to dedicate the game to George Murphy, the 1942 team captain who had been killed in action on Okinawa in May 1945. Leahy, oddly enough, had the team spend Friday night at the Bear Mountain Inn, just off the grounds of the United States Military Academy. He wanted nothing to do with the tumult of New York. Jerry Nason, writing from New York for *The Boston Globe*, said, "The local hotel association has thrown up its hands in resignation, warns latecomers to camp under a billboard. There are no rooms, no tickets, no hope. There is a terrific amount of wagering." Nason did not exaggerate. *The New Yorker* magazine reported a "sort of insanity seemed to seize the city... Thousands of people from all over the country wandered the streets day and night, many of them without a place to sleep, to eat, or even just to sit down for a while."

As the Army players rode buses to Yankee Stadium, the Irish beat cops would spot them and yell, "Beat Army!" When the players emerged from the bus, they saw a man standing on the curb holding a fistful of $100 bills, trying to buy two tickets. Another man drove around the stadium for an hour, holding a sign offering $200 for a ticket. He didn't find one. At Baker Field, fifty-seven blocks northwest, where Penn and Columbia would kick off a half hour after Notre Dame and Army, ushers didn't allow ticketholders to bring their portable radios into the game, so fans sat in their cars listening. WCBS, WNBC, and WJZ, the three most powerful stations in the city, each broadcast the game. NBC estimated that 150,000 viewers in New York, Washington, and Philadelphia saw its telecast, a remarkable number given that only 44,000 homes in the nation had a TV set by year's end. At the Waldorf-Astoria, during day six of a meeting of the "Big Four" foreign ministers (including the USSR, the United Kingdom, and France), Secretary of State James F. Byrnes held the Saturday meeting in the morning so that he could get to Yankee Stadium for kickoff.

The unseasonably warm (high of sixty-six), muggy weather appeared to be a plus for the Irish. The Black Knights had a celebrated team of starters but not nearly the depth of talent of their opponents. "I don't see any reason why Notre Dame should not win," Blaik said. "They have no weakness, unless it's the fact that they are only three deep at quarterback." Not to be outdone, Leahy predicted publicly that Army would win, 27–14.

Privately, Leahy prepared his players to be at a psychological peak on Saturday afternoon. For easy games, Leahy would talk at length in the pregame locker room. For Army, Leahy kept quiet, the tension that had built for months permeating the walls of the Yankee locker room in which the Irish dressed. Then, he looked at his players and said, "Army is out there."

Frank Leahy coached 129 games in his thirteen seasons as a head coach. The most memorable game of his career, this 1946 game against Army, owns that designation because Leahy did not make the same shrewd decisions he made on all the other Saturdays. "I did a bad coaching job on that game," he said in 1959. "I had been away [in the Navy] and had gotten out of the habit of doing things right."

For one thing, Leahy was so impressed with Army's starting eleven that he did not play his second team nearly as much as usual. All season he had played the first team in the first and third quarters, the second team in the second and fourth quarters, similar to what Rockne had done. The second team dominated, especially this season, when the entire Notre Dame roster could have started at most schools. Against Army, Leahy used only eighteen players. Krause kept calling from the press box to the sideline to urge Leahy to take advantage of Army's run defense by putting in the second-team offense with George Ratterman at quarterback. Leahy ignored the advice.

For another, when Notre Dame drove down to the Army 4-yard line in the second quarter, facing 4th-and-goal, Leahy refused the opportunity to kick a short field goal. He thought Notre Dame needed more than three points. Besides, the Irish had scored 35.4 points per game in their first five games. If they didn't score, they would drive down the field again.

Only Army stopped the fourth-down play and the Irish never came closer.* Lujack may have been able to play all sixty minutes, but he threw four interceptions, three to his counterpart on Army, Arnold Tucker. The story went that when Leahy asked Lujack why he threw so many passes to Tucker, Lujack responded, "He was the only man I could find open." Actually, though Lujack ran well straight ahead on his injured ankle, he had trouble setting up to throw.

Notre Dame also lost three fumbles. The Black Knights got as good as they gave, coughing up the ball four times and never penetrating the Irish 15. That, too, qualified as field-goal range, but Blaik didn't believe in field goals. He hadn't called for an attempt in three seasons. In the third quarter, Blanchard appeared to break away on a long run. Lujack, the only man who could have caught him, brought him down after a 21-yard gain at the Notre Dame 37. The game ended as it started, with the scoreboard reading 0–0.

Leahy and Blaik both tried to hide their disappointment after the game. They said all the appropriate things, although Blaik believed he had blown his clearest shot. "Army will never have another chance to beat Notre Dame," he said. Leahy kept the locker room closed for thirty minutes. "You played your hearts out," Leahy told his team, "but you were not quite good enough today. Remember one thing now—the

---

* Three years later, Leahy told reporters that the Army defense should have been called for clipping on the play. Clearly, it stuck with him because of the final score.

test of a champion is how he reacts to adversity on the days when it is bound to come."

Krause tried to console the head coach. "I told Frank that it wasn't the end of the world," he said. "We hadn't even lost the game, but he sat there and cried anyway. Every time we lost he would go into a corner of the locker room and cry."

When Leahy opened the door to the writers, he took questions for ninety minutes, speaking softly and courteously. "The boys are a little bit depressed. We really expected to win. I really was amazed at the display of fine defensive football by both teams. I thought they would both score at least two or three touchdowns."

Wallace, the writer and Notre Dame graduate, said of Leahy, "He replayed the game, offered no alibi, took responsibility for the conservative strategy of his team, admitted he might be more daring if the game were to be replayed."

When the writers left, Leahy continued to sit in the locker room, keeping his coaches with him, going over and over the decisions he had made, trying for another three-plus hours to figure out why Notre Dame hadn't won. By the time he finally let go long enough to trudge out of an empty Yankee Stadium, there wasn't a cab to be found. Leahy and his coaches began walking the 120 blocks south to midtown. They finally found a cop, who went to a phone and made a call. A few minutes later, a cab arrived.

"Let's face it," Martin, the left end, said of his head coach many years later. "He just chickened out. They had a great first unit, but we could have worn them down with our squad."

From 1941 to 1946, Blaik had coached against Leahy four times, and Army had yet to score a point. Many years later, Blaik went to lunch with Red Smith and Terry Brennan, a freshman on the 1946 Notre Dame team. They discussed all the missed opportunities, and Blaik finally said, "You're right. We both screwed up." He said he and Leahy had discussed the game some years afterward and agreed that their personal animus had overtaken their good sense. "[W]e often criticized ourselves in the sense that we were too interested in not losing... We took the wrong psychology. 'He's not going to beat us' rather than 'We're going to win this game.'"

Blaik made that comment to the Associated Press in 1973 when called for a reaction to Leahy's death.

A few years after the game, Joe Doyle of *The South Bend Tribune* recalled an afternoon in the early 1950s when he walked into the Notre Dame locker room unannounced and found Leahy sitting alone on a bench, lost in thought. "Then he said out loud, 'If only we'd kicked the field goal,'" Doyle said.

The team returned to South Bend on the New York Central train known as the Commodore Vanderbilt, arriving at six a.m. Monday. It may have been Armistice Day, a national holiday with no classes scheduled at Notre Dame, but per tradition for the Army rivalry, the entire student body greeted the players and coaches in the predawn darkness as they stepped off the train.

Eight of the eighteen players who played against Army came out of the game with varying degrees of injury. But there would be no more Armys on the Notre Dame schedule. The Irish defeated Northwestern, Tulane, and USC by large margins to end the season. After the 41–0 rout of the Green Wave in New Orleans, Tulane coach Henry Frnka said, "They made us look like a high school team at times, but it wasn't because we were so bad; it was because they were so good."

LEAHY, WORN DOWN PER USUAL, CAUGHT A VIRUS, GOT LARYNGITIS, and stayed home in bed for the USC game. Leahy put Krause in charge of the game. Krause, who possessed all the warmth that Leahy did not, ran a looser practice. Late in the week, he appropriated one of Leahy's pet sayings while watching film, telling the offense, "Run that play again." The players, mimicking film being reversed, ran backward into their pre-snap positions. The entire team dissolved into laughter, and no, that never would have happened had the boss been on the field.

Something similar happened in the locker room before the game. That morning Krause and the other assistants had gone to Leahy's house to discuss the game plan with him. In the locker room, Krause tried to bring the team to an emotional high by telling the players how sick Leahy was, that he had gone days without shaving. Livingstone interrupted by suggesting everyone chip in and buy their head coach some razor blades. The locker room broke up, Krause included, laughing so hard that he forgot to announce the starting lineup.

There the story would end, with Notre Dame rushing for 517 yards en route to a 26–6 victory, except that Krause had found a star. Before the war, Coy McGee played one season at Tulane but got run off by Frnka because McGee didn't weigh 150 in full pads with pockets full of coins. After the war, McGee, weighing all of 160 pounds, enrolled at Notre Dame in aeronautical engineering and reported to football tryouts. He got as high as third team but hadn't even made the traveling squad for the Navy game. Krause put in McGee against USC, and he ran six times for 146 yards and two touchdowns, including a 77-yarder. Krause used to tell the story that when he called Leahy after the game, the head coach said, "Who the hell is this Coy McGee you put in my starting lineup?" But Leahy had seen McGee return a kick for a touchdown in practice, and given that the coaches met the morning of the game, it's safe to assume that Krause always knew how to tell a story for laughs.

While the Irish cruised past the Trojans, No. 1 Army needed a last-second goal-line stand to overtake a 1-7 Navy team. The Black Knights held on to a 21–18 lead only when the Midshipmen ran out of time on the Army 4-yard line. Win the game, lose the war: The AP voters dethroned two-time national champ Army (9-0-1) and awarded Notre Dame with its second title under Leahy.

Blaik, however, won the *New York World-Telegram* Coach of the Year vote. That poll of football coaches did not at all follow the AP vote. Blaik received 112 first-place votes, Leahy 30. In fact, Leahy finished fourth in the vote behind Bert LaBrucherie of UCLA and John

Barnhill of Arkansas. One writer called the vote a "gratuitous slight" against Leahy but in the same piece labeled him as "dour, peevish." It was another popularity vote by his peers that he did not win.

Before the year ended, Leahy, Blaik, and their schools took a joint public relations hit. On December 30, Notre Dame and West Point released a statement that after the teams played each other in 1947, the rivalry would be "temporarily interrupted." The decision came after weeks of discussion that began when the administrators of the two schools convened in New York for the 1946 game. It was a joint decision in the way that a divorce is joint; if one side wants out, there isn't much the other can say. A few days before the 1946 game, General Taylor had written a letter to General Dwight D. Eisenhower, by then the Army Chief of Staff, suggesting that Army retreat. Ending the rivalry would give Army more schedule flexibility, Taylor said. He added that the public had begun to view the rivalry as West Point vs. the Catholic Church, which would never turn out well for the Academy. Also, Taylor wrote, Notre Dame was simply too good. The rivalry "has ceased to be fun," Taylor said.

Eisenhower suggested that Army play a final game, which, for appearance's sake if nothing else, sent the message that the schools parted on good terms. The priests and the brass agreed in New York that they would end the rivalry six weeks before they announced that agreement; in fact, Leahy knew it when the 1946 game kicked off. That may add a sharper focus to Leahy's upset over the tie, although it's difficult to know for sure. Some frustrated Notre Dame fans wondered why Leahy had not used that information to motivate the team. As if the team needed any more motivation.

If the generals thought they were hated before the announcement, they had it confirmed afterward. "The animosity that descended on us was heavy and it lingered for at least three years," Blaik said.

The only place that Leahy remained popular was the only place that mattered. In January 1947, two weeks after the Army cancellation, and one week after Floss gave birth to James, the Leahys' fifth child, Father

Cavanaugh gave a lengthy defense of the success of Notre Dame football and its coach at the annual football banquet.

"We at Notre Dame make no apologies about wanting winners," he said. "We want our students to go out and win in debates, on the basketball floor, in track, in baseball, and in the much more important battles of life. We shall always want Notre Dame men to play to win so long as there is a Notre Dame. But with even more emphasis, we want Notre Dame men to play to win cleanly and according to the rules, and because Notre Dame men are reared here on this campus in this spirit and because they exemplify this spirit all over the world, they are the envy of the nation."

Father Cavanaugh spoke sixteen paragraphs before he got to defending Leahy. "Frank Leahy deserves unqualified credit for his coaching record, which is just about the most impressive ever made by any coach in the country. Confidentially, and speaking softly among ourselves, much of the distress about Frank Leahy is due to the fact that he is admittedly the most able coach in America.

"At a football banquet given by the St. Joseph Valley Alumni in 1943, I heard a nationally known coach say that, for Frank Leahy's ability to condition his team, for his imagination in devising an effective running and passing game, for his uncommon power to teach fundamentals, for his extraordinary success in holding a team up to a high standard of perfection week after week, Leahy deserves to be ranked along with the peerless Rockne.* It is apparently envy that inclines critics to say that Frank Leahy's success depends upon his choice of material... Reactions such as that envy emanated from the 'dismal tradition' of viewing successful people with suspicion because they are successful. The condition of the loser is not improved in the estimation of the public by criticizing the winner."

Cavanaugh pointed out that in two of his six seasons as head coach, his first at Boston College and his first at Notre Dame, Leahy coached

---

* The coach in question appears to be Clark Shaughnessy. See the quote in Chapter One.

rosters made up largely of players he did not recruit. On and on the priest in charge of athletics at Notre Dame went, defending his friend and the man who had become the face of the university. Leahy, thirty-eight years old, remained a young coach and yet had reached the top of his craft. He had won a national championship in the last two seasons he coached. He had entered the prime of his career. His teams would not lose a game in the next three seasons. That he would win national championships in only two of them is a result best laid at the feet of the poll voters.

If the reign of Frank Leahy's Notre Dame Fighting Irish peaked with his 1949 team—his last national champions, his last unblemished record—the seeds of the fall from greatness were planted in 1947. A lot of fans believed the Irish to be too successful. Only one person who thought so was in a position to do something about it. The culprit was the priest who befriended him, the university president who defended him so vigorously.

CHAPTER TWELVE

A LOOK IN THE MIRROR

THE WAR HAD ENDED, NOTRE DAME STOOD ASTRIDE COLLEGE FOOTball, and therefore to the Irish fan the world had jumped back upon its axis. To the rest of the country, Notre Dame may have been a small Catholic school in an anti-Catholic world with an endowment that passed for the change Harvard found under its sofa cushions, but socially and culturally, Notre Dame football became a metaphor for excellence. They didn't write a Broadway musical comedy about Harvard, did they? *Toplitzky of Notre Dame* opened at the New Century Theater on December 26, 1946, and ran for sixty performances. *Toplitzky* made a run at the plot that *Damn Yankees* perfected nearly a decade later. The play involved an angel descending from on high to help Notre Dame defeat Army. Leahy had a presence in the play, if not a role. A character named McCormack, an Irish immigrant, arrives in America and promptly calls Leahy to wish him "a fine year of Catholic action." *Time* reported that in the McCormack character's brogue, the second word came out as "foine."

On Monday, April 14, the university held its twenty-fourth annual Universal Notre Dame Night, on which more than a hundred alumni clubs across the country and overseas gathered to hear from the university. The main program, broadcast nationally by Mutual Radio, took place in Denver with three speakers: Father Cavanaugh, the president of the university; Thomas E. Braniff, president of Braniff International Airways; and Leahy. Before an audience of five hundred, Leahy spoke for four patriotic, platitudinous minutes. He promoted the academic standards of the university, gave tribute to the priests and professors who taught them, and tied the benefits of competition to the success of America on Wall Street and in the war:

> American business is advanced by the executive ability of leaders whose competitive courage, whose adherence to the rules of American fair play, were fostered on the fields of sport. The ability to produce, the will to win, the intense determination to lead at the final gun no matter what the obstacles, are familiar to sports readers and fans in this country. Translated into the grim business of the recent war, they spelled ultimate victory.

Leahy's speech, a serving of red meat delivered across the country, may have been written for him, but it came straight from his heart. He genuinely believed in American ideals, in the might and decency of American business, and he gladly espoused those beliefs. For all the Notre Dame detractors who believed the last thing the Irish utilized was fair play, America pushed its chips in on Leahy. *The American Legion Magazine*, which had a circulation of 1.25 million for its ex-servicemen members, published a glowing profile of Leahy. Back home in Winner, they renamed the high school stadium Leahy Field, a ceremony for which Leahy returned in June, joined by his mother and his brothers Gene and Tom. Leahy expressed his gratitude as he said he didn't deserve it. He also emphasized that "I want to stay at Notre Dame as long as they'll have me."

Once again, he had the opportunity to leave. At the end of 1946, just as in the year before, a team in the All-American Football Conference made a run at him. Then it had been Cleveland, this time the Chicago Rockets. If Leahy succumbed to the temptation of the pros, Chicago would be the most convenient destination. But Leahy had no interest. Instead, he threw himself into promoting Notre Dame football and the university itself.

Only now, when it came to the product on the field, Notre Dame pulled back. Leahy's wealth of talent on the roster, a product of the crush of talent that came back from the war to resume their college careers, was draining university resources. Even with the largesse of the new GI Bill, which paid for the tuition, living expenses, and books of the servicemen, Notre Dame felt squeezed. Cavanaugh decided to cut the number of scholarships that Leahy could offer to incoming freshmen from thirty-two to eighteen. Leahy, late in his life, said Cavanaugh had acted because he had been spooked by teams leaving the Irish's schedule: "Father Cavanaugh told me that we were winning ourselves out of a schedule, that Army, Michigan, Illinois, and Northwestern had already dropped us and that Navy and USC were about to. He pushed the panic button."

Leahy warned Cavanaugh what the on-field consequences would be. But over the next three seasons, with that core group of war veterans who would be there through 1949, Leahy's warning sounded like one more dollop of undue pessimism from a coach known for it.

In August Leahy returned to Chicago as the head coach of the College All-Stars for his friend Arch Ward. The All-Stars took on the Chicago Bears in the Windy City's Soldier Field, on a day when the thermometer took its time dipping below ninety degrees. The high that day was ninety-four. The temperature on the field at eight thirty that night was eighty, which failed to discourage a record crowd of 105,840.

Glenn Davis of Army, who won the 1946 Heisman Trophy, could not play because of a knee injury. But Leahy still had Davis's backfield mate Doc Blanchard, Charley Trippi of Georgia, Buddy Young of Illinois, and George Ratterman, who backed up Lujack at quarterback the previous year. In case anyone doubted Ratterman's ability, Leahy started him—one of seven Notre Dame players on the roster—and he threw a 46-yard touchdown pass to Irish teammate John Zilly in the first quarter. That was the second touchdown the All-Stars scored.

Bears coach George Halas, ever the wily one, had brought his team into town from its Indiana training camp and dispatched a friend to find a portable air conditioner for the Bears' locker room. When the Bears came out of their chilled locker room into the swelter of the field, they wilted like greenhouse orchids. The young players, who had practiced hard under Leahy, handled it much better. The All-Stars, having jumped out to a 13–0 lead, never slowed, winning 16–0. They outgained the Bears 340–116, and rushed for 189 yards compared to the Bears' 35.

Young finished with eight carries for 73 yards, worth mentioning because he became the first Black player to start for Leahy since Lou Montgomery at Boston College. Leahy saw to it that the player who got the most playing time was his favorite, Bob McBride. The guard lost fifteen pounds over the course of the game.

Leahy, per usual, took the success of the All-Stars as a bad omen for the 1947 Irish. After all, if Notre Dame lost seven players good enough to beat the Chicago Bears, well, you may as well call off the season. "We have not got the reserve strength this year that we had last year," he told Dick Hyland, who returned after the war to the *Los Angeles Times*. By the time Leahy talked to Hyland around the beginning of the season, Leahy had inflated in his own mind what his players had done in the All-Star Game. "I never did realize that until the All-Star game against the Chicago Bears. Seven—one, two, three, four, five, six, SEVEN—of our boys started that game. You can't lose that many players of that caliber."

Actually, only three of the Notre Dame players started the game, not to mention that McBride, the iron man of the All-Star Game, had been a third-team guard in 1946. All of which was preamble to Leahy's main point to Hyland: "I'll be very happy if we can squeeze past Purdue with a one-point win. Then, if we can beat Nebraska by one point next week, I'll be delighted. After that, we'll see. We may have a good ball club by that time."

And this, in September: "Army will come out here undefeated on November 8. As for us, who knows? No telling how many games we'll have lost."

Notre Dame might have lost players good enough to lead a victory over the Chicago Bears but Leahy had so much talent returning. There was Lujack, a twenty-two-year-old senior with a season and a half of starting experience. There was twenty-three-year-old sophomore halfback Emil "Red" Sitko. And there was nineteen-year-old junior Terry Brennan at halfback as well. And that was just the backfield. The line included Czarobski, Bill Fischer, and captain George Connor, and at end Jim Martin and Leon Hart. All eight men are in the College Football Hall of Fame.

Shortly before the season began, Leahy gathered the team on Cartier Field. He had a prop, a large mirror.

"I see by the newspapers we're already accorded the national title," Leahy began. "We don't even need to play our games. Everybody says we'll wallop Army, Navy, Purdue, Tulane, Iowa, and USC by seven or eight touchdowns, whatever margin we like."

Having made the point that the players should not take a national title for granted, Leahy made clear that he expected nothing less.

"We're going to have to work for these victories," the coach continued. "We won't win 'em on paste-ups or cover shots of Lujack. But you can do it with hard work and team play. Now if you fellows don't win that title"—here Leahy held the mirror high—"you'll be ashamed to look yourselves in the face in the mirror after the season is over."

Leahy's counsel against complacency manifested itself in more than one preseason speech. He made them scrimmage again and again, spinning the players' physical odometers at such a rate that two weeks into the season, they appeared spent. The toll that Leahy took could be seen during the games. The Irish won the opener at Pitt largely by attrition, scoring four touchdowns in the second half for a 40–6 victory. A trip to Purdue came next. The Boilermakers had a new coach, Purdue hiring Stu Holcomb off of Blaik's staff at Army. Leahy's woe-is-us pealing never grated on Holcomb the way it did on others. His attitude with Leahy amounted to you-can't-bullshit-a-bullshitter.

"Stuart," Leahy said to him before the game, "at the termination of this contest you are going to be very proud of your athletes."

"You mean we're going to hold you to 60 points, Frank?" Holcomb replied.

"Stuart, next year Purdue will win the Western Conference championship."

This year, the Boilermakers lost to the Irish, 22–7. The AP voters dropped Notre Dame to No. 2 behind Michigan. The Irish didn't look crisp, and they hadn't played crisply. Leahy redirected any criticism of his team by again beating the drum to settle the debate on the field. "I just wish we had the opportunity to beat Michigan," he said. "We'd be happy to play them any time, on any Saturday, during any fall."

But anyone who followed the team could see something had gone amiss. Warren Brown, a longtime Chicago sportswriter, paid close attention to the Irish. One son, Roger, backed up Lujack at quarterback; another, Pete, covered the team for the *Scholastic*, the student magazine. Warren Brown approached Connor, the team captain, and asked him why the team appeared to be misfiring. Connor's answer has been reported in two interpretations. According to Connor's brother Jack, in his 1994 book *Leahy's Lads*, Connor replied to Brown that the coaches had fallen in love with scrimmaging at the expense of drills that focused on fundamentals. The team had begun to get sloppy. Put that way, Leahy needed only to choose from this bag of coaching tricks instead of that one.

The way that Terry Brennan explained it, Connor, in his role as team captain, went to Leahy and told him if he didn't back off of scrimmaging, the players would mutiny. Leahy had a team of veterans who knew what to do. The constant scrimmages had become a matter of maintaining survival, not sharpness. After Connor left, according to Brennan, Leahy remained unconvinced. When Brown came to him and told him the same thing, only then did Leahy cut back. Brown may have been a parent of a player but Leahy saw him as a knowledgeable, independent voice. Leahy eased up on the amount of scrimmaging, and, Brennan said, that decision saved the season.

He may have been right. The Irish shut out their next three opponents—Nebraska, Iowa, and Navy, climbing over Michigan back to No. 1, all the time knowing full well that the week after Navy would be the last scheduled game against Army. Two weeks before the showdown, the Army players figured out a method to really upset their nemeses in South Bend—the Black Knights lost their first game in four years, and lost it to someone else. Columbia upset Army, 21–20, ending Army's thirty-two-game unbeaten streak. That disappointed the Irish players, who wanted to end Army's winning streak themselves, but didn't lessen their ardor. They knew full well that Notre Dame had not beaten Army since 1943 and they felt, especially after the scoreless tie the season before, that they had some unfinished business.

In reality, the 1947 game couldn't have carried the charge of the previous season's game, one that teemed with the energy of a country scrabbling to get back to a "normal" life after so much war and sacrifice. The 1947 game, being the last in an annual rivalry that dated to 1913, had an elegiac air about it. The era actually ended a few months earlier with the graduation of Army backs Doc Blanchard and Glenn Davis, quarterback Arnold Tucker, and tackle Hank Foldberg, each of them All-Americans. Still, Army arrived at Notre Dame with a record of 4-1-1 (the tie against No. 6 Illinois) and a No. 9 ranking, enough to keep the top writers and broadcasters of the day riveted. They descended upon the South Bend campus early in the week and established camp, forcing Leahy to hold more daily briefings in the Rockne Memorial Lounge on campus. In the Monday presser, when asked for a prediction, Leahy asked the writers for theirs. The consensus came in at Notre Dame by a couple of touchdowns. "If we can luck out by one point," Leahy said, "you'll see one smiling Irishman on Saturday night." Leahy often referred to himself ethnically in an era when ethnic bloodlines were not only a matter of pride but also a badge of identification.

The total for Saturday included 103 newspapers, six press associations, four national magazines, and, as Notre Dame publicist Charlie Callahan described, "all five major newsreel companies." On the electronic side, twelve radio broadcasts—three of them national—and two telecasts covered the game. The rivalry had been played in New York City for nearly a quarter-century (one game in Chicago), so General Taylor loosened the rules for the team's departure for South Bend. He allowed the cadets on post, as the West Point campus is called, to leave their barracks in their bathrobes and go to the train station to send their football team off. An eleven-gun salute—one for each starter—boomed as the team began its trip west.

Given the uneasy nature of the end of the rivalry, Notre Dame wanted to be the consummate hosts. When the Army team arrived at Notre Dame Stadium for its Friday walkthrough, Leahy and Father Cavanaugh stood outside to greet them. Leahy and Blaik still had a prickly relationship, if they had any relationship at all, but Leahy stuck to his good manners. He said to the opposing coach what he had said to Holcomb right before the Purdue game.

"Earl, I think you and your lads are going to be very happy after tomorrow's contest."

Blaik would have none of it.

"Let me tell you something, Frank," Blaik said. "The Cadets will give you a battle!" With that, he turned and strode into the stadium.

Notre Dame installed a total of 1,200 bleacher seats behind the two end zones and welcomed a record crowd of 59,171 despite a thermometer that struggled to rise past freezing. The delay of the train carrying

General Taylor and thirty first-classmen (seniors) caused them to arrive at the stadium fifteen minutes before kickoff. Just as they settled into their seats, Notre Dame established control. The Army kicker sent the opening kickoff out of bounds. Brennan grabbed the re-kick at the 3-yard line, took off running and never stopped. It turns out that Leahy had a wrinkle ready.

"For some reason or other, coaches designed most plays to go to the right and that included kick runbacks," Leahy said. "On that return, we designed it to go to the left. He was never touched. I've never seen so many bodies on the ground." Leahy may have been an accidental genius. Connor remembered that as he ran upfield to block, he tripped and fell, the man he intended to block tripped over him, and the two of them sprawled on the ground tripped another Army player. "Brennan ran right through the hole for the touchdown," Connor said.

Leahy toyed with the idea of putting Lujack and Tripucka in the same backfield, moving Lujack to halfback so that he could emphasize his running ability. But unlike the previous season, when Leahy over-coached his way to not winning the game—remember he played his second team very little?—this time he stuck with what the team had done to reach 5-0.

The Irish followed up Brennan's touchdown by scoring another on their first offensive possession. With 8:50 to play in the opening quarter, Notre Dame led, 13–0, and the only remaining suspense hovered over whether an Army team by Blaik would ever score against a Notre Dame team coached by Leahy. The answer turned out to be yes, late in the third quarter of Blaik's fifth game against Leahy, narrowing Notre Dame's lead to 20–7. The Irish immediately added a final score, and won going away, 27–7. Blaik and Leahy endured a perfunctory post-game handshake then walked, 10 yards apart, toward the same stadium portal to their locker rooms.

Across the nation, Notre Dame alumni, real and subway, celebrated the slaying of the Army dragon. That's not what happened at the Leahy home in Michigan City. Leahy had what Floss called his typical postgame meal—tomato soup and crackers. He was in bed by nine p.m. "You know," she said, "nobody gets less fun out of a Notre Dame victory than he does."

For the rest of his time at Notre Dame, Leahy publicly professed his wish to play Army again, just as he never stopped priming the pump for Notre Dame to play Michigan again. Army may have taken the brunt of the public displeasure over the end of the rivalry, but Leahy felt it, too. Deep in the season, with nerves and lack of sleep and poor eating habits eating away at him, Leahy usually edged toward exhaustion. That's the Leahy that Joe Williams of the *New York World-Telegram* and Harry G. Salsinger of *The Detroit News* wrote about after the Army game. Williams had established a voice in New York. He had been a columnist for twenty years. He had gotten to know Leahy when he coached at Fordham and he liked him. They had a rapport.

"I always found him an all-right gent," Williams said. "I'll concede it may take a little time to know him but in the end it's worth it...I recall discussing Leahy with a colleague who had just interviewed him at length. It was the first time they'd met. His comment was rather typical: 'You can have him. He's too nice for me.' But being gracious is not always a pose. Some people actually come by it naturally. I like to believe Leahy is one."

Three days after the Army victory and what amounted to the divorce decree of two great rivals, Williams wrote a copyrighted column that made national news.

"This is a delayed action news bomb but don't handle it too carelessly. It has its full quota of explosives," Williams said. "Frank Leahy is quitting Notre Dame for professional football. He may not step down until the end of the '49 season but The Master is definitely, positively on his way."

Williams cited a source "as close to the famous coach as the hair on his head." In other words, Leahy.

Williams wrote that the "brush-off" by Army had a role in Leahy's disenchantment; Salsinger cited the toll of several schools bailing on

Notre Dame. Williams said Leahy went to his superiors and told them that if they believed his presence caused Army to want to end the series, he would resign immediately. He said that the decisions by a number of schools (Army, Michigan, Ohio State, Illinois, Minnesota, and Stanford in recent years) to not play Notre Dame had caused Notre Dame to lose stability and "no little prestige." But Williams also made a point both obvious and necessary for any objective discussion of Leahy.

"Some people find it difficult to understand Leahy," Williams wrote. "Others don't at all. But if personal antipathy to Leahy enters into this situation it is not directed at his personality so much as at the fact that he's just too tough to handle. They can't beat him... You never would hear anything about Leahy's personality if his teams dropped three to four games a year."

At a moment of what appeared to be personal and team triumph, Leahy needed to vent and did so. But the reporting upended Notre Dame for days. The AP story sent out over the national wires led with a question: "Is Notre Dame becoming a football Frankenstein, too powerful for its own good?" Leahy's office took seventy-three calls, presumably from journalists, looking for a response. Arch Ward, the *Chicago Tribune* sports editor who never wanted to appear as anything less than the authoritative voice on Notre Dame, wrote that the story was a year old and occurred when Army first broached the subject of ending the rivalry.

That said, Ward considered the story important enough to call Father Cavanaugh for a comment. The president denied that Leahy had tried to resign and said, "Surely the reward for outstanding service should not be dismissal from one's job," Cavanaugh said.

The university released an official statement from Leahy on Wednesday in which he said he would consider it "a great honor and privilege" to continue as head coach and athletic director for as long as the priests considered him an asset. And, with an undertone of I-really-don't-have-time-for-this, he added that "Right now we are concentrating just as diligently as possible for our forthcoming opponent, Northwestern

University." He also told Jim Costin of *The South Bend Tribune*, "I'm not going to quit, nor have I considered quitting."

Journalists generally aren't fond of being hung out to dry. Williams and Salsinger both stood by their stories, and eighteen months later, in the relaxed time of April, when the optimism of spring practice is blooming as brightly as the flowers, Williams interviewed Leahy again. This time, Williams wrote that Leahy had been the source.

"That's true," he quoted Leahy. "I did tell you that and I sincerely meant to. I felt that, in some way, which I couldn't understand, maybe I was responsible for Army dropping us from its schedule. And if that was so I wasn't doing the university any good. Therefore I was determined to go elsewhere. Later I was persuaded to change my mind."

The writer Francis Wallace recalled Leahy describing the teams that pulled themselves off of Notre Dame's schedule. Leahy, in a calm tone, assured Wallace that their alma mater had no reason to worry. The coach's phone rang. He answered it, had a quick conversation, and hung up. "She was reminding me of a dental appointment," Leahy said. "I ground the cap off a tooth in my sleep last night." Wallace said Leahy gave no indication of understanding the possibility that the stress he felt over the schedule controversy might be powerful enough to grind his cap to pieces.

Leahy, of course, could look at new asphalt and see potholes. In the case of the Northwestern game, coming the week after the emotional win over Army, he had reason for concern. On a rainy Saturday in Evanston, the Irish had trouble putting the Wildcats away, winning 26–19. The poll voters responded by again dropping Notre Dame to No. 2 behind Michigan, which had gone to No. 9 Wisconsin and overrun the Badgers, 40–6. Given the state of diplomatic relations between Michigan and Notre Dame, or more accurately, between Leahy and Crisler, the battle for the love of the poll voters took on added tension. The Irish responded by humiliating Tulane for the fourth consecutive season, this time by the score of 59–6, a game that Leahy feared so little he traveled to Los Angeles to scout the Irish's next and final opponent, USC, as it defeated UCLA. The Los Angeles writers got in a quick question to Leahy at halftime of the game, which the Trojans won, 6–0, wanting to know if there were any substance to the rumor that he would become the head coach of the Los Angeles Dons in the AAFC. At this moment in his career, someone attached Leahy's name to just about every prominent vacancy save the Boston Red Sox, who had just hired former Yankee skipper Joe McCarthy as manager.

Even though Michigan concluded its regular season by defeating Ohio State 21–0, the voters returned Notre Dame to No. 1 by a narrow margin. The Irish held a narrow edge in first-place votes, 58.5 to 54.5. The national championship would be decided two weeks later, when No. 1 Notre Dame played at No. 3 USC (7-0-1). The Trojans had more than Michigan's interest at heart. They would be playing the Wolverines in the Rose Bowl on Jan. 1, which meant that USC had a straight path to the national championship as well.

The Irish would have to play the Trojans without Brennan, the halfback who made up in speed and smarts what he lacked in size and power. Against Tulane, Brennan tore ligaments in his left knee which, per the medical wisdom of the day, was put in a cast. Leahy said the team would miss Brennan "tremendously" on both sides of the ball. What he didn't say is that he intended for the team to miss Brennan completely. Leahy had no intention of taking Brennan to Los Angeles. Brennan was a halfback, he couldn't play on Saturday, so why would he make the travel roster?

Connor, tipped off by a student manager, made sure Leahy understood why. The team captain didn't like this piece of news one bit. Connor and the other war veterans liked Brennan. They treated him a bit like a younger brother (Terry's older brother Jim played on the team as well). Connor saw how hard Brennan worked. Connor believed that Brennan had earned the trip to Los Angeles. Perhaps buoyed by the results of speaking up against the scrimmage workload early in the season, Connor went to see Leahy and asked about the travel roster. When Leahy confirmed that Brennan wouldn't travel because he couldn't play, Connor said, "I know he's injured, and so does the rest of the team. I want to tell you that if Terry doesn't make the trip, none of us makes the trip."

Connor could pack a punch whether in pads or not. He stunned Leahy. He also got a change in the travel roster. Brennan went to Los Angeles.

As one might expect given the stakes, not to mention the crowd of nearly 105,000 in the Los Angeles Memorial Coliseum, the Trojans played the Irish evenly for a while. Notre Dame led 10–7 at the half. Leahy knew how good a team he had, and as he had been reminded that week, the war veterans he coached held an atypical level of maturity. To motivate them, Leahy didn't need sarcasm or an emotional plea about the Lady on the Dome. He spoke to them directly.

"Gentlemen, you have an opportunity no other Notre Dame football players have enjoyed in seventeen years," Leahy said. "For the rest of your lives you can derive great personal satisfaction from having been a member of an unbeaten and untied team. Think of all the hours of toil that have been put in on the practice field. You've worked hard for an unbeaten season. Southern California had you on the run near the end of the period. You have thirty minutes, gentlemen, in which to achieve the goal we all want. You seniors have thirty more minutes of football at Notre Dame. That's all gentlemen."

Well, there was one other thing. Leahy didn't normally call plays but he "suggested" that the offense open the second half with a run over right tackle. From the Irish 24-yard line, Sitko took a handoff, ran behind Czarobski at right tackle and Hart at right end, and broke into the open field. As he moved to the right, the left side of the line—Martin, Connor, and Fischer, ran ahead of him to escort. Connor, a tackle, took out the last defensive back at the USC 25, 50 yards downfield. The 76-yard touchdown broke open the game and the Irish steadily added to the lead with power football throughout the second half. In fact, the Notre Dame offense scored two more touchdowns without throwing a single pass. In the final fifteen seconds, fourth-string tackle Al Zmijewski, who got on the field about as often as you would expect, intercepted a Trojan lateral and ran 30 yards for a touchdown to make the final score Notre Dame 38, USC 7.

Zmijewski's score pushed a joyous locker room into overjoy. The Irish finished 9-0-0. When Leahy walked in, the players—*his* players—ambushed him. They put him on their shoulders, crumpled his fedora over his ears and carried him in front of a mirror. They had not forgotten his preseason motivational ploy.

"All right, Coach!" one of them yelled. "Here's the mirror. Take a look at yourself!" The players chanted, "Take a look! Take a look!"

Leahy, whether politicking, truth-telling or both, said, "I have never seen a better intercollegiate team than my boys who beat Southern Cal." He pretty much said that at the end of every championship season but in this case, others agreed with Leahy. Fifty years later, Fischer, asked to pick the better of the consecutive national champions, chose the '47 team. "We were better. We'd played two years together," he said.

Nick Saban, the recently retired coach who won six of his seven national championships in a twelve-season period at Alabama, became known for the focus and self-discipline that he imparted to his team. Saban would hold recruiting meetings on the morning after winning the national championship. He left the celebrations to others.

Leahy didn't even wait for the sun to rise. The night of the USC victory, he invited his five assistant coaches to his hotel room. When they arrived, he pulled out a bottle of whiskey and poured each a celebratory drink. After they downed the drinks and prepared to leave for a party, Leahy pulled out a pen and notepad and said, "Now, let's start planning for next year." The assistants managed to escape.

When the AP released its final poll on the Monday after the game, Notre Dame received 107 of the 132 first-place votes. Two days later, the nation's football coaches sided with Crisler, voting him first in the *New York World-Telegram* annual poll. The Michigan coach received 68 of the 271 votes. Leahy finished fourth, receiving 21 votes. That means that eleven of twelve of Leahy's colleagues believed that the man who coached Notre Dame to its first unblemished record in seventeen years, winning its games by an average margin of four touchdowns, did not qualify as the best in the country.

Michigan, feeling snubbed, tried to get the final word with a 49–0 victory over USC in the Rose Bowl. Resounding, surely, but not loud enough to change anything. The AP, in the finest tradition of journalists making a hot story hotter, conducted an unofficial poll of the sports editors of its member newspapers, which Michigan won. USC coach Jeff Cravath, having been beaten decisively by both teams, chose Notre Dame. An enterprising United Press correspondent in Los Angeles polled twenty-two Trojan players, who voted 17–5 in favor of the Irish. Several proposals for a charity postseason game between the two teams died quietly.

Crisler gave a statesmanlike, everyone's-a-winner response. "The men who voted couldn't have made a mistake if they had picked either team," he said. He called Leahy a "superb coach."

Leahy sent a telegram that skillfully slid a verbal needle right into Crisler's solar plexus.

"Congratulations to you and your squad on your amazing football achievements of 1947," Leahy wrote. "I regret that I did not have the opportunity of seeing your great team in action. Regards…"

Notre Dame head coach Knute Rockne loved Leahy more for his football mind than for his playing ability. Leahy missed most of his junior and senior seasons with injuries. *Courtesy of the Notre Dame Archives*

Appointed head coach at Boston College at age 30, Leahy was the picture of youth and vigor. He went 20-2 in two seasons. *Courtesy of Boston College Athletics*

The Eagles stunned Tennessee with a second-half comeback to win the 1941 Sugar Bowl, 19–13. *Courtesy of Boston College Athletics*

Leahy and his well-bundled up staff at his first Notre Dame practice in March 1941. From left, Bill Cerney, Ed McKeever, Leahy, Joe McArdle, Johnny Druze. After a public chiding from Leahy, his assistants never wore coats on the field again. *Courtesy of the Notre Dame Archives*

Leahy began his career as a hands-on assistant and continued to coach by example at Notre Dame. *Courtesy of the Notre Dame Archives*

Leahy (*left*) enlisted in the US Navy in the spring of 1944, well after many other prominent coaches. He attained the rank of lieutenant commander and served in the Pacific theater. *Courtesy of the Notre Dame Archives*

Fleet Admiral Chester W. Nimitz (*second from left*), commander in chief of the US Pacific Fleet and of the Pacific Ocean Areas during World War II, shakes hands with Lt. Commander Leahy. They became friends and competitors at horseshoes. *Courtesy of the Notre Dame Archives*

Time magazine, October 14, 1946. Though the quote echoed Leahy's sense of humor, when his drollery went public he tried to distance himself from it. *From TIME. © 1946 TIME USA LLC. All rights reserved. Used under license.*

A late 1940s photo of the Leahys with the first five of their eight children. From left to right: Susan, Frank Jr., Florence, Frank Sr., Jerry, Floss, Jimmy. *Courtesy of the Notre Dame Archives*

Though one assistant said that Leahy cared little about clothes, he proved to be quite the dandy on game day. To his left and behind him is Fred Miller, Leahy's volunteer assistant and the president of Miller Brewing Company. *Courtesy of the Notre Dame Archives*

Leahy, flanked by Rev. Theodore Hesburgh, the Notre Dame president (*left*), and Leahy's successor, Terry Brennan. The bonhomie depicted here didn't last. Leahy had fraught relationships with both men. *Courtesy of the Notre Dame Archives*

After retirement from Notre Dame, Leahy worked in television for many years. Here, a publicity shot for his first show, a 1954 pilot about Cleveland Browns quarterback Otto Graham picked up by ABC-TV for its show *Cavalcade of America*. Leahy hoped to sell more episodes as a separate series; the networks did not bite. *© Bettmann via Getty Images*

The January 1969 dinner to honor Leahy at Notre Dame's new Convocation Center. Among the dignitaries to Leahy's right are Father Hesburgh, US Rep. John Brademas, then–ND head coach Ara Parseghian, and 1947 Heisman Trophy winner Johnny Lujack. *Courtesy of the Notre Dame Archives*

After the College Football Hall of Fame finally elected Leahy to membership in January 1970, he is honored at a game that fall by university vice president Father Edmund Joyce, holding the framed Hall of Fame scroll. At right is athletic director Moose Krause. *Courtesy of the Notre Dame Archives*

In 1997, thanks to the fundraising efforts of the former Notre Dame players who called themselves Leahy's Lads, the University of Notre Dame unveiled this statue of Leahy outside Notre Dame Stadium. *Courtesy of the author*

CHAPTER THIRTEEN

THE COACH

As a daily communicant, Frank Leahy regarded the basilica and the grotto on the Notre Dame campus as sacred spaces. As a coach, as a leader and developer of athletically gifted young men, he considered the football field to be the same, with a bit of classroom and laboratory mixed in for good measure. As a man who took little pleasure from food and less from alcohol, who idealized the priests on campus, Leahy held a high standard for his players and accepted no excuses when they failed to meet it. Given his history of health issues it may be redundant to say that he held himself to live the same high-standard, no-excuse way of life. The price of success may have been hard work and dedication. For Leahy it would also be health and family life. He paid in full.

Charlie Callahan once published the coach's daily schedule. The sports publicist described Leahy working a fourteen-hour day that began with an eight a.m. staff meeting and ended at ten p.m. In reality, during the season, he rarely went home. The priests who served as firemen at the firehouse on campus saved room seven, a small upstairs nook with a cot, for Leahy. He would work in his office, often to midnight, just him and a journalism student who knew how to run a film projector. "Run that over again, will you, John?" Leahy would say, again and again. And then, after a nineteen-hour day, he would walk down the street to the firehouse, fall into the cot, rise at five a.m. and go at it again.

There's another word for this—insomnia. Krause said that Leahy would compel the coaches to return to the office after dinner to watch the film with him. One night Krause wanted to go home so badly that he handed out cigars to the other assistants, which they all lit, breaking Leahy's rule about smoking in meetings. Leahy sent them home. Assistant coach Bernie Crimmins remembered when Leahy didn't go home he would ask to borrow clothes. "Sometimes he slept in them," Crimmins said. "Then he'd wear them around the campus the next day."

"He simply had a fear of losing, and it manifested itself in hard work," Creighton Miller said. "It drove him. He just wasn't going to lose." Through Leahy's first six seasons as a head coach, he had lost five times: twice at Boston College without a key (Black) player; twice at Notre Dame when he switched the Irish to the T, and once at Notre Dame on a Hail Mary.

As a freshman end in 1946, Leon Hart played well enough to get a lot of playing time on a team loaded with war veterans. As a senior, he won the 1949 Heisman Trophy. "Get down on the ground and dig for it. Get dirty," Hart said. "As hard as he made you work, you knew he was working twice as hard. And he expected the same thing from his coaches." Hart called Leahy, the man who made him run a lap around the field for every minute he arrived late for practice, "the greatest man I ever met." The vast majority of players from Hart's generation venerated Leahy, although most of that veneration came as men when they looked back and understood more clearly what the coach's work ethic had done for them.

"While you were there," Bertelli said, "you sometimes had the feeling that this guy was the toughest taskmaster in the world."

Many of them reported to practice as war veterans, therefore, perhaps, with a higher threshold of withstanding discomfort, physical exertion, mental pressure. They certainly knew how to work.

"Frank Leahy, more than any human being I have ever been connected with, worked tremendously hard to prepare himself for anything he did," McBride said. "His biggest goal in life was to teach other people the value of dedicated hard work. Ultimately, human beings are governed and formed by their habits. We are slaves to habit. If a person learns as much as he can about what he wants to do, and then dedicates all of the hard work he can possibly muster in that direction, nothing in the world can keep him from being successful. I learned that from Frank Leahy. He was the greatest teacher I have ever known in my life."

Leahy inculcated that work ethic into his players through conditioning, through rote learning, through discipline, example, sarcasm, expectation, rule-skirting, and whatever other method he thought might work. Of course, the incentive to endure any or all of that in order to play football for Notre Dame carried a lot of water, too.

"The only way to cause a lad to strive to achieve physical perfection is to sell to him the idea of what that physical perfection will mean to him both on the field and in later life," Leahy said. "The thought of achieving physical perfection—which isn't easy—requires a lot of tough, grinding, grueling hard work—the thought must emanate from the individual himself. You can shout and scream at him, have clubs and bats in your hands as threats, and you can stomp up and down in blind rages but the individual must *want* to do it, must realize that the price must be paid for perfection... It has to come from within, though, and nobody can force him to do it."

Practice began at three thirty, and Leahy let the players know that the coaches would be on the field at three o'clock for anyone who needed additional tutelage. They would stay late, too. In other words, a player had no excuses for a lack of proficiency. In fact, Leahy didn't believe the opportunity to improve ended when practice did. He told his players that when they stood before the mirror shaving, they should ask themselves how they are better today than yesterday. When they went to bed, they should ask how they had made themselves a better man or a better player.

When a player came through the Cartier Field gate, he ran—he did not walk, saunter, trot, or jog—to his position group. Practice began with calisthenics, then moved to fundamentals, and concluded with scrimmaging. During the season, those who played extensively on Saturday got Monday off. Scrimmages dominated Tuesday and Wednesday. Thursday focused on goal-line play, calisthenics, and wind sprints. Conditioning, Leahy told his players, would propel them to be their best in the fourth quarter, when the opponents tired.

Snow, wind, rain, it didn't matter. In spring 1947, when torrential rain transformed Cartier Field into mud, Leahy told his players, "Men, this may be just the kind of field on which you will play Army in the last game of the series next November." For years, he didn't allow his coaches to wear coats because he didn't want his players thinking it may be cold.

When Dick Szymanski, who played on Leahy's last two teams at Notre Dame, reported to Baltimore Colts training camp in 1955, he couldn't believe how the conditioning drills failed to measure up to what he had endured under Leahy. "All the guys were moaning and groaning about how tough it was," he said. "I never saw a practice anywhere that could compare with one run by the Old Man."

Leahy considered himself and his assistants to be teachers, hands-on teachers, although the only position he coached once he got to Notre Dame was quarterback. A local writer once asked him one question about tackling and got a tutorial on keeping the legs spread, the chin back, the body relaxed as it moved forward, churning the grass with your cleat once you made contact. "I learned more about tackling in that three minutes than I had ever known," the writer said in the piece.

Leahy talked a good game of physical football. His line coaches taught their linemen by getting down into a stance and blocking them, just as Leahy had done at Fordham a decade before. The *New York Herald Tribune* used to hold a "Football Coaching School" in Manhattan before each season. Top coaches in the New York area would lecture to several hundred attendees. Leahy became a featured speaker at the 1941 school, held just before his first season at Notre Dame. "There are some coaches who have the gift of teaching by telling their men what to do," Leahy told the assemblage. "But I find that I have to show them how to do it." With that, he took off his coat and tie, rolled up his sleeves, and using his assistant John Druze as a foil, began to demonstrate guard play—the shoulder block, the body block, how to move outside to block an end, how to get downfield to block a linebacker or defensive back, open-field blocking, pass protection. He didn't draw an X or O on the board.

"They really gave you pressure and encouraged you to stay mean and aggressive, and keep the legs moving, and be fundamentally correct, and to really come after them," McBride remembered of the assistant coaches during his playing days. A story in *The South Bend Tribune* from Leahy's first spring described how Druze and McArdle also taught the linemen some skills not in the rulebook under the reasoning that they needed to know how to defend themselves against holding, clipping, etc. This was fuel for the detractors who accused Leahy's Notre Dame teams of dirty play, but the story's explanation is plausible.

If Leahy wandered over to watch the drill, the assistant might stealthily give ground to make the player look good. Bill Fischer said Krause, his coach, did just that in front of Leahy one day, and that when the head coach moved on, Krause suggested they go one more time. At the signal, Krause slammed an elbow into Fischer's throat, walked him off to the side and told him, "Don't you ever forget who's boss here." The coach blocked to demonstrate skill. Sometimes, he blocked to demonstrate authority. And sometimes, he blocked to administer discipline. Off to the side of Cartier Field sat a mound of dirt that the players called Bunker Hill. If McBride deemed one of his linemen a slacker, McBride would take him over to Bunker Hill and tell him, "OK, block me." McBride would proceed to pummel him one-on-one, snap after snap, sometimes until the player could not stand up.

Leahy drilled into his players his Five Cardinal Sins of Football: laziness, missed assignments, penalties, fumbles, and a lack of team play. Committing such sins, he said, "would not be tolerated!" exclamation point included. He gave them his expectations—academics first. The grade point average of 77 that he had to maintain as an undergrad still applied. "The university owes you something for all that you've done," Leahy would say. "The best thing it can do to repay that debt is to make sure that you young lads who come to Notre Dame to participate in football get the best education you possibly can. You'll be glad you've sacrificed and worked hard in the classroom when your four years are over."

Leahy warned his players not to go downtown looking for fun, encouraged them to make sacrifices for the team, and insisted that they comport themselves as gentlemen on and off the field. That meant that anyone wearing a Notre Dame uniform didn't throw a punch on the field. Throwing a punch, Leahy believed, proved the lack of toughness necessary to compete, not to mention that you would be thrown out of the game. "If you want out of the contest, you let us know," Leahy said. "We'll substitute somebody for you. Don't be belting somebody and giving Notre Dame a black eye for illegal tactics and showing you don't have enough gumption and courage and character to stay out there and be a part of the fight."

Art Donovan played football at Notre Dame in 1942. Actually, he never got farther than spring practice that year. He told an offensive lineman to quit holding him during a scrimmage, and when it happened again, Donovan started a fight, although the fight didn't anger Leahy as much as Donovan's refusal to shake hands with the lineman afterward. "The guy was a jerk, and shaking hands with him wasn't going to make him any less of a jerk," Donovan said. "But Leahy told me right in front of the whole team that he didn't need or like my type around there."*

Being a gentleman also included language.

"You are never allowed to curse or swear," Leahy would tell them. "All of our lads here at Notre Dame have proven that you have the capacity for learning. You have shown this by what you have done up until the time you have been accepted. You have to show that you have the capacity to be a good student. Anyone who is a good student has taken a number of English courses in high school and has to have a decent command of the English language. When you curse or swear, you are announcing that you do not have a command of the English language. This can't be allowed at Notre Dame."

In Leahy's first week as head coach on the Notre Dame campus, a guard performing a tough drill responded to the difficulty by yelling out a curse word. It was the last play the guard, who had won a letter the previous season, ever played at Notre Dame. There is a more famous story regarding the use of foul language. It has been told often enough that it's difficult to pin down the actual players. One version involves Robert Neff. Another version, Lujack used to tell on himself. He said that when Livingstone missed a block in a game, Lujack yelled, "Livingstone, you son-of-a-bitch!"

Leahy raced over to him to castigate him over his "unthinkable" epithet.

"Another profane outburst like that, Jonathan Lujack, and you will be asked to disassociate yourself from our fine Catholic university," Leahy said. "You might well remember that when I recruited you, I promised your parents you would have a fine Catholic upbringing."

Lujack slumped onto the bench and tried to hide in his parka. A few plays later, Livingstone missed another block. Leahy walked toward the

---

* Art Donovan joined the Marines, played for Boston College after the war, and went on to a Hall of Fame pro career.

bench and said, "Gentlemen, I fear that Jonathan Lujack is right about Robert Livingstone."

When Lujack went to play for the Chicago Bears, he couldn't believe the language that came out of owner/coach George Halas's mouth. "I didn't know anything about pro ball, and I thought, 'This is the way they do things?'" Lujack said.

When Leahy signed Lujack out of Connellsville (Pennsylvania) High in 1942, he also took Lujack's fellow All-County teammate, a back named John Schroyer. During the recruiting, Schroyer, who had a big personality, put his arm around the coach and addressed him, "Frank, old boy." Leahy didn't want to take him but got talked into signing both boys. Schroyer didn't last long under Leahy, who said he left without saying goodbye. Schroyer enrolled at Penn State a few days later, where he played enough to earn a letter in the 1942 season. Any further comparison to Lujack abruptly ended on the battlefield at Anzio, where Army Private John Schroyer lost his right leg.

A friend of Frank's brother Gene, Dr. John Broz, once asked Frank, "Your reputation as a coach is as a severe disciplinarian, and you demand extreme effort from your players, with very hard workouts. Do they like you?"

"John, I do not care too much whether or not they like me. But the question I am concerned about is, do they respect me?"

On the practice field, Leahy would follow the play down the field, coaching aloud as he ran. In his memoir, McBride reconstructed how, if a coach stopped practice to ask a question, deliver criticism, point out a nugget of information—in other words, to coach—the player(s) on the receiving end had to maintain eye contact. For a black-and-white coach in a black-and-white world, eye contact meant the coach had the player's attention, interest, and respect.

"Any criticism that comes for you from a coach at Notre Dame is constructive criticism," McBride recalled. "You have to learn to take constructive criticism and react properly to it by hard work and dedication to overcome your faults and to improve yourself. Without proper criticism, a person can't possibly be educated to the extent that he is capable of being educated. At Notre Dame, you're going to be criticized often; don't get down. Be concerned if you aren't criticized."

The coaches told the players to never use an alibi or explain why they made a mistake, to be attentive, to look the coach in the eye and listen, to learn the skill and execute it. Leahy would remind his players that the coaches pointed out mistakes to improve the players, not embarrass them. He encouraged his players to admit their shortcomings and then do something about them. "Egotism is the anesthetic which dulls the pain of stupidity" would become one of his favorite maxims.

"Don't start tomorrow. Start today. Don't put it off," Leahy would say. "Don't talk to opposing players on the field or from the bench. Concentrate on the football game and what you can to do help the situation on the field at any time. Don't use your mouth. Football isn't played with the mouth. It is played with the arms, legs, and the heart and the fundamentals of football, not with a lot of talk."

No coach ever worked a team harder on fundamentals. Quarterbacks executing a fake in practice drills had to keep their eyes on the defender intently enough to report to Leahy how many fingers the defender had extended. He had quarterbacks kneel and throw the ball as if they were throwing a dart, a drill he learned on annual offseason trips to clinics in Texas, the home of the great passers Sammy Baugh and Davey O'Brien. "It keeps the passing arm right out in front all the time," Leahy said.

He had quarterbacks practice their spins and cuts in sneakers on the basketball court; he believed the traction would give them confidence in their fakes. Receivers honed their reflexes by catching footballs that caromed wildly off the basketball backboard. He told centers he wanted them to snap the ball so hard that they drew blood from the quarterback's hands.

Leahy typically didn't criticize the player. Instead, he would address the coach: "Coach Crimmins, look what your man is doing there," or "Coach McArdle, that man isn't blocking properly." The assistant might be quite a bit more direct than Leahy. McArdle, in particular, earned the nickname Captain Bligh, the tyrant in the movie *Mutiny on the Bounty*.

Leahy drilled the players on the plays over and over so that they became instinctive. He might call for the same off-tackle play to be run seven times in a row in order to teach one player one thing, never mind what the repetition did to the other twenty-one players. But that second nature is what Hart remembered most fondly: the timing of the blocks, the artistic beauty of eleven men moving in sync. Boston College quarterback Charley O'Rourke recalled practicing a sprint-out pass play for hours. They used it twice all season. "The thing was, if we ever needed it in an emergency, Leahy had drilled it into us so deep that we could execute it from memory." Lujack said that Leahy didn't like to send in plays from the sideline. He expected the quarterback to have learned enough during practice to know what to do. Leahy considered it a demonstration of loyalty. "You can't let your linemen or your backfield down in football any more than a third baseman can let down a first baseman in baseball."

Of course, if the quarterback made a poor decision, Leahy took it as an insult, an indignity meant for him. Notre Dame, nursing a 14–0 lead over Army in 1947, had a 4th-and-1 at midfield. Quarterback Frank Tripucka decided not to punt. The team emerged from the huddle into formation to go for the first down. Tripucka heard Leahy on the sideline say, "Oh, no, Francis." Tripucka handed the ball off, there was a fumble, and there was no first down. Tripucka came off the field, hoping to join the French Foreign Legion.

Leahy bored right in. "You hate me," he said. And then, "You hate your teammates." And then, as if he hadn't made his point, "You hate the lady on the Dome."

Tripucka didn't play another down the rest of the game.

When Jim Schrader came off the field after missing an extra point that would have given Notre Dame the lead against Pittsburgh in 1952, Leahy grabbed him by the shoulders and said, "Oh, Jim Schrader, you'll burn in hell for this!"

It's not fair to say that the heat of competition caused Leahy to come unglued on the sideline. He arrived unglued and remained that way, constantly steeling himself for the worst. Leonard Tose, a Notre Dame alum who made a fortune in the trucking business, bought the Philadelphia Eagles, then lost them because of gambling debts, became close enough to Leahy that he received Friday night invitations to room seven. "He used to make me believe the worst," Tose said. "I've seen Notre Dame three touchdowns ahead with three minutes to go and him walking up and down in front of the bench saying, 'We're going to lose the game.'"

Leahy didn't yell at his players like a drill sergeant; often he chastised, usually in the form of sarcasm or disappointment, always in precise diction and, sometimes using the player's full name.

- "Ah, Robert. Robert Williams. You'll never be a Notre Dame quarterback until you learn to throw the ball softer."
- At Boston College, a player came off the sideline, told him that Georgetown was playing dirty and asked permission to fight fire with fire. "You can," Leahy said, "but if you do, it will be the last game you play for Boston College."
- Mike Holovak, a fullback on Leahy's BC teams, said they watched the game film on Monday after a game and Leahy ran the same missed block over and over again. Then he turned to the player who missed the block and said, "I am now going to run that film one more time. If you still miss the block, turn in your uniform."
- This story may be on the spectrum of Yogi Berra sayings never uttered by Yogi Berra. Nevertheless, a player came off the field after losing several front teeth in an on-field collision. When Leahy tried to return him to the game, the player balked. "Are you here to play football or eat a sandwich?" Leahy asked.
- When guard Joe Signaigo suffered a broken nose against Northwestern, he didn't report for practice two days later. Leahy sent for him. Signaigo arrived with his nose encased in bandages. Leahy asked why he didn't report for practice. Signaigo pointed out that

he had a broken nose. "I don't consider that a valid excuse," Leahy said. "After all, what else can happen to you?"

- "Hold it, everyone! Now, Joe, who were you blocking on that play? Well, that's a new one. We haven't put that play in our book yet, Joe, so please cooperate and run the simple one we gave you."
- "You there, number 68, how did you expect your ball carrier to get through left tackle when you failed to take out your man? Give them the same play later on, and I'll not settle for anything under 12 yards, or I'll keep you boys here all evening." Five plays later, the same play gains 18 yards. "See how easy it is when you play according to instructions?"

He might ask the player who lost his footing if he tripped over a newspaper clipping, or ask if a player was thinking or sleeping, or suggest to linemen that they move faster so that their teammate with the ball doesn't run over them. He used sarcasm in that halftime speech of the 1941 Sugar Bowl against Tennessee—"The heroes! The worthy representatives of New England!"—when Boston College trailed 7–0.

Sometimes, Leahy simply reminded his players of what they had at stake. As a senior in 1953, Johnny Lattner remembered a halftime talk Leahy gave at what was likely the 1951 USC game, in those days the traditional season-ending opponent. "Well, you have just thirty minutes of college football left," Leahy said. "It can end up dismally or it can be something you'll be proud of the rest of your lives. It's up to you." The Irish came from behind in the second half to win, 19–12.

On other occasions, Leahy appealed to the players' heartstrings. In the locker room before the game, he would tell his team that he would rather have his son—didn't specify which one—lose his right arm than lose the game. The next week, it might be the son's left arm. "By the end of the season, we had that kid totally dismembered," George Connor said.

Sometimes Leahy ran out of ideas. He once described to his coaching pal Wally Butts of Georgia a talented player whom Leahy could not figure out how to motivate. "Oh, Wallace, what would you do if you had a young lad like that?"

Butts, ever the pragmatist, said, "Pray to God that he stayed healthy for every game."

It may be true that Leahy didn't recruit as much as he selected. It was said that every American boy grew up wanting to play football for Notre Dame just as every American girl wanted to go to Hollywood to be a movie star. Top athletes wanted to go for the challenge. Hart said the more that other schools warned him how tough it would be to win a starting job at Notre Dame, the more he wanted to go there. The Catholic boys wanted to go there as a matter of pride. Leahy said one look at the lady on the Golden Dome usually did the trick. Sometimes it took one look at Leahy. Dick Lynch recalled that when he met Leahy during recruiting, "It was like the Pope walked into the room. He said, 'Son, do you want to go to Notre Dame?' I said, 'Yes, sir.' He said, 'I'll see you on August 15,' and he shook my hand."

In the industrial heartland of the Midwest, the sons of central European immigrant coal miners and steelworkers saw Notre Dame as a way to a college education. The plethora of Polish, Russian, and Lithuanian last names on the roster of the "Fighting Irish" led to plenty of jokes, including on *The Jack Benny Show*, the highest-rated radio series of the time, in 1947. When Jack said he had a difficult time getting tickets for the Notre Dame–USC game, Dennis Day said he had no problem.

Jack: How'd you get yours?
Dennis: From my cousin. He plays for Notre Dame.
Jack: Notre Dame? Oh, of course. Certainly. You're Irish. What's your cousin's name?
Dennis: Kazikowski.
Jack: Kazikowski?
Dennis: His real name is McNulty.
Jack: What?
Dennis: He changed it to get on the team.

It was about this time that Leahy would step into the huddle on the practice field and ask Czarobski to tell a Polish joke. Czarobski would tell a joke, in Polish, and a good number of players would dissolve into laughter. For all that he demanded, Leahy understood the value of a lighter moment on the field.

Leahy used to promote the democratization of the locker room, where no one cared about your nationality as long as you helped the team win. Shortly after he arrived at Notre Dame, he pointed out that his 1940 team at Boston College included "the following nationalities on our squad: Russian, Lithuanian Polish, German, French, Irish, Italian, and an American Negro. While the kinsmen of these men were shooting each other in Europe, they were fighting for each other here in the United States." This was a bit of a stretch for Leahy, who readily acquiesced to benching Lou Montgomery at Boston College and took a decade to integrate his Notre Dame roster. Say this for Leahy—when he signed Wayne Edmonds in 1952, Leahy promised Edmonds's mother that on the first Sunday after her son's arrival in South Bend, he would be taken to meet the Baptist minister. Edmonds became the first Black football player to earn a monogram at Notre Dame.

The NCAA didn't allow tryouts during Leahy's tenure but Leahy employed them until he got caught. When a recruit showed up on campus, he would change into sweats and football shoes and go into the field house, where an assistant coach would work him for thirty minutes or so to assess talent and skill. "We would teach them a few things to see how coachable they were," McBride said. "One of the things we would always teach them was the lunge . . . We would have them lunge out and hit us with their shoulder to see how quick they were and how hard they could hit. We could see their physique and what kind of abilities they had."

Occasionally there would be a vanity tryout. Leahy once called McBride into his office and found him sitting there with university trustee Joseph P. Kennedy, the former ambassador to Great Britain and the father of Congressman John F. Kennedy. Kennedy had brought to campus his youngest son, Teddy, a football player at Milton Academy near Boston. Leahy instructed McBride to give Teddy a workout in such a way that McBride understood the politics of the situation. It took no time at all for McBride to assess that Teddy didn't have the skills to play at Notre Dame, but McBride worked him out anyway. Teddy Kennedy had a very good football career at Harvard, which just may have boosted his political career.

Jim Crowley, Leahy's boss at Fordham, considered Leahy excellent at making tactical adjustments during the game. Leahy did not consider himself a good strategist. "I've never had any flair for improvisation, for devising something new," he said. Leahy would pour energy into watching film, a relatively new tactic in the forties. He would organize, delegate, hire good assistants, recruit, and develop talent. If a head coach can accomplish all of those tasks, he doesn't have to be a good strategist.

And yet Leahy found ways to innovate. He became an early adapter of the defensive huddle. In the late 1940s, as Michigan State emerged as a national power, Leahy wanted Hart to defend the strong side of the Spartan formation and Jim Martin on the weak side. Leahy had his defense not break their huddle until they saw where the Spartan tight end lined up. He also created the two-quarterback system in the fourth quarter of the season opener against Purdue in 1948. Plenty of coaches have played two quarterbacks. But at the same time? Both lining up under center? Either Williams or Tripucka took the snap. They both turned their backs to the defense in unison, dropped back 5 yards, and Williams completed a pass. They did it again, and one faked a pass while the other handed the ball off. The experiment succeeded in making the Boilermaker defense hesitate. But the tactic came to a halt shortly after the snap went past both of them in an I-got-it, you-take-it manner.

Leahy also remained smart enough to seize a play that dropped in his lap. Lujack recalled a play in which he was supposed to take the snap, spin, and hand off to the halfback. But Lujack reacted so slowly that he missed the handoff. As the defense quickly converged on him, he pitched the ball to the fullback trailing him as a decoy. The fullback ran the ball wide for 50 yards.

"Let's try that play again!" Leahy said. "It worked!" After the play succeeded in the next game, on the following day Leahy called his defensive coordinator and told him to come up with a plan to stop that play.

Leahy kept thinking, kept scheming to improve his team. His mind went so many places that he would forget to eat. He once left campus to drive home and started thinking about a play. He stopped thinking about the play when he looked up and found himself in Chicago, ninety-five miles away. "I knew that had to be a great play," quarterback John Mazur said. "We waited for the right spot to use it, and that came in a game two weeks later. It lost 5 yards."

His players joked about how Leahy would have a conversation with them and not be present at all. Here again, the names change depending on who repeated the anecdote—sometimes Jim Mello, sometimes Lujack. When Leahy saw a player on campus, he would ask the same two questions: "How's your weight?" and "How's your family?"

On this day, Leahy asked, "How's your weight?"

Mello/Lujack replied, "Two hundred eighty-four pounds, Coach."

"And how's your mother?"

"She's dying."

Leahy nodded and kept walking.

CHAPTER FOURTEEN

THE GRAND OLD MAN

If it was hiring time in pro football, someone would make a run at Leahy.

As 1947 became 1948, a group of businessmen including Harry Wismer, the irrepressible radio impresario, bought the Detroit Lions. Wismer went to see Leahy with an offer of $100,000 a year for ten years, 10 percent of the team, and an automobile dealership in Detroit. Leahy declined, and the Lions moved downstate to hire Indiana head coach Bo McMillin. Years later, Frank Jr., Leahy's oldest child, said he asked his father "a thousand times" why he didn't take the offer "and he's never known why himself."

Leahy always said his goal was to fulfill his ten-year contract with Notre Dame without losing a game. He did lose one in the spring of 1948. The alumni "Old-Timers" team, led by Lujack, beat the Irish, 20–14, at the end of spring practice, the varsity's first loss since Devore coached them in 1945. Leahy rather liked the outcome. He made sure every year to hold a particularly tough scrimmage on the Friday before the Old-Timers Game. Then he removed all but the most vanilla plays from the varsity playbook on Saturday. Sure, he assumed that the upcoming opponents had people watching in the stands. But more to the point, Leahy liked the idea that the team would struggle in its last spring practice. He wanted his players to understand how much work they had to do during the summer. He wanted them to arrive at fall practice with a desire to improve.

A few weeks before the Old-Timers Game, toward the end of a meeting of the Michigan athletic board, Fritz Crisler announced he had one more item: He would coach the Wolverines no longer. "Fritz, we didn't know you were getting that old," one of the board members teased. Crisler, forty-nine, remained as athletic director and no one argued when he suggested that he be replaced as head coach by long-time assistant Bennie Oosterbaan. Within two years, Crisler became chair of the NCAA Football Rules Committee. In July, a wire service sent out a photo of Crisler at a coaching clinic at Adams State in Alamosa, Colorado, looking crisp in a shirt and tie, sitting attentively next to . . . Leahy.

"I don't know why I don't like Frank Leahy. I don't know why I do like Frank Leahy," Crisler told the *Detroit Times*. "He's a total enigma. One morning you see him and he's full of fun, full of life. The next morning you see him, he's morose and gloomy. The next day he's telling you he's going to destroy you. Some say his teams play rough but don't play dirty. I'm never sure what Leahy thinks is the difference between rough and dirty. I just don't know what to make of the man."

It doesn't seem as if Crisler made much of an effort. When Northwestern's contract with Notre Dame neared its end—the last game would be in 1948—the uproar over the Big Nine Conference's* attitude toward its Catholic neighbor started anew. Officials from the league

* Long known as the Western Conference, the league began using Big Nine in earnest after the war. When the conference invited Michigan State to join in December 1948, it became the Big Ten.

and from Notre Dame, speaking on the record, came up with all manner of reasons why there was nothing to see here. Northwestern athletic director Ted Payseur said the school needed flexibility so it would take at least a three-year break. "But I want to make it clear that we're not breaking relations with Notre Dame," Payseur said. "All this fuss is being made simply because it happens to be Notre Dame." Commissioner Kenneth "Tug" Wilson blamed the media for stirring the pot, pointing out to *Time* correspondent Serrell Hillman that as conference schools began using planes to travel, they became more open to playing teams farther away. Charlie Callahan, the Notre Dame spokesman, just flicked the question away. "Everybody is talking as though we were poor, heartbroken little boys," Callahan said. "We're doing all right... There's no more obligation on our part than on theirs to renew. We like a little freedom, too."

Leahy, still smarting from the controversy over his *Time* cover story two years earlier, didn't speak to Hillman, but the conference public relations head, a young man named Walt Byers, speaking on background, acknowledged what seemed obvious. "The situation probably wouldn't have developed the way it has except for Leahy. Nobody minded losing to Rockne the way they do to Leahy. They just don't like the guy. Take [Iowa coach] Eddie Anderson, who always wants to play Notre Dame. He keeps wanting to lick 'em. Well, how do you think Anderson felt last year when he had a lousy team, and the week he was to play Leahy, out comes Leahy [saying] he'll consider himself very lucky if he beats Iowa by one point? [Final score: Notre Dame 21, Iowa 0] You won't find the Big Nine eager to play Notre Dame as long as Leahy's there—and it looks as though he'll be there for a long time."

Byers, voluble to the point of gossipy, would become Walter Byers, the notoriously private executive director who over three decades built the NCAA into a monolithic institution that began to lose its power only when the US Supreme Court stopped its monopolistic hold over the TV rights of its member schools in 1984.

Francis Powers, who covered college football for the *Chicago Daily*

News, also speaking not for attribution, told Hillman that the Big Nine coaches' attitude toward Leahy consisted of "45 percent of fear, 45 percent of jealousy, and 10 percent of plain, old-fashioned dislike."

It would take another year, but at long last a prominent national sportswriter came to Notre Dame's defense in the schedule debacle. Henry McLemore, the Hearst Newspapers columnist and (since he wrote for Hearst, this may be redundant) a red-meat, red-blooded conservative, wrote in a way that read like a love letter to the Irish head coach.

"There was a time in this country when the hard way was the way that was wanted, because it offered a challenge," McLemore wrote. "...I wonder if the coaches who don't want to schedule the Irish ever consider the possibility that Frank Leahy might be a better coach than they are.

"I wonder, too, when it became wrong in this country to be the best...

"Notre Dame just plays the game a little harder, a little smarter, and a little better.

"More power to you, Frank. Lay it on 'em."

Leahy didn't want to return to Chicago to coach the 1948 College All-Stars. But Arch Ward leaned on him hard; Leahy acquiesced and walked into an untenable situation. Ward handed Leahy a roster of seventy-one players, a roster acclaimed by one and all to be the greatest amalgam of talent in history. The problem was that all seventy-one players expected to play in one sixty-minute game. Leahy tried to soothe the egos by preparing two different units. Lujack and Bobby Layne of Texas would play quarterback in the T formation; Charlie Conerly of Ole Miss and Bob Chappuis of Michigan would run the single wing. The idea looked good on paper. In reality, it split the team in half. The Cardinals used two long drives to score touchdowns in the first quarter and dominated the All-Stars, winning 28–0.

Leahy's five losses as a college head coach had been by a cumulative margin of 34 points. He was so upset after the game that he couldn't go into the locker room. He viewed it as personal humiliation, and so did the section of the public always eager to see the unvanquished vanquished. Even *The South Bend Tribune* ran the headline: "Cardinals Humble Leahy, Stars by 28–0."

The headline captured the relative star power of Leahy and the NFL in the firmament of American celebrity. *The Sporting News*, at the time the only national sports weekly, annually published the *National League Football Pro Record and Rule Book*, which didn't even use the abbreviation "NFL." The cover of the 1948 edition featured a portrait of Leahy towering over an unidentified player sitting or kneeling alongside him; inside was a sixty-plus-page hagiography of Leahy written by Callahan.

Leahy left Chicago and went on a fishing trip in Wisconsin, his last respite before the season. He returned home to celebrate his fortieth birthday with his family on the following Friday. And then he slipped into coaching mode again. With the Notre Dame opener a month away, Leahy could not dwell on the All-Star loss or his milestone birthday. He had Purdue to worry about, the Purdue that he had predicted would win the Big Nine. The day before the game, the syndicated column written by Callahan with Leahy's byline on it contained the line, "One point will assume major proportions in our game." The eternal pessimist, like the boy who cried wolf, was bound to be right one day.

Between coach Stu Holcomb's matter-of-fact attitude, and three months of preparation, the Boilermakers played the Irish evenly for the entire game. Outplayed the Irish for a while, in fact, thanks to three extra points and two field goals missed by new Irish kicker Steve Oracko. When Purdue edged ahead, 13–12, in the third quarter, it marked the first time that Notre Dame had been behind in a game since Leahy returned to coaching from the Navy. In the fourth quarter, Leahy tried the two-quarterback ploy with Frank Tripucka and Bob Williams. Late in the game, with Notre Dame holding an 18–13 lead, Leahy sent Oracko onto the field to attempt a 24-yard field goal that would give the Irish a two-score margin (the two-point conversion would not be admitted to the rule book for another decade).

What happened next became the source of a staple of Leahy's banquet anecdotes for years.

"Father Cavanaugh comes the closest of anybody I've ever met to being the perfect priest, the perfect man," Leahy said. "He was a beautiful, beautiful person. His manner and his speech were impeccable. He never used profanity."

But not even the president of Notre Dame could stomach it. When Father Cavanaugh watched the kicker run onto the field, he stood in the stands and screamed, "Frank! Frank! Jesus Christ! Not Oracko!"

As Oracko's field goal sailed through the uprights, assistant coach Joe McArdle jerked open the window in front of him in the press box and yelled, "God bless you, Steve Oracko!" and yanked it shut. At the reception at Leahy's home that night, two fans, a little worse for the alcoholic wear, told the coach they heard the yell, looked up and saw no one. One of them concluded, "It could only have been the voice of Rockne himself."

Notre Dame won the game more comfortably than the 28–27 final score indicated—Purdue scored a touchdown as time expired to pull within a point—but the game had ramifications for the rest of the season for both teams. Purdue, crushed by the narrow loss after preparing for so many weeks, never recovered emotionally. Two weeks later, Michigan defeated Purdue 40–0, the first of several comparative scores that bent the race for No. 1 toward the Wolverines.

Notre Dame sailed through six non-competitive games. Leading Navy 28–0 at the half, Leahy told Tripucka as they headed out of the locker room, "Francis, come here for a minute. Now you know we don't want to embarrass the United States Navy, so you're not going to play in the second half." Williams came in at quarterback, did not pass the ball once, and the Irish won, 41–7. The most peril Leahy confronted in that stretch occurred when he and Floss got stuck in the elevator at the team's Davenport hotel for more than fifteen minutes before Notre

Dame defeated Iowa, 27–12. The Irish popped back into No. 1 when Michigan struggled to win at Illinois. The Wolverines regained the top position a week later, won their last three games handily, and finished the season atop the poll.

Notre Dame did not play on the Saturday that Michigan closed out its season by winning at No. 18 Ohio State, 13–3. Leahy traveled to Los Angeles to scout USC, whom the Irish would play two weeks later, as the Trojans defeated crosstown rival UCLA, 20–13.

In those days schools held cocktail parties on the Friday night before a home game for the visiting writers and radio men, parties deemed important enough that the head coach would attend. It was the end of the season, and Leahy had run out of gas yet again. He didn't contract a virus and take to his bed, but he was exhausted. On the night before the Irish's last home game, against Washington, Jack Clowser of *The Cleveland Press* came away from a conversation with Leahy believing he had a scoop. Clowser waited until the Monday after Notre Dame's 46–0 victory to write that Leahy would resign as athletic director after the 1949 season and that he would only coach a year after that.

"I don't think I can take it for more than another couple of years," Clowser quoted Leahy. "I'll have to give it up. It just gets me down and leaves me feeling poorly every year."

Leahy labeled the coaching resignation as a misunderstanding, but Clowser had stumbled on some news regarding the position of athletic director. The custom of the time had head coaches serve as athletic directors as well. But the latter job had become more than a formal acknowledgment of the head coach's primacy among a university's coaches.

With a third consecutive national championship foreclosed, the Irish had to depend on personal pride to win the season finale at USC. Pride and backup quarterback Bob Williams, that is. Tripucka went down on the last play of the first half. Williams had played a lot for a freshman but had yet to take a snap when the outcome of the game was in doubt. "Usually when I went in," Williams recalled, "the last thing Leahy said was, 'Don't pass!'"

The Irish lost six fumbles, and when the Trojans scored late in the fourth quarter to take a 14–7 lead, Notre Dame was in danger of losing the game and its twenty-seven-game unbeaten streak as well. When Irish kick returner Billy Gay went onto the field for the ensuing kickoff, he asked an official how much time remained in the game.

"Two minutes and thirty-six seconds," the official said.

"Thank you, sir," Gay replied. "That's enough."

Gay took the kickoff and returned it 86 yards to the USC 12-yard line. The Irish shoved the ball into the end zone with thirty seconds to play and salvaged a 14–14 tie. The official, Jimmy Cain, found Gay's comment so extraordinary that he stopped by Leahy's room at the Hotel Biltmore after the game to tell him. Just as in the 1943 loss to Great Lakes Naval Training Station, Leahy failed to win the final game, and just as in 1943, it had no effect on the national championship. A few days after the season ended, Frank and Floss, with Frank Jr. (twelve), Susan (ten), and Florence (eight) in tow, boarded the SS *Lurline* in Los Angeles for a coaching clinic at the University of Hawaii. The Leahys spent nine days in Honolulu, and that was all the relaxation/family time that Frank could stand. On Christmas Eve, they flew back to the mainland. Four days later, *The South Bend Tribune* ran a photo of Leahy in Miami, sleeves rolled up, kneeling next to his closest coaching friend, Wally Butts of Georgia, as the Bulldogs prepared to play Texas in the Orange Bowl.

The idea that Leahy surrender the athletic director job emanated from a push by Father Cavanaugh to streamline the administrative side of campus life. But Leahy readily accepted it. For one thing, being athletic director had become a real job now that the university had a student body of 5,000, as opposed to 3,200 before the war. For another, Leahy didn't enjoy the gladhanding part of the job. He would be replaced as AD by Moose Krause, Leahy's one-time assistant and also the head coach of the basketball team. Leahy understood that Krause never met a stranger.

"I don't seem to be the type," Leahy told Joe Williams of the *New York World-Telegram*. "I try it but it just doesn't come off."

So why wait? In mid-January, Krause told the *Binghamton Press* (New York) the announcement would come in two weeks. Krause, ever the schmoozer, spoke frankly about Leahy to sports editor Charles Peet.

"Like all coaches, Leahy is a great worrier," Krause said. "Before every game he is so nervous and jumpy he says, 'This is the last game for me. I'm going to quit.' "

While Krause spoke upstate, Leahy went to New York to be inducted into the Knights of Malta, the highest honor available to a Catholic layperson. The membership of the order added up to only 245 men worldwide. Francis Cardinal Spellman, the archbishop of New York, conferred the honor onto Leahy on behalf of Pope Pius XII in a ceremony at the Waldorf-Astoria Hotel. The Vatican didn't make a habit of honoring American sports figures. Leahy was the first, a tribute both to him and to Spellman's political sway in the church hierarchy across the Atlantic.

Two days later, Leahy, speaking to a 1,500-person dinner put on by the Norfolk (Virginia) Sports Club, said he would step down as AD "this year."

Leahy also gave one of the first public indications of his political leanings as the "red scare" began to heighten tension across the country. Later in life, Leahy would give ardently anti-Communist speeches to any gathered crowd. In Norfolk, he just wrapped himself in the flag.

A Notre Dame team, he said, "represents Americanism on display. Every boy, regardless of his creed, can play for our team [four years before a Black player stepped on the field for Leahy at Notre Dame] . . . We should start now eliminating all form of 'isms' in this country except one—Americanism."

Leahy discussed the dire prospects of the 1949 Irish, with a little twist on the always-simmering schedule issues. "We're going to make a lot of friends next year," Leahy said. "We lost seven regulars off last fall's team and we're going to lose some ball games. In fact, after next season everybody in the country probably will be calling us for games."

Leahy also denied he had come to the area to interview for the Washington Redskins head coaching job, even though he did meet with team attorney Leo Deorsey. Leahy told *The Washington Post* he had no interest in the job, even as published reports said the team would pay as much as $50,000 to the right coach.

Just to make sure everyone understood, at the team's annual banquet on January 20, Leahy said, "It is an enormous honor to serve Notre Dame as football coach. I'm the luckiest Notre Dame man in the United States of America. I hope I can stay here for a long period of time. If I couldn't coach at Notre Dame, I would never want to coach anyplace else in the United States."

Leahy went on a speaking tour in early February, bouncing from Detroit to Bethlehem, Pennsylvania, to Leroy, New York, to Aurora, Illinois, with an invitation for dinner at the White House with President Harry Truman wedged in as well. The dinner had been arranged by Leahy's old friend and patron from Norwalk, Judge Paul Connery, a prominent Democrat.

In February, Notre Dame announced that Krause would take over as athletic director. Father Cavanaugh described Leahy as "the finest football coach in the country," but that also serving as AD had forced Leahy to work as many as eighteen hours a day. Cavanaugh said this as if freeing Leahy of one of the jobs would make him work less. Wishful thinking, perhaps.

And, God bless Leahy, this quieted talk of him leaving Notre Dame for several . . . weeks.

Red Smith, not a writer who threw stuff against the wall to see what stuck, wrote in the *New York Herald Tribune* that Leahy would resign after the 1950 season and go to work for Fred Miller, his Notre Dame teammate and close friend. That's Miller, as in president of Miller Brewing Company.

"The story goes that Frank Leahy, the Grand Old Man of football, is tired and has a bright business opportunity with Freddy Miller, another former Notre Dame player, and so has completed arrangements to retire as Notre Dame coach after the 1950 season," Smith wrote on April 27. "There is one difference between this story and a dozen earlier rumors that the Grand Old Man was ready to quit. This one happens to be true."

Smith pushed in all his chips on this tip. Smith grew up in Green Bay and graduated from Notre Dame in 1927. Miller grew up in Milwaukee and graduated from Notre Dame in 1929. That could be a coincidence. Or it could be that Smith got the story from Miller. Leahy shot it down.

"Miller is one of my closest friends and I have no doubt he'd put me up in business if I ever left football," Leahy told Williams the next day, "but the truth is, and please believe me completely, I haven't the slightest idea of giving up football."

No, Leahy wouldn't think of leaving Notre Dame for several... months.

But a couple of other points should be made from Smith's column. One, referring to Leahy as the Grand Old Man is revealing, if only because Leahy remained all of forty years old and had been a head coach for a total of eight seasons. It must be said that the nickname represented Smith's puckish sense of humor. Through the years, Smith also referred to Leahy as "the gloomy dean of American football," "the unhappy archbishop of Notre Dame," "Uncle Frank," and as "a gentleman of deep and abiding melancholy." Smith's description of Leahy's job captured why Leahy may have looked like a Grand Old Man.

"There is no bigger job in football than the one at Notre Dame," Smith wrote. "There is no coach of whom more is demanded. It is a twelve-month job, and there are not eight-hour days. It is a job to tire anybody."

That is where Fred Miller came in. Leahy and Miller rekindled their college friendship when the coach returned to South Bend. Miller loved their alma mater as few men did. And he loved Leahy, too. Miller commuted from Milwaukee to Notre Dame twice a week as the pilot in a two-seat Ercoupe plane. By the 1948 season, not only was he president of the Monogram Club of former athletes, he was listed as a "volunteer coach" alongside the assistants. His chief purpose appeared to be deflecting attention, fans, writers, and broadcasters away from Leahy. Where Leahy stepped, Miller wasn't far away. When a civic group wanted Leahy as a speaker, they went to Miller. When Leahy barked a comment during a practice or a game, Miller served as stenographer. With the players, he served as a confidant.

"He always seemed to give me a little added strength, a little extra feeling of confidence," Leahy said.

A few weeks later, Leahy reiterated that he had no thoughts or plans to quit after two more seasons, "but you never know when a man's health may go bad on him. I was sickly in 1942. If that condition comes back, I would ask for my release." In August, Leahy attempted to put an end to the speculation about his future with a ghostwritten piece in *Sport* entitled "The Truth About My Future," in which he reiterated, "I enjoy coaching here, and health permitting, I will remain as long as the University authorities so desire."

In sickness or in health, Leahy always could be counted on to spout forth a pessimistic view of his football team. At this point in his career, he began to lean into it with a bit of self-awareness, thinking that if the writers wanted fodder, then he would provide it. "I felt the press and the public were welcome to them if they contributed anything in the way of color," Leahy said. "For color was a quality I fell short in, not only compared to Rock but to so many others." This was the spring when he said, "We'll have the worst team Notre Dame has ever had. We'll lose seven games." Remember, Leahy, in eight seasons as a head coach, had lost a total of five games. In for a dime, in for a losing record.

He knew how good his top-line players were. Given the age and experience of the ex-servicemen players—six seniors ranged in age from twenty-three to twenty-five—Leahy understood what an advantage they provided. Leahy also knew that as good as his entire senior class was—and Notre Dame had six senior linemen—his team lacked depth, the kind of depth provided by the scholarships that Father Cavanaugh had taken away from him. Leahy wrote Father John Murphy, the vice president in charge of athletics, a two-and-a-half-page, single-spaced letter in which he pleaded for the university to grant the football program thirty-three scholarships for the class entering in the fall of 1949. Notre Dame needed that many, he said, because "I am most anxious for Notre Dame to preserve the fine name she has achieved in the football world." Leahy also played the money card. Winning football meant more donations, he said. "I do feel that in view of Notre Dame's limited endowment it would be very imprudent for us to field a football team that would not draw capacity crowds... We both know, Father, that the overhead expenses on the stadium remain fairly constant and must be paid whether it is sold out or not."*

Leahy promised he would ask for no more than fifteen scholarships for the 1950 class, but his plucking of the financial violin strings failed to sway Murphy, who had the strength of Father Cavanaugh behind him. It was a rare "no" from Father Murphy, who didn't have the personality to rein in Leahy. Father Murphy tried. He would write Leahy a long letter, reminding him to send a travel roster for approval, reminding him to file the list of absentee players with the campus prefect for discipline, reminding him to suggest the right amount of travel money per player for road trips. Leahy didn't make time to be bothered with Father Murphy's approval. With the notable exception of the scholarships—a change that Cavanaugh himself had made—the coach had what amounted to carte blanche over the football program.

Leahy told Williams in June that the 1949 Irish would be "representative," an allowance of success that rarely emanated from Leahy's mouth. Before the season began, Leahy called in the seniors and went

* The football program made a profit of nearly $357,000 in 1948 and would make $376,469.95 in 1949. That was nearly 10 percent of the university endowment of $4.1 million in 1948.

through the entire schedule, game by game. He told them that if they beat Tulane in the fourth game of the season, they would win the national championship.

A decade earlier, Leahy had told his Boston College players that they would beat Florida and they did not, turning him into a career-long public pessimist. This time, when Leahy said aloud that his team would be "representative" of the name Notre Dame, he ventured toward a different sort of self-awareness, what in modernspeak became self-actualization. Might as well say we have a good team. It was the summer, a long way from the pressure of fall Saturdays, when everyone on campus and in the stadium, all those nuns across the country leading their students in novenas for the Fighting Irish, all those subway alumni sitting by the radio, rosary in hand, loaded their hopes and dreams on his back and expected him, Frank Leahy from Winner, South Dakota, to maintain Notre Dame as king of the college football mountain.

Leahy made that statement within days of Father Cavanaugh announcing a change in how the university would be run. His determination to make the university run more smoothly resulted in him creating a new office, an executive vice president whose job would be to oversee the four university vice presidents. Another of the EVP's duties would be to oversee athletics. In that job, Cavanaugh appointed a confident, spirited, handsome thirty-two-year-old priest named Theodore Hesburgh.* He had been on campus only four years, but in that time he had made a difference in student life and an impression on Father Cavanaugh. Hesburgh professed to Cavanaugh that he didn't want to be an administrator. But that confidence and that spirit went hand-in-hand with ambition. Hesburgh made sure to get from his boss the promise that in any conflict with Leahy that Cavanaugh would back Hesburgh. Cavanaugh gave it, an indication that even he, who had befriended, counseled, and supported Leahy for two decades, had become wary

* In his autobiography, *God, Country, Notre Dame*, Father Hesburgh wrote that after being named EVP, the first thing he did was appoint an athletic director. Krause was named AD in March 1949. Hesburgh became EVP in July, four months later.

of how football had become synonymous with Notre Dame. The year before, the writer Francis Wallace, an alum who dearly loved the place, assessed the university's bifurcated personality by saying, "Most people do think of Notre Dame primarily as a football school, identify it *with* football. That's not as we want, nor as it is; but Notre Dame made the situation; and it's up to Notre Dame to correct it." Of course, Wallace's profile ran in a football preview magazine. Sigh.

Father Hesburgh didn't much care for or about football. But he understood the charge that Father Cavanaugh had given him. Early in the season, Leahy would find out that Father Hesburgh was no Father Murphy.

With five children and a sixth on the way, the Leahy household in the summer of 1949 proved to be a whirlwind of activity. At age five, Jerry already showed signs that if Mom or Dad told him to zig, he would without hesitation zag. One day Floss told him that if he didn't listen to her, he would end up in jail. Three days later, Frank walked into the house and Floss told him, "I have news for you. Jerry's in jail."

He had broken a window in nursery school. His teacher saw a town police car driving by and waved him down. The cop took Jerry to jail, proving without a doubt that this story took place in 1949, not in the present day.

"I learned later," Frank told Williams, "that Jerry didn't want to leave the jail."

Two months later, a series of thunderstorms pounded northwest Indiana on the last night of August, when assistant coaches Bill Earley and John Druze had a post-practice dinner at the Leahy home in Long Beach. Floss may have been due any day, but Frank brought the guys home for dinner, and so dinner appeared. Earley and Druze left the Leahys' at nine thirty p.m., shortly before the storms cut off the house's electricity, which happened to be right about the time that Floss went into labor. Frank called two doctors, hoping one would get to the house quickly. He helped Floss upstairs and into bed, where she lay for, by Frank's estimation, about thirty seconds before she gave birth. Neither doctor arrived in time to aid Floss, although one did treat eleven-year-old Sue, who, dispatched downstairs in the darkness for something by her father, tripped and broke her toe.

"If you think a football game is exciting," Leahy said at Cartier Field the next day, "you should have been at our house last night."

They named their fourth son Frederick, after Fred Miller. The story so captivated the editors at *Life* magazine that they published a near-full-page photo of Floss, Frank, and Fred in the next week's issue. The headline read "Life Congratulates..."

Fred would not be the last. They followed quickly with Mary, born in 1951, and Christopher, the eighth and final, who arrived on February 25, 1952, a month early, so early that Frank wasn't even in town. He had a speaking engagement.

LEAHY MAY HAVE BENT UNDER THE STRESS OF COACHING AT NOTRE Dame, but to the depths of his soul he still believed in the institution. At the pep rally before the 1949 opener against Indiana, he addressed the freshmen in the crowd, among them a young man from the Bronx named Regis Philbin.

"He began to speak in a voice that could cut through steel," Philbin recalled. "This was a serious, no-nonsense guy who had a magical way with a motivational turn of phrase. He [began] telling us in particular of the university's wondrous tradition and of the spirit that would soon consume us, and also what Notre Dame would mean to each of us later in our futures and how we should enjoy every moment of our time there because we would never again experience a place like this for the rest of our lives... With each declaration he made, I'd feel my scalp tingle and more goose bumps rise. He simply inflamed us and, frankly, I was ready to go join the team that very instant—to make that tackle, catch that pass, run for that touchdown! We began to cheer the coach onward, one sentence after another. I had never felt such wild enthusiasm in my life. And so, through the hypnotic power of Frank Leahy,

Notre Dame had begun to overtake my soul so deeply that it would never let go."

The Notre Dame fans responded to Leahy's success on the field. In 1941, Leahy's first season at Notre Dame, every alum who ordered even the maximum of four tickets between the 30-yard lines had his offer filled. In 1949, less than half of the alumni who received tickets got seats between the 30s, and by then the alums had been limited to two tickets apiece. They got to see exactly what they came to see.

The 1949 Irish raced through the schedule with an abundance of older talent and a modicum of luck. North Carolina back Charlie "Choo-Choo" Justice and SMU back Doak Walker, the 1948 Heisman winner, both first-team AP All-Americans, missed playing against Notre Dame because of injuries. Only in two games did Leahy find trouble. In the second game of the season, the first away game, Notre Dame played at Washington, returning the trip the Huskies had made to South Bend the previous season. The trip proved troublesome from start to finish.

Leahy had vowed after the game at USC the previous November that the Irish would begin flying to games in 1949. He had asked Father Murphy for permission for the team to fly home from Seattle in order to get the students back to campus for Monday classes. He didn't get it. Leahy didn't ask for permission to fly back to campus himself. He informed Father Murphy he needed to do so in order to begin preparation for Purdue the following week. The team made the round trip to Seattle via train, which doubly irked Leahy because Washington traveled to and from its opener at Minnesota the previous week by air. That would turn out to be the least of Leahy's concerns.

Father Hesburgh decided to go ahead and establish ground rules with the iconic coach now under his charge. He wanted a copy of the thirty-eight-man travel roster. He soon learned that Leahy intended to take forty-four players on the train. When Hesburgh dispatched Herb Jones, the athletic business manager, to Leahy's office to get the roster, Leahy told Jones he was too busy preparing for the game. Hesburgh sent Jones back with an easier request—just provide the names of the six extra players, because if they go, they will be dismissed from the university for cutting classes.

Hesburgh warned Father Cavanaugh that there might be a showdown, and that if the university didn't back Hesburgh, he would resign. Cavanaugh promised his support but Hesburgh didn't need it. Leahy acquiesced. However, on the long train trip west, Leahy did not speak to Hesburgh once.

By now these trips looked like whistlestop tours. In Threeforks, Montana, school was dismissed so the children could come to the train station to see the team. In Butte, a local high school played the Notre Dame Victory March as the team train pulled into the station deluged with fans.

When the team got to the Olympic Hotel in Seattle, Leahy met a ten-year-old fan named Patrick Carr Murphy, who had written him a letter offering to be the team mascot or Leahy's errand boy while Notre Dame was in town if it meant that he could see the game.

> *Your recent letter pleased me immensely. It was most enjoyable hearing from you. Kindly call on us at the Olympic Hotel in Seattle and we will see that you witness the game.*
>
> *Sincerely,*
> *F. Leahy*

Young Patrick saw quite the spectacle. As soon as the game started at Husky Stadium, the yellow flags started appearing. The four-man officiating crew called three penalties on the Irish in their first nine snaps and a fourth one on the next possession. At halftime, Notre Dame led Washington in total yards, 243–43, but also led in penalty yards, 75–10, which explained why the score stood at 7–7.

Early in the second half, Notre Dame blocked a punt that led to one touchdown and recovered a fumble that led to another, but the defense got called for holding twice in a three-play span. The Irish won the game, 27–7, and the penalty yards finished 135–10. Leahy, usually the most politic of men, called out the officiating afterward. He told *Seattle Times* reporters Emmett Watson and Alex Shults, "The officials today—all four of them—tried their best to even up a football game. How could it be a good game when we had to play four extra men?"

Leahy may have been reacting to what had been a tense week on campus with Father Hesburgh. He may have been reacting to the flags paving the way for critics to again claim that the Irish played dirty. Former Washington State coach Babe Hollingsberry, watching from the press box as a guest columnist for *The Seattle Times*, wrote that Leahy should consider himself fortunate that the crew didn't flag the Irish four or five more times for unnecessary roughness. A UW regent said after the game that the school "can get plenty of games with name teams without having to subject our players to the kind of football we saw Saturday."

Or it could have been merely that Leahy wanted a fair fight and didn't think he got one. He did not have a record of carping about officiating. Given a day to cool off, Leahy remained hot, repeating the accusation. "The officials did their best to protect [Pacific] Coast Conference football," and that he was "tired of accepting incompetence politely and without comment." He stayed hot on Monday, when head linesman W. H. Frazier revealed that the officials had watched Notre Dame film in the days leading up to the game with Washington head coach Howie Odell there "to point out what they [Washington] thought about holding by Notre Dame players." Frazier, who happened to be a coach at Gonzaga High, a Catholic school in Spokane, said afterward that the film session hadn't been a good idea. The meeting didn't look good, especially being held without Notre Dame's knowledge, much less presence. Leahy vowed that none of the four would ever call another Notre Dame game as long as he coached. That lined up nicely with the attitude of Washington athletic director Harvey Cassill, who on the Monday after the game wrote a letter to Moose Krause in which he said that, in light of Leahy's comments, Notre Dame can forget about any future games with Washington.

Forty-six years passed before the two schools played again.

Father Hesburgh, who traveled to the game and saw for himself the one-sided officiating, immediately and vigorously defended Leahy, privately and publicly. The priest politely jousted via letters with University of Washington president Raymond B. Allen. Hesburgh wrote Allen that he himself had watched the game film "for several hours, frontwards, backwards, and slow motion" and had detected no underhanded tactics. He also pointed out that, while Leahy violated university policy by speaking publicly about the officiating, Hesburgh agreed that his comments had been justified.

Hesburgh not only thought Notre Dame had been wronged, he seized the opportunity to pave over the rocky start with his celebrity coach. Leahy appreciated the gesture, and their relationship began to thaw. It had been a tough trip for Hesburgh, too. He took umbrage at the fact that only sportswriters attended his press conference in Seattle. When the local photographers asked him to get into a center's stance with a football, Hesburgh bristled. "Would you ask the president of Yale to do that?" Hesburgh asked. They didn't get the shot.

Perhaps Leahy genuinely believed that Tulane would be the toughest opponent that one of his teams had ever faced. Or maybe he said that to add more kindling to the fire he built in the preseason. In week four, against the No. 4 Green Wave that Leahy had told his players stood between them and the national championship, the Irish scored four touchdowns in the first quarter. The 46–7 victory over the eventual SEC champions served as a marvelous display of Leahy's ability to focus his players, as well as their respect for him. But Leahy already had begun to wear himself down. Even though the team had an off week, theoretically a time to take a midseason breather, by the following week Leahy had become sick enough to stay in bed as his team prepared to play Navy in Baltimore. The newspapers at the time reported it as the flu. In later years, Leahy said he suffered an attack of pancreatitis during the season.

On Saturday morning, Miller served as pilot and at seven thirty a.m. flew Leahy down to Baltimore for the game. After fighting traffic, they made it to Municipal Stadium forty-three minutes before kickoff. For the second season in a row, Leahy didn't allow his quarterbacks to throw a pass in the fourth quarter. The 40–0 victory gave Notre Dame a national record thirty-three-game unbeaten streak.

The following week, after No. 10 Michigan State made Notre Dame work well into the second half before succumbing, 34–21, Spartan coach Biggie Munn declared that the Irish may turn out to be the greatest team in the history of the sport. Leahy's analysis differed. He told Red Smith that his team had made eighty-eight mistakes in the game. "And if you know anything about Leahy and his meticulous attention to detail," Smith wrote, "you know Notre Dame made eighty-eight mistakes in East Lansing, Michigan, not eighty-seven or eighty-nine."

The bond that Leahy had established with this older team, this locker room led by war veterans, showed itself on Thanksgiving Saturday, the final game before the AP voters awarded their national championship. The Irish closed out their home schedule with a 32–0 rout of USC in which they outgained the Trojans on the ground, 316 yards to 17. The Notre Dame players punctuated the victory by lifting Leahy upon their shoulders and carrying him off the field. None of the writers could remember seeing that before.

Four teams finished the regular season undefeated, yet the AP voters ignored Oklahoma, California, and Army. Notre Dame received 172 first-place votes from the 190 voters. A lot of football teams got ignored that season. When the Irish played North Carolina at Yankee Stadium, their first visit to the Bronx since the 0–0 tie with Army three years earlier, 67,000 fans turned out to see Notre Dame win, 42–6. The next day, the New York Yanks of the All-American Football Conference drew 9,091. "Nobody cares about anything except the Notre Dame score," Yankees/Yanks owner Dan Topping said.

Notre Dame finished No. 1 for the third time in four seasons but still had a game to play at SMU. As had become the norm for Leahy's

Irish, both he and his players struggled to finish out the season. The team struggled because it already had achieved its goal. In the days leading up to the game, Hart, Martin, and Sitko made the AP All-America team, the UP named quarterback Bob Williams its Back of the Year, and Hart later won the Heisman Trophy. Leahy was tired, so tired that he contemplated the SMU game being his final one. The Mustangs came into the game with a mediocre record (5-3-1) and without Walker, who that day would watch the game in street clothes from the sideline. He had suffered a severe muscle bruise, then universally known as a charley horse, during an early November game and aggravated it the previous week.

"The only reason my boys will show up," SMU head coach Matty Bell said, "is because all the tickets have been sold."

Dallas threw a party to celebrate Notre Dame's first game there anyway. The visitors' pep rally at the Baker Hotel drew 1,800 people, and that didn't include the fans turned away. Bob Hope and singer Tony Martin entertained. Father Cavanaugh spoke. And the following day, in a dank drizzle, SMU gave Notre Dame its first close game of the season. Walker's replacement, Kyle Rote, almost singlehandedly kept the Mustangs on even footing with the national champs. Rote ran and threw for 261 yards. He carried the ball on 24 of SMU's 30 rushes. He completed 10 of 24 passes. And early in the fourth quarter, when Rote ran for his third touchdown of the game, the extra point would have put Notre Dame behind, 21–20. But linebacker Jerry Groom blocked the point-after try. "For the first time all fall," Leahy said, "we had only a few minutes to prove we were really a championship team."

On the road, before a hostile crowd, with all the college football world wanting to see them lose for the first time in four years, the Irish gathered around Leahy before they went out on the field. Williams, as young as he was, asked Leahy if he had any advice. The coach looked at his team, could sense the players' tension as they prepared for a situation that they hadn't experienced all season. It is one of the rare times Leahy opted for humor.

"Yes," Leahy said. "I have some very good advice for you. Don't ever enter the coaching profession."

The players laughed, ran onto the Cotton Bowl grass, and drove right down the field for the winning touchdown. In the locker room after the 27–20 victory, Leahy tried to put the game into perspective for his players.

"Something happened to you today for which we've prayed. Let's show our gratitude to God. I want you all, players and coaches, to go to that church where we prayed this morning, and pray again.

"We have won what they call the national championship in football. Perhaps, you think that calls for a celebration. But before you celebrate, I want each of you to write a letter to [your] parents. I want you to thank them for sending you to Notre Dame. And I want you to thank them for giving you the physical attributes for playing football at Notre Dame."

And then he told his players, "You are my greatest team. God bless you, everyone."

The players had no intention of pausing before they celebrated. They crowded around Leahy, and Martin, the twenty-five-year-old war veteran, the senior who had switched positions this season and still made All-American, yelled, "Who is the greatest coach in the world?"

The players responded in unison, "Leahy!"

Leahy later told the writers, "It has guts. It has character. It's the greatest team I've ever coached." Bell and Walker later came into the Irish locker room to pay their respects. Walker, every bit as famous a player as Hart, Sitko, and the other Notre Dame stars, riveted the attention of the room. Before Walker left, he acceded to the request of an autograph from a young boy: thirteen-year-old Frank Leahy Jr.

"I wish I could have played," Walker told the Notre Dame team. "But it was an even greater game to watch."

Groom, a junior, already had begun to think about the following season. He knew what Leahy knew and so few outside of the program realized. Notre Dame would no longer have the wealth of talent the

Irish had enjoyed in the four years since the war ended. Not only were the veterans graduating, but Leahy would be playing with four classes limited in number by Father Cavanaugh. Groom looked at Leahy and saw the fatigue that overtook the head coach at the end of every season.

"Coach, you aren't as happy as usual," Groom said. "You aren't thinking of quitting, are you?"

Leahy told him that he was thinking about it.

"When you recruited me," Groom said, "you promised my mother you would coach me for four years and I'm only a junior."

In that moment, Groom pushed the one button that would force Leahy to reset. Leahy did not want to be a man who shirked responsibility, who could not be depended upon, who made a promise and broke it. He considered himself a man of his word.

"All I could say," Leahy said years later, "was, 'See you in the spring.' "

And yet stories here and there began to be written that Notre Dame would falter in 1950, and Leahy didn't want to be there when it happened. Three weeks after the 1949 season ended, Dick Hyland, the *Los Angeles Times* writer who never walked past a Fighting Irish pot without stirring it, wrote a column in which he declared that Notre Dame was about to de-emphasize football, that Leahy "is quietly looking" for a new job, and the first place that Leahy looked was USC. According to Hyland, on the cusp of the 1949 season, as the coaching gossip held that Cravath had to win or else, Leahy put the word out among his USC contacts that he didn't want the job at Cravath's expense, but that if the school intended to remove him, Leahy would be interested.

One other source confirmed Leahy's interest, albeit many years later. Leahy told Twombly that someone connected to USC had "approached" Leahy at three points in his career, and that the only serious consideration he ever gave came right about the time the bottom fell out of his program. In an interview with Bud Furillo of the *Los Angeles Herald-Examiner* three years before Leahy died, the coach said if he had known that he would have to deal with scholarship cutbacks, he would have taken that Cleveland Browns job offered right after he returned home from the war. As for the cutbacks themselves and the resultant slump, Leahy called it "the great disappointment of my life." He firmly believed he could have fulfilled his goal of completing the ten-year contract he signed upon returning from the war without losing a game.

"They shouldn't have done that to me," Leahy said.

For the fourth time, Leahy's peers in the American Football Coaches Association watched him win a national championship and selected someone else as Coach of the Year. This time, the AFCA chose Bud Wilkinson of Oklahoma. But even the coaches must have felt sheepish about the snub. The AFCA named Leahy "Man of the Year," a distinction that didn't have enough of a difference to survive as an award for many more years. The Washington Touchdown Club honored Leahy as Coach of the Year, which gave him the opportunity to mingle on the dais with political powers such as Sam Rayburn, the Speaker of the House; Chief Justice Fred Vinson, and Attorney General J. Howard McGrath. Heady stuff, and maybe just enough recognition to tamp down the impulse he had to chuck it all.

CHAPTER FIFTEEN

GETTING BACK UP AGAIN... AND AGAIN

On the weekend following the 1949 season, Leahy stood before a microphone in Los Angeles, appearing on Jack Benny's radio program on CBS. Benny's on-air character fed his fragile ego by trumpeting skills he didn't remotely possess. After meeting Leahy on a train, Benny realizes he has prattled on about his football expertise without recognizing he is talking to *the* Frank Leahy.

Benny: I must apologize for making a fool of myself. Imagine me not knowing what business you were in.
Leahy: Well, Jack, don't let it worry you. When we played SMU last week, up until the last quarter I didn't know what business I was in either.

Leahy had never been more popular nor more recognizable than after the 1949 season. Arthur Godfrey, a singer whose genial on-air presence on CBS captivated the country, had a business relationship with attorney Leo Deorsey, who had taken on Leahy as well. Godfrey and Deorsey made a deal with Leahy for him to appear on radio. Newspaper accounts said that Leahy would take home anywhere from $25,000 to $50,000 per year for his appearances, well more than what Notre Dame paid him. Leahy already had a fifteen-minute radio show each week during the season. He may have been a little stiff on the air—after all, he was a little stiff in person—but people wanted to hear him and see him.

Leahy maintained his long affiliation with Keds. Full-color cartoons of him promoting the shoes became a fixture in the Sunday comics of newspapers across the country ("Coach Frank Leahy says, 'WIN IN KEDS!' "). He continued to be a sought-after speaker to Catholic and to lay sports-oriented audiences in the offseason. On the first weekend of June, Leahy played in the annual National Celebrities Golf Tournament at the Army-Navy Country Club in Washington. The charity event featured male and female pros (including Gene Sarazen, Ben Hogan, and Babe Didrikson), entertainers (among them Frank Sinatra, Milton Berle, and Bob Hope), Cabinet members and Supreme Court justices. At that time in his life, Leahy played a little social golf, and a little celebrity golf. Hogan received little acclaim for winning the rain-shortened event as he continued his rehabilitation from the near-fatal car accident he had suffered sixteen months earlier. A week later, Hogan would win the US Open and be lionized as a walking miracle.

In the wake of the victory over SMU that closed out the previous season, Leahy looked ahead and said he thought Notre Dame would lose five games in 1950. No one gave the comment a second thought. Typical Leahy, always pessimistic, who is he kidding, etc. Even his players, who knew as well as their coaches what the team no longer had, had trouble believing that they could lose.

"We were young and this was Notre Dame," quarterback Bob Williams said. "Losing never entered our minds. We couldn't be beaten. Maybe we should have gotten an inkling in the spring game. All the seniors played against us and beat us pretty bad."

The Old-Timers Game amplified the alarm that had been ringing in Leahy's ears all spring. Not only had the Irish lost so many seniors, but injuries and academic probation had prevented a number of younger players from participating as well. Inclement weather also allowed only one good practice before Easter (April 9). After the Old-Timers Game, Leahy vented his worries in a letter to Father Hesburgh. "We have only one team this year that bears any resemblance to a typical Notre Dame club. There will be absolutely no depth in 1950. In view of our rugged schedule this defect could prove disastrous." He suggested that the administration consider suspending the 77-point GPA requirement for freshmen. There is a note on the letter, in what appears to be Father's Cavanaugh's red pencil, that the policy should be discussed. But it didn't change.

A few writers heeded Leahy's warning. But no one outside of the program saw the mediocrity that lay ahead. He would turn forty-two a few weeks before the season began. He looked older. Crow's feet had begun to radiate from his temples. Above those striations his hairline had begun to recede. The taut, physical specimen who once demonstrated line play to his players looked a little jowly. The bow tie he had adopted as part of his wardrobe added a few years as well. And the coming season would age anyone. By the end of it, Leahy wondered aloud if he had become too old to coach. Again, at age forty-two.

The secret to Leahy's success had been not only quality but quantity. He wore down even the best opponents because the second-best team on the field usually was the Irish second team. Recall Jim Martin's sentiment that Notre Dame didn't beat Army in 1946 because Leahy uncharacteristically stuck with his starters for most of the game.

Playing so many players paid the immediate benefit of pounding a tired opponent into submission. It also provided an atypical amount of experience to the backups, who slid into the starting lineup in subsequent seasons with a minimal amount of adjustment.

When the university reduced Leahy's scholarships in 1947, however, the well of talent began to dry. By 1949, Leahy leaned on his starters. Judging by the number of awards they won, well he should have. End Leon Hart won not only the 1949 Heisman Trophy and the Maxwell Award, the two most prominent individual college football prizes, but AP Male Athlete of the Year, beating out professional stars such as National League MVP Jackie Robinson and golfer Sam Snead, who won the Masters and the PGA Championship. Halfback Emil Sitko won Back of the Year from the Washington Touchdown Club; United Press gave the same award to Williams. It helped that the core of leadership—Sitko, Martin, South Bend native Ernie Zalejski, end Ray Espenan, and others—were men in their mid-twenties, the last remaining war veterans.

But Leahy also leaned on them because he didn't have a lot of talent behind them. As a result, the team that reported to Leahy for spring practice included a total of twelve players with varsity experience. Williams and Jerry Groom, who played center/linebacker, were the only returning starters.

"I don't think Notre Dame ever had fewer athletes on the campus than we had in 1950," McBride said.

Shortly before spring practice began, Espenan, a senior who had been Hart's backup and a physical education major, demonstrated a backflip on a trampoline to a gymnastics class at Central High School. He didn't complete the flip, landing on his head and breaking his neck. "I'm paralyzed," he said to another teacher. "Don't let anybody touch me. Send for an ambulance and a padre." Espenan died a few days later. Leahy, on a yacht off the coast of south Florida taking a rare fishing vacation, could not get back to South Bend for the funeral. There is no comparison between a teammate's death and poor results on the football field. Maybe Espenan's death gave Leahy and his players a little bit of perspective later that year. But anyone who ever thought Notre Dame got more than its share of luck never considered the year 1950.

LATE IN THE SUMMER, LEAHY TRAVELED TO BOISE FOR A HIGH SCHOOL coaches' clinic. He predicted Army would win the national title, with North Carolina second and Kentucky and Oklahoma right behind the Tar Heels. As a prognosticator, Leahy did very well. Oklahoma won the national title, then lost to Kentucky in the Sugar Bowl. Army finished second, losing after the final poll to Navy in a major upset, 14–2. Leahy could be excused for including North Carolina, which finished 3-5-2; the Fighting Irish opened against the Tar Heels.

Three weeks before the season opener, Krause delivered his annual report on the state of Notre Dame athletics to Father Hesburgh. "There is no football coaching staff that is as well organized as ours is at the present time," Krause wrote. "We are rated No. 1 in this department. The quality of our athletes is comparable to any large University, even though we do not get the quantity in numbers that other institutions receive, but because of our excellent coaching we can compare the quality of our team with any institution in the Country."

Krause's report looked backward. Leahy, looking forward, didn't like what he saw.

"I'm convinced our winning streak is going to be broken," Leahy said. "Nineteen-fifty will test the loyalty of our alumni."

He allowed that Notre Dame had a talented first string. On the line, he said, "If injuries set in we'll be finished." Two linemen, right tackle Bob Toneff and left guard Paul Burns, suffered injuries in preseason practice. Sure enough, in the opener, Notre Dame had no running game to speak of. A touchdown pass in the last three minutes secured a 14–7 victory over North Carolina. The loss of talent, Allison Danzig wrote in *The New York Times*, "seems to have been too great for even the master to repair."

Leahy didn't try to mask his team's issues. "We will be just about even with just about everybody we play," he said. And still no one believed him. Five days later, Leahy, lunching with John Carmichael of the *Chicago Daily News*, told him that Purdue, the Irish's next opponent, would win easily.

"Cut out the bullshit, Frank," Carmichael said, "and get out the bottle."

The gods knew just how to set the tableau. On an overcast Saturday, the Boilermakers dominated the line of scrimmage from the opening whistle. Purdue, behind a wisp of a sophomore quarterback named Dale Samuels, scored three touchdowns in the first half as the Irish struggled to cross midfield. In the second half, Notre Dame scored two touchdowns to provide false hope for fans who couldn't make sense of what they were seeing. Just to complete the scene, a steady rain enveloped the stadium in the fourth quarter as Samuels threw a fourth touchdown to put the game away. Final score: Purdue 28, Notre Dame 14, and a thirty-nine-game unbeaten streak came to an ignominious end.

On the same day that the ascendant New York Yankees won the second of what would be five consecutive World Series, the Notre Dame Fighting Irish relinquished their hold on a similar form of domination, what Francis Wallace would describe as "the annual infallibility of the Irish as a symbol of permanence." Notre Dame had not lost a game since 1945. Leahy had not lost a game since 1943, when the freshmen on campus were eleven years old.

After suffering the sixth loss of his collegiate coaching career, Leahy walked into the equipment room for his postgame presser holding a cup of coffee. He found the writers speaking to each other in whispers.

"Gentlemen, we lost to a better team than we were today," Leahy said. "But if we had to lose I am glad it was to a time-honored foe like Purdue. That Purdue team was great. They didn't make any mistakes . . . offensively, they were superb."

Someone asked him about the ball bouncing Purdue's way. "We have no alibis," Leahy said. "We lost to a team that was better than ours."

And what does this mean for next week's trip to Tulane? "I haven't thought about that yet," Leahy said. "But one thing is certain—we'll show up."

He left the writers and walked slowly through the locker room, doling out reassurance to his stricken players that the sun would rise on Sunday. Outside, the players' fellow students—none of the undergrads had ever seen a loss—had been slow to leave the stadium. When they did, hundreds drifted to the area outside the Notre Dame locker room door. They stood in the rain, calling for their coach to come outside. One student climbed to the top of a tree to get a better look.

Leahy emerged from the locker room and, as the rain continued, began addressing the young people before him.

"Men, a lot of people will be watching how we take this adversity," Leahy said. "It's a real test of real men to lose like champions."

Leahy continued to talk, and the impact of his words stuck with sophomore Regis Philbin for the rest of his life. Philbin remembered thinking Leahy looked more haggard than he had ever seen him.

"He told us about defeat and how sometimes during our lives, we, too, would be defeated by something or someone," Philbin said. "We would lose out or take it in the chops and it would hurt—but we should use what happened on this day to remind us that a defeat can always come your way. He explained that what had occurred on the field that day should only make us stronger, make us want to win even more, make us understand that that's what life is all about. It was all about getting back up again.

"Then," Philbin said, "suddenly it didn't hurt so much." Of Leahy's talk, he wrote many years later, "I always thought it made me a better man."

On his drive home, Leahy, who didn't enjoy an abundance of self-confidence in the best of seasons, wondered what he had done wrong. If he was The Master, as the sportswriters referred to him, he should have figured out a solution to the lack of talent and experience. "The pain was indescribable," he recalled. "I wondered if, perhaps, I was simply a creation of my own recruiting. Oh, could it be that I simply was sitting on top of a situation where fine young players went to Notre Dame because it was Notre Dame and not because they respected me as a coach or because I was an especially good coach. I suffered much self-doubt that autumn."

Three days later, Father Hesburgh sent Leahy a typewritten letter thanking him for his impromptu speech to the students. "I think it is at moments like this when greatness is much more apparent than in the moments of great glory and victory," Father Hesburgh wrote, adding that now that the young team no longer had to carry the burden of the thirty-nine-game unbeaten streak, "I felt somehow that this year's team was being put in a very unfair position like that of a younger brother who is always being reminded of what his older brother did. We know that this year's team is not the greatest from the point of view of talent and experience, but I am sure that they will do very creditably with the powers they have." Hesburgh concluded with the notion that acting as a champion in defeat showed the true Notre Dame spirit and told Leahy, nine years his senior, to "keep up the good work." The following day, Leahy dictated a quick thank-you in return, adding in his own hand, "I dislike sounding gloomy—looks as tho [sic] we're destined to be defeated several times in 1950."

The Irish seesawed through the season, never winning more than two straight, never losing more than two straight. Leahy felt the weight of mediocrity on his shoulders, yet there seemed to be enough blame to spread around. In late October, after a 20–7 loss at Indiana dropped the Irish to 2-2, the number of students who attended Saturday Communion had fallen 25 percent. "The best way to wreck a season," the campus chaplain scolded in the Religious Bulletin, "is to prove you do not deserve a winning team."

The angst felt by the student body paled before that of their football coach. Leahy suffered more than he had in any season since 1942, the year he switched the Irish to the T formation and lost two games. He had not experienced mediocrity like this since 1928, his sophomore season playing for Rockne, when his excitement over getting onto the field as a backup tackle overcame any disappointment he felt over the Fighting Irish going 5-4.

More than two decades later, the whole country knew this was his team. He had tried to warn them. After a 14–14 tie at Iowa guaranteed that Notre Dame (4-3-1) would not finish with a losing record, Leahy told *New York Post* columnist Jimmy Cannon, "No one would believe me. I cried wolf too often, I guess. But when I said what type of club we had... no one would believe me."

At the end of even the best seasons, Leahy's health gave out. In this, his worst season, between the worry and the sleepless nights and the lack of success, Leahy's nerves were shot. Cannon, who came to South Bend to visit Leahy during Notre Dame's off week, was a brawler of a columnist. He reflected his upbringing, a poor, tough Irish kid from New York. When he grew up, college football seemed to take place in another universe. But he remembered the saloons handing out free drinks when Notre Dame beat Army. Cannon came straight at his topic. He didn't mince words. At times he walked right up to the line between writing and overwriting. Other times he sprinted across it. But the reader never had to wonder what Cannon thought.

He spent time with Leahy in his office and came away describing Leahy as "probably sport's hardest loser." Leahy gave him the testimony to back up that assessment.

"It hurts me a lot to lose," Leahy told him. "The headaches and the heartaches of this season... several times I thought I was going to black out. I don't know what causes this. Nerves, I guess. But several times I've been so weak I've had to call for smelling salts while the game was in progress. If I hadn't I'm sure I would have passed out."

And this:

"I hate to show up. I'm tired physically every Saturday morning. I sleep badly on Friday nights."

And this:

"If we have another year like this. If we have a third one...I think they might want to try it with someone else."

Cannon came away stunned by Leahy's demeanor.

"In the years when he was building his reputation, Leahy was a morose and apprehensive man," Cannon wrote. "There were times when I believed his grief was an act which delighted him. But never before have I known him to suspect his skill in these moods of gracious depression."

The simple fact remained that the Irish were undersized and young. Their inexperience could be measured by their record in their four games decided by fewer than seven points—one win, two losses, one tie. They gained 526 yards against No. 15 Michigan State but lost, 36–33, on a touchdown scored by the Spartans' Don McAuliffe, a Navy washout who wanted to attend Notre Dame so badly that after he left Annapolis, he paid his own way to South Bend and spent five days on campus. The university wouldn't accept him. In the season finale Notre Dame limited USC to 74 yards of total offense but gave up a kickoff return for a touchdown, had a punt blocked out of the end zone for a safety, and lost, 9–7. More to the point, the more experienced Trojans physically beat the Irish into submission, knocking six Irish players out of the game, including Williams at quarterback, John Petitbon at halfback, and Groom, the center and captain.

Leahy was not in Los Angeles to witness the season-ending loss. The university put out the word that he had contracted the flu. It would seem much more likely that it was a stress-related illness; either way, he was in no shape to travel across country. He invited his doctor and close friend, Nicholas Johns, and his wife, Doris, to come to the Leahy home on Saturday to listen to the radio broadcast of the game.

When his guests arrived, Leahy did not come downstairs to greet them. They ended up in the kitchen, chatting with Floss as she made lunch for everyone. At game time, Leahy came downstairs, and barely spoke. Early in the game, Johns recalled, Leahy got upset at an official's call. He stood, pointed his finger at the radio and began berating all the officials. "You sons of bitches! You bastards! You hate Notre Dame! You hate Notre Dame!" Leahy wheeled around, walked back upstairs and got into bed, where he listened by himself.

In the fourth quarter, Bob Houser of *The South Bend Tribune* stopped by, went upstairs to Leahy's room, and found the coach in bed, his English setter Peppy at his side. They listened together as a late field goal attempt to win the game fell short. As the game ended, Floss brought in Fred, by then fifteen months old, to try to distract her husband.

"We left behind a sad man," Houser wrote.

The week before the USC game, Leahy traveled to Los Angeles to scout the Trojans as they played crosstown rival UCLA. That same week *Los Angeles Examiner* columnist Vincent X. Flaherty wrote that Leahy would leave Notre Dame at the end of the season to become coach of the Los Angeles Rams. Team owner Dan Reeves shot the story down, and a few days after the season, Leahy released a column in his name saying that he would never leave Notre Dame for any coaching job. "I couldn't possibly leave Notre Dame with the won-lost record such as we compiled this last fall," Leahy said. "And, I am not about to do it."

After the season, Leahy underwent a physical performed by Dr. Stephen J. Donovan, who wrote him a letter on December 27 telling him that "no serious defects were discovered." Then Dr. Donovan began, "However," and started on a three-paragraph harangue that Leahy simply had to cut back on his schedule. The green light was no longer lit, the doctor said; the yellow light was flashing. Just to sledgehammer his point, he concluded, "I am enclosing a few obituary notes from this week's medical journal. I thought it might be a good idea to draw your attention to their ages." Dr. Donovan also sent a copy of the letter to Floss. The following week, Leahy wrote a letter to Father Hesburgh asking to be excused from speaking at the university's Marriage Institute, which he had done successfully the previous year.

Leahy and his assistants had a keen eye for talent, but they didn't have a perfect record. In the spring of 1951, two dozen prospects came to campus for what amounted to a tryout, which was against both NCAA and Notre Dame rules but also how programs conducted business. Among the prospects was a 137-pound quarterback from Louisville. Assistant coach Bernie Crimmins worked him out and liked him. Crimmins told the prospect, "God, you're so small . . . We're liable to be sued for manslaughter up here." Crimmins called a few Ivy League schools on the prospects' behalf, but grades were an issue. So John Unitas went home and enrolled at Louisville.

A bruising back from Wisconsin also came to visit that spring. He began chatting with a freshman player from Milwaukee named Neal Worden. The recruit liked Notre Dame, at least until Worden began describing campus life. "I told him there were no girls here," Worden said, "and that the studies and the football practices were really tough." So Alan Ameche stayed home and went to Wisconsin, where in 1954, his senior year, he won the Heisman Trophy.

Leahy and his assistants did take chances on undersized players, such as Coy McGee. In 1949, Bob McBride fell for a small but feisty lineman from Cleveland. However, the lineman suffered an epileptic seizure on the practice field, and Leahy refused to go any further with him. So Chuck Noll left and enrolled at Dayton, played seven years in the NFL, and won four Super Bowls as coach of the Pittsburgh Steelers.

The truth was, Leahy didn't have to recruit much. He didn't believe in the flattery and toadying that characterizes so much of modern recruiting, most likely because he didn't have to use it. Players often tried to recruit him. After the final game of the 1952 season, a defeat of USC, all the visiting recruits lined up to file past Leahy and shake his hand. A few of them later got to meet Leahy, including a senior quarterback from Louisville named Paul Hornung and his high school teammate, Sherrill Sipes.

"We were taken to a room where Leahy was sitting on a big chair, like some kind of king," Hornung said. "...I remember him looking at Sherrill and me and saying, 'You lads would look splendid in green.'

"And that was it, the only contact with him."

Kentucky coach Bear Bryant enlisted the governor of the state, Lawrence Wetherby, to help recruit Hornung and Sipes to play for the Wildcats. McBride went to Louisville and offered both of them a Notre Dame scholarship. They didn't accept. A Notre Dame bird dog convinced the pair to make one more visit to South Bend. They came during spring break, to a cold, empty campus. They agreed they weren't going to attend Notre Dame.

"But then," Hornung said, "we saw Leahy."

Flattery? No. Inspiration? Motivation? Absolutely.

"Lads, Our Lady needs you here," Leahy told them. "Lads like you belong in a Catholic college. You belong to Notre Dame. You should matriculate at the finest university in the world. If you're going to play professional football, there's a back door and a there's a front door. You'll be nationally recognized.

"Paul, not only will you get a good education here, but I think I can make you the greatest football player in the country."

Sipes asked Leahy, "Where do we sign?"

"We don't sign," Leahy said. "We shake hands."

Leahy did have a hole card—Hornung's mother.

"If I hadn't picked Notre Dame," Hornung said, "I think it would have broken her heart."

And yet the freshmen whom Leahy did recruit for the fall semester in 1951 injected life into the program. For one thing, because of the manpower demands of the Korean War, the NCAA reinstituted freshmen eligibility for the 1951 season. For another, Leahy, in an excellent example of "working the officials," got an increase in scholarships from eighteen to twenty-one.

When Father Hesburgh learned that Leahy had received commitments from twenty-one recruits, he told Leahy to cut three. Leahy lobbied for time, explaining that there was no way that all twenty-one recruits actually would decide to come to Notre Dame. The administration agreed to let nature take its course—and all twenty-one recruits enrolled at Notre Dame.* To illustrate the talent dearth, twelve of them earned monograms that fall. They had to—fully forty-five of the seventy-five players on the roster were sophomores or freshmen. Leahy joked that season that on one road trip he conducted a luggage check of the suitcases of his freshmen and found a total of one razor.

It is fair to say that with this young a team, Leahy's prowess made a big difference. The Irish finished 7-2-1, stealing a tie from Iowa and a victory from USC. Leahy installed the split T, a T-formation variation that Bud Wilkinson used to drive Oklahoma to the national championship the previous season. Unlike the move to the T nine seasons earlier, Leahy heard little objection from the Notre Dame fan base. This time, he wasn't despoiling Rockne's memory, he was just trying to escape mediocrity. The split T favored a quarterback who could run and throw on the run, and Leahy had discovered those skills in a freshman named Ralph Guglielmi.

Leahy worried about the opener against Indiana, a team that had defeated Notre Dame 20–7 the previous year. He needed his young team to gain confidence quickly. Leahy prepared his team for the Hoosiers as if they were the NFL Champion Cleveland Browns, and the Irish responded with a 48–6 rout. Two weeks later, the Irish lost at home to SMU by the same 27–20 score that the Irish had beaten the Mustangs two seasons earlier. The Irish took a 5-1 record and a No. 11 ranking into East Lansing to play unbeaten, No. 5 Michigan State, a team that showed Notre Dame just how inexperienced it was. The Spartans delivered the worst beating that Leahy ever suffered, a 35–0 rout so decisive that Red Smith wrote "the score might as well have

* Hesburgh recalled in his memoir that Leahy signed forty-one players instead of thirty, and that he insisted that Leahy sign only nineteen the following year. I would think McBride's memory more accurate than the administrator's.

been 70–0." Michigan State ran 88 yards for a touchdown on its first play from scrimmage and the young Irish players never recovered.

Leahy poured on the compliments to Michigan State head coach Biggie Munn and his team. "Their boys didn't make a mistake and when we made any, they were quick to pounce on them," Leahy told the writers. "... [I]t was obvious from the start that we had little hope against such a keyed-up, perfectly poised team."

Shirley Povich praised Leahy in *The Washington Post* for exemplifying a brand of sportsmanship "all too rare in college football." Povich did not witness Leahy at halftime, trailing 21–0, when the coach demonstrated little perfect poise or any other kind. In a frenzy, Leahy called his players "gutless" and all but accused them of throwing the game. When the team returned home, Leahy remained so traumatized that on Sunday morning, he refused to get out of bed. Floss called Father Hesburgh, who drove out to Leahy's home in Michigan City, counseled the coach, and pretty much dragged him out of bed to get him going again.

As the season progressed, however, Leahy began to get a sense of the vast potential his team possessed. The week after the Michigan State debacle, in the hotel before the game at North Carolina, Leahy asked Guglielmi, the freshman quarterback, how he felt. "Naturally, I told him I was feeling fine. Then he told me I was going to start the next day," Guglielmi said more than forty years later. "I was pretty nervous, but our captain, Jim Mutscheller, came up to me and said, 'Don't worry about a thing. Whatever you call, we'll make it work.'" The young players had gumption. Guglielmi toughed out a 12–7 victory. In the season-ending game at USC, Guglielmi came off the bench to lead the Irish to three touchdowns and a 19–12 victory. Between those two games, Notre Dame played its final home game against Iowa. With the Hawkeyes leading 20–13 late in the fourth quarter, Leahy signaled for sophomore Johnny Lattner to punt. Mutscheller overruled Leahy in the huddle and instructed Lattner to pass the ball to him instead. Lattner, who had never thrown a collegiate pass, obeyed his captain instead of his coach and wobbled the ball to Mutscheller, who had to come back toward the line to catch it but still muscled his way to a first down. The Irish continued downfield with the help of a pass interference call on the Hawkeyes and, with fifty-five seconds to play, Lattner ran 1 yard to score a touchdown and salvage a tie.

"Coach didn't say much," Lattner said. "He couldn't."

Seven wins, three more than the previous season, didn't get the praise it should have, although the AP voters did not recognize it by including the Irish in the final poll.

In the summer of 1952, Father Cavanaugh decided to retire as an administrator, and Father Hesburgh, thirty-five years old, replaced him as president. Cavanaugh had done a great deal to modernize the university, but he understood how much work remained. The university budget in 1952—not the football program but the entire university—came in slightly under $10 million. Hesburgh possessed the vision and the energy to transform Notre Dame into a leading academic institution.

"He is a distinctive person, who believed right through his life, that he came to contribute to the situation," said Father Wilson D. Miscamble, a retired Notre Dame professor and author of *American Priest*, a 2019 biography of Hesburgh. "Whether it was world hunger, the arms race, civil rights, he could bring something to it. So, it's not just his vision for Notre Dame. Enormous self-confidence. There's no other word for it. He just believed that he could do it. But in this early stage he does have his vision for Notre Dame as a great Catholic university in his mind and getting football in the right balance is part of the vision."

Over three years, Hesburgh and Leahy had developed a working relationship. They sometimes took walks around the lake on campus to discuss whatever issues needed discussing. But Hesburgh invested so much into his determination to put academics before football that his ego clouded his judgment.

A decade after his death, Hesburgh is all but canonized on the Notre Dame campus. Father Miscamble's biography is notable for seeing Hesburgh as a great man, but a man, not a saint. An incident shortly after Hesburgh became president illustrates the difference.

Less than two weeks before the opener at Penn, General Dwight D. Eisenhower, the Republican nominee for president, and his wife, Mamie, made a campaign stop in South Bend, one of thirteen that day on the Eisenhower Special train. Eisenhower and Leahy's friendship went back some years. Eisenhower's motorcade made two stops on campus. About 2,500 people attended the general's rally in front of the administration building, where Father Murphy, the university vice president, greeted him. Father Hesburgh had left town to attend the funeral of a university trustee in Cincinnati, a hiccup in the priest's schedule that had unfortunate ramifications for his head coach. Eisenhower directed his remarks toward the newly arrived freshman class. He also discussed Notre Dame's 35–13 victory over his Army team in 1913, the game that put Irish football on the national map. Eisenhower said that based on that game he thought Notre Dame men stood fourteen feet tall and weighed 420 pounds. In truth, as he said to Leahy later, he sat on the bench for that game, having suffered what amounted to a career-ending knee injury.

The motorcade moved on to the Rockne Memorial Building, where Leahy appeared with Eisenhower and Mamie. The candidate and the football coach shook hands and chatted, which proved to be catnip for the photographers. The impression that the photograph left was that Eisenhower met with the most prominent man at Notre Dame—the football coach. That did not sit well with the new president, this young man on a mission, this priest determined to take Notre Dame to the heights of academe.

Fred Leahy, Frank's son, said that through the years he had been told by a number of people that "I guess it just really, really pissed Hesburgh off... It was just Dad was too big for Notre Dame at the time."

Father Miscamble said that the impression Eisenhower's meeting with Leahy made "would only confirm for Father Ted—again, this is my speculation—who's the big man on campus? It's Frank Leahy, not Father Hesburgh," Father Miscamble said. "Father Hesburgh wanted it to be Father Hesburgh, and then the football coach." Six weeks later, Senator Adlai Stevenson, the Democratic presidential candidate, came to campus and made sure to pose for a photo with Leahy. This time, Hesburgh posed with the candidate, too.

The Irish finished with the same 7-2-1 record in 1952 as the year before, which proves how misleading a record can be. Notre Dame defeated the champions of four major conferences (Texas, Oklahoma, Purdue, USC). One of the losses came at the hands of national champion Michigan State (which didn't join the Big Ten in football until the following season), the other to Pittsburgh. Johnny Lujack, who retired from the NFL and came back to Notre Dame as an assistant to Leahy, recalled how, on the eve of the Pitt game, Callahan came in to inform the coaches of the death of another coach's father. "Well, Charles," Leahy said, "at least that man won't have to undergo the humiliation of being defeated by Pittsburgh tomorrow."

The team revolved around the quarterback play of Guglielmi and the do-it-all play of Lattner, one of the best football players that Leahy ever coached. The junior halfback, big (six foot one, 190) for his day, wasn't particularly fast. But he could run, catch, block, and he understood the game so well that he instinctively knew where to be and the fastest route to get there. Two-platoon football—separate units playing offense and defense—had been made legal in the wake of the war, yet Leahy started Lattner on offense and defense. He punted, too.

As the opener at Penn neared, Leahy ratcheted up his woe is-me patter. Even his own spokesman, Callahan, said, "If you have water wings, prepare to inflate them now. Here comes our tear-stained leader." Red Smith called it "the art of crying hunger with a standing rib roast under each arm."

Perhaps Leahy realized he needed a distraction. On the night before the No. 10 Irish played the No. 12 Quakers,* Leahy visited the New York Yankees in their locker room at the Philadelphia A's Shibe Park. They needed one victory to clinch their third consecutive American League pennant. Center fielder Mickey Mantle, an Oklahoma native and a diehard Sooner fan—had he chosen to accept Bud Wilkinson's scholarship offer, he would have been a senior and likely starting in the Oklahoma backfield—puffed out his chest about the Sooners in Leahy's presence.

"Huh," Mantle said to Red Smith, "Oklahoma would flog the ears off Notre Dame this season."

This being American journalism circa 1952, odds are Mantle did not say "flog the ears."

"Why don't you tell him so?" Smith replied.

"You think I won't?" Mantle said. He got up and marched into the next room to confront Leahy, whereupon he turned into a polite young man.

"Mr. Leahy," Mantle said. "How about Oklahoma?"

Leahy smiled and gave Mantle his best woe-is-us smile. The Sooners, who had replaced the Irish as the most powerful program in the sport, would come to Notre Dame Stadium in early November.

"Why, Mickey, I think Oklahoma may have the finest team in the nation," Leahy said. "I know they're far out of our class."

Mantle melted right into the palm of Leahy's hand. He and his teammates spent an hour talking college football with their guest, then went out and won the pennant. Mantle hit his twenty-third homer, and the Yanks scored three runs in the eleventh inning to beat the A's, 5–2.

The next day, Notre Dame and Penn finished regulation tied, 7–7, only there would be no extra innings. A late fumble killed the Irish's last chance to win the game. After the game, Leahy retreated to his

* Before the Ivy League formed in 1953, its schools competed at the highest level of the game.

room at the Warwick Hotel, locked the door, and refused to speak with anyone.

For most of his career at Notre Dame, Leahy didn't need to utilize any sort of tactical acumen for the Irish to win. He had better players, so much better that they didn't usually need the entire sixty minutes afforded them to show it. After the scholarship reductions, however, Leahy had no such luxury. He had to engage his entire coaching toolbox—tactics, motivation, preparation—to get the victories that defined his life. The 1952 season may have been the best demonstration of Leahy's ability with those tools.

In the second week of the season, Notre Dame played at Texas. The forecast for the game was ninety degrees and sunny. Leahy purposely waited to fly into Austin until late Friday night, where they stayed at the Commodore Perry Hotel downtown, mainly because the hotel had air-conditioning. Upon arrival, Leahy issued each of the thirty-seven players on the travel roster a pith helmet, the sun hats made famous by the British Army, to wear on the sideline.

Texas athletic director D. X. Bible, the former Longhorn head coach, was known throughout the game for being a gentleman. Given that the game would be played early in the year, in all that heat, Leahy asked if it would be all right if the Irish shared the shady sideline of Memorial Stadium with the Longhorns. Bible readily agreed. And could they be on the left side? Bible agreed to that, too.

In the first half, Texas dominated the line of scrimmage, but the Longhorns lost two fumbles inside the Notre Dame 15. A third trip stalled at the Irish 3; Texas kicked a field goal and went into halftime leading, 3–0. Notre Dame had not crossed its own 40-yard line. The Irish had gained 55 yards of total offense and made two first downs. Leahy made his displeasure known at the half. He adjusted the offensive line and went to quicker-developing runs. As for an inspirational pep talk, he said exactly seventeen words.

"You're not playing like Notre Dame men," Leahy said. "Get out there now and play like Notre Dame men."

The Irish took the second-half kickoff and ground out a 74-yard drive for a touchdown to take the lead. Midway through the quarter, as the sun began to sink behind the press box, the Irish, to the left of the Longhorns, stood in the shade. The home team continued to bake in the sun. In the fourth quarter, Texas fumbled on its own 5-yard line, which Notre Dame converted into a touchdown on the next snap.

Late in the game, Notre Dame's 14–3 lead safe, Texas head coach Ed Price had taken all he could take. He looked down to Leahy and yelled, "Anything else we can do for you, Leahy? How about a fan? Or a milkshake? Or a cold beer?"

The visitors did not wilt in the sun. The home team did. Texas committed five turnovers and made one first down in the second half. "I didn't want the lads looking into the sun more than was necessary," Leahy said.

After a narrow loss to Pitt, Notre Dame came back on the road and stunned No. 9 Purdue, 26–14, a game that is famous not because the Irish snapped the Boilermakers' seven-game unbeaten streak dating to the previous season, but because Notre Dame won despite five fumbles by Lattner. The game stories didn't mention Lattner's fumbles, probably because the teams combined for 21 of them, 11 by Purdue. But it became legendary because of Leahy's reaction to Lattner's sacrilege.

The junior, mortified by his performance, didn't go back to South Bend on the team bus. He got permission to go home to Chicago with his brother. When the team met Monday afternoon, Lattner discovered all he had done was delay the inevitable.

"Oh, my goodness gracious," Leahy said to the team. "Last Saturday against the enemy, lads, there was a young man who disgraced his teammates. He disgraced the coaching staff here at Notre Dame by his five fumbles." Leahy didn't stop there. He spent untold minutes demonstrating handoffs, how the quarterback should give the ball to the halfbacks. Leahy finally brought the meeting to a close—for everyone but Lattner.

"Oh, Mr. Lattner. I'd like to have a little chat with you, if you wouldn't mind."

"Sure, Coach."

"What in the world happened to you last Saturday, John? Why, a boy of your caliber. Why would he fumble five times?"

"Coach, I don't really know. I really don't have any reason for it."

"I was wondering. Do you have any type of girl problems back in Chicago that would cause you to fumble five times?"

"No, Coach. I have no girl problems."

"I understand, John, back in Chicago, you and your dad used to go to the horse races. Did you ever bet on a horse?"

"Sure, I did when I had the money, Coach."

"Did you have any money bet with the bookies back in Chicago?"

Leahy finally relented, but not without handing Lattner a football and telling him that if anyone saw him without that football anywhere on campus that week, he would lose his scholarship.

"Coach made sure that I made at least one visit to Lattner's room to be sure he had the ball in his arm," McBride said.

One of his teammates very helpfully attached a handle to the ball. On the first play of the next game, Lattner took a handoff—and fumbled. But he recovered it, and Notre Dame drove down the field for a touchdown en route to a 34–14 rout of North Carolina.

A month later, the Irish had a 5-1-1 record and a No. 10 ranking as they prepared for No. 4 Oklahoma to come to Notre Dame Stadium for the first time. Notre Dame had agreed to play a home-and-home with Oklahoma because Krause believed that Wilkinson, a Minnesota native and a former Golden Gopher player, would return to his alma mater as head coach (he didn't). Krause saw a good relationship with Wilkinson as a way, someday, to get Minnesota back on the Notre Dame schedule (not yet).

Oklahoma at Notre Dame, ballyhooed as the game of the year and televised nationally to 30 million viewers by NBC, lived up to the expectation. On the day before the game, Grantland Rice asked Leahy about Lattner, the team's best player according to anyone who saw Notre Dame play, with the notable exception of Leahy, who hadn't quite forgiven the halfback.

"John Lattner is a fine boy," Leahy told Rice. "He is a conscientious student. John Lattner observes his religion. He respects and helps his parents. He is active in student affairs and a credit to Notre Dame. But, unfortunately, Granny, John Lattner is not a football player."

Lattner was famous for not having an ego, so Leahy didn't downplay his talent to trim his ego. Perhaps he knew that Lattner possessed an enormous desire to prove himself. Against the Sooners, Lattner rushed 24 times for 98 yards. He averaged 38 yards a punt. And he led the two-touchdown underdog Irish to a 27–21 upset.

Oklahoma had been running the split-T long before Leahy adopted it. The Sooners gave a recital of the offense at Notre Dame Stadium. Billy Vessels rushed for 195 yards, a record by an Irish opponent that stood for more than twenty years. He rushed for touchdowns of 62 and 46 yards, caught a 28-yard touchdown pass, and made an interception. In other words, he pretty much clinched the 1952 Heisman Trophy.

The offense, Lattner said, "was all new to Leahy and none of us really understood it. I think he was surprised that we did as well as we did. When we played Oklahoma in '52, we learned more about the split-T in one afternoon than we did in all of '51."

Three times Oklahoma scored, and three times Notre Dame came back and tied the game. After the third touchdown tied the game 21–21 midway through the fourth quarter, hundreds of Irish fans outside the stadium marched in a circle saying the rosary in support of their team. Sooner returner Larry Griggs gathered in the kickoff and sprinted upfield. Irish fullback Dan Shannon came downfield just as fast, and at 190 pounds and with a bigger head of steam (he had been running 40 yards), collided with Griggs with such force that both players lost consciousness. Griggs, however, also lost the ball, Notre Dame recovered at the Oklahoma 19 and went on to score what proved to be the winning touchdown.

No one argued that the play was dirty. In fact, in subsequent years, Wilkinson paid tribute to the play by referring to tackling drills as "Shannonizing." But the play surely turned the game in Notre Dame's favor. After the game, the fans remained in the stands for nearly half an hour, unwilling to leave behind the magic they witnessed.

Wilkinson won three national championships at Oklahoma. He would call the 1952 team, which finished second to Michigan State, his best. Leahy, after he retired, called the Sooners the best team he ever coached against and that upset "my greatest coaching thrill." And he beat them with a bunch of sophomores.

That said, the Sooners didn't go home without a complaint. When Oklahoma defensive lineman Ed Rowland got injured, his departure allowed the Notre Dame blockers to pay more attention to All-American guard J. D. Roberts. Oklahoma claimed that Notre Dame guard Manil Mavraides began hitting Roberts after the whistle, trying to provoke him. Something provoked Roberts: He took a swing at Mavraides and got ejected. That left a lot easier path for Lattner's runs up the middle.*

Oklahoma also claimed that a late offensive shift by Notre Dame near the Oklahoma goal line goaded the Sooners into jumping offside. Rather than launch into their blocks at the sound of Guglielmi's voice, the Irish linemen moved a step to one side. Purdue had made the same claim that the Irish had used what became known as the "sucker shift," and three weeks after the Oklahoma game, USC would claim that the Irish used it in their 9–0 victory over the Trojans as well. USC head coach Jess Hill said, "That shift is an evasion of the spirit of the rule. I thought it was definitely uncalled for."

Leahy said he used the shift near the goal line to try to make easier a 2-on-1 block on a defensive lineman. Baloney, of course. Years later, Guglielmi, the Irish quarterback, said that his line worked very hard to

* Roberts, from Dallas, wanted to attend Notre Dame, and Leahy wanted to sign him. But Roberts wanted his brother to come to school with him. Notre Dame said no to that. The Roberts brothers enrolled at Oklahoma.

launch into their blocks at the sound of his voice. "We were quick off the ball and everyone who played us knew it. So when we used the shift they jumped."

He claimed that Pitt (a 22–19 winner) and Iowa (a 27–0 loser) both had used the same tactic against his team. Yet Notre Dame, or more to the point, Leahy, bore the brunt of social opprobrium for living between the lines of the NCAA Football Rulebook.

Dick Hyland wrote in the *Los Angeles Times* that you couldn't blame Leahy for using the same tactics that had been used against Notre Dame. But Hyland went ahead and blamed him anyway. "Frank Leahy was wrong, in my judgment, teaching that kind of football," Hyland wrote. "The officials, however, were much worse. They let him get away with it." The following week Leahy responded, telling Red Smith that there would be no complaint forthcoming from Notre Dame about the shift being used against the Irish. "There was nothing wrong in it and I felt it was very sound football," Leahy said.

The season ended with Notre Dame third in the nation, despite that 7-2-1 record. Notre Dame fans were overjoyed with Leahy's development of the young team. With so many stars returning, led by Lattner, the Heisman runner-up and winner of the Maxwell Trophy, the drumbeat for 1953 began. Leahy's health again failed to withstand the stresses of the season. He did not make the trip to Iowa for the next-to-last game of the season, the school again announcing it as the flu. Francis Wallace, the writer and Notre Dame grad, said that in Leahy's tenth season at the school, the coach's ability to control himself on the sideline had begun to slip. Nail-biting, yelling to the field, accosting his players had become part of Leahy's repertoire. Quarterback Tom Carey remembered Leahy telling him to keep the ball on the ground, but Carey threw a pass anyway, and the Irish scored a touchdown. He felt good as he came to the sideline right until the moment Leahy swatted him in the back.

"You're a disgrace! You're a disgrace to those beautiful nuns who taught you! You're a disgrace to the Blessed Mother!" Leahy shouted.

"He didn't even care we scored a touchdown," Carey said. "It was all about me disobeying him."

"The crowds had gradually become aware of his sideline reactions," Wallace wrote. None of this was written in real time. But Wallace, in hindsight, saw how fragile the Notre Dame head coach had become. After the season, Leahy sought treatment for what he later called "nervous exhaustion." That treatment entailed doctors ordering him to relax during the offseason. But there was always so much to do.

In March 1953, Leahy hired his former halfback, twenty-four-year-old Terry Brennan, to coach the Irish freshmen. That sounds young—Brennan wouldn't graduate from DePaul University Law School until June—but Brennan had never been young. He started for Notre Dame in 1945 as a seventeen-year-old freshman, and when all those men came back from the war the following season, Brennan didn't relinquish his job.

Brennan had been taking night classes at DePaul. During the day, Brennan coached Mount Carmel High, a Catholic school, to an unprecedented three consecutive Chicago city championships. To say that his success caught the eye of President Hesburgh wouldn't quite be accurate; Hesburgh never lost sight of Brennan after he graduated in 1950. Hesburgh had taught Brennan in a religion class. He came away more impressed with Brennan's intellect and classroom presence than any football player he had taught at Notre Dame. Hesburgh pushed for Leahy to hire Brennan, and he pushed Brennan to take the job.

"I'm not too smart, but when the president of a university goes out of his way to visit you, it must mean something," Brennan wrote in his memoir. "He was sincere, but there was something I didn't know then. He had a hidden agenda."

CHAPTER SIXTEEN

CRACKING FAST

PRACTICE FOR THE 1953 SEASON AT NOTRE DAME BEGAN WITH A renewed sense of optimism, which had less to do with the returning talent that Leahy had at his disposal than with the changing rules of the sport. A philosophical debate over the future of the game developed. Should college football be played by eleven men playing offense and defense—one platoon in the shorthand of the sport—or twenty-two men, eleven playing offense and eleven playing defense—two-platoon?

College football had been a one-platoon game for most of its history, the idea best captured by the saying that players should know how to block and tackle, not block *or* tackle. With the passage of a peacetime military draft in 1940, college football suddenly had a manpower shortage. The following year, the NCAA Football Rules Committee relaxed its substitution rules so that coaches could utilize the skills of every player on their diminished rosters. After the war, with so many men pouring onto college campuses, playing two-platoon football provided more opportunities to put more players on the field.

Two-platoon football made for a more explosive game. From 1940 to 1952, the average scoring in the game jumped nearly 38 percent; the average passing yardage, 43 percent. But the old guard viewed these changes as temporary accommodations. Older coaches managed to get themselves appointed to the NCAA Football Rules Committee, and in 1953 the committee voted unanimously to abandon what the most vocal among them, the recently retired General Robert R. Neyland of Tennessee, called "chickenshit" football.

The vote changed more than the rule; it changed the game. It made depth less important, and the athletic talent of a team's best players more important. Given that Notre Dame fell from its heights because of the scholarship limits imposed by Father Cavanaugh several years earlier—Notre Dame would have only forty-seven scholarship players in the 1953 season—the change to one platoon provided a boost to Leahy.

Leahy campaigned against the change. He believed the allowance of twenty days of spring practice insufficient to teach his offensive players how to play defense and vice versa. That didn't apply to the whole roster. Lattner made All-American and won the Maxwell Award while playing both sides of the ball in 1952.

"He made mistakes," Leahy said of Lattner, "oooooh, but how he hated to make them twice."

The shrewdest assessment of Lattner's talent came from an unexpected scout. On the second day of practice, Floss Leahy fell as she ran up the stairs at the house and broke her leg. When she told her husband, she said, "Frank, it could be a lot worse."

"What do you mean by that, Floss?"

"Frank," she said, "suppose it had been Lattner?"

He played offense, defense, special teams, and big brother to the freshman Hornung, who made it quickly clear that he could have contributed to the Irish that season if freshman eligibility had not been rescinded. One week, Hornung ran the scout team offense so well in the first half of a midweek scrimmage that Leahy congratulated him, then told the starting defense he didn't want to see Hornung standing by day's end. Perhaps Hornung stood out among the freshmen not only because of his own talent, but because of the lack of talent among his classmates. Brennan, the freshman coach, described his team as "woefully weak in talent and numbers."

Leahy didn't have a roster of Lattners, but he had other veteran stars—Guglielmi, Worden, and at left tackle after two seasons at offensive guard, Frank Varrichione. He fit the stereotype of the feeder system of Catholic boys, first- and second-generation Americans, who made their way to South Bend to play football. He came from Natick, Massachusetts, the youngest of ten children of Italian immigrants, and Leahy signed him out of St. Thomas Aquinas Prep in Rochester, New York, one more parochial school that sent a boy to play for Leahy, to play for Our Lady, to perpetuate the idea of the American melting pot.

Stereotypes aside, the fact is that Notre Dame never applied a religious requirement to its locker room. In the famous 18–13 come-from-behind victory at Ohio State in 1935, it was often remarked that a Catholic centered the ball, a Protestant threw the winning last-second touchdown pass, and a Jew caught it. Rockne made sure to publicize his open-door policy. A quarter-century later, the university did not publicize how many Catholics suited up on the football team and discouraged any such reporting. When *Time* magazine sent a correspondent to Notre Dame early in the 1953 season to write a cover story on Lattner, he sent a file back reporting that ten to twelve Irish players—about 20 percent of the team—were not Catholic (that correspondent, Jim Murray, eventually landed at the *Los Angeles Times*, where he became one of the best-known, best-loved sports columnists of the second half of the twentieth century).

It had been four years since the Fighting Irish had met the high standard of success that Leahy established during the 1940s. Yet the popularity of Notre Dame football remained high. The power and allure of the brand—if people had spoken that way seven decades ago—could be measured by the 115 radio stations that made up the so-called Irish Network and the thirteen movie theaters that preempted showing of a Saturday afternoon feature to instead take the television feed of a Notre Dame game. As many as eighty-one newspapers and wire services covered one game at Notre Dame Stadium that season.

The product heard, seen, and written about that fall would meet Leahy's high standard.

After three seasons in which the Irish lost eight games—keep in mind that in his thirteen-season coaching career, Leahy lost thirteen games—Notre Dame stood poised on the threshold of reclaiming greatness. That would be wonderful for the Irish fans, the subway alumni responsible for making Notre Dame into the only college football team with a national fan base. But as Leahy embarked on the 1953 season, whatever emotional dams that Leahy had constructed to hold back the pressure began to crumble.

"All jobs have tensions," Leahy said. "But coaching eats out a man's insides. At Notre Dame, the pressure is the worst. Not from within the school. My bosses were always telling me not to worry if we lost some games. But Notre Dame's millions of followers expect us to win. Our football tradition was built on victory under Knute Rockne, the greatest coach who ever lived. I felt myself, I should try to maintain that tradition.

"Anyhow, I hate to lose," Leahy said. "Always did and always will."

That hate, as he described it, fueled his success. But it ate up his insides. In retrospect, it seems clear that Leahy demanded more of himself than millions of Irish fans around the country would ever expect. He would not allow himself to fail, and when he did, in the form of an Irish loss, he would collapse from within. Years later, Lattner would look back on 1953, his senior season in which he won the Heisman Trophy, and say of his forty-five-year-old coach, "I thought he was a lot older." Frank Graham, the *New York Journal-American* columnist and one of the most well-respected press box voices of the day, wrote that as Leahy fell ill, he "couldn't" recuperate long enough to make himself better.

"If he thought of it at all," Graham wrote, "he probably hoped that if he kept on working and kept quiet, the pain would go away."

Leahy rarely stopped to eat. Sleep came fitfully if it came at all. He had too many what-ifs to answer, too many scenarios to consider.

Notre Dame began the season ranked atop the Associated Press poll, then proved the wisdom of the voters by winning the opener at No. 6 Oklahoma. Leahy and Sooners coach Bud Wilkinson appeared on the cover of the game program. The photo appeared to represent two generations of coaches, even though Wilkinson was only eight years younger. Both men wore gray suits with white pocket kerchiefs. Leahy, graying at the temples, gazed into the distance, while standing to his left, Wilkinson, blond and handsome, gazed at Leahy.

The Irish won, 28–21, even though the Sooners limited Lattner to 22 yards on 13 carries. They didn't limit his tackling, though. Late in the game, Lattner split two blockers to take down end Carl Allison on what appeared to be a breakaway screen pass. The Sooners would not lose again until 1957. A week later, the Irish went on the road and overran Purdue, 37–7, gaining 307 yards on the ground. Leahy, who distrusted success almost as much as he feared failure, groused, "I did not see a running back out there all afternoon."

"Don't know what game you were watching, Frank," the writer Tim Cohane replied. "I saw a hell of a lot of them. Now I know you're going undefeated. You're agonizing again and you look just terrible. Those are both good signs for Notre Dame."

That night, during a celebratory reception at his home, Leahy felt pains in his chest and lower back and quietly slipped upstairs. He didn't want to break up the party.

The next difficult opponent loomed two weeks later. When Michigan State, which had played Notre Dame the previous five seasons, needed the schedule slot for its first season in the Big Ten, Leahy made a deal for a home-and-home with Georgia Tech. The good news was that Michigan State had won the 1952 national championship. The bad news was that Georgia Tech had finished second to the Spartans and brought to Notre Dame Stadium a No. 4 ranking, a 4-0-1 record, and a thirty-one-game unbeaten streak that dated to the 1950 season. Put another way, no player on the Yellow Jacket roster had ever lost a game. And yet the oddsmakers established the Irish as seven-point favorites.

The local hotels sold out early in the summer. The last game ticket sold a month or so later. On game weekend, the New York Central added special trains from as far away as Buffalo. The Grand Trunk Railroad did the same from St. Louis, Chicago, and Atlanta. Georgia Tech had sold its allotment of 3,500 tickets. There would be one section of Notre Dame Stadium awash in Confederate flags, a rediscovered token of Southern pride in the face of the burgeoning civil rights movement.

On the day before the game, Yellow Jackets head coach Bobby Dodd stopped by Leahy's office and found the head coach with McBride. It was not merely a social visit. Dodd wanted to discuss an Irish return visit to Atlanta the following year. The two Black players on the Notre Dame roster, guard Wayne Edmonds and halfback Dick Washington, could not play at Grant Field on the Tech campus. They couldn't even suit up and remain on the sideline.

It wasn't because he or Georgia Tech had an objection, Dodd explained, "but we really couldn't guarantee their safety." Oh, sure.

Thirteen years after Lou Montgomery had to watch his Boston College teammates play the Sugar Bowl from the press box, Leahy reacted differently. Maybe he was older. Maybe he and Notre Dame were more established than he and Boston College had been in 1940. Leahy didn't accept Georgia Tech's rules. He and Dodd agreed that the players deserved to be with the Notre Dame team. And the Irish did not play at Georgia Tech until 1967.

Leahy lightened the team's practice load during Georgia Tech week, eliminating live scrimmaging and instead working on situational football. He didn't frame it that way to the players. Leahy touted the Yellow Jacket defense to Guglielmi, his quarterback. Georgia Tech hadn't allowed a touchdown pass in twenty-two games. "There's no use in practicing this week, Ralph. They're just too good," Leahy said.

"He made me want to prove that I could pass against Georgia Tech," Guglielmi remembered nearly four decades later.

Oddly enough, Leahy mimicked the week-in, week-out strategy of Dodd, a master strategist and motivator who bucked the conventional wisdom that demanded that players pay a physical price on the practice field. Dodd preferred to keep his players fresh. He coached as a unicorn; Bear Bryant said he didn't want to coach against Dodd, he wanted to coach against the guy who tried to imitate him. But it worked for Dodd. He coached at Georgia Tech for twenty-two seasons. He won 165 games.

Leahy didn't coach like Dodd very often. But he did have a stratagem for Georgia Tech. The week before, while preparing for Pittsburgh, the coaching staff had discovered a defensive wrinkle, lining up one lineman behind another to disguise which one would cover which gap. The Panthers gained only 3 yards in the second half of the Irish's 23–14 victory. The defensive "I formation" would come in handy on Saturday.

Leahy saw that his team needed rest that week, but he didn't afford himself the same consideration. Film of the team's practice that week show the collar of his white dress shirt loose, his face thin, his bow tie askew. On Friday night, Leahy chose not to stay in the campus firehouse he called home during the season. He didn't want to drive home the thirty-five miles to Long Beach, either. An intestinal virus had begun traversing through the Leahy children, a classic hazard of a houseful of kids. Instead, Leahy stayed at the South Bend home of a close friend, Julius Tucker. "I knew the strain Frank was under," Tucker would say. He implored Leahy to take something to help him sleep the night before such an important game. The following week, when Tucker visited Leahy at St. Joseph's Hospital, Leahy said, "I should have taken your advice about the sleeping pills. I didn't get to sleep until seven thirty in the morning and I was up at eight."

The sunny, mid-fifties weather boded well for the Southern visitors. Notre Dame, following its custom of dedicating each game to a different saint, chose the Queen of the Holy Rosary for Georgia Tech. Before the game ended, it looked as if the rosary prayers would be needed.

The New York Times described "an overflow crowd of 58,254" in Notre Dame Stadium, gathered on the twenty-first birthday of Lattner, their team's star. Drawn, sleepless, and in pain, Leahy put on his suit, tie, and overcoat and began to coach the game. The Irish caught a break when the Yellow Jacket starting quarterback Pepper Rodgers got injured on the opening kickoff. Behind Rodgers was a freshman, Wade Mitchell, thrown into action at one of the toughest stadiums in the game. Notre Dame edged out to a 7–0 lead.

In the second quarter, Leahy began to falter. He felt exhausted, went to the bench, sat down, and gasped for breath. He felt a sharp pain in his chest. "I thought I was dying," Leahy would say later. Of course, he refused to leave the sideline. "I thought for a while that I wouldn't be able to make it off the field at the half," Leahy recalled from the safety of his hospital bed the following week. "Things started to whirl around in my head."

Like this: At halftime, Leahy stood up and thought, "So this is what a heart attack is like."

He didn't want to give in to the pain, just as he taught his players. Leahy struggled to climb the stairs up to the Irish locker room in the end zone. Assistant coach Bill Earley helped him the last few stairs, alarm bells ringing in his head, and sent for Dr. Nicholas Johns. Leahy made it into the equipment room. He sat down and experienced "an awfully severe pain" in his left side and chest. He tried to make some notes about the first half but he couldn't grip the pencil. He slowly bent down and picked up the pencil, then dropped it and the notepad.

As he reached down to pick them up, Leahy pitched forward onto the floor. One account said that Leahy blacked out. McBride recalled Leahy writhing in pain. One of the assistant coaches ran into the main locker room and yelled, "Get a priest!" Ed Kelly, a junior team manager, stood closest to the locker room door.

"I don't ever remember a priest sitting on the sidelines. I knew they had their own section. That's where I ran and got one," Kelly said. "I said, 'Father, I need to have you come to the locker room. Coach Leahy's having a problem.' "

"What happened?" the priest asked.

"Coach Leahy collapsed. He's awful white-looking," Kelly said.

The priest happened to be Father Edmund Joyce, the executive vice president of the university and the right-hand man to Father Hesburgh. Joyce, a big, athletic man, had been the first South Carolina native to attend and graduate from Notre Dame. He started his professional life as a CPA, then entered divinity school at age twenty-eight. By age thirty-five, not only was he a priest, he had risen to become second-in-command of his alma mater.

Father Ned, as he was known, strode through the locker room and into the equipment room, where he found Leahy, conscious. Equipment manager Jack McAllister, who had placed a jersey beneath Leahy's head as a pseudo-pillow, stood there crying. Dr. Johns diagnosed Leahy as in shock, cold, clammy—classic symptoms of a coronary event. Earley remembers someone asking Leahy if he thought he was having a heart attack. "I don't think so, but there is a big pain in my left side," he said. Someone handed Leahy a cup of whiskey—a janitor had a pint in his pocket—and he downed it. A wave of pain came over Leahy, and he nearly passed out again.

Leahy thought he was dying. So did Father Joyce, who began to administer the last rites of the Catholic Church. So did Kelly, the junior team manager. "He looked to me like he was going to die," Kelly said. "Pale, no color in his face. He was just lying there. I don't really think he was fully conscious. He may have been going in and out. I didn't really know what the hell I was seeing. But I knew it wasn't good."

The players saw the commotion. End Don Penza, in his role as team captain, went into the equipment room, came out, and began to spread the word that Leahy was dying. Not all of them took the news somberly.

"I was sitting next to my good buddy, Bobby Rigali," Lattner recalled years later. "Now his dad played for Rockne back in 1924 and used to hear all the Rockne stories, the halftime stories of how Rock would get the team up. So as Don Penza comes back, he says, 'The coach is dying, the coach is dying,' Bobby Rigali gives me the elbow. He says, 'He's pulling a Rockne! Don't believe him. He's pulling a Rockne to get us up for the second half.' I started laughing, and everybody looked at me."

Worden recalled thinking it was another arrow in Leahy's quiver of emotional tricks to gain an emotional reaction from his players. "We said, 'Look at this Academy Award,'" Worden remembered.

As halftime ended, assistant coach Joe McArdle took over the team and led a prayer. Earley, the assistant who had helped Leahy into the locker room, stood before the players and asked, "Anyone want to win this one for the Coach?" As the players absorbed the news, the tears began to flow.

Then as now, Notre Dame Stadium has only one end zone tunnel. It serves as the portal to both locker rooms. The Irish emerged from their locker room and waited behind the Yellow Jackets.

"I heard the clatter of their cleats," Mitchell, the Georgia Tech freshman quarterback, said, "And above the cleats I could hear all this, 'Sniff, sniff, sniff.' I turned around and looked at these guys. And they were monsters—weighed 240 pounds. And every one of 'em had tears just running down their faces like that."

Mitchell turned to assistant coach Frank Broyles, who would go on to a long, distinguished career as head coach and athletic director at Arkansas, and said, "Frank, it's gonna be a long second half. Somebody gave 'em one of those 'Get this one for the Gipper' speeches."

Not right away. The Irish team that returned to the field had yet to control its emotions. The Yellow Jackets struck quickly for a touchdown to tie the game, 7–7. The entire stadium began to feel unsettled. In the press box, *South Bend Tribune* managing editor Paul Neville scanned the sideline with his binoculars and announced, "Leahy's not down there." Other writers noticed that McArdle, who usually coached from a perch atop the scoreboard, had moved to the Irish sideline. As fans began to notice the coach's absence, the news of his illness didn't spread nearly as quickly as the rumors. In the stands and in downtown South Bend, word spread that Leahy had died.

In the locker room, Leahy began to feel better. Johns found that his blood pressure had risen to normal. "Is the team still here?" he asked.

"Take it easy, Frank," Father Joyce answered. "It's the middle of the third quarter."

Leahy protested that he taught his players not to quit and he wasn't about to start himself, which Dr. Johns solved by giving him a sedative. As he began to pass out, Leahy thought to himself, "I will never coach football again. Oh God, what am I going to do with the rest of my life?" An ambulance crew loaded him up, and Leahy awoke in St. Joseph's Hospital.

The Tech touchdown reoriented Notre Dame, and the Irish began to play, Earley said after the game, "the hardest ball I've seen them play this season." The Notre Dame linemen outweighed their smaller, quicker visitors by twenty pounds per man, an advantage that extracted its toll in the fourth quarter, as the bodies of these one-platoon players began to tire. McBride remembered "some of the most vicious contact I had ever seen." In addition to the starting quarterback, three Yellow Jacket guards suffered injuries that kept them out of Georgia Tech's game the following week at Vanderbilt.

For all the domination, Georgia Tech began the fourth quarter trailing by only a touchdown, 21–14. After the Irish drove to the Yellow Jacket 1-yard line, Notre Dame tackle Art Hunter got into his stance and said to his opponent, "You better look out, boy, Johnny's coming through here."

After Lattner scored through that hole, Hunter said, "See, what did I tell you?"

"In the stands," Red Smith wrote in the *New York Herald Tribune*, "Confederate flags drooped unwaved."

Notre Dame finished the 27–14 victory with 323 rushing yards to Georgia Tech's 131. Whether the Yellow Jacket offense sputtered because of the necessity of playing a freshman quarterback or because the Irish employed that I-formation defensive front can't be measured, although Tech gained 70 of those rushing yards when Notre Dame didn't employ the wrinkle.

Lattner celebrated his birthday by rushing for 101 yards, more than he had gained in the first three games combined. His postgame soft drink shower would be the only celebrating done in Notre Dame's locker room. Dr. Johns returned from St. Joseph's to tell the players and coaches that Leahy had not had a heart attack and was resting comfortably in the hospital. Leahy's younger brother Tom talked his way into the locker room and found Penza, the team captain, drying off after a shower.

"Frank asked me to congratulate the team on its wonderful showing," Tom began, "and hopes you can come see him this evening. He said, 'Have Don tell the boys I'm proud of them. I wish I could have been there.' "

McArdle, the assistant whom Leahy had put in charge of the team, went to the hospital, wary of what awaited him. What he got was an earful.

"What the hell happened with that [Georgia Tech] belly series, Joe?" Leahy began. "Why the hell did you let 'em [photographers] in the dressing room to take Lattner's picture?"

Doctors made a first diagnosis of a gastrointestinal issue, reported as an inflammation of the stomach lining in some stories, a severe abdominal spasm in another. Johns believed it to be a manifestation of the virus that Leahy's kids had passed around the house that week. As the wire services spread the news, calls and telegrams began streaming into South Bend. Army coach Red Blaik, Leahy's former rival, called Notre Dame athletic director Moose Krause after his team's 40–7 victory over Columbia. "We can't afford to lose a figure like Frank in college football today," Blaik told Krause. "Be sure and force him to take it easy."

When Floss went up to see her husband in the hospital, she said,

"Frank, you're going to have to get into a more relaxing form of work." She later said, "I guess I shouldn't say this, but gee, I'm relieved. That boy was cracking. He was cracking fast."

More tests led Dr. Johns to set aside the earlier diagnosis and conclude that Leahy suffered from acute pancreatitis, "which could have been fatal in a lesser man."

Dr. Johns used an odd sort of logic to explain that nervous strain had nothing to do with Leahy's illness. "I have never seen a man who gave himself a worse beating than Leahy does," Johns said, "yet he is also the toughest man emotionally that I've ever seen. He has to be, to take that beating."

In other words, Leahy must be tough because he beats himself up so often, and yet Johns diagnosed that as not nervous strain. Whatever the doctor called it, he had to come up with a way to get Leahy to rest in the hospital. At the *Tribune*, which also owned the local television station WSBT, managing editor Neville had an idea. He enlisted Indiana Bell, the local phone company, to help.

Neville visited Leahy in the hospital and asked him, "Frank, how would you like to see practice tomorrow?"

"Oh, Paul," Leahy said, "I've got to get out there."

"I mean," Neville said, "would you like to see it right here in your room on a closed TV circuit from Cartier Field?"

Leahy raised up on one elbow, energy returning to his frame. "Do you really mean it? Oh, thank God, that would be wonderful."

The station mounted a TV camera on the back of a pickup truck, ran a cable four hundred yards from Cartier Field to a microwave station atop Notre Dame Stadium, and sent the signal to a microwave dish atop St. Joe's. Cables trailed down to new receiving equipment in the hospital attic. From there, it became a question of getting the signal to Leahy's room, two floors below. More wires solved that issue. And there Leahy was, Tuesday afternoon, in bed, watching a silent practice—with notebook in hand. At the end of their workout, the players crowded in front of the camera for their coach to see them.

He marveled at how much more he could see through the camera than he could from his tower. Leahy noticed that Guglielmi's trouble taking the snap without a bobble occurred because he had drifted four or five inches farther from the center. The issue not only contributed to Guglielmi's increased fumbles, Leahy explained, but it prevented center Jim Schrader from blocking as crisply as the situation demanded. He traced Lattner's diminished punting stats to a lack of follow-through.

Doctors decided on Thursday to send Leahy home, not so much because he had recovered but because he hadn't. Well-wishers entered Leahy's room throughout the day, including a random fan from Los Angeles. Leahy treated them all with grace, at least until the nurses chased them away. The only way he could get the needed rest would be to go home.

With the announcement of his release came the news that he would not attend the home game two days later against Navy. On the morning of the game, workmen arrived at his home thirty-five miles away in Long Beach to install a seventy-foot-high antenna to pull in a clear picture of the game telecast.

While his boys Jerry, ten, and Jimmy, six, cheered from the sideline, Leahy had to find a way to watch calmly. Someone turned the sound down on the telecast. That helped, especially on the opening play of the game, when Lattner's pitch to Worden went awry and Navy recovered at the Notre Dame 15-yard line.

Leahy became "awfully tense and very quiet," a guest told *The South Bend Tribune*. Three plays gained 9 yards, and Leahy predicted the Midshipmen would run wide. Instead, Navy plunged into the line, the Irish held, and that was pretty much the ball game. Notre Dame led, 26–0, at the half, and won the game, 38–7. The *Tribune* gave an account of Leahy's in-game analysis:

> Leahy, viewing the game on television, noted some lapses on pass defense in the first half and communicated this information to Earley [a practice

> since outlawed by the NCAA, which decided that coaches shouldn't receive information from outside the stadium]. The head coach noticed that the middle linebacker was playing too much to the inside, thus leaving the outside open for "flare" passes.

The acute pancreatitis cleared up, but Leahy still needed rest. Dr. Johns allowed him to attend the road game at Penn the following Saturday but advised him not to return to practice until Wednesday. With forty-degree temperatures and the typical bitter South Bend winds, Leahy stayed in an extra day. He showed up Thursday in a winter coat, buttoned all the way up, while his assistants wore their usual sweats.

Six inches of snow and a record low of twenty-nine degrees surprised Philadelphia on Friday. The airline canceled the Notre Dame flight, allowing the ailing coach to remain in a warm, cozy train from Friday afternoon until a Saturday morning arrival into Philly. It's a good thing. One man en route to the game dropped dead at the corner of 32nd and Chestnut.

A traffic jam to Franklin Field further delayed the Fighting Irish. When they arrived late onto the field, referee George Pennix assessed a 15-yard penalty. Penn coach George Munger tried to talk Pennix out of being a stickler for the rulebook; he didn't want to give Leahy any fuel to fire up his team.

With the snow piled up on the sideline, and the temperature hovering at thirty-five degrees, it was no weather for a self-described "convalescent" (the term that PR man Charlie Callahan used in the column he ghostwrote for Leahy). Before the game, Leahy sat on a yard-marker at the 30, fedora on, the collar of his overcoat turned up. Once the game began, Leahy limited himself to cheerleading and questioning the assistants who had prepared his team while he recuperated. Still, he paced and he sat until he regained the energy to arise and pace again. He had a reason to pace. It was that kind of game.

The Irish won because Lattner wouldn't let them lose. After the Quakers took advantage of that pregame penalty to drive for a touchdown, Lattner returned the ensuing kickoff to tie the game. After Penn scored twice in the second half to pull within 21–20, Lattner returned a kickoff 53 yards to set up an insurance touchdown. And with the score 28–20 late in the game, Lattner's goal-line interception curtailed Penn's last threat. He finished with 258 rushing, receiving, and returning yards. Smith, in the *Herald Tribune*, described him as "the finest advertisement for the one-platoon game."

In the postgame locker room, Leahy took questions from the throng of sportswriters while sitting on a bench.

"I've never been so tired and completely exhausted in my life," Leahy said.

His demeanor and his appearance—he would finish the season ten pounds lighter than he began—fueled speculation that he would retire. That sort of speculation, constructed of common sense but void of fact, is difficult to tamp down. The players worried about him. One player recalled that late in Leahy's career, Fred Miller, the assistant coach in charge of being the head coach's close friend, would all but hold Leahy up as he spoke in the halftime locker room. Lattner recalled Leahy distraught on the sideline during games, kneeling and praying.

On Monday after the Penn game, at the Football Writers Association of America weekly luncheon in Manhattan, athletic director Moose Krause said, "Leahy will be the Notre Dame coach for a long, long time. His health is coming back fast." Later that week, Leahy addressed the issue.

"I feel good physically now," he said. "I'm confident my health will permit me to finish this season and the remaining two years of my contract. If my doctor should say otherwise, that might change things, but I have never discussed the subject of the long-range future with him. After 1955, I'll await the pleasure of the officials at Notre Dame. They always have treated me exceedingly well."

Notre Dame went to North Carolina and dominated the rebuilding Tar Heels, 34–14. Next up—an Iowa team that had bedeviled the Irish even as it struggled to beat anyone else. In 1950, a three-win Hawkeye team tied the Irish, 14–14. In 1951, a two-win Hawkeye team tied the Irish again, 20–20.

This time around, under second-year head coach Forest Evashevski, you could see Iowa improve from Saturday to Saturday. In Detroit, Leon Hart, starring for the Lions as he had for Notre Dame four years earlier, warned in a newspaper interview that Iowa would be the spoiler. The Hawkeyes came to Notre Dame Stadium for the last game of their season without allowing a point in the month of November. That defense would be primed for Lattner and his teammates. Iowa shut down Notre Dame so well that the Irish players again resorted to the gray area of the black-and-white rulebook to keep from losing. Their decisions, in and of themselves, may not have been heinous. But as often happens with sensational news stories, the players' actions set into motion a series of events that generated their own momentum and became a national scandal. It's not fair to say that the Irish players caused the university to force Leahy's resignation. But the public opprobrium directed at Notre Dame and Leahy after the Iowa game, given Leahy's fading health and the vision of Father Hesburgh to mold Notre Dame into an academic powerhouse, served as the last weight on a scale tipped against the coach.

CHAPTER SEVENTEEN

FAREWELL AND THANK YOU

THE STORY GOES THAT IN SEPTEMBER, WITH THE 1953 OPENER against Oklahoma days away, Leahy announced to the starters, "Oh, lads. Let us practice the injury play."

Frank Varrichione, the lineman who served as the injury designee, collapsed to the ground, flopping like a reeled-in trout. Leahy ran onto the field, peered down at Varrichione and said, "Frank, I think we better make it total unconsciousness."

That story appeared in print for years. It may be true and it may be a wee bit of Irish humor. But it foretold an event that left a smudge on the pristine image that Notre Dame strove to present and accelerated Leahy's way out the door.

The "injury play" provided a way to stop the clock for a team that had used all of its time-outs. A designated player faked an injury, and the trainers came out to minister to him and "help" him off the field. The trainers made sure to minister to him at a pace deliberate enough to ensure that his substitute had ample time to get to the huddle, hear the play call, and get to the line of scrimmage before the trainers and the "injured" player left the field.

To this day, faking an injury is considered a breach of ethics, a dark art, and an essential tool of every college football team. Its history extended well before Leahy ever employed it. Under Leahy, Notre Dame practiced stopping the clock in every Friday practice.

"I will tell you," McBride said, "that every major collegiate football team in America had a plan like this. Not every team was as successful as we were."

In the end, the controversy that swallowed up Leahy at the end of the 1953 season had its roots in that success, and in the schadenfreude that American popular culture takes in cutting down whoever is standing tall.

Before the season, *The Notre Dame Scholastic*, the student publication, nailed how the Iowa Hawkeyes' year would unfold. "Last year, the Iowa frosh squad was the talk of the Midwest," the *Scholastic* said. "This season those fellows will be sophomores. In Forest Evashevski, the Hawkeyes have one of the finest young coaches in the collegiate ranks. With a heavy dependency on sophomores, the Iowans may start slow but by November they could very well be the most improved team in the Big Ten."

Iowa lost two of its first three games but came into South Bend for the final game of their season having won four of five, including shutouts of Purdue and Minnesota the previous two weeks. Leahy, as ever fearing the worst in the best of times, didn't try to hide his assessment of his diminished state with one more big game headed his way. He told a midweek conference call of Chicago writers, "I am nervous, weak, and weary."

In 1952, Notre Dame led Iowa, 13–0 late in the first half. After the Hawkeyes crossed midfield, their All-American guard Calvin Jones looked up at the end zone scoreboard, saw that fewer than thirty seconds remained, and keeled over in the huddle. The clock stopped, and trainers helped Jones off the field, but Iowa did not score before the half ended. The injury play didn't work.

The Hawkeyes didn't score before the second half ended, either. Notre Dame won, 27–0.

A year later, no one expected an Irish rout. The nervous, weak, and weary head coach surely did not. Four weeks earlier, when legs were fresher, Leahy practiced his players lightly to prepare for Georgia Tech. Not this week. Not against Iowa. "He worked us so hard that week, we came out flat," Worden recalled, four decades later.

Not only that, but when Notre Dame neared the Iowa end zone, the Irish coaches got cute with their play calling, choosing passes and trick plays rather than the running game the Irish had used to get into that position. Guglielmi, who told no one he didn't feel well, threw three interceptions in Iowa territory, one of them in the Hawkeye end zone. After the game, he discovered he had strep throat.

All of which explains why the Irish never held a lead in the entire game, and all of which also makes Guglielmi's play at the end of each half all the more thrilling. We take for granted in modern football, when every team has a two-minute offense (and some offenses play that style for sixty minutes), that teams are capable of scoring quickly. In the 1950s, the way that Guglielmi led the Irish downfield begged for adjectives. If Notre Dame hadn't needed Varrichione's skills as a thespian, what the Irish achieved might be remembered as one of the great finishes in Irish history.

Late in the first half, with Iowa ahead, 7–0, Guglielmi methodically drove Notre Dame 48 yards in 11 plays. The Irish, out of time-outs, didn't move quickly enough; as the seconds ticked away, the quarterback tried to stop the clock by intentionally fumbling the ball out of bounds at the Hawkeyes' 11-yard line. Varrichione returned to the huddle thinking the clock had stopped. But the officials, like everyone else paying attention, saw through Guglielmi's ruse and refused to stop the clock. In the huddle, Guglielmi started yelling at Varrichione to do his thing. He collapsed to the ground with two seconds to spare.

Varrichione came out—"nearly trotted off the field," *The Des Moines Register* drily noted—and on the last play of the half, in the time Varrichione had saved, Guglielmi found end Dan Shannon crossing from right to left through the end zone for an 11-yard touchdown pass.

The same stage set itself at the end of the game. Iowa scored with 2:06 to play and went ahead, 14–7. From the Irish 42-yard line, Guglielmi threw five consecutive passes. Lattner caught the fifth one and fought his way for a 10-yard gain to the Iowa 9 but could not get out of bounds. Fewer than thirty seconds remained, and the Irish, abandoning their typical discipline, did not look to Varrichione to fall. Reports vary of how many Notre Dame players went to the ground. "Actually, Guglielmi recalled, "there were about five guys down. We had to go around kicking them in the ass and telling them to get up."

The epidemic worked—the officials declared that only two, tackle Art Hunter and end Don Penza, needed to leave the game—and the Irish had time to reset themselves. After two incompletions, Guglielmi sent everyone left, while Shannon quietly rolled to the right. Guglielmi threw the touchdown, and Notre Dame salvaged its tie with six seconds to play.

A few days after the game, *The Des Moines Register* published an interview with game umpire Don Eiser. "Naturally, there's always a possibility that a player is faking an injury when his team needs a timeout," Eiser said. "But what is an official to do? Your first duty is to protect the players. You have to protect them. You have to assume that the man is hurt."

In the locker room, Leahy appeared so clearly spent that one writer described him as "near exhaustion" and another said that "it seemed the sound of someone's voice would bowl him over." The coach understood what he had witnessed. In his opening statement, he said, "I'm extremely proud of our team and its terrific spirit. It simply would not lose."

A team that used its two-minute offense to score a tying touchdown at the end of each half might be recognized for its talent and mental fortitude by more people than its head coach. If the Irish had failed to score in either half, no one would recall that they faked injuries to do so. Yet focus quickly settled on the inconvenient fact that the Irish scored both tying touchdowns on borrowed time.

Two hours after the game, an Associated Press reporter went to the dorm room in Dillon Hall that Varrichione shared with junior nose guard Jack Lee. "A reporter found the husky tackle lying down and looking the picture of health," the story said of Varrichione. "He would not admit anything. He said he had no comment whatsoever."

"We saw you get up after the play just previously," the reporter said. "Then you went back to your position and started screaming and holding your back or leg. Were you really hurt?"

"What do you think?" Varrichione replied.

Evashevski, the Iowa coach, fumed after the game, yet held his tongue. He gave the writers only one anodyne sentence: "It was a wonderfully played game."

The Associated Press poll voters treated the tie like a loss—dropping the No. 1 Irish to No. 2 behind undefeated, untied Maryland. The Hawkeye student body treated the tie like a victory. Several hundred students greeted the train that carried the team home to Iowa City. The university president ordered a dance and rally to be held on campus Monday night. Evashevski, having had a three-hundred-mile train ride and a couple of days to consider the game, stood before the students at the rally and let go of his tongue. His doggerel skewered the Irish not with outrage, but with humor.

When the One Great Scorer comes
To write against your name,
He won't write whether we won or lost
But how we got gypped at Notre Dame.

Funny that Evashevski chose to riff on the famous poem written in 1908 by Grantland Rice. The Fainting Irish controversy didn't get national legs until Monday, when the Godfather of American Sportswriting made a comment.

In November 1953, the writers who worked alongside Rice in the nation's press boxes knew he was slowing down. Friends like Red Smith and Frank Graham and Fred Russell would bring him quotes from the locker room because they knew he no longer could easily leave the press box. Rice had just turned seventy-three years old. He would not see seventy-four, dying the following summer, a column half-written sitting in his typewriter, waiting for his return. For more than a half century Rice blended a classical education with enthusiasm and a genuine fondness for people. For the way that he made athletes larger than life while ignoring their flaws, he became known as the progenitor of the "gee-whiz" school of sportswriting.

"Those who flagrantly copied his style failed in their imitations because they couldn't steal from him his unshakable belief in the integrity of the human race," Jimmy Cannon, a proud practitioner of the "aw-nuts," cynical brand of copy, wrote after Rice died.

Even as he had slowed down, in that last football season of his life, Rice continued to have a following. He still wrote the annual story in which *Look* magazine presented the Football Writers Association of America All-America team. He still wrote a weekly column of football picks. The previous Friday, Rice's column included:

> **NOTRE DAME–IOWA**
>
> A terrific meeting. We are picking Notre Dame, but with deep misgiving. Iowa has a fine chance. However, we must stick with the Irish until they lose.

On the Monday after the Notre Dame–Iowa tie, Rice attended the weekly football writers' luncheon at Toots Shor's in Midtown Manhattan. The luncheon, a journalism fixture since at least the thirties, gathered the New York writers with local college and pro football coaches.

The consensus opinion at Toots's that Monday saw nothing amiss with what Notre Dame did to tie the game.

Columbia's Lou Little, who had been a head coach for thirty years, defended Leahy—sort of. "Notre Dame should not be criticized because Frank Leahy's men acted well within the rules." He posited that if the rule needs to be changed, it should be, or that the American Football Coaches Association could address it in their code of ethics. "If enough fans, coaches, and writers clamor for a change, I am reasonably certain one will be made."

Arthur Daley of *The New York Times* called it Saturday's "biggest eye-raiser," yet made the point that players had been faking injuries to stop the clock since football began. "Common usage makes it acceptable even if it never can be fully condoned."

"The consensus seems to be that it is a legitimate dodge under the rules and not unethical per se;" Red Smith wrote, "that if some relatively obscure team had tried it, as many have in the past, nobody would give it a second thought; but that Notre Dame, because of its preeminence in the game, ought to make like Caesar's wife and studiously avoid the appearance of evil."

The loudest griping ("pretty cheap trickery") had been in the Iowa papers, of course, but the consensus among the attendees at the New York luncheon, writers and coaches alike, was that Notre Dame acted within the rules of the game. These luncheons were working affairs—writers had stories to write, about the Saturday before and the Saturday to come—but there was also a high level of bonhomie, especially in Toots's place, which served as Grand Central Station to the sports world. Writers speak freely among one another. A lot of opinion swapped back and forth in the press box, or in the postgame bar, or in a shared car going to and from the game, never sees the light of day.

Rice didn't write a column that week about Notre Dame. He didn't have to. He made a comment about the Irish at the luncheon. Given his stature and that of Notre Dame, perhaps because three decades earlier he had named the Irish backfield "the Four Horsemen," the Associated Press picked up Rice's comment and wired it to its clients across the country.

"I consider it a complete violation of the spirit and ethics of the game," Rice said of the clock-stopping, "and was sorry to see Notre Dame, of all teams, using this method. Why in Heaven's name was it allowed? If this violates neither the rules nor the coaching code, let's throw them both out the window. Notre Dame was on the shady side of sportsmanship. They did not get any good out of tying the game in that manner. Some people are calling it smart playing. I'm calling it disgraceful playing. Especially after last year when the Notre Dame 'sucker shift' had to be legislated against."

Not that anyone had any question, but in that last season of Granny Rice's life, his voice still carried. Rice's comments brought the controversy to life, made it a permanent fixture in the story of Leahy's last season. The feigned injuries would serve as a Trojan horse for a variety of people who took issue with Leahy. Writers with cynical pens, frustrated by Leahy's sanctimony and pessimism, pounced on the easy hook of "the Fainting Irish." Opposing coaches roasted Leahy—or watched silently as he roasted—for his team's success with a tactic that their own players failed to master. Father Hesburgh employed the controversy as one more lever to expedite Leahy's departure.

Arch Ward, Leahy's fiercest defender in print, didn't come to the coach's aid in his *Chicago Tribune* column until four days had passed. Ward equated feigning injury with a player stepping out of bounds—just another method of stopping the clock. "It becomes a matter of controversy," Ward wrote, "only when it works." Without mentioning Leahy by name, Ward wrote, "There always will be some inventive genius coming up with a new touch to bedevil the slower thinkers... Instead of trying to match wits with their more progressive rivals, the latter group wants to meet the competition thru legislation."

American League umpire Cal Hubbard, to this day the only man elected to the Hall of Fame of college football (1962) and baseball

(1976), gave a speech in which he asked, "Hell, where do they get off trying to give all the credit to Leahy? I invented that trick thirty years ago and everybody's been using it since."

Little comment came from Notre Dame. For one thing, the Irish had two games to play, the first being their biannual trip to Los Angeles to play USC. For another, Leahy didn't say a word. The crush of the season, the strain of his illness, and the toll he had to pay for standing on a chilly, fall sideline for three hours in his diminished state hampered his ability to return to full strength.

Leahy did not attend practice on Monday.

No comment came from the administration, even as the school received letters from its own constituency decrying Leahy's adhering to the letter of the law and not the spirit. Years later, after he retired, Father Joyce said the incident meant "absolutely nothing" because so many coaches used fake injuries to stop the clock. "So under the circumstances, we thought Leahy did the smart thing," he said.

It would have been nice for Leahy if Father Joyce had chosen to be so matter-of-fact in the heat of the moment in front of a microphone. In fact, there would come a time when Joyce not only didn't speak up but forbade Leahy to do so.

But first, the end of the season awaited. Notre Dame always took USC seriously. Between the lackluster performance against Iowa and the Trojans' own struggles—they had lost two of their last three—the circumstances favored the Irish. The coaches, scarred by their overcoaching against Iowa, stripped the playbook to five running plays and seven passes. The coaches explained to Guglielmi that if he strayed from those twelve plays, he would be taken out of the game and sent to the locker room.

"Southern Cal has been sort of a sputtering team throughout the season," said the fifteen-page scouting report the Notre Dame players received that week. "The potential is there, but for some reason or other there doesn't seem to be the consistency that is needed to make this an outstanding team. But remember the where-with-all is there."

When the team left for the West Coast on Thanksgiving Day, Leahy stayed behind with the idea, or more likely, hope, that he would follow twenty-four hours later. But Friday came and went with Leahy resting at home, where he planned to follow the game on radio. McBride and Joe McArdle ran the team. One night that week, Ward later wrote, he received a phone call from Leahy, who asked him to drive over and visit him in Long Beach. Ward came to the house for dinner, where they discussed Leahy's health and his future.

"We urged him to get out of coaching," Ward wrote. "He agreed."

Ward, who had much more interest in influence than he had in journalism, kept the evening quiet until after Leahy resigned. Ward is the only one who says Leahy decided to leave in November.

On Saturday, another very close friend spoke about Leahy coaching the following season. Dr. Johns told *The South Bend Tribune*, "I have advised Frank to take a complete rest after the first of the year and cancel all commitments. That's what he needs most—rest. Then he will be able to carry on in fine shape when spring football drills start."

For the next two months, Leahy danced on both sides of the issue, one day talking about being too old to stay in the job, and another day saying he had every intention of returning for the 1954 season.

The Irish did it up big in Los Angeles. They stayed in the Ambassador Hotel, where Lena Horne was performing in the second week of a three-week gig at the Cocoanut Grove nightclub. And the Irish did it up big at the Memorial Coliseum on Saturday, overrunning the Trojans, 48–14. The Irish, running their simplified offense, took 112 snaps. Joe Heap started the scoring with a 94-yard punt return for a touchdown, and Lattner finished it in the fourth quarter with a 50-yard scoring run. Talk about timing—three days before the voting deadline for the Heisman Trophy, Lattner rushed for 157 yards and scored four touchdowns, while his chief competition, Paul Giel of Minnesota, sat idle. The Gophers' season had ended the previous week.

One of Leahy's Chicago buddies, Frank Scobie, threw a postgame dinner party for the two teams and coaching staffs. Trojans head coach Jess Hill walked over to McBride.

"Last Sunday morning," Hill told him, "I called Eddie Erdelatz at Navy to ask him if he had any suggestion on how we should play Notre Dame. Eddie said, 'Notre Dame is not a very bright or intelligent football team because they'll actually run something other than handoff plays against you when they really don't have to.' I thought Coach Erdelatz was pulling my leg until today. As you recall, we ran a 7-2-2 defense against you and our deepest men were 4 yards off the ball. You just knocked us all over the field. I have never seen anything like that and couldn't believe that any team could do that."

The victory didn't do enough to convince the AP voters to return unbeaten, once-tied Notre Dame to the top of the poll. Maryland won its first national championship. But Lattner did squeak past Giel to become the fourth Irish player in Leahy's eleven seasons to win the Heisman. Notre Dame would play its final game at home against SMU with a chance to finish unbeaten for the sixth time under Leahy. But the concerns about Leahy's future had begun to seep out into the public discourse. *Newsweek* put Leahy on the cover that week. It wasn't the first time that a tired Leahy said aloud at the end of the season his doubts about how much longer he could perform his job. The season always drained him. But it was the first time he gave voice to his doubts a couple of weeks after he had received last rites in the locker room. He was spent.

"At forty-five," Leahy said, "I can't work eighteen to twenty hours a day and bounce back as easily as I once did. Almost all the time, I feel so awfully tired. Consequently, I have thought that perhaps a younger man might be able to do a better job." He told *Newsweek*, echoing Dr. Johns, that when the season he ended he planned to "sleep for a good, long, long time."

A remarkable senior class, who arrived in the turmoil of the scholarship reductions and the mediocrity of the 1950 season, closed out its career with a flourish. Notre Dame dominated SMU, winning the nationally televised rout, 40–14. Lattner, the newly crowned Heisman winner, rushed for 84 yards, scored twice, and threw a 55-yard pass to Shannon to set up the opening touchdown. Worden scored three times, extending his career total to 29 touchdowns, a school record.

When the game ended, the players swooped Leahy atop their shoulders and carried him in front of the box that held Floss. The stadium serenaded him with the traditional "He's a Notre Dame man" cheer, just as the students had done on the first day of his tenure nearly thirteen years earlier.

He went into the locker room, where he told the writers, "I'll be back next season if they want me." It's easy to say in hindsight that perhaps Leahy felt some unease about his employment; more likely, the tone is simply Leahy's trademark self-effacement. Across the dressing room, Father Hesburgh told reporters, "Frank has been told he can stay as long as he wants to stay."

And yet those reporters considered the possibility that Leahy might be done. They had eyes. *Indianapolis Star* writer Frank Anderson described the coach as a "gaunt, fever-cheeked Irishman" with a "lined face, the shoulders that had been broad at season's start and now sagged—the shirt collar that hung away even though the collar was buttoned..."

Talking to the writers, Leahy announced, "The 1953 football team is the greatest Notre Dame ever had." Surely he meant it, just as he meant it when he said it after other seasons, but that doesn't do a lot for his credibility. Leahy stuck to that assessment for years. He had rebuilt the team from the mediocrity of the scholarship diminished 1950 team. They had played as tough a schedule as anyone in the nation. As they proved with the opening defeat of Oklahoma, and with the late-season tie with Iowa, they would not be beaten. Late in life, McBride, too, would look back and call it the best team he had ever seen.

When Leahy finished with the writers, they lined up to shake his hand. Anderson said he wanted to say something, just in case this was Leahy's last game, but the words didn't come. He heard the man behind him say, "God bless you, Frank."

Leahy went home, greeted his guests, and went to bed at eight p.m. Ward would say afterward that he and Floss quietly toasted the end of an era. On campus, Guglielmi and Heap were busted for violating campus curfew after the SMU game. The university expelled them for the rest of the semester. They had to attend summer school the following year in order to regain their eligibility.

The team held its annual postseason dinner on the Wednesday after the SMU game. Evashevski was originally announced as the guest speaker, but at some point after the Iowa tie and before the banquet, he discovered a conflict in his schedule. Iowa director of athletics Paul Brechler replaced him and brought nothing but bouquets.

Evashevski's comment about being cheated at Notre Dame? He said it for laughs. "Notre Dame did what they did within the time allowed and within the rules," Brechler told the sellout crowd in the campus's east dining hall. "What's important, they scored the touchdowns. You'll hear no beefs from Iowa. None was made and none will be made."

The Irish players had moved on as well. During the awards portion of the evening, they awarded Varrichione an Academy Award for Best Actor. The two-plus weeks since the usually anonymous lineman became nationally known had been a dizzying sprint through celebrity life, circa 1953.

Mail poured into the Notre Dame campus, a lot of it with Varrichione's name on it. He and Lee served as the mailmen for Dillon Hall. "Honest to God, we were getting bags of mail for Frank," Lee said. "I mean, bags of mail. I remember one guy sent him flowers. The note said, 'Rest in peace, you bastard.'"

A columnist in Indianapolis wrote a Shakespearean ode to Varrichione; a Madison columnist wrote poetry. "Strange things have come to pass, I think/At proud old Notre Dame,/When lying on the ground reflects/Undying football fame."

Years later, Varrichione would recall a magazine photo of a Harlem Globetrotter player lying on the court with text that described him as "pulling a Varrichione." To a certain subset of fans, he carried the nickname "Fainting Frank" throughout his playing career. Varrichione enjoyed pointing out that he played eleven years of pro football, made five Pro Bowls, and never suffered a serious injury. In later years, when the statute of limitations on outrage had expired, Varrichione joked about it. "If you were on the ground and looked at the scoreboard and saw your team trailing with time running out, wouldn't you feel sick?"

Leahy, eventually, told a similar joke. But in the moment, he did not laugh away so easily at the fallout that accumulated around him. The unreachable standard to which he held himself compelled him to publicly justify his innocence. He would not stand for being regarded as a cheater when all he had done was coach his team to execute an accepted stratagem—the injury play—as well as it executed most plays in that undefeated season. On January 7, 1954, the Scripps-Howard newspaper chain, based in Cincinnati, planned to hold a Coach of the Year dinner, with the award portion of the evening being nationally televised as a thirty-minute show at nine p.m. EST by ABC. Jim Tatum, the Maryland coach, had won the award. Leahy asked to speak at the dinner in order to clear his name before a national audience. The program director, no fool, rearranged the schedule, which had been devoted to honoring Tatum, to give Leahy four minutes of airtime.

Joe Williams, the show host and a *New York World-Telegram* columnist, worked with Leahy on the content of the speech and wrote a column about it on the day of the show.

Leahy planned to suggest that the NCAA, or perhaps the AFCA, "protect coaches from themselves." Either the NCAA should codify a ban on faking injuries in the rulebook or either/both of the bodies should have the coaches take an oath not to do so. He would close by taking the oath himself on national television: "This much, gentlemen, I can faithfully assure you: No member of the Notre Dame football team will ever resort to such tactics again."

Leahy never made the speech. Father Joyce had gotten a copy of Williams's column. He may have defended Leahy's honor in November, but he wanted no one affiliated with Notre Dame to keep the issue alive in January. He called Leahy, heard him out, then forbade him from making the speech. Leahy was presented on the show but adhered to his boss's demand.

If Leahy's final days had a starting line, the TV show may have been it. The next day, the AFCA ethics committee released a statement decrying fake injuries "as a violation of the code" and recommended that coaches stop. Leahy arrived home from Cincinnati and said to his wife, "It's all over, Floss. Whatever it was that was working before, isn't working anymore."

His longstanding feud with Crisler, the Michigan athletic director, played a role. Crisler began his fifth year as chair of the NCAA Football Rules Committee when it convened on January 11, 1954, at the Lido Biltmore Hotel in Sarasota, Florida, for its annual meeting. A few days before, Crisler received a scathing letter from Nebraska written by Leahy's oldest brother and benefactor, Gene.

Fake injuries and the Notre Dame shift "become a CRIME only when Notre Dame uses them," Gene Leahy wrote. ". . . Why don't all of you, Mr. Crisler, who hate to see Notre Dame win, make a New Year's resolution to be FAIR WITH NOTRE DAME in the interests of true sportsmanship?"

Crisler responded to Gene, calling his letter unfair and slanted. He cc'd a copy of his response to Frank. Once the rules committee convened, the discussion by the eleven members quickly crystalized around the difficulty of legislating feigned injuries. The committee passed a resolution, to be printed in the official 1954 rule book, to lend its weight to the AFCA resolution passed a few days earlier "with full confidence in their ability to find effective means of eliminating this unethical practice" from the game.

"We prefer to rely on the integrity of and sportsmanship of the member coaches rather than use legislation," Crisler said.

After Crisler made his statement, Gene Leahy wrote him another letter that made his first one sound tame. Three times he compared Michigan or Crisler to the Communists in the USSR. Example: "If YOU are a shining example of sportsmanship and lily-white ethics in sports, then STALIN should have become POPE. And even YOU must realize how impossible that was."

The Michigan athletic director chose not to answer that one.

The rules committee debated whether to change the rule but had no real desire to do so. Little, appearing as a representative of the AFCA, urged that the committee allow the coaches to handle the matter themselves. He proposed that AFCA president George Munger of Penn write a letter to each member of the organization asking that they no longer use fake injuries as a tool. The rules committee decided to pass a resolution putting the "serious problem" in the hands of the AFCA and expressed "full confidence" that the coaches would eliminate the "unethical practice from the great American game."

The committee didn't single out Leahy. Then again, it didn't have to. The whole college football world knew what had caused the committee to take up feigned injuries. The season had been over for a month, and yet the stress that plagued Leahy every fall had yet to abate.

Dr. Johns said he didn't urge Leahy to stop coaching, just change how he did it. He described Leahy's health issue as functional, not organic. He had to put a governor on his adrenaline. If Leahy did that, Johns felt he could continue without a problem.

If Leahy did that, he wouldn't be Leahy. Moose Krause recalled urging and failing to convince Leahy to take a vacation. Late in life, Floss said she didn't think that Frank should have left coaching, that if he had just had time to relax and rejuvenate, he would have been fine. In real time, however, she was quoted more than once as saying that he couldn't take the stress of coaching any longer. In real time, Leahy was exhausted, he felt wrongly accused in the court of public opinion, and he had a boss who saw him as an impediment.

Frank Sullivan filled the job of publicity director and administrative aide to Leahy once held by his brother Billy. Frank Sullivan regaled his sons with tales of Leahy's drive. "The intensity of the man was both a blessing and a curse," Bob Sullivan, Frank's son, said. "He just could not let go. When [longtime Indiana basketball coach] Bobby Knight threw that chair across the court, my dad couldn't help but think that if Leahy had continued coaching, he might do something like that."

Father Hesburgh always maintained that he did not fire Leahy, and technically, Leahy did resign. But Hesburgh, only months into his presidency, wanted Leahy out. Hesburgh wanted to build a Notre Dame known for academics. Not only was Notre Dame known for its football excellence but in each of the past two seasons it had been mired in controversy for using specious tactics. Leahy's program was in the way. The young president orchestrated Leahy's departure with political skill that belied his inexperience, and didn't bother to wipe his fingerprints off what he engineered. Professor Robert Burns, who wrote the definitive, two-volume history of the first 110 years of Notre Dame, said when he joined the faculty in 1957, the consensus among the faculty was that Hesburgh had fired Leahy. Terry Brennan, speaking in the 1990s, said he knew why Leahy had been fired but would never tell because he had promised silence to Father Hesburgh. Brennan, in his autobiography, published in 2020, the year before he died at age ninety-three, said that in 1955, Father Hesburgh questioned him about the athletic department billing an alum for a $2,000 payment to a player. Brennan didn't have enough evidence to connect the payment to Leahy in the book. But late in life, he told a friend Father Hesburgh got rid of Leahy because he paid players.

Hesburgh said he believed Leahy should stop coaching because he was relatively young and the father of eight, and he was concerned for the coach's health. He also said he didn't think that he could convince Leahy to leave. In other words, Leahy didn't want to quit. And he wouldn't have quit if he had felt that he had Hesburgh's support.

Leahy had a speaking engagement in Clearwater, Florida, with the top executives of U.S. Rubber. He didn't feel up to it and asked Bob

McBride to go replace him. Bob and his wife, Mary, made a vacation of it, leaving their children with their grandparents and driving down to the Gulf Coast.

On the last weekend in January, Hesburgh enlisted two of Leahy's good friends, Arch Ward and Art Haley, the university director of public relations, to meet with Leahy and Floss at Ward's apartment in Chicago. Over dinner, they convinced Leahy that for his health he should surrender the job. Leahy called Dr. Johns from Chicago and asked for his permission to say that he had told Leahy to resign. Dr. Johns agreed. They exchanged quick pleasantries and Leahy got off the phone.

"I knew at that time," Dr. Johns said, "that he was being fired."

Joe McArdle, a member of Leahy's staff since his first year at Boston College, fifteen years earlier, didn't have to think about it. He immediately thought that Leahy had been forced out. The decision caught the assistants by surprise, especially those whom Leahy failed to get hold of before it became public. The coach felt the worst about McBride, for whom he had lobbied Hesburgh to name McBride the new head coach. Hesburgh had brought Brennan back to campus a year earlier to place him in position to take over for Leahy. It may have happened prematurely—top college programs had stopped hiring twenty-five-year-old head coaches a generation earlier—but perhaps Hesburgh, ten years Brennan's senior, saw something of himself in a young leader.

On Sunday, January 31, the top college football story in the sports section of *The South Bend Tribune* discussed how new Minnesota head coach Murray Warmath would bring the split-T offense to the Gophers, who had been a single-wing team under Bernie Bierman since the 1930s. No hint of the meeting in Chicago, no hint of an era ending.

At five p.m. Sunday, Notre Dame issued a press release that "regretfully announces the resignation of Mr. Frank Leahy for reasons of health" and the appointment of Terry Brennan to replace him. The release glowed with praise for Leahy. Father Hesburgh said he "has distinguished himself as a fine Christian gentleman who represented Notre Dame's ideals to millions of Americans, young and old." The university would provide scholarships to Leahy's five sons, although it did not say that they would have to qualify academically just like anyone else (three of them graduated from Notre Dame). "We regret the illness... but fully agree with the medical advice that recommends a less strenuous occupation for his future."

The first line of Leahy's three-paragraph statement began with him saying that the doctors had advised him to stop coaching. He said that he and Father Hesburgh agreed "in view of the dangers to my health that would come from continued coaching" that the time had come for him to stop. And Leahy thanked Father Hesburgh, Father Joyce, and Krause "for the very kind consideration they are now showing to me. Among the happiest memories I take away from this coaching position is that of their support..."

Bob and Mary McBride, driving home from Florida, were somewhere between Connellsville and Lancaster in western Pennsylvania when they heard the news on the radio. Mary never forgot how the shock turned Bob pale as he drove west.

"Our world crashed," Mary said.

"Thank God, we didn't," McBride said. When they arrived in Lancaster to pick up their daughter from Bob's mother, she told him that Leahy had been trying to reach him.

"Bob," Leahy told him over the phone, "I have suggested as strongly as I can to the university officials that you replace me but I believe Father Hesburgh has other intentions on his mind." Tim McBride, years later, described his father as disappointed but never bitter.

Johnny Lujack, a rumored head-coach-in-waiting who had been on Leahy's staff only two years, said, "I just can't believe it... I never thought he'd leave Notre Dame."

Notre Dame didn't hold a press conference until Tuesday. Both Brennan and Leahy appeared at the Morris Inn on campus. Leahy first met with the players for a tearful goodbye. He spoke with Joe Williams of the *New York World-Telegram* for an hour, explaining that "since tension is my greatest peril I must leave football."

In the bowels of the stadium, caretaker Joe Dierickx, who had been on the job dating to Leahy's days as a student, went there with his comparison. "It was different with Rock—he was killed," Dierickx said. "But the reaction is the same—the same stunned atmosphere."

At some point during the day, Leahy, in topcoat and fedora, said goodbye to the stadium from the field, newsreel cameramen and still photographers in tow. When Brennan and Leahy appeared before the press, Leahy stayed on the high road. He promised Brennan that he was just one phone call and thirty-five miles away. And then the old coach gave one final pep talk.

"Remember this, lads. Never, never, never give up. It is too easy to quit, to lie down and say that you are defeated. Go out and win one more victory for Our Lady. I am leaving as head football coach at Notre Dame," he said, "... but I will never leave Notre Dame. Farewell and thank you."

When Leahy concluded the press conference, many in the audience were in tears. The last hand he shook on his way out of the building belonged to South Bend Police Sergeant Leni Krulewitz, who was crying along with everyone else. "He was the best friend I had," Krulewitz said. Leahy walked out of the press conference to find 2,000 people, mostly students on this campus with an enrollment of 5,600, and a small pep band waiting for him. Someone had rigged up a platform for him. Leahy thanked the gathering for their support through his career. "Believe me, it is the one thing that makes Notre Dame different than other places," he said. "Other schools try to match our spirit but you people just won't let them."

Leahy climbed into a car driven by Frank Jr., and they took a last tour of campus. He got out of the car at the statue of Mary, bowed and said a prayer. He touched his hand to his mouth to throw a kiss, climbed back into the car, and departed.

CHAPTER EIGHTEEN

THE PEOPLE-PLEASER

"I always knew, even all through high school, that the only thing I wanted was athletics," Frank Leahy said, looking back at his life. "I wanted to be a great coach—and I never cared about history, or language, or mathematics, etc. Nothing else interested me but athletics—all forms of it."

And then, the life he had built in football over nearly three decades skidded to an abrupt halt. At age forty-five, too old to coach and too young to retire, Frank Leahy had to decide how to fill his days.

"He was kind of a lonesome man," Lujack said. "Football and his life around football were the only things he really knew. Out of coaching he was kind of lost."

Leahy hobnobbed with the president and went to bat for one of the wealthiest men in the country. He parlayed his celebrity and his expertise into a television career. He got suckered into a series of bad business deals. He broke the First Commandment of Coaching Retirement

(Thou Shalt Not Criticize Thy Successor). When his health improved, and his mind produced the amnesia that clouds the memory of the day-to-day grind, he pursued being a head coach again. For a man who had pushed himself hard and harvested the fruit of that labor in the form of wins, the ensuing years would be immensely frustrating. Leahy continued to work hard. He just didn't win every Saturday. Far from it.

Leahy whisked Floss down to Tampa for a few days in March smack in the middle of spring training. He held a press conference, and baseball managers and execs showed up just to shake his hand, including ninety-one-year-old Connie Mack, still the owner of the Philadelphia A's.

He traveled to the California desert and played some golf with President Eisenhower and Ben Hogan at Tamarisk Country Club in Rancho Mirage, where Hogan had been the first head professional. Eisenhower pursued their friendship, inviting Leahy to a gathering of Republican businessmen and fundraisers in April, later that spring to an "informal stag dinner" of fourteen men at the White House, and in the summer to play golf again in Colorado, where the president established a western White House for two months. They played a round at Cherry Hills, along with Colorado Governor Dan Thornton, and the next day Leahy visited with the president for a half hour in Eisenhower's makeshift office at Lowry Air Force Base.

Afterward, Leahy stood before the news cameras and said, "I feel free to state with a very strong amount of conviction that Mr. President is definitely one of the all-time great leaders that this nation of ours has ever had. And for my part, I think all of us ought to get down on our knees every night of our lives and thank God for his great leadership. I've never known anyone more sincere in trying to do an All-American job for the nation."

He liked Ike, and no wonder Ike liked him. America loved him, too. In the spring of 1954, a list of a dozen actors, sportsmen, and statesmen ranked as the most wanted celebrities for endorsements included Eleanor Roosevelt, Henry Fonda, and Leahy. Television wanted him.

ABC-TV had shown *The Frank Leahy Show* on Sundays during the 1953 season.

The agent for Lucille Ball and Desi Arnaz, whose *I Love Lucy* sitcom was in its second consecutive season as the number one show on American television, recruited Leahy to participate in a drama about high school coaches that would run on ABC. The pilot, part of the *DuPont Cavalcade of America* series, featured Browns quarterback Otto Graham and his high school coach. But no network picked up the series.

Rather than continue to take time to decompress, Leahy fell back on the industriousness he had learned as a child. He threw himself into the business world with the same fervor that he had for coaching. The one difference is that Leahy didn't have the innate understanding of a balance sheet that he had for an unbalanced line. He had spent more than twenty-five years sharpening his football mind. He didn't know how to operate a business, and over the next decade, as each venture proved more painful than the last, he proved he didn't know how to recognize someone who could run a business, either.

In Leahy's second year as Notre Dame head coach, when opposing coaches accused him of poaching recruits and players, Father John Cavanaugh blamed the issue on Leahy being a people-pleaser. Cavanaugh warned Leahy that some of those people would try to use him for their own ends, and the result could be damaging to him and the university. The best priests become astute judges of human nature. Cavanaugh pegged Leahy, whose desire to trust those who tried to befriend him in the business world proved to be his undoing.

"So at age forty-five, and then maybe fifty, he was like a fish out of water. And it just killed him," Fred Leahy said of his father, "Dad was not a good businessman. In fact, he was horrible." Fred said that his uncle Tom, a successful insurance man, would tell his older brother what to do to check the people who wanted Frank Leahy as a business partner. "Dad was so headstrong. I guess if you're forty-five and one of the most successful coaches, you're kind of confident."

When Leahy left Notre Dame, he already had several business

ventures. He continued to be a spokesman for Keds. He had a public relations business with his former aide Billy Sullivan, whom Leahy had known and worked with for more than a decade. He had an interest in two insurance agencies with the financier Louis Wolfson, a friend for several years. In 1950, Leahy invested in a drugstore in Burbank, California, with a Notre Dame classmate, Lou Berardi. That sounds like a lot, yet as soon as he stopped coaching, Leahy became national sales director of a South Bend business run by his neighbor. Exothermic Alloys produced material for steelmaking.

Leahy brought Bob McBride with him to that job, and just to make sure that McBride would stay, Leahy sold him a home that Leahy owned in Long Beach, near Michigan City, for $26,500. McBride, who had been making an assistant coach's salary, didn't have the money for a down payment, much less the purchase price. Leahy told McBride to pay him for the house when he could he afford it. Leahy then made a deal with *Life* magazine to write a story about the best small college football players in the nation. He asked McBride to do the research, and when *Life* magazine sent Leahy his author's fee of $2,000, Leahy endorsed the check to McBride, who gave it right back to Leahy as part of a down payment.*

In the days leading up to the 1954 season opener against Texas, Leahy repeated what he had been saying about his successor for eight months. "I predict that ten years from now Brennan's record will be comparable to that of any coach who ever coached Notre Dame," he said. As an aside, he added, "I've really never felt quite so good in the last ten years."

After the 1954 Fighting Irish opened the Terry Brennan Era with a 21–0 defeat of the Longhorns, *Life* magazine ran a full-page photo of a beaming Frank Leahy standing with Brennan in front of the sportswriters. "I'm the happiest coach in the United States today," Leahy said. Of course, Leahy was not the "coach." Brennan stared downward,

* Leahy could be remarkably generous in that fashion. When McBride told Leahy that academic advisor Bill Burke and his wife used to come to the McBrides' house to watch television, Leahy had a TV sent to the Burke home.

which *Life* described as modesty. Actually, Brennan couldn't have been more angry.

Brennan asked Leahy to speak to the team in the pregame locker room. He did so as a peace offering. Brennan knew that Father Hesburgh had pushed Leahy out the door. He wanted to honor Leahy, smooth things over, move forward.

A first-time head coach has thought about the moments before his first game as head coach, oh, no more than a thousand times. Brennan handed Leahy his team, and Leahy preceded to wind the players up with an emotional speech that wasn't anything close to how Brennan intended to prepare them. Brennan later called the speech a "disaster" and a "dumb thing to do," which is curious, given the dominance the Irish displayed on the field. Leahy watched the game in the stands with Floss and their six oldest children, an experience he called "wonderful… especially since Terry's lads played so well."

At age twenty-six, humble or not, you could tell Brennan but you couldn't tell him much. On the Tuesday after the game, he felt compelled to reassert control of the team that only he felt he had lost. Brennan told the players that this was *his* team, and that what had happened on Saturday with an "intruder" in the locker room would never happen again. The speech made Brennan feel better. It also cost him the trust of the seventeen seniors, the leadership corps of the team. They respected Leahy, and didn't understand why Brennan would disrespect him. They felt deflated, and they played like it against Purdue four days later. It may not have helped that Leahy, uninvited, came into the pregame locker room again. The guy working the door let him in, mainly because he was Frank Leahy.

Purdue won the game, 27–14. Brennan laid blame for the loss at the feet of the seniors, and demoted both starting quarterback Ralph Guglielmi and fullback Joe Heap.

"Hey, you can say what you want about Leahy," Guglielmi said years later. "But when a Leahy team lost he took the blame. I never heard him blame the players."

The man working the locker room door received a reprimand. Leahy never entered Brennan's locker room again.

Brennan and the seniors eventually made peace. The Irish, on the backs of those seniors, won their last eight games to finish 9-1. Leahy put a smile on his face but he didn't have a lot of respect for Brennan. It bothered him that the players called Brennan "Terry." It bothered him that Father Hesburgh had given the team to someone he could control rather than to McBride or to Lujack.

Late in the season, Leahy and Arch Ward walked into the Morris Inn, the two-year-old campus hotel, and went upstairs with senior Jack Lee to say hello to his parents. Amid the small talk, Lee's mother said, "Frank, what happened? Why did you leave Notre Dame?"

"They didn't want me anymore," Leahy said. His emotions overwhelmed him, and he teared up. Mrs. Lee ushered him into the bathroom, gave him a wet washcloth, and helped him compose himself.

In 1955, Leahy found a TV role more suited for his talent. He hosted a fifteen-minute syndicated preview show, *Frank Leahy and His Football Forecasts*, also sponsored by DuPont. Leahy, in trademark suit and bow tie, sat at a desk and introduced the preview segments of highlights, aided by an animated football named Fumble. After the highlights, he would come back and select the winner of the game. The show ran in most of the upper Midwest towns and cities where Notre Dame ruled supreme—Chicago, Pittsburgh, Buffalo, Youngstown, Erie—but also in Atlanta, Sacramento, San Antonio, etc. It usually ran on Friday at 10:15 p.m., eastern time, although WAGA in Atlanta put Leahy on Thursday night opposite *The Groucho Marx Show*, one of the top-rated programs on television. Leahy made a successful career scheduling better than that.

One of the goals that Leahy vowed to achieve after he left coaching was to spend more time with Fred Miller. In the first six years after the war, Leahy's former "assistant coach" quadrupled sales volume at Miller Brewing. He seemed to be indestructible. Twice he walked away from planes he crashed—once, in 1946, while bringing Brennan, then a sophomore running back, from a speaking engagement in their hometown of Milwaukee back to Notre Dame.

Miller put Leahy on the brewery payroll and helped make his friend wealthy. After Leahy retired, Miller began to press him to go on a hunting trip with their boys, twenty-year-old Freddie Jr. and nineteen-year-old Frankie Jr. They couldn't make their schedules sync until December 1954, when they decided to hunt near Winnipeg, Canada. A few days before the trip, something came up and Frank postponed again. The Miller Brewing plane, with two pilots and Fred Sr. and Jr. on board, crashed less than a mile after taking off. Fred Sr. survived long enough to be taken to the hospital. He was forty-eight years old. His son and his pilots died, too.

Leahy, a private man by nature, lost one of the few close friends he had. He turned even farther inward, a response that would produce a lasting impact on his family.

Though Louis Wolfson grew up Jewish in Jacksonville, Florida, and Leahy grew up Catholic in Winner, South Dakota, the similarities between them explained why they took to each other. Leahy described Wolfson to *The Wall Street Journal* as a "very, very fine gentleman."

Both men boxed as teenagers. Both were handsome introverts whose aloofness was misinterpreted by the public at large. Wolfson played football at Georgia but, like Leahy, had a college career curtailed by injury. Leahy had an intuitive understanding of football; Wolfson could look at a balance sheet and instantly understand how to make it put money in his pocket. At the age of twenty, in 1932, Wolfson started a construction supply house and made it a success in the depths of the Depression. Once World War II kicked into gear, Wolfson's business did $4.5 million annually.

Wolfson, devoted to Georgia, doted on Bulldogs coach Wally Butts, Leahy's closest coaching friend (Wolfson once offered to purchase the

Baltimore Colts and have Butts run the team, but Butts didn't want to leave Georgia). After the war, Wolfson asked Leahy to go into the insurance business with him. He cut Leahy in on his investments; one $20,000 stake returned $200,000. When Leahy collapsed at halftime of the Georgia Tech game in 1953, the first telegram he received in the hospital came from Wolfson.

Shortly after Leahy retired, Wolfson tried to buy up enough stock to take over Montgomery Ward, the department store chain and catalog business that dated to the nineteenth century. When Ward management began to excoriate Wolfson in the press, Wolfson recognized that he needed a respected public celebrity to represent him. He enlisted Leahy, who spoke on Wolfson's behalf to investors and to the financial press. Leahy presided over what became a raucous presentation to 2,800 stockholders at a New York hotel. "Boy, I've seen a lot of alumni meetings," Leahy said, "but nothing whatever to compare to this," an offhanded comment that captured how Leahy found himself in an unfamiliar sport playing for much higher stakes.

Wolfson lost the proxy battle but hired Leahy as a vice president of trade relations for his biggest company and paid him close to $100,000 per year, so much that Leahy left Exothermic Alloys. The position may have given Leahy false confidence. Wolfson proved to be one of only a few business partners who didn't take advantage of Leahy.

In the summer of 1956, as President Eisenhower prepared to run for reelection, he told his political staff to offer a speech seconding his nomination to either actress Irene Dunne, a prominent California Republican, or Leahy. Once they decided on Leahy, Eisenhower called him from the White House—called him off the Cherry Hills Country Club golf course in Denver—and asked him what he would be doing in a couple of weeks.

"Anything my president wants me to do," Leahy said.

Leahy spoke as one of eight seconders at the Republican National

Convention at the Cow Palace just south of San Francisco. He appeared directly after a thirty-two-year-old housewife from Houston.

"Frankly, I am not directly affiliated with either political party," Leahy told the delegates. "I have always believed that an individual should vote for the person most qualified for public office. But you will recognize, ladies and gentlemen, before I proceed very far, that I am definitely prejudiced towards our great leader, Mr. Eisenhower. I am more grateful than words can express that our gifted leader will again give his badly needed, his desperately needed leadership to Americans and free-loving people the world over."

(This being San Francisco, a local columnist teased Leahy for saying "free-loving" instead of "freedom-loving.")

Leahy succumbed to the temptation of using his former career as metaphor for only one paragraph.

"You know, in football and in other walks of life, the quarterback, the leader who can rise instead of fall under great pressure, has a priceless quality. It's that quality of leadership, it's the mark of a strong man, a great competitor. Our president has been forced many, many times during recent years to call exactly the right play at the right time, and under the toughest kind of competition, and regardless of circumstances or geographical location, he has always come through with exactly the right play at the right time. He exemplifies the phrase which has always been near and dear to my heart. It goes like this: When the going gets tough, the tough get going."*

Seconding speeches generally do not make history. Just short of the four-minute mark, as Leahy wrapped up his remarks, NBC Radio cut him off for news coverage of a Navy plane being shot down off the coast of Formosa (now Taiwan). The *Time* magazine correspondent who covered the speech reported, "For once, Leahy seemed to think his team would win." Eisenhower greatly appreciated the speech. When

---

* Leahy had also used that bit of coaching wisdom in a get-well-soon letter to Eisenhower following the president's heart attack the year before.

Leahy stopped by the president's room at the St. Francis Hotel on Union Square, Eisenhower stirred from a nap at the sound of Leahy's voice, came out in his robe, and had a drink with him.

Leahy, for the rest of his life, held that day close to his heart. "I felt like a true patriot," he said. Red Smith, covering the convention for the *New York Herald Tribune*, attempted to capture the fish-out-of-water nature of Leahy's speech. "Delegates waited in vain," Smith wrote, "for Frank to exhort them to win this one for the Gipper."

Little did Smith know whom the Republicans would nominate in 1980.

At the outset of the 1956 season, Leahy wrote a piece for the *Scholastic* in which he bragged that he had missed attending only one Notre Dame game in retirement. "I believe it goes without saying," Leahy said, "I shall continue to be an avid and loyal Notre Dame fan for as long as God permits me to remain on this earth."

Avid? Yes. Loyal? In the eye of the beholder. Notre Dame had Hornung and little else in the way of seniors. Hornung played well enough to win the Heisman Trophy. The Irish went 2-8 anyway. They lost close games. They lost routs. Brennan's career mimicked Leahy's in one sense. Father Hesburgh restricted his scholarships, too. That, coupled with what Brennan decried as the lack of talent among his senior class—the players he coached as freshmen three years earlier—set up the young coach for a huge fall. He didn't have the players he needed to win.

Leahy commuted to Los Angeles every weekend in 1956 to do his television show. He envisioned it would work out perfectly. Notre Dame closed out the season at USC, so Leahy asked Brennan to allow Hornung to appear on a special show on the Friday night before the Trojan game. Leahy would announce his All-America team. Chrysler, the sponsor, would fly Hornung's mother from Louisville to Los Angeles.

Brennan said no.

Most football coaches would have said no. In those early days of television, when people didn't quite know what to make of the medium's invasiveness and reach, the last group that would readily alter habits to make room for television were tradition-bound football coaches, even those who had yet to turn thirty.

Maybe Leahy had promised his producer he could get Hornung on the air. Maybe he didn't like what had happened to Notre Dame football. Maybe he had a bad day. But Leahy didn't take the refusal well. Brennan pointed out to Leahy that he had asked him to allow something that Leahy the head coach never would have allowed. Leahy, Brennan said, spewed forth his anger and then hung up. Leahy called Father Hesburgh to ask that he intervene. Leahy called Hornung's mother. He got nowhere.

A night's sleep didn't cool him off. In an interview the following day with an AP reporter, Leahy, without naming Brennan, took him apart. Leahy said he had watched the 48–8 loss to Iowa the previous Saturday in disbelief.

"There was no fight, no will to win," Leahy said. "It's not the losses that upset me; it's that attitude. What has happened to the old Notre Dame spirit? Those great fourth-quarter finishers? That old try right down to the final whistle even if there were no chance of winning?"

The backlash rose swiftly. It wasn't just that Leahy had criticized his successor. He had kicked Brennan when he was down. Leahy sounded like every "downtown coach" who ever sat in a barber shop. Leahy's predecessor, Elmer Layden, called the remarks "in poor taste" and suggested that Leahy missed the headlines. Joe Williams, who usually fawned over Leahy, said in the *New York Journal-American*, "Frank could have dynamited the Board of Trade Building [in Chicago] and still come off better."

After the initial fusillade of criticism, Leahy doubled down, saying, "I can only reply: Isn't it true?"

For years, Leahy had spoken of Notre Dame only in reverence. His devotion to the university provoked mocking among the cynical. He would never dream of uttering a syllable that could be construed as critical of what he lovingly called "Our Lady." Until he did.

In the first couple of years after retirement, few rumors surfaced regarding Leahy returning to coaching. He was busy working for Wolfson. He insisted he would not reopen the door to his coaching career. In 1956, as Texas began looking for a replacement for Ed Price, the feelers went out to Leahy. He told them he would be interested in being athletic director. The university wanted one man to be AD and head coach. Texas hired a young coach at Washington named Darrell Royal. In twenty seasons he won three national championships.

But the flirtation must have awakened whatever coaching urge lay dormant in Leahy. During the 1957 season, Billy Sullivan began working behind the scenes for Leahy to return to Boston College. It didn't matter that Leahy would be replacing his former fullback, Mike Holovak. The alums wanted to get back to undefeated seasons and bowl games, and they believed Leahy was the answer. Holovak had the gall to thwart their scheme by leading the Eagles to a 7-2 record. "His friends tried to get him the job," Holovak would say. "They knew it. I knew it. Just one of the hazards of coaching. It is a business like anything else."

A few weeks later, after Texas A&M narrowly missed out on the national championship, coach Paul "Bear" Bryant left to coach Alabama, his alma mater, with what became an iconic two-word explanation: "Mama called." The Aggies, never at a loss for bravado, set out to hire a coach who would outshine Bryant. They made a run at Red Sanders of UCLA, who had led the Bruins to a national title three years before. He said no.* Then they set their sights on Leahy. Four years off the sideline appeared to be enough. Leahy initially suggested the same deal that he had pushed at Texas the previous year. He would become athletic director and bring Bob McBride with him to be head coach. On the weekend before Christmas, Leahy and McBride flew down to

* Sanders would die eight months later of a heart attack.

College Station. That's where Leahy learned that he didn't comprehend Aggies. They wanted *Frank Leahy* as head coach.

After four hours, Leahy and the university president, Dr. M. T. Harrington, made a handshake deal, which Leahy described as "99 percent definite." He loved the vibe on campus. Though A&M in those days was a military school, the all-male student body felt familiar to him. "Texas A&M is about the closest thing you'll find to Notre Dame," he told *Sports Illustrated*. He said the locals had impressed upon him that their school spirit rivaled what he had in South Bend.

In the course of the coaching interview, Leahy was asked if he believed that his health would allow him to do the work. Leahy decided the best thing to do for all parties would be to go home and get a thorough physical.

The United Press ran with the story, saying that Texas A&M had named Leahy as AD and head coach, quoting Harrington that the contract would be signed by the end of the week.

"I've never felt better in my life than I do now," Leahy said. "The layoff got me over all the trouble that I had and my local doctor has told me that I am healthier than I've been in ten years."

Leahy told *Sports Illustrated* that he would be "delighted" to play Notre Dame, that he still had recruiting contacts in Texas, and wouldn't you know it, "seven lads" from outside of Texas played for the 1957 Aggies.

Leahy flew home to spend the holiday in the winter wonderland of northwest Indiana. He detoured to Champaign, Illinois, to attend the funeral of Bob Zuppke, the longtime Hall of Fame coach at Illinois. On Christmas Day, Leahy pulled into his driveway, unloaded the car, and began carrying a tower of presents into the house. He didn't make it. Leahy slipped on the ice and broke his right ankle.

He spent the rest of the holiday in St. Anthony's Hospital in Michigan City before heading to Chicago for his Texas A&M examination by Dr. Clifford Barborka, who had tended to Leahy's gastric ailments several years before. The results, developed over two days, blindsided the patient. Whether it came from the stress of the negotiation, the stress of breaking his ankle, or the pace at which his mind had begun to race over the task of taking over the Aggies and reentering coaching, Leahy began to experience some gastric issues. Dr. Barborka told him he could not recommend that Leahy return to coaching. In fact, he wanted Leahy to remain in Passavant Hospital in Chicago for treatment.

Out of an abundance of caution, Leahy tested himself right out of a coaching job. He had allowed himself to be seduced by the excitement of a return to the arena. He had forgotten what he had told a college buddy two years earlier: "The pressure was terrific, as you say, Jim, but in my case the pressure was self-imposed."

Leahy called A&M with the news. He offered to come as athletic director but the school turned him down. Nearly three weeks later, after he left the hospital, Leahy told Joe Williams that he "was most distressed by the outcome of the medical checkup. I was anticipating with great pleasure my resumption of coaching. I was never more sincere about anything in my life." Leahy said he missed dealing with young men, he missed the excitement and, just as he had thought when he left coaching, that a return to coaching might be better for his home life. "I find I have to travel more now than I ever did as a coach," he said.

He would never come so close to another coaching job again.

After the sniping with Brennan, a Cold War truce took hold. During the 1958 season, Leahy made a hindsight-aided apology of sorts. "I guess I'll never live that down. I was still too close to the team... Well, I just flipped, as the youngsters say." Yet in his weekly newspaper column, he heaped praise upon the Fighting Irish, even as they were in the midst of a 6-4 season, the implication being that this team should be better. And who was to blame that it wasn't?

"He would be horrible to Terry Brennan, the things he said," Fred Leahy, Frank's son, remembered. "Even Moose Krause said, 'Coach, you got to stop. You're horrible.' I always wanted to reach out to Terry

Brennan through [longtime *Blue & Gold* writer] Lou Somogyi. But Lou said no, he doesn't want to talk to any of the family members."

At the conclusion of Brennan's five-year contract in 1958, Hesburgh fired him. Brennan, thirty years old, had a record of 32-18. He never became a head coach again. He appeared to forgive Leahy, even serving as toastmaster at the First Annual Frank Leahy Pro Sports Award Dinner in Chicago in 1972, a peace offering to a dying man. But Brennan didn't forget. Leahy could have made Brennan's job easier. He did not. "I sincerely believe that he didn't want anyone who followed him to do well," Brennan said.

As the years passed, Leahy's attitude reverted to the fact that a twenty-five-year-old kid replaced him at all. "He considered it a slap in his face," Frank Jr. said.

Notre Dame replaced Brennan with an NFL coach, Joe Kuharich, who had even less success than Brennan. Leahy considered Kuharich a friend, too, but the pride that Leahy took in Notre Dame football superseded friendship. In four seasons, Kuharich's teams never did better than 5-5. After the 1961 season, Leahy said, "I don't think Kuharich would take advice if Rockne himself leaned down from heaven to give it." When the beloved Hughie Devore, who had coached the Irish in 1945, returned as a placeholder for the 1963 season, Leahy didn't spare him, either. After Notre Dame lost to Pittsburgh, 27–7, Leahy described to the Daytona (Florida) Quarterback Club the tradition of Rockne, of George Gipp, of the Four Horsemen, and said, "For some reason, that feeling doesn't exist today." Even Arthur Daley, the venerable columnist for *The New York Times* who rarely threw a journalistic punch, said, "It's time Frank shut up."

Father Hesburgh, feeling secure about the academic progress of the university, hired Ara Parseghian away from Northwestern for the 1964 season. "I think down deep, my father thought that ten years after Brennan and Kuharich, Notre Dame may come calling again," Fred Leahy said. "They never did."

Parseghian revamped the Irish much as Leahy had twenty-three years before. He moved players to different positions. He infused them with new energy and gave them confidence. The Irish went 9-1. Leahy, asked to speak at the pep rally on the eve of the Stanford game, the fifth game of the season, predicted that Notre Dame would win. Moose Krause followed him and said, "You never talked that way on Friday nights when you were coach, Frank."

In the late 1950s, Leahy engaged more deeply in the insurance business. He took on some publicity work for John MacArthur, the Chicago-based insurance titan. Leahy and MacArthur soon became part of a new insurance business in Colorado with the state's former governor, Dan Thornton, with whom Leahy had played golf in the Eisenhower foursome a few years earlier. Thornton and Leahy also decided to throw in with a new Denver firm, Hamilton Oil & Gas, Thornton as a director, Leahy as an executive vice president who would drum up business.

Leahy didn't perform any due diligence on men who approached him to invest. He met them and if he liked them, that was his due diligence. That naïveté cost him hundreds of thousands of dollars and probably shaved years off of his life. There weren't a lot of Fred Millers or Louis Wolfsons out there. Men looking out for themselves, men who sized up Leahy and saw a pigeon in a suit and bow tie, sniffed him out like a coyote sniffs out a deer.

The Hamilton Oil & Gas plan was simple: The company provided Leahy with one hundred thousand shares of stock, worth a total of $50,000. He turned around and sold it to investors for $150,000. Leahy didn't hit the streets to sell the stock. He went through his Rolodex. He sold stock to Iowa coach Forest Evashevski. He sold three thousand shares to Congressman Thomas P. "Tip" O'Neill (D-Mass.), who had been a student at Boston College when Leahy coached there. He sold stock to his brothers and sisters, to Notre Dame equipment manager Jack McAllister. There was only one problem. Hamilton Oil & Gas didn't have access to the oil reserves that it suggested it did. Not long after Leahy sold the stock, the price dropped to twenty-five cents per share. The Securities and Exchange Commission smelled a rat.

The SEC held hearings in which it established that Leahy had used "false and misleading information" to sell the stock, that he and the firm president had misrepresented the stock, and that Hamilton Oil & Gas should have registered the stock with the SEC.

Syndicated columnist Drew Pearson made a career of taking on—and taking down—the high and mighty. On Leahy, he utilized pity instead of venom. "Thereby hangs a tale of what can happen to sports figures, actors, writers, et al., when they barge into the field of high finance," Pearson wrote in his column "Washington Merry-Go-Round," adding, "Actually, SEC officials don't plan to be too hard on Leahy. They know he's better at football than high finance." In the end, the SEC charged only that Leahy had made "misleading" statements.

As he sank deeper into the morass of the Hamilton deal, Leahy decided it would be a good time to take one more job. In October 1959, Leahy found what appeared to be a safe haven in the upstart American Football League. Barron Hilton, the thirty-two-year-old playboy son of hotel magnate Conrad Hilton, hired Leahy as general manager of what would become the Los Angeles Chargers. When the old AAFC began after the war, Leahy had turned down a chance to become who Paul Brown had become, a coach and part-owner of a lucrative franchise. The Detroit Lions tried to hire him and give him a piece of the team. Maybe Leahy saw the AFL starting up and didn't want to pass up another opportunity.

The NFL did what it could to stymie the AFL. When the new league met in Minneapolis, dangling a team to the city fathers, the NFL suddenly granted the expansion franchise that became the Vikings. The AFL needed a home for its eighth and final franchise for the inaugural season of 1960. Leahy, one of three members on the league's expansion committee, called Billy Sullivan, who had tried in vain to interest the NFL in coming back to Boston. Leahy told him if he could raise $25,000 by either the next day or the following Monday, depending on who's retelling the story, then he could be an owner in the AFL. Sullivan had $8,300 in the bank. He and his wife had been saving to buy a cottage on Cape Cod. Sullivan came home and told her they were buying a professional football team instead. He passed the hat among friends and business associates for the remainder of the buy-in fee.

The next month, Leahy lured McBride out of the business and back into coaching, announcing that his favorite assistant would be the first head coach of the Chargers. The hire didn't go over well in Los Angeles. Leahy saw McBride as an able football man. The writers saw a businessman who had been out of football for five years. Once McBride slept on it, the hire didn't go over well with him, either. He realized, his son said, that his love of football and his love of Notre Dame could not be separated. McBride promptly resigned, which made Leahy look like a buffoon. He saved himself a few weeks later by hiring Sid Gillman, whom the crosstown Rams of the NFL had just fired.

And then it all came apart. Gillman, a brilliant coach and a tough infighter, liked doing things his way. For instance, Leahy had signed several players to no-cut contracts. Gillman didn't believe in them. Gillman clashed with Leahy. So did Tom Eddy, Hilton's right-hand man. It could be that their personalities didn't mesh. But that wasn't it. Leahy was coming apart at the seams. The collapse of the Hamilton Oil deal ate away at his fragile insides.

Five weeks before the Chargers' first preseason game, on July 1, 1960, Leahy resigned as general manager. The next day, he checked himself into the Loretto Hospital in Chicago. His brother Tom readily described Frank as having suffered a "nervous breakdown."

"I've been close to Frank for the last year and I know he's been terribly worried about oil stocks he sold to friends which hadn't turned out well," Tom said. "He feels responsible." Tom said he had watched his brother undergo "a complete personality change. He's just the reverse of everything he was. Once he was a quick decider. Now he doesn't want to make decisions. Previously once he made a commitment he'd break his neck to keep it. Now his promises mean nothing to him."

There's no context available for knowing which promises Tom referenced. He did eventually keep one promise. He vowed to the SEC that he would repay every single investor to whom he sold Hamilton stock "if it's God's last act on Earth for me."

Maybe that search for cash led to his worst debacle. Or maybe Leahy would have fallen to one more charlatan, anyway. A fast-talker in Southern California convinced Leahy to put $125,000 down on a title company out there. The Southern California of the early 1960s resembled a second coming of the Gold Rush. Never mind that the drugstore in which Leahy invested in Burbank went bust. Tom begged his older brother to let him check out the title business. Frank waved him off. A few months later, the partner said they needed another couple of hundred grand to operate. Leahy invested it. It may have cost Leahy as much as $500,000 before the business went under.

His professional life was a shambles. His reputation had been severely bruised. And there was one other thing—his marriage was in tatters.

CHAPTER NINETEEN

A GREAT AMERICAN FAMILY

In the fall of 1955, the one-year-old magazine *Sports Illustrated* sent writer Gerald Holland to Michigan City to write a story about Frank Leahy in retirement. Holland chose to be a fly on the wall amid the tumult of an autumn Sunday morning, the day after a Notre Dame game, in a home with old friends stopping by and eight children, ages three to nineteen, coming in and out of the room.

Leahy told Holland that he and Floss called their home "The Stadium" because of its size. Fred Leahy recalls growing up there had its moments of feeling as if they were surrounded by spectators.

"It would be, 'C'mon kids, gotta go home, get baths, showers, whatever because *Life* magazine is here to take pictures,'" Fred, sixth in birth order, remembers of his childhood. "A lot of posed pictures. *That* was different. Our friends are saying, 'Where you going?' 'I don't know. People are coming to take pictures of us and do a story.'"

Holland portrayed Leahy as a kindly, benevolent father who ran a strict home but gave his children wide latitude. "Dad would say, 'Never belittle or embarrass Our Lady on the Dome,'" Fred said. "Even as we were growing up, 'Act like a Notre Damer.'"

When Frank Leahy turned forty-six in 1954, shortly before the first autumn without football in his adult life, he called the celebration "wonderful and strange." Now, in Holland's account, Leahy had embraced his identity as a former coach.

Floss remained offstage throughout the seven-page piece. Holland made a brief mention of her being elsewhere in the house.

"Sometimes, publicly, our family was listed as a Great American Family," said Sue Moustakas, the Leahys' second child and oldest daughter. In the *Sports Illustrated* piece, Holland refers over and over again to the politeness of the Leahy children, all of them executing their dad's instruction to look strangers in the eye as they shake hands. Sue, seventeen at the time, walks in and says, "Excuse me, gentlemen," before she asks Dad for the Oldsmobile. Sue is in her mid-eighties now, a kind, sweet woman who clearly has her father's spine.

She remembers the gulf between the Great American Family and the Leahys.

"As children who were raised to be smart, wise, honest, we fought it," Sue said. "We weren't polite and humble, I don't think."

Great American Families don't have problems. The Leahys had problems that plenty of families had in the 1950s, just not the ideal families that blanketed the national culture. Thanks to the sudden ubiquity of television, shows such as *Father Knows Best* or *The Adventures of Ozzie & Harriet* provided weekly examples of what a family is supposed to be. No one on those shows had the problems that the Leahys and so many others had.

"Do you know anything about my mother?" Sue Moustakas said. "Well, it was kind of a sad story. She was an alcoholic. So life was difficult, because people expected us to be beyond that, or not part of that. I think her problem was, he was famous, and she was Mom at home with all of us."

American culture promoted traditional roles, traditional values.

In the fall of 1949, Leahy spoke to Notre Dame students about the institution of marriage. The priest who introduced him called him "a national figure, but before the eyes of God and His Blessed Mother, a perfect Catholic gentleman and father." That's what an American man intended to be, especially Catholic men, as part of a group still on the edges of Main Street. After the war, America had been thrust into the role of leader of the free world. Americans had to show strength, lest Communism win. The magazines and newspapers depicted Frank and Floss as Ozzie & Harriet & Football. But Frank and Floss had issues. Frank grew up in a family in which vulnerability was a flaw. He grew up on the prairie with a father who taught him to project strength. He told Floss next to nothing about his problems. Getting squeezed out by Father Hesburgh? He said nothing. The post-coaching problems in business? He said little. Floss knew something had gone awry. She described Frank as "miserable." But he shut her out. "He wouldn't let me be a part of anything personal," she said to biographer Wells Twombly. When he coached, he wasn't home. When he quit coaching and began working, he traveled. Floss couldn't travel. She had kids at home, and besides, she didn't like airplanes.

Alcoholism ran in Floss's family. Her parents drank. She drank. Frank's brother Jack, the smallest and fiercest of the four Leahy brothers, drank. Three of the Leahy children struggled with alcohol throughout most or all of their adult lives.

When Frank coached at Notre Dame, and Floss lived a quasi-public life, she managed the ups and downs. Floss became friends with Bonnie Rockne, Knute's widow, perhaps the only woman in America who had walked in her shoes. But Frank quit coaching, and Fred Miller died the following year, a loss that made a private man withdraw even more. Bonnie Rockne died a few months after Miller. Floss told Twombly that she became an alcoholic the way that so many people do: a drink here, a drink there, two drinks here, three drinks there, and pretty soon, the bridge club didn't play bridge anymore. They just got together for afternoon cocktails.

"A lot of drinkers there," Sue said of her Long Beach neighborhood.

"A lot of Irish Catholic people and they're all drinkers. It was just, everybody thought it was OK."

All the Leahy kids wanted was to be what every teenager wants to be—like everyone else. But they had a famous dad. That brought unwanted attention. And they might come home from school to a mother who hadn't waited for happy hour to open a bottle.

"She would drink anything," Fred said. "Mostly wine. Growing up, you always knew. We would come home from school. There was that atmosphere in the house. And you knew right away. She'd be either on the floor passed out, or at the table with her head down. That was tough. When Mom wasn't drunk, she'd be making cookies, dinner. The radio would be going."

Moose Krause, Leahy's former assistant coach and still the athletic director at Notre Dame, kept an eye on Floss and the kids while Frank traveled, even after Frank no longer coached. That helped—Fred Leahy reserves a special place in his heart for Moose's memory—but Moose wasn't much more than a Band-Aid. Fred remembers his sober mom as loving, caring, happy, a "cuddlebug." She went to church. She took care of people. He thinks he got a lot of those traits. He did not get the alcoholism trait. Fred guesses that if he added up every beer he has ever had, it wouldn't fill a case.

The kids fought back the only way they knew how. They would bury their mom's bottle in the yard, hide it in the attic, throw it out. One of them would pour out a bottle of gin, and a taxicab would arrive at the house with a new bottle as passenger. One time, Fred said, his mom resorted to drinking a bottle of Lavoris mouthwash.

"We would do mean things, tough love, back then," Fred said. "We'd say, 'You know what, Mom? You're horrible.' It was just kind of a vicious cycle."

"By the way, we all have Irish tempers," Sue said. "So everybody spoke their piece. We didn't let it lay low. We fought about it. My older brother Frank went away to [high] school. He wasn't home very much. I was very critical of my mother. I was telling her that it's not something a mother should do, to be drunk. She really did not like that I said these things to her. But I felt like she needed to hear them."

Floss kept drinking. Frank kept withdrawing. He put a padlock on the liquor cabinet. She broke it. They argued about Floss's drinking. When the Chargers' general manager job came open, Frank leaped at it. He went to California, a de facto separation if not a legal one. Frank, by himself on the West Coast, started drinking, too. Sue idolized her father, who wasn't around. She saw her mother's struggles every day. "I thought in a way it was her fault," Sue said of Frank's absences. "Why would he want to be here when there was nothing but fighting about it [Floss's drinking]?"

Sue wasn't the first daughter to ever have trouble getting along with her mother. Sue grew up as a Daddy's Girl. "I would say that he was a good father," she said. "You know he and I used to take walks. I used to ask him a lot of questions about a lot of things. And he said, 'Why do you ask so many questions?' And I think I said, 'I wanna know.' And he said, 'Well, I'm glad to tell you.' "

As she got older, she said, "We used to go walking together, walking down the beach road. I was then thinking, I would like to be a success, so I was finding out what are the tasks that have to be accomplished in order to be a success. I think that's what I was thinking. So we talked a lot, and he liked that."

Perhaps those walks stand out in her mind for their rarity. Leahy told Holland that, when he coached, that is, during Sue's childhood, "I can remember coming to the house, and the children would come in and speak to me and I would look at them without seeing them or without hearing what they said. I was that preoccupied."

And yet, Sue said of her and her seven siblings, "I know the elders of us got the best of it," she said, "the best of his wisdom."

The dad in Fred's memory is a more forbidding figure. Fred remembers his father giving him a total of three compliments. One was for showing the initiative to go cut a Christmas tree for the family. A few minutes later, the doorbell rang, and an irate man informed Frank that Fred had cut the tree down in the man's yard.

Leahy described the family unit to writers as akin to a team, with regular meetings in which each child received grades for his or her performance of chores. The child who graded out the highest received a monetary prize; the child who graded out at the bottom would lose privileges.

"We believe all children are happier when they have a clear idea of what is expected of them," Leahy said.

> *"The Leahy home-coaching system may sound formal and old-fashioned, but it works wonderfully well. His children are happy, spontaneous, and secure."*
> —Hal Boyle, AP, April 8, 1952

Two flaws developed in this system. One, Leahy traveled so much in his post-coaching life that he remained a distant presence in his kids' lives. Two, children aren't players, motivated to do what they must to get playing time and keep their scholarship.

"Dad would come home," Fred said. "We'd go to him for our allowance. He'd say, 'Son, come in here. I want you to tell me what have you done this week to earn your allowance.' It was like an inquisition. Finally, we just stopped. We'd go to Mom."

Or the story about the letters.

"He was gone a lot. We'd write him letters. He'd bring them back graded for spelling, punctuation, legibility. So we stopped writing him. He'd come back, 'Lads, how come you've stopped writing me?' None of us had the guts to say, 'Because you're a prick. You grade them.' "

Fred said that with a smile, not bitterness. He is in his mid-seventies now. He loved his father and knows that his father loved him. He does not resent his dad's absences, the strictness or the spankings (Dad used a hairbrush). Fred appreciates the values that his father so wanted to instill in his children. He speaks proudly of how Frank used to get up from the table after a family dinner in a restaurant and walk into the kitchen to thank the staff, of how the ushers at Notre Dame Stadium used to tell Fred that anytime Coach Leahy heard one of them had run into a rough patch, he would send over a signed football, of how Fred once complained about his shoes, and Frank put him in the car and drove nearly to Gary, forty minutes away, to show him poor children who had no shoes at all.

And, of course, manners.

"When you met somebody, it was shaking the hand, 'Yes sir,' 'No sir,' 'Pleased to meet you, sir,' " Fred said. "When he had a group come over, a few days later, Dad would always say, 'Lads, come into the den.' "

Time for the test.

"Who were the guests we had two days ago?"

"Man, if we didn't remember their names, we were grounded and spanked and everything," Fred said. "I remember Vince Lombardi coming there once, and I was terrified to walk into Dad's den where Vince Lombardi was. He had a presence like Dad did."

He imitates his father straight down to Frank's prefacing his statements with a clearing of the throat. Fred is wistful that his dad died when Fred was twenty-three years old, that he didn't get to talk football with him.

"He was the most intense human being I've ever known," Fred said. "Competitive, driving."

He remembers his dad asking him and his brothers about getting into fights in school, an echo of what Frank's father had asked him in his adolescence. If they answered yes, Frank would ask, "Did you win?"

He wanted his sons to be tough. Fred remembers being nine or ten years old, playing baseball in the front yard, when one of his brothers lost control of the bat, which flew into Fred's face. He ran inside for help. Frank said, "Just hold it with your fingertip long enough and it will heal." Fred went to the doctor anyway. The wound needed eighteen stitches. It's not that Frank was a Christian Scientist. Lord knows that doctors healed him over and over again. But he had a great belief in a person's ability to strengthen himself. Take Fred's nearsightedness. His father discouraged him from wearing glasses.

"He said, 'You know, a person on crutches, they're not going to improve their leg strength,' " Fred recalled. So he didn't always wear his glasses. Fred recalled how his father sent him and his brother to the other end of a practice area to shag golf balls for him.

"He'd start out with a hundred golf balls and we'd come back, with, like, fifty-six," Fred said.

" 'God, son, where have all these golf balls gone?'

"I said, 'Well, Dad, I can't see!'

"He said, 'That's no excuse.' "

When high-schooler Frank Jr. got a job at Sears selling shoes, Frank, the man who had taken a class on the foot from Dr. Scholl himself, told his son to go to the library and get a book about the skeleton and musculature of the foot, "because I want you to become the best shoe salesman in the history of Sears."

Frank Jr. looked at his father as if he had three heads.

"That's who Dad was," Fred said.

Every activity had to have a purpose, and that purpose was to be better. That's how Frank Leahy lived. That's not how most people live. That's not how children live.

"We had this huge house, huge front yard," Fred said. "So it was always the place where my friends, my older brothers' friends, would come play football in the front yard. Dad would come out." Fred does the throat clearing, then imitates his father.

"Lads, let's stop playing now. Let's work on fundamentals."

"Here was twelve of us," Fred said, "age seven, eight, nine, ten, and he would have us doing passing drills, centering drills. Finally, my friends said, 'We're not playing football at your house anymore.'

"And that's who he was."

Sue became a substitute mom to her younger siblings. She and her boyfriend Deno Moustakas, who lived in the neighborhood, would take the kids out of the house when Floss was drinking. They would go to the beach, go horseback riding, go to the movies.

"I had the greatest older brothers and sisters of them all," Fred said. "They would take me, my younger sister [Mary], my younger brother [Chris], everywhere with them. Back then, we had drive-ins. In fact,

I used to tell my older sisters. I'd say, I don't know how you guys ever had sex or kissed. You always had us three kids in the back seat."

But eventually Sue had had enough. When Frank decided to move the family west, he planned on Sue coming with them, continuing her role as au pair. That's when Deno and Sue decided to elope. Sue didn't want to ask permission, because she didn't want to hear the answer that she didn't want to hear. When they discussed it with Frank, he told Deno that he couldn't marry Sue until he got into the boxing ring with Sue's uncle Tom.

"He was a Golden Gloves boxer," said Luke Moustakas, Sue and Deno's son. "My dad was like hell, no. Tom would take silver dollars and bend them with his fingers."

Telling Frank Leahy no was never an effective solution. Deno put on the gloves, took one punch from Tom and went down. That was sufficient.

The five boys lived with the athletic pressure, either societal or self-induced or both, of being the son of the great Frank Leahy. Frank Jr., who was slight of stature, started out at Notre Dame and went out for football. But he could see he would not play and eventually gave it up. Jim, whom the family called Jub, most resembled his father. Frank told Jim he had neither the size nor the speed to play at Notre Dame, just as Frank had been told by his high school friend. And Jim toughed it out there for four years to prove he could make it, just as his father did. Jim appeared in one game in 1968, his senior year, as a guard in the last two minutes of the last home game, a 34–6 rout of Georgia Tech played in what *The South Bend Tribune* called "some of the worst weather conditions in Notre Dame Stadium history."

His father delighted in telling the story that when the game ended, Jim reached over and grabbed the football as a souvenir. "That was," Frank said, "the first time in history that a football player awarded himself the game ball."

Jim did enjoy the glory of having a son, Ryan, play four seasons on the offensive line for Lou Holtz and serve as co-captain in his junior and senior seasons, 1994 and 1995. It took three generations to produce a Leahy who could thrive on the field for the Fighting Irish.

Jerry seemed to live to not do what his father said. He had some prankster in him. He once beaned Frank with a snowball. Frank, furious, wanted to know which boy threw it. When no one confessed, he walked into the house with snowball still on his head, sat down at the Monopoly board, and began playing with the other kids, waiting for Jerry to crack. He finally did.

Jerry always looked for a shortcut. In his twenties, he owed his dad some money, so on a trip to the Netherlands, Jerry mailed home forty pounds of hashish hidden in cuckoo clocks. His arrest humiliated his father, not to mention unleashing a fountain of schadenfreude for all those still out to avenge Frank Leahy's dominance on the football field.

"I never, ever, ever wanted to get in trouble, because I thought Dad's name would be ruined," Fred Leahy said. "I remember when my brother Jerry was arrested, Dad called me, my brother Jim, and I was a senior in college, and it just mortified me, because the headline in Portland was, 'Frank Leahy's Son Arrested.' And Dad wanted to leave the country. So embarrassed." Jerry served a year and a day in prison.

Though Frank had left the Chargers in 1960, a year later he moved the family to Southern California. A year after that, they moved to Denver. Two years later, in 1964, they moved again, to Portland, Oregon, this time where Frank opened an insurance business in which he enlisted Frank Jr. Through it all, Floss drank.

"So many parents gave up on their kids, and do now," said Fred Leahy, who works with troubled adolescents in Arizona. "Dad never gave up. He would put Mom into program after program. And it was hard growing up, because back then, alcoholism was thought of as mental illness. They would go and they would do, what's the word I'm thinking of, where they zap the brain, shock treatment. We'd go visit Mom, and she was a zombie. That was tough... So she'd come home, be good for a couple of months, drink a bottle of Listerine. Go back, more shock, but Dad never gave up on her."

Floss finally found a program in Portland that worked. She remained sober for the rest of her life. Without alcohol as an accelerant, Floss and Frank quit lashing out at each other. They repaired their marriage. Floss told Twombly that when she saw how proud Frank was of her sobriety, she knew she would never drink again.

Frank remained in business, bouncing from insurance deal to insurance deal. In 1966, he tried to merge football and business, getting involved with a group trying to get an AFL franchise in Anaheim, California, for the following year. The NFL quashed the AFL expansion by agreeing to merge with the ten-team AFL, and ten teams was it. Leahy's ownership group pivoted to align itself with a group promoting a third professional league, but a lack of interest from the TV networks put an end to that.

Leahy continued to do television work, one indication that his name, however tarnished by his business woes, still carried some heft among the American public. In 1962, he co-produced and hosted a short documentary on Sonny Liston, who in September of that year became the heavyweight boxing champion of the world. *The Other Side of Sonny Liston*, released days after Liston won the title in a first-round knockout of Floyd Patterson, carried a jazz soundtrack, showed Liston training, and included an interview of the champ conducted by Leahy. The pairing of the host, with his formal manner of speaking, and the introverted subject sent off few sparks.

Leahy: Sonny, what advice would you give to a young lad who came to you and said, "I want to become a boxer." What would you tell him as regards training and so forth?
Liston: Well, they always told me anything you want to do, do your best and be the best at it.
Leahy: And the training part? He has to pay a price, doesn't he?
Liston: Yes, he do. You have to really train. Anything you go after, you have to train at.

But the two of them hit it off, at least enough that a New Orleans columnist ran with a story a month later reporting that Liston planned to dump his manager and hire Leahy. Leahy shot the story down.

In the mid-1960s, Leahy began doing sports for WBBM-TV, the CBS affiliate in Chicago. He shot off a zinger or two at a subpar player. Leahy once said about Bears tackle Frank Cornish, "The only time that Cornish crosses the line of scrimmage is when teams changed goals after the first and third quarters. Only very occasionally does he abrogate his non-aggression pact."

After a long losing streak of investing with and banking on the wrong people, late in life Leahy found another benevolent sponsor. Pat O'Malley ran Canteen Corporation, a company that operated concessions around the country. Leahy became an assistant to the president, and O'Malley sent him around the country as a goodwill ambassador, speaking to civic groups and to young people on the attributes of America and the evils of Communism. The American way of life in the 1960s descended into a cultural and political maelstrom. Leahy manned the ramparts of the old guard, blaming the upheaval on the Communists.

"Many, many countless, innumerable people are not aware of the facts," Leahy would say. "They're just shocked speechless when you talk to them about the precarious situation in which we find the United States today. They really say they don't know what's going on. But they better find out and do something about it immediately. This man Lenin started out with twenty thousand. Now he has over two billion people under Communistic slave rule. And they're after us, very scientifically, very cunningly, very brilliantly and they are succeeding."

Leahy carried that torch, making speeches to football coaches who wanted tips from The Master, making speeches to players who had no idea how successful he had been.

"Those virtues I talk about are no longer popular," Leahy said. "That is why I have to live. If I die, those virtues may die with me."

As he approached sixty years of age, his body began to give out on him. No one stood over him, imploring him to stand and resume the fight for Our Lady. No one had to. Leahy had never stopped paying the price.

CHAPTER TWENTY

THE CARDINAL SIN: HE BEAT THEM ALL

It's impossible to know whether the wear and tear that Leahy put himself through wore down his immunity, but at some point in 1967 he began to notice numbness in his leg. Soon after doctors diagnosed him with a form of leukemia. Life expectancy for leukemia six decades ago measured in months, not years. But Leahy had built a life by not giving in to discomfort, misfortune, or bad diagnoses. Leahy told Los Angeles columnist Bud Furillo that doctors told him not to expect to get any better but that he intended to live another ten to fifteen years anyway. "It's embarrassing to get up from a luncheon table and find my feet don't want to go the way I want them to go," Leahy said. "That's what Coach Rockne used to say. 'Leahy, your feet aren't going in the right direction.' "

Leukemia had a fight on its hands. Leahy refused to let the disease slow him down. In 1969, an intestine became gangrenous, and Leahy's heart stopped on the operating table—twice. The following January, he flew from Chicago to Dallas to see Notre Dame end its forty-five-year bowl ban by playing in the 1970 Cotton Bowl.

The College Football Hall of Fame named its first class in 1951. The Hall had been created by the new National Football Foundation, itself the brainchild of Red Blaik, General Douglas MacArthur, and Grantland Rice. Through more than seven decades the Hall has steered clear of even the hint of scandal. In most years, the NFF Honors Court selected one coach to join the class of honored players. Leahy did not become eligible for election until 1956, three years after retirement. The headlines engendered by Leahy's business disasters that began in 1959 gave succor to those coaches and administrators looking for a reason not to honor him. Whether scandal or spite, the court did not nominate Leahy for inclusion on the Hall of Fame ballot again until 1965. The court did not elect him that year or in the next four.

Billy Sullivan, the Patriots owner, stopped contributing to the NFF and let them know why. Newspaper columnists took up the cause. David Condon of the *Chicago Tribune*, who had attended Notre Dame in the 1940s, wrote, "Leahy still cannot fathom why his contemporaries shun him . . . Most of the rest of us understand. The folks in college football still are jealous of Frank Leahy, the greatest coach of modern times. A super-Rockne. Frank Leahy must live with the cardinal sin: he beat them all."

Before the January 1969 meeting in Los Angeles, Furillo wrote of Leahy, "If he doesn't qualify for the College Hall of Fame, Cooperstown should have second thoughts on whether a mistake might have been made in honoring [Babe] Ruth so fast."

The court named five finalists. Bud Wilkinson of Oklahoma won the vote. Leahy came in a distant fifth.

Two weeks later, Notre Dame held the dinner to honor Leahy, the dinner at which speaker after speaker implored the Hall of Fame to right the wrong of Leahy's exclusion from the court. Fred Russell, the

Nashville Banner sports editor who chaired the court, decided to take up Leahy's cause. So did Blaik. Newspaper columnists continued to pipe up. The omission began to attract more attention, not the kind that the NFF liked. Leahy had the credentials, he was sick, and not voting for him reeked of pettiness.

The minutes of the Honors Court meeting on January 15, 1970, held in the Ohio Room of the Statler Hilton in Washington, DC, state that the members opened with a discussion of the passage in the court's rules regarding a nominee's post-football life. "All agreed that by honoring... only men who had excelled in their chosen profession after their playing careers are over, the Honors Court could make their National Football Foundation and Hall of Fame selections meaningful—and if we did not do so—the comparison between what we said and what we did would be unfortunate."

Having covered its collective rear for posterity, the Honors Court voted in Leahy. Russell wrote the letter that Leahy had waited to receive for thirteen years.

> *Dear Frank,*
>
> *This is the greatest honor that can come to a former college player or coach, and I wish to congratulate you...*

Jerry Nason of *The Boston Globe* celebrated Leahy while raising an eyebrow at the entire process. "Guys passed him on the way in who should call him 'Sir.' "

Doctors began computer searches looking for blood for Leahy's regular transfusions. The arthritis that had plagued him since the 1940s bore down on him. Diabetes joined in. In the summer of 1971, Leahy lapsed into "extremely critical" condition. Surgery to remove fatty tissue from his kidneys and liver saved him. That fall, he flew to Boston to see his friend Billy Sullivan's New England Patriots play their first game in Foxboro Stadium. "He weighed about 144 pounds and was doing something that he never would have done when he was in his prime," Sullivan said. "He was accepting the arms of people who wanted to help him up the steps."

LEAHY MADE ONE LAST TRIP TO BOSTON, IN THE SPRING OF 1973. Sullivan drove him over to the *Globe* office to see Nason, and the three of them sat in the cafeteria for two hours, reminisced, and drank iced tea. Nason said Leahy's thirst for memories of the Boston College upset of Tennessee in the 1941 Sugar Bowl could not be slaked. Nason recounted how Leahy leaned heavily on him as went to the elevator to leave. "He was just a shell of the virile Leahy of yore," Nason wrote. And this: "He was all pride and guts."

On June 10, in his home in Lake Oswego, a suburb of Portland, Leahy received an oil portrait of himself purchased for $500 by students at St. Michael's in Schererville, Indiana, where he had spoken at a father-son banquet two years earlier. A week later, an old acquaintance, Father Hesburgh, came to visit, perhaps to minister to a dying man, perhaps to tie up loose ends, more likely both. Over two days, they told stories, laughed together, cried together. The day after that, Leahy gathered himself, walked to the pool outside his apartment, eased in, and swam five laps. He shuffled back to the apartment, got in bed, and a short time later he returned to St. Vincent's Hospital. He died the next afternoon, June 21, 1973, seven weeks short of his sixty-fifth birthday.

The encomiums to Leahy flowed from coast to coast. "I loved the man," Sullivan said in Boston. "God was having a good day when he made Frank Leahy. He was a fighting Irishman until the very end." That's when Sullivan broke into tears.

"It took me several years to understand Frank Leahy," Red Blaik said, "and I am better for the experience as Leahy was a genuinely fine and inspirational man. Frank only had one problem: His teams won too often, and even Rockne had no better record. Indeed, I am saddened by the passing of my old friend."

President Richard Nixon, who had endured a hellish week in which his former counsel John Dean testified to all of Nixon's Watergate misdeeds, wrote a lovely condolence letter to Floss. "His death is a profound loss to American collegiate athletics and to all of us who were proud to count him as a friend," the president wrote.

Notre Dame inquired about holding the funeral and burial on campus. Floss declined. She said that Notre Dame had him for so many years, and now he belonged to her. They are buried together in Portland.

The family held the funeral on a stiflingly hot day in Portland. Johnny Lattner, one of the eight former players who served as pallbearers, remembered all of them sweating and gasping for air as they carried the casket to the hearse. Lattner turned to fellow pallbearer George Connor. "Oh, George," he said, "Leahy always said that the last 10 yards were the hardest."

On Thanksgiving Day, at Notre Dame's last home game of the 1973 season, the university held a memorial of its own. Father Hesburgh celebrated the memorial Mass before the game, and Floss sat with him to watch Notre Dame defeat Air Force, 48–15. The Irish finished 11-0 that season, their first undefeated, untied record since 1949, the last year that Leahy won a national championship.

Floss Leahy died in 1977 of cancer. She was only sixty-four years old.

"It was horrible," Fred said. "I would hear her in pain. I used to pray, 'God, end it. Take her.' And it just went on and on."

The family that had watched Jerry go to prison for drugs made its peace with weed.

"My brother was a pot smoker," Fred said. "He gave Mom marijuana. And her last week, she was pain free. Never moaned. Never groaned. Never anything. I got confused, because I viewed it as illegal. 'OK, God, I'm confused. Did you send my brother marijuana to do this?' "

"I WOULD NOT TRADE ONE MINUTE OF MY LIFE FOR A DIFFERENT ENDing," Leahy told Twombly. "So man suffers some. The only thing that matters is: To what end does that suffering come?"

No one knows how or why Leahy's accomplishments receded among the Notre Dame faithful. Surely it had something to do with his rocky relationship with the university that he never stopped loving. Lujack recalled that years after Leahy retired, he and Creighton Miller had dinner with Leahy in South Bend. Afterward, as they drove by campus, Leahy spotted the moonlight illuminating the golden dome of the administration building. He told Lujack to stop the car. The three alums stared in awe at the sight before Leahy broke the silence. "Gents, there might be the greatest sight the world has ever known," he said. "It's a shame that everyone can't see it."

Ara Parseghian, Dan Devine, and Lou Holtz won four national championships for the Irish among them, from 1966 to 1988, and President Ronald Reagan, who christened himself the Gipper, appeared on the scene to burnish the legend of Rockne. By the mid-1990s, the graying men who had played for Leahy decided they must act. Leahy's Lads, as they called themselves, began raising money to establish a scholarship in Leahy's name and erect a statue of him at Notre Dame Stadium. It stands in front of Gate C.

The statue, dedicated in 1997, has Leahy kneeling on his right knee, holding a football with both hands above it. By 2002, Leahy's Lads had raised nearly $1 million, enough to pay for the statue and award four scholarships per year. That gave a permanence to Leahy's legacy. Yet it remains clouded, perhaps by time.

"The difference between him and Rockne," Beano Cook said in 2010, "is Rockne didn't have to chase any ghosts . . . It's phenomenal what Leahy did. And yet he's forgotten."

Some of the fog emanates from recency bias. To commemorate the 150th anniversary of college football in 2019, ESPN commissioned a poll of administrators and journalists to name the 150 greatest coaches. Leahy finished tenth. Five of the nine coaches ahead of him coached into the 1990s or later.

The clouds even hover over Notre Dame. Every season, the student government creates The Shirt, a tee sold to unite the fan base and raise funds for needy students and campus organizations. In 2006, on the heels of Charlie Weis's glorious 9-3 debut season, the back of The Shirt featured photos of Rockne, Parseghian, Holtz, and... Weis. "It says TRADITION on the front and ignores it on the back," a fan told the *South Bend Tribune*.

The Leahys noticed. "Nobody had an answer," Fred Leahy said. You could blame it on college-age students, to whom Frank Leahy may as well be Abe Lincoln. You could blame it on how Leahy's heyday took place before television dominated American culture. But it's as if Father Hesburgh's decision to pivot the university away from Leahy's success left the coach in a football purgatory.

If Leahy departed a beloved figure on campus, the prickly nature of his relationship with the coaches who followed him lessened that affection. While the university and Leahy officially reconciled with the dinner that opened the Convocation Center in 1969, Leahy's death coming only four years later prevented him from being showered with the love that legends on other campuses receive. Alabama, for instance, recently honored Nick Saban by putting his name on a venue already named for Bear Bryant. Saban Field at Bryant-Denny Stadium may be a mouthful but it guarantees that the legends of both Bryant and Saban are not written in pencil.

Notre Dame plays in Notre Dame Stadium. On a campus where change is made carefully if at all, Rockne-Leahy Stadium, Leahy Field at Rockne Stadium, or whatever combination you like, isn't going to happen anytime soon. That doesn't diminish the fact that they are the two coaches who made Notre Dame football what it is. Rockne created it out of whole cloth, taking his "Ramblers" to the people, Notre Dame's people, the Catholic masses in New York and Chicago, Philadelphia, and Baltimore.

Leahy? Leahy poured the concrete to set the foundation of Notre Dame football. Amid the anti-Catholic bias in postwar America, the success of Leahy's teams established Notre Dame as a metaphor for success in a nation that hungered to honor it. Over the course of his sixty-five years, Leahy proved himself all too human. He struggled to connect with people, up to and including the ones in his own home. The struggle to connect continues more than a half century after his death. Former NFL coach Bill Parcells is famous for saying, "You are what your record says you are." Frank Leahy's record is second in the history of college football only to Rockne. Leahy must be the exception that proves that rule.

ACKNOWLEDGMENTS

During the three years I worked on ESPN's College Football 150, a commemoration of the sport's 2019 sesquicentennial, I noticed Frank Leahy had the second-best record in the history of college football yet did not get elected to the College Football Hall of Fame for thirteen years. That is the thread that I began to pull. The more I researched, the more I wanted to know about a man whose life captured the growth of college football, and America, in the first two-thirds of the twentieth century.

Fred Leahy has been an email friend for many years. His openness about his father convinced me I could write biography, not hagiography. Fred's older sister Sue Moustakas and her son Luke tried to help me learn what made their father/grandfather tick in every way they could. They informed this book greatly.

Former Notre Dame athletic director Jack Swarbrick showed an early enthusiasm for this project. At the university's Hesburgh Library, head archivist Patrick Milhoan, sports archivist Greg Bond, Joe Smith, Elizabeth Hogan, and Rachel Bohlmann patiently answered a multitude of questions and requests. All letters referenced in the text, as well as so much more material that built this book, are housed in the university archives. Current athletic director Pete Bevacqua, deputy AD Aaron Horvath, associate AD Katy Lonergan, and assistant AD Alan Wasielewski opened doors for me on campus, most important, their own. Thank you to Irish superfan Cappy Gagnon, whose Notre Dame arcana is a collection surpassed only by what he stores between his ears. Author Jim Lefebvre, who runs the Knute Rockne Memorial Society, lent his support and knowledge.

This book benefited greatly from the unpublished memoir of Leahy's former player and top assistant Bob McBride, entrusted to me by his sons Bob, Pat, and Tim. I owe them thanks, as well as Jeanie Knudtson, the niece of Frank Leahy and daughter of Frank's older brother Gene. Her father's memoir revealed and explained a great deal about Frank Leahy's upbringing. Pat Sullivan and Bob Sullivan, the sons of brothers Billy and Frank Sullivan, respectively, helped me with both family memories and scrapbooks of their fathers' relationship with and respect for the coach they worked for and adored for so many years.

Ed Kelly, Notre Dame '55, who served as a manager on Leahy's last Irish teams, shared his time, memories, and scrapbook with me. Father Wilson Miscamble, a retired Notre Dame professor who wrote a biography of the late university president Father Theodore Hesburgh, shared his knowledge of Father Ted over a long interview/lunch at the Morris Inn. Much appreciated.

The New York Historical Society houses the former editorial libraries of *Time* and *Sports Illustrated* magazines. Librarian Gina Modero unearthed four folders of raw reporting and published material related to Leahy.

My former colleague at On3, Ryan Tice, the editor of *Blue & Gold Illustrated*, gave me access to more than four decades of back issues. Steve Hatchell and Matt Sign of the National Football Foundation, which operates the College Football Hall of Fame, opened the foundation's archives to me, illuminating the annual snubs of Leahy in the Hall voting. I lived on Newspapers.com as I wrote and researched this book. What a godsend. The same goes for Phillip Bahr of the Fairfield Public Library, who chased down a gaggle of wild geese for me.

My agent Nena Madonia is a treasure. I value her bottomless well of enthusiasm and knowledge of the book business. I would like to thank Dan Ambrosio, formerly of Grand Central Publishing, for his belief in the book. Grand Central editorial director Brant Rumble, a fellow native of Alabama, brought this ship into port with a light hand and unflagging good humor. Marketing director Allison Schuster and publicist Staci Burt politely absorbed my pep talks and applied their expertise anyway. So did copy editor Rebecca Maines and production maven Mari C. Okuda, a proud Domer.

Thanks as well to friends and cheerleaders Gene Wojciechowski, Dave Wilson, David Duffey, Mark Schlabach, Pete Thamel, Heather Dinich, Mark Blaudschun, and John Dahl. Author Tom Reilly, who loves Notre Dame so much you would think he attended the school, remains a great sounding board. Thank you to my golf buddy Tom Buccellato and his wife, Elizabeth, who made their South Bend home available to me. My friends Brian and Linda Barlaam and Karen and Ken Ferleger have been there when I needed to push away from the laptop.

For more than three years, my wife, Meg Murray, and our daughters, Sarah and Elizabeth, indulged me by pretending to hang on every word of my Leahy anecdotes. I read the room and kept talking anyway. Meg is a wonderful cheerleader, a skill she pursued at neither Nottingham High nor Cornell University, as well as a life partner who makes me feel fortunate every day. Our son, Max, died a decade ago. I'd love to know who he would be. We miss him so.

NOTES

Chapter One: A Name in a Record Book

Buck Shaw took himself out: Buck Shaw, *The Life and Sportsmanship of the Legendary Football Coach,* Kevin Carroll, McFarland & Company, 2022, 108–109.

"I was a contemporary": Arch Ward, *Frank Leahy and the Fighting Irish,* G. P. Putnam Sons, 1944, 217.

"In the old culture": Lance Morrow, "When Time's 'Man of the Year' Meant Something," *Wall Street Journal,* Dec. 2, 2022.

pegged the high-water mark: Mark S. Massa, *Catholics and American Culture,* Herder & Herder, 1999, 10.

The testimonial dinner: Robert J. and Mary M. McBride, "The Story of Bob & Mary," unpublished memoir, 2013, 224.

Telegrams poured in: David Condon, "In the Wake of the News," *Chicago Tribune,* Feb. 3, 1969.

"The reason Red didn't show up": Quotes from Lujack, Lucian, Butts, Leahy derive from story by Joe Doyle, "Leahy's Lads Pay 'Master' Tribute," *South Bend Tribune,* Feb. 1, 1969.

"Have I really been there?": *Congressional Record,* House of Representatives, Jan. 9, 1969, 367.

Chapter Two: Vow on the Spot

The details of Frank Leahy's childhood: The family history is derived from these self-published books: Carol Bennett, *Peter Robinson's Settlers,* Global Heritage Press, 2011; Rosemary McConkey and Suzanne Allen, *Call Back Yesterday: The Allen Family History,* 2013; and Gene Leahy's undated family memoir, used here with the permission of his daughter, Marie J. Leahy Knudtson. The latter, much of it typed single-spaced on business letterhead, appears to be a principal source of much of Leahy's childhood as presented in Arch Ward's 1944 book *Frank Leahy and the Fighting Irish.*

His younger sister: Maury White, "Frank Leahy's Success Story Got Early Start," *Des Moines Register,* June 29, 1973.

"I never got much": Frank Leahy, "Paying the Price," ed. Edmond G. Addeo, unfinished memoir, 1965, Notre Dame Archives, 24.

"My dad would buy": Ed Fitzgerald, "Frank Leahy: The Enigma," *Sport,* Nov. 1949, reprinted in *The Glory of Notre Dame,* Fred Katz, ed., Bartholomew House, Ltd., 1971, 83.

As a boy: White, "Frank Leahy's Success Story."

"He was a brilliant person": Leahy and Addeo, "Paying the Price," 24.

"I thought my job": Leahy and Addeo, "Paying the Price," 6.

"What do they give you": Charles G. Johnson, "Pop Leahy Frowned on Grid Pretty Boys," *The Tidings*, Oct. 15, 1954, 18.

Mr. Leahy backed down: "Charlie Long Puts Ray Carter Away in the Fifth Round," *The Frontier* (O'Neill, NE), July 10, 1924.

"As soon as the bell rang": Leahy and Addeo, "Paying the Price," 11.

More than three decades later: "Leahy's Fight Career Ended in '21", *The Frontier* (O'Neill, NE), Sept. 13, 1956.

"Perhaps my reputation": Leahy and Addeo, "Paying the Price," 14.

"I suppose that resentment": Leahy and Addeo, "Paying the Price," 24.

"I know that Balfany": Leahy and Addeo, "Paying the Price," 7–9.

Chapter Three: A Certain Courage

"A man should always know": Leahy and Addeo, "Paying the Price," 22.

"I'll relate an incident": Gene Leahy, *Memoirs*, 18.

Chapter Four: Under Rock's Wing

"I do not have to leave": Gene Leahy, *Memoirs*, 18.

Not for nothing: Gene Leahy, *Memoirs*, 18.

Chapter Five: Seven Blocks, Two Jobs—and Floss

"By now I began to feel": Wells Twombly, *Shake Down the Thunder*, Chilton Book Co., 1974, 153.

In 1932, the average salary: Statistics of Income for 1932, U.S. Department of Treasury, 7.

"You fellows will never": Tim Cohane, *Great College Football Coaches of the Twenties and Thirties*, Arlington House, 1973, 61.

"I was so in love": Twombly, *Shake Down the Thunder*, 309.

"I was young in those days": Condon, "In the Wake of the News," *Chicago Tribune*, Oct. 27, 1971.

"Lombardi was just another player": Bill Mulflur, "Leahy Rates Johnny Lujack His Best Player at ND," *Oregon Journal*, Dec. 24, 1971.

In the late 1940s: Charlie Callahan, *NFL Pro Record and Rule Book*, Spink Publishing Company, 1948, 27.

Between coaching and selling: Ward, *Frank Leahy and the Fighting Irish*, 137.

"I always felt Leahy": Interview with David Zeitlin, *Time*, Sept. 20, 1946, file, New York Historical Society.

Chapter Six: Young, Scrappy, Tough, Brilliant

In December 1938: Red Smith, "Tale of Two Cities," *New York Herald Tribune*, Nov. 18, 1952.

A couple of years later: "'Mickey' Connolly Lauded for His Football Playing," *Norwalk Hour*, Feb. 11, 1941.

"I guessed that he would": Joe Doyle, *Blue & Gold Illustrated*, Nov. 9, 1987.

"He was young, scrappy, tough, brilliant": Mike Holovak, *Violence Every Sunday*, Coward-McCann, 1967, 24, 34.

Crowley once told: Lindsey Nelson, *Hello Everybody, I'm Lindsey Nelson*, Beech Tree Books/William Morrow, 1985, 330.

Leahy made a lot of changes: Victor O. Jones, "New 'Atmosphere' Aids Boston College Players in Gridiron Drilling," *Boston Globe*, Oct. 2, 1939.

He bunked with Druze: Jack Connor, *Leahy's Lads*, Diamond Communications, 1994, 8C.

Some schools had taken: "1939 Track Article," University of Wisconsin–Madison Athletic Department, https://uwbadgers.com/sports/2015/8/21/GEN_20140101918.aspx?id=918.

The year before: Al Williams, "Sideline Salvos," *Santa Barbara News-Press*, Oct. 22, 1938.

If Leahy pushed: *Tackling Jim Crow*, thesis by Kevin Gregg, Boston College Libraries, 2005.

In the second week: *The Heights*, Dec. 13, 1940.

The Boston College group: Tim Cohane, *New York World-Telegram*, Dec. 12, 1940.

"It's embarrassing to talk about": Marty Mulé, *Sugar Bowl: The First Fifty Years*, Oxmoor House, 1983.

"There can never be": Holovak, *Violence Every Sunday*, 31.

Nearly 50 years later: Glenn Stout, "Jim Crow, Halfback," *Boston Magazine*, December 1987.

"We had nightmares": Jerry Nason, "The Leahy Chuckin' Charlie Remembers," *Boston Globe*, June 24, 1973.

"Team looked too good": Andrew Kozar, ed., *Football as a War Game*, Falcon Press, 2002, 282.

"the best team I ever had": Henry Super, UPI, "Tennessee, Boston College Take Great Teams to Bowl," *Green Bay Press-Gazette*, Dec. 26, 1940.

Leahy named it: Mulé, *Sugar Bowl*, 43–44.

When the team left: Condon, "In the Wake of the News," *Chicago Tribune*, June 24, 1973.

"they were a different ball club": Mulé, *Sugar Bowl*, 44–45.

"Can you imagine": Mulé, *Sugar Bowl*, 45; Beano Cook, *ESPN College Football Podcast*, Sept. 8, 2010.

When the train pulled into: Bill Doherty, *The Heights*, Oct. 5, 1956.

Chapter Seven: A Dream Realized, Messily

More to the point: Thomas B. Littlewood, *Arch: A Promoter, Not a Poet: The Story of Arch Ward*, Iowa State Press, 1990, xi, 106.

"an unusual step to take": Francis Wallace, *Notre Dame: Its People and Its Legends*, D. McKay Co., 1969, 175–176.

"We lost 16": Thad Holt, "Pooley Hubert Defends 'Bama at Dinner Here," *Atlanta Constitution*, Jan. 18, 1941, 9.

had enough prominence: Peg Boland, *Joe Boland: Notre Dame Man*, NSP Publishing, 1962.

But another Layden assistant: Beano Cook, *ESPN College Football Podcast*, Sept. 8, 2010.

the resentment lingered: David Zeitlin, *Time*, interview with Curley, filed to *Time*, Sept. 26, 1946, New York Historical Society.

"When Coach Leahy went": Pat Sullivan interview, Mashpee, MA, Aug. 18, 2023.

Chapter Eight: No One Will Ever Outgame These Boys

Leahy learned quickly: McBride, "The Story of Bob & Mary," 149–150.

A practice field dusted: Jerry Nason, "Leahy Starts Reign in Irish Gym Where He Played Janitor," *Boston Globe*, March 12, 1941.

In his small office: Edward W. "History at the Gold Dome," *Boston Herald-American*, March 29, 1941.

Six weeks after his hiring: Nason, "Leahy Starts Reign."

"At the end of next season": Charles L. Egenroad, "Cavanaugh and Coach Leahy Address Elks at Banquet," *South Bend Tribune*, March 12, 1941.

"All of us pulling together": Ward, *Frank Leahy and the Fighting Irish*, 169–171.

The assistants eyeballed: McBride, "The Story of Bob & Mary," 47–48.

"My coaching staff": Connor, *Leahy's Lads*, 10.

"the most photographed man": Jerry Nason, "Leahy Says He'll Pattern N.D. Play After Eagles'," *Boston Globe*, March 13, 1941.

In response to the deluge: Jack Ledden, "Seen and Heard in the Sports Realm," *South Bend Tribune*, March 26, 1941.

At one point during spring ball: Ledden, "Seen and Heard in the Sports Realm," April 27, 1941.

Every new head coach: McBride, "The Story of Bob & Mary," 44–46.

"No one wanted to get cut": Moose Krause and Steven Singular, *Notre Dame's Greatest Coaches*, Simon & Schuster, 1993, 70–71.

"You're pretty soft": Bill Cunningham, *Boston Post*, June 3, 1941.

Lillis slimmed: Eugene "Scrapiron" Young, *With Rockne at Notre Dame*, G. P. Putnam's Sons, 1951, 240.

"It taught us": McBride, "The Story of Bob & Mary," 49.

"At Boston College": Earl Hilligan, Associated Press, "Leahy May Throw Game Wide Open," *Alexandria Daily Town Talk*, March 13, 1941.

Leahy shifted the positions: Connor, *Leahy's Lads*, 8.

Leahy's emphasis: Jack Ledden, "11 Touchdowns Registered During Irish Scrimmage," *South Bend Tribune*, March 30, 1941.

"I thought my basketball practices": Swen Nater, *You Haven't Taught Until They Have Learned*, Fitness Information Technology, 2005.

After the team worked out: McBride, "The Story of Bob & Mary," 48.

The Notre Dame track and field team: Dave Hicks, "Frank Leahy Without Peer," *Arizona Republic*, June 24, 1973.

"by a sophomore left halfback": Ledden, "11 Touchdowns Registered."

Leahy had tried to recruit: Connor, *Leahy's Lads*, 17.

"I'd heard that McKeever": T. Nicholas Dawidoff, "A Half-Season Heisman," *Sports Illustrated*, Dec. 7, 1987.

So of course it was McKeever: Whitney Martin, Associated Press, "Leahy Must Take Spot Among Top '41 Coaches," *Atlanta Constitution*, Nov. 13, 1941.

"It was extremely important": McBride, "The Story of Bob & Mary," 52.

Leahy had attempted: Doyle, *Blue & Gold Illustrated*, Nov. 9, 1987.

"He must grapple": Bob Considine, *Washington Post*, Sept. 12, 1941.

"Memories can't block": *Washington Post*, Oct. 8, 1941.

He told quarterback Harry Wright: Jim Beach and David Moore, *The Big Game*, Random House, 1948, 225–226.

"Look me in the eyes": McBride, "The Story of Bob & Mary," 81; Connor, *Leahy's Lads*, 26.

"Like everything else": *Football: The Great Years*, 1966 documentary, produced/directed by Art Lieberman and produced by Frank Morriss, PeriscopeFilm.com.

Chapter Nine: The Guinea-Pig Team

"When a man is young": Bill Lee, "With Malice Toward None," *Hartford Courant*, March 20, 1954.

"You are the finest passer": Twombly, *Shake Down the Thunder*, 226.

"We practiced hours": Bud Maloney, *Blue & Gold Illustrated*, preseason issue, 1992, 42.

"Which eye": McBride, "The Story of Bob & Mary," 53–54.

The war permeated: Robert E. Burns, *Being Catholic, Being American*, University of Notre Dame Press, 1999, 219.

"Johnny didn't throw": Mulflur, "Leahy Rates Johnny Lujack."

Lujack's memory: Twombly, *Shake Down the Thunder*, 235.

"an unsolicited appointment": John H. Whoric, "Sportorials," *Daily Courier* (Connellsville, PA), June 8, 1942.

"at first denied": John M. Taylor, *General Maxwell Taylor: The Sword and the Pen*, Doubleday, 1989, 152–153.

"I didn't think": Fayette (PA) County Sports Hall of Fame, http://fayettecountysports halloffame.com/hall.html.

"It was a shock": Mort Berry, "Dove, Notre Dame 'Immortal,'" *Philadelphia Inquirer*, August 5, 1948.

One discovery he made: Connor, *Leahy's Lads*, 56.

"That football team had to learn": McBride, "The Story of Bob & Mary," 54.

Shortly before kickoff: Hank Casserly, "Badgers Tie Irish, 7–7," *Capital Times*, Sept. 27, 1942.

Leahy blamed it on: Associated Press, "N.D. Victory Cheers Leahy, Ailing Coach," *South Bend Tribune*, Oct. 11, 1942.

When he had suffered: Ward, *Frank Leahy and the Fighting Irish*, 186–187.

listening to his team's games: Jim Costin, "Jim Costin Says . . . ," *South Bend Tribune*, Oct. 30, 1942.

Wright also had developed: Letter, Fr. John Cavanaugh to Leahy, Jan. 30, 1943, Notre Dame Archives.

the official version of events: Jim Costin, "Irish Curtail '43 Football Schedule," *South Bend Tribune*, March 8, 1943.

"I have never seen": Louis Banks, *Time* correspondent file, Sept. 25, 1946, New York Historical Society.

Al Masters still held: Memo, Father Hesburgh to Father Cavanaugh, May 1, 1952, Notre Dame Archives.

The rivalry didn't resume: Dick Hyland, "The Hyland Fling," *Los Angeles Times*, Aug. 14, 1946.

After this procedure: Ward, *Frank Leahy and the Fighting Irish*, 187.

Leahy's description: Costin, "Jim Costin Says...".

One fourth-stringer: Connor, *Leahy's Lads*, 47.

"Against the Seahawks": Maloney, *Blue & Gold Illustrated*, 1992 preseason issue, 1992, 42.

"a good case of the miseries": William Gildea and Christopher Dennison, *The Fighting Irish: Notre Dame Through the Years*, Prentice-Hall, 1976, 71.

"worried himself into": Jack Cuddy, "Today's Sports Parade," United Press, Nov. 6, 1943.

In Yost's later years: John Kryk, *Natural Enemies*, Taylor Trade, 2004, 119–123.

"that kind of football": Banks, *Time* file, Sept. 25, 1946.

"Frank was so technically superior": Twombly, *Shake Down the Thunder*, 245.

Cavanaugh also urged: Francis Wallace, *Notre Dame from Rockne to Parseghian*, D. McKay Co., 1967, 97–100.

Chapter Ten: Wartime

"Notre Dame, like all other": George V. Kelly, "Leahy Emphasizes Value of Football to Notre Dame U.," *Wichita Catholic Advance*, Mar. 12, 1943.

"Coach Leahy and his staff": McBride, "The Story of Bob & Mary," 57.

"He made it a point": Twombly, *Shake Down the Thunder*, 238.

the Navy's huge presence: Paul Fussell, *Wartime*, Oxford University Press, 1989, 53.

"I always felt": Kryk, *Natural Enemies*, 2007, 161.

"The boys then went out": Jim Costin, "U.S. Rating Baffles N.D. Players," *South Bend Tribune*, Nov. 25, 1943.

"I was crying one moment": *Blue & Gold Illustrated*, August 1987.

"No inch was an easy one": Elliot Cushing, "A Closeup of Frank Leahy, The Man," *Rochester Democrat & Chronicle*, Dec. 1, 1943.

Maybe that softened: Don Hassett, "Leahy 'Sells' Irish, Football; Rejoices Over Fourth Crown," *Rochester Democrat & Chronicle*, Dec. 7, 1943.

A submarine that dived: Max Hastings, *Retribution*, Alfred A. Knopf, 2007, 269–271.

Were it not for the cooling effect: Admiral I. J. Galantin, *Take Her Deep!*, Algonquin Books of Chapel Hill, 1987, 121.

"The closest I ever came to a battle": Associated Press, "Leahy Optimistic About Notre Dame's Football Outlook for This Year," *Berkshire Evening Eagle*, Feb. 22, 1946.

Leahy spent time at Pearl Harbor: Jim Costin, "Leahy, Home, Says G.I.s Need Sports," *South Bend Tribune*, Jan. 14, 1945.

"I took him to the officers' club": Krause and Singular, *Notre Dame's Greatest Coaches*, 75.

As luck would have it: Tim Prister, *Blue & Gold Illustrated*, July 18, 1983.

"Commander Leahy would like": Paul Zimmerman, *Sports Illustrated*, Nov. 24, 1997; and Bud Maloney, *Blue & Gold Illustrated*, Sept. 21, 1992.

"I'm just looking": Dick Hyland, *Los Angeles Times*, quoted in "Sporting Comment," *Kansas City Star*, July 17, 1946.

"an old friend": Paul Gardner, "The Mad Maestro of Football," *American Legion Magazine*, Sept. 1947, 59.

"I pledge that to Our Lady": Littlewood, *Arch*, 156–157.

"listening to the radio": Red Smith, "Well, Well, Well, Leahy Sees Trouble Ahead," *New York Herald Tribune*, Nov. 5, 1946.

"He asked if he could sit down": Bud Maloney, *Blue & Gold Illustrated*, May 1992, 25.

he signed a 10-year contract: Wallace, *Notre Dame from Rockne to Parseghian*, 102.

This was Army and Notre Dame: Bill Pennington, "Army–Notre Dame Stirs Yankee Stadium's Ghosts," *New York Times*, Nov. 16, 2010.

Chapter Eleven: Army Is Out There

"If young McBride fails": Sid Keener, "Football Outlook Hazy at Notre Dame for 1946," *St. Louis Star-Times*, Sept. 18, 1946.

Leahy arrived with a football: Tim Cohane, "Frank Leahy... The Classic Gridiron Battler," *The Sporting News*, June 27, 1970.

"It was easier to get into the Kremlin": "To See or Not to See the Irish," *Sports Illustrated*, July 30, 1956.

When the university constructed: Jim Murray, *Time* magazine correspondent file, Oct. 29, 1953.

Leahy scraped off a little rust: Don Stull, Associated Press, "South Defeats North 26–21 in All-Star Grid Game," *Massillon Evening Independent*, Aug. 17, 1946.

The Ziggy stories: Connor, *Leahy's Lads*, 186.

Leahy looked the other way: Michael Haggerty, *Blue & Gold Illustrated*, Nov. 21, 1983.

At several points over the next four years: Steve Delsohn, *Talking Irish*, William Morrow, 1998, 27–28.

That's not the only scouting: Delsohn, interview of George Connor, *Talking Irish*, 30.

"Lads, we all know": Delsohn, *Talking Irish*, 29.

As the train headed east: Jack Sher, *Sport*, October 1947.

"I don't see any reason": Dick Hyland, *Los Angeles Times*, Nov. 9, 1946.

"Army is out there.": Wallace, *Notre Dame from Rockne to Parseghian*, 108.

The story went that: Ed Fitzgerald, "Glamour? Spell It L-u-j-a-c-k," *Sport*, Dec. 1951, reprinted in *The Glory of Notre Dame*, Katz, 119.

When the writers left: Krause and Singular, *Notre Dame's Greatest Coaches*, 77–78.

"Then he said out loud": Delsohn, *Talking Irish*, 31.

Something similar happened: Tom Dennin, *Blue & Gold Illustrated*, Feb. 1993, 24.

There the story would end: Red Smith, "The Story of Coy McGee," *New York Herald Tribune*, Nov. 24, 1949.

"Who the hell is this": Twombly, *Shake Down the Thunder*, 48.

One writer called: Davis J. Walsh, International News Service, *Washington Post*, Dec. 7, 1946.

A few days before the 1946 game: Taylor, *General Maxwell Taylor*, 153.

If the generals thought: Earl H. Blaik with Tim Cohane, *You Have to Pay the Price*, Holt, Rinehart and Winston, 1960, 239.

"At a football banquet": Rev. J. J. Cavanaugh, CSC, "Danger of Gambling Not Involved in Notre Dame–Army Game Break," *The Tidings*, January 17, 1947.

Chapter Twelve: A Look in the Mirror

"a fine year of Catholic action": *Time*, "The Theater," Jan. 6, 1947.

"I want to stay": Associated Press, "Leahy Visits His Home Town," *Rapid City Journal*, June 14, 1947.

"Father Cavanaugh told me": Bill Mulflur, "10 Unbeaten Seasons? That Was Leahy's Goal," *Oregon Journal*, Dec. 25, 1971.

"Army will come out here": Zimmerman, *Sports Illustrated*, Nov. 24, 1997.

A trip to Purdue: Twombly, *Shake Down the Thunder*, 245.

The way that Terry Brennan explained: Zimmerman, *Sports Illustrated*, Nov. 24, 1997.

"If we can luck out": Red Smith, "Meditation, Prayer and Good Works," *New York Herald Tribune*, Nov. 4, 1947.

The total for Saturday: Callahan, *NFL Pro Record and Rule Book*, 60.

The rivalry had been played: Beach and Moore, *The Big Game*, 285–290.

Given the uneasy nature: Cohane, "Classic Gridiron Battler."

"For some reason": Mulflur, "Leahy Rates Johnny Lujack."

Leahy may have been: Maloney, *Blue & Gold Illustrated*, Sept. 21, 1992.

That's not what happened: Frank Graham, "Case Study of Frank Leahy," *New York Journal-American*, Oct. 27, 1953.

"I always found him": Joe Williams, *New York World-Telegram*, April 27, 1949.

The writer Francis Wallace: Wallace, *Notre Dame from Rockne to Parseghian*, 117.

Well, there was one other thing: Maloney, *Blue & Gold Illustrated*, Sept. 21, 1992.

Leahy, whether politicking: Zimmerman, *Sports Illustrated*, Nov. 24, 1997.

Crisler gave a statesmanlike: Associated Press, "Either Team Tops—Crisler," *Philadelphia Inquirer*, Jan. 7, 1948.

Chapter Thirteen: The Coach

Charlie Callahan once published: Callahan, *NFL Pro Record and Rule Book*, 65.

The priests who served: Buzz Bissinger, *The Mosquito Bowl*, Harper Perennial, 2023, 67.

"Run that over again": Beach and Moore, *The Big Game*, 284–285.

There's another word for this: Krause and Singular, *Notre Dame's Greatest Coaches*, 67–68, 78.

As a freshman end: Krause and Singular, *Notre Dame's Greatest Coaches*, 108.

"While you were there": NFL Films, *Wake Up the Echoes*.

more than any human being: McBride, "The Story of Bob & Mary," 112.

"The only way": Leahy and Addeo, "Paying the Price," 2–3.

Practice began at 3:30: McBride, "The Story of Bob & Mary," 41.

"I only know": Leahy and Addeo, "Paying the Price," 13.

"Men, this may be": Gardner, "Mad Maestro of Football."

"I learned more about tackling": Dave Gallup, "It Was a Pleasure," *South Bend Tribune*, Nov. 28, 1948.

Top coaches in the New York area: Jesse Abramson, "300 at Opening of Football Coaching School Hear Leahy Outline Duties, Technique," *New York Herald Tribune*, Aug. 26, 1941.

If Leahy wandered over: Zimmerman, *Sports Illustrated*, Nov. 24, 1997.

The coach blocked: Delsohn, *Talking Irish*, 47–48.

"The university owes you": McBride, "The Story of Bob & Mary," 41.

Leahy warned his players: McBride, "The Story of Bob & Mary," 44–45.

Art Donovan played football: Arthur J. Donovan Jr. and Bob Drury, *Fatso*, William Morrow, 1987, 94.

When Lujack went: Jeff Davis, *Papa Bear*, McGraw-Hill, 2004, 221.

When Leahy signed Lujack: Bill Diehl, "Leahy, Stepping Out as ND Athletic Director, Won't Leave," *Norfolk Ledger-Star*, Jan. 19, 1949.

Schroyer enrolled: "Ex-Gridder Badly Hurt," *Pittsburgh Post-Gazette*, Sept. 25, 1944.

The coaches told the players: McBride, "The Story of Bob & Mary," 42.

He encouraged his players: William Brashler, "The Hard Fate of a Zealous Man," *Notre Dame Magazine*, Oct. 1983.

"Don't start tomorrow": McBride, "The Story of Bob & Mary," 45.

No coach ever worked: Associated Press, April 3, 1947.

He had quarterbacks: *Time*, "T-Secrets," Sept. 19, 1949.

Leahy drilled the players: Ken Rappoport, *Wake Up the Echoes*, Strode Publishers, 1988, 211.

But that second nature: Zimmerman, *Sports Illustrated*, Nov. 24, 1997.

"The thing was": Nason, "Leahy Chuckin' Charlie Remembers."

Lujack said that Leahy: Hal Bock, Associated Press, "Leahy's Teams Recall His Legacy," *South Bend Tribune*, Dec. 17, 1995.

Leahy considered it: Clifford B. Ward, *Fort Wayne News-Sentinel*, May 7, 1947.

It's not fair to say: Frank Dolson, "How Many Sleepless Nights?" *Philadelphia Inquirer*, Dec. 20, 1979.

"Ah, Robert": Bud Maloney, *Blue & Gold Illustrated*, May 1993, 24.

a player came off the sideline: Eddie Dooley, "Football's Fair-Haired Boy," *Liberty Magazine*, July 3, 1941.

Mike Holovak, a fullback: Holovak, *Violence Every Sunday*, 33.

This story may be on the spectrum: Bill Dwyre, "Leahy Had Irish Stand Tall—Or Else," *Los Angeles Times*, Oct. 20, 2012.

When guard Joe Signaigo: Tim Weigel, *Chicago Daily News*, June 24, 1973.

"Hold it, everyone": Ledden, "Seen and Heard in the Sport Realm," *South Bend Tribune*, April 10, 1941.

Leahy simply reminded: Jim Murray, *Time* magazine correspondence file, Oct. 28, 1953.

Sometimes Leahy ran out of ideas: Joe McGuff, "Sporting Comment," *Kansas City Star*, June 24, 1973.

It may be true: Wallace, *Notre Dame from Rockne to Parseghian*, 137.

Dick Lynch recalled: Bock, "Leahy's Teams Recall."

In the industrial heartland: *The Jack Benny Show*, Dec. 7, 1947.

It was about this time: Jim Klobuchar, "Nobody Beat Frank and Saints," *Minneapolis Star*, June 22, 1973.

Leahy used to promote: Dooley, "Football's Fair-Haired Boy."

The NCAA didn't allow: McBride, "The Story of Bob & Mary," 169.

Occasionally there would be: Tim McBride interviews, Dec. 18, 2023, and Feb. 1, 2025.

Jim Crowley, Leahy's boss: Sid Ziff, "Leahy Bares Secret Self," *Los Angeles Mirror*, Sept. 24, 1954.

And yet Leahy found ways: Condon, "In the Wake of the News," *Chicago Tribune*, Feb. 3, 1969.

"I knew that had to be a great play": Condon, "In the Wake of the News," *Chicago Tribune*, Jan. 10, 1969.

Chapter Fourteen: The Grand Old Man

"a thousand times": Twombly, *Shake Down the Thunder*, 298.

He made sure every year: McBride, "The Story of Bob & Mary," 154–155.

A few weeks before: *Time*, "Fritz Quits," March 29, 1948.

"But I want to make it clear": Serrell Hillman, *Time* magazine file, Oct. 20, 1948.

"45 percent of fear": Hillman, *Time* file, October 21, 1948.

With a third consecutive: Maloney, *Blue & Gold Illustrated*, May 1993.

The official, Jimmy Cain: Scoop Kennedy, *New Orleans Item*, undated clipping, Notre Dame Archives.

The membership of the order: Fitzgerald, "The Enigma," *Glory of Notre Dame*, Katz, 87.

"It is an enormous honor": Bob Houser, "'I'll Coach No One But Irish,' Leahy Tells 1,200 at Banquet," *South Bend Tribune*, Jan. 21, 1949.

"He always seemed to give me": Charles G. Johnson, "Fred Miller Began Fatal Day with Mass, Communion," *Lake Shore Visitor*, Aug. 19, 1955.

"but you never know when a man's health": Ted Smits, Associated Press, "Leahy Weary but He'll Stay at Notre Dame," *Chicago Tribune*, June 13, 1949.

"I felt the press": Weigel, *Chicago Daily News*, June 24, 1973.

"We'll have the worst team": *Time*, "People," April 11, 1949.

Cavanaugh appointed: Interview, Father Wilson D. Miscamble, April 19, 2022.

"I learned later": Joe Williams, "Notre Dame Looks Forward to Great Year," *New York World-Telegram*, June 29, 1949.

"If you think a football game": Paul Neville, "Coach Leahy Demonstrates Versatility," *South Bend Tribune*, Sept. 2, 1949.

"He began to speak in a voice": Regis Philbin, *How I Got This Way*, It Books, 2011, 136.

The Notre Dame fans responded: *Notre Dame Alumnus*, Jan.–Feb. 1950, 12.

"Would you ask the president of Yale": Joel R. Connelly and Howard J. Dooley, *Hesburgh's Notre Dame*, Hawthorne Books, 1972, 19; and Doug Bedell, *Dallas Morning News*, April 15, 1987.

"I have some very good advice": Rappoport, *Wake Up the Echoes*, 282.

"All I could say": Mulflur, "10 Unbeaten Seasons?"

Chapter Fifteen: Getting Back Up Again . . . and Again

"We were young": Maloney, *Blue & Gold Illustrated*, May 1993.

"I'm convinced our winning streak": Inez Rabb, *New York Journal-American*, Aug. 7, 1950.

"if injuries set in": Jim Kelly, "Fighting Irish of 1950, In Spirit and in Truth," *Catholic Advance* (Wichita), Sept. 29, 1950.

"We will be just about even": Allison Danzig, "Humpty-Dumpty Act of Football's Big Teams Mars Pigskin Parade," *New York Times*, Oct. 2, 1950.

"Cut out the bullshit": Twombly, *Shake Down the Thunder*, 262.

"The pain was indescribable": Twombly, *Shake Down the Thunder*, 264.

He reflected his upbringing: Bob Callahan, ed., *Big Book of American Irish Culture*, Viking, 1987, 204–205.

"You sons-of-bitches": Delsohn, *Talking Irish*, 45–46.

So Alan Ameche stayed home: Doyle, *Blue & Gold Illustrated*, Oct. 27, 1986.

"If I hadn't picked Notre Dame": Paul Hornung, *Golden Boy*, Simon & Schuster, 2004, 34–35.

The administration agreed: McBride, "The Story of Bob & Mary," 167.

"Their boys didn't make a mistake": Shirley Povich, *Washington Post*, Nov. 13, 1951.

"gutless": Delsohn, *Talking Irish*, 49.

Floss called Father Hesburgh: Interview, former Notre Dame athletic director Jack Swarbrick, April 19, 2022.

"Coach didn't say much": Rick Blaine, *Go Irish!*, Oct. 11, 1982.

The university budget: Doyle, *Blue & Gold Illustrated*, August 1986.

"He is a distinctive person": Miscamble, interview, April 19, 2022.

Father Hesburgh had left town: James Carroll, "Eisenhowers' Smiles Set Couple Apart," *South Bend Tribune*, Sept. 15, 1952.

Eisenhower told the students: Associated Press, *Los Angeles Times*, Sept. 16, 1952; and Joe Doyle, "According to Doyle," *South Bend Tribune*, Sept. 16, 1952.

"Well, Charles": Brashler, "Hard Fate of a Zealous Man."

Mantle melted: Red Smith, "Mr. Leahy Meets Some Winners," *New York Herald Tribune*, Sept. 28, 1952.

Leahy retreated to his room: Dolson, "How Many Sleepless Nights?"

Texas athletic director: Kenneth Levenidos, John Lattner interview, IrishUnderground .com; and Bob Broeg, "Frank Leahy: Overlooked by Football Hall of Fame?" *St. Louis Post-Dispatch*, Feb. 8, 1970.

The Irish took the second-half kickoff: Fred Williams, "Statistics Tell Tale of Irish Victory but Leahy's Pep Talk Turning Point," *Austin American-Statesman*, Oct. 6, 1952.

"I didn't want the lads": Bob Broeg, "Leahy Won Like Rockne—But No Charisma," *St. Louis Post-Dispatch*, June 24, 1973.

"Oh, my goodness gracious": Interview, *Heisman Heroes*, ESPN, 1995.

"Coach made sure": McBride, "The Story of Bob & Mary," 170–171.

the fans remained in the stands: McBride, "The Story of Bob & Mary," 171.

"my greatest coaching thrill": Frank Leahy, with Tim Cohane, "Farewell to Notre Dame," *Look*, March 23, 1954.

Roberts: Dick Cullum, *Daily Oklahoman*, undated clipping, Notre Dame Archives.

"We were quick": Bud Maloney, *Blue & Gold Illustrated*, Oct. 26, 1992.

"You're a disgrace": Delsohn, *Talking Irish*, 51.

"The crowds had gradually become aware": Wallace, *Notre Dame from Rockne to Parseghian*, 148.

Chapter Sixteen: Cracking Fast

"it could be a lot worse": Leahy with Cohane, "Farewell to Notre Dame."

He played offense: Hornung, *Golden Boy*, 39.

"woefully weak in talent and numbers": Terry Brennan and William Meiners, *Though the Odds Be Great or Small*, Loyola Press, 2021, 26.

Chapter Seventeen: Farewell and Thank You

a similar joke: Gerald Holland, "Subject: Frank Leahy," *Sports Illustrated*, Oct. 31, 1955.

Chapter Eighteen: The People-Pleaser

"I always knew": Leahy and Addeo, "Paying the Price," 19.

Television wanted him: Charles G. Johnson, "The Sports Front," *The Tidings*, Oct. 2, 1953, 35.

The agent for Lucille Ball: "Leahy Puts Spirit in Movie Series," *North Hollywood Valley Times*, May 4, 1954; and "Judge" Carberry, "The Sports Front," *The Tidings*, June 18, 1954.

Leahy brought Bob McBride with him: McBride, "The Story of Bob & Mary," 193.

"I predict that 10 years": Ziff, "Leahy Bares Secret Self."

"especially since Terry's lads played so well": Johnson, "Leahy Frowned on Grid Pretty Boys."

"you can say what you want": Delsohn, *Talking Irish*, 70–72; and Maloney, *Blue & Gold Illustrated*, Oct. 26, 1992.

"They didn't want me anymore": Delsohn, *Talking Irish*, 62.

Frank postponed again: Leahy and Addeo, "Paying the Price," 41.

The Miller Brewing plane: Tim John, *The Miller Beer Barons*, Badger Books, 2005, 336.

"very, very fine gentleman": *Wall Street Journal*, March 28, 1955.

Wolfson, devoted to Georgia: *Saturday Evening Post*, July 24, 1954, via *Super Lou!*, by Marcia Wolfson, Waterside Press, 2017.

"I felt like a true patriot": Twombly, *Shake Down the Thunder*, 36.

"I've never felt better": United Press, "Leahy OKs 3-Year Pact to Coach Texas A&M," Dec. 26, 1957.

"The pressure was terrific": Holland, "Subject: Frank Leahy."

"I guess I'll never live that down": Joe Williams, *New York World-Telegram*, Nov. 6, 1958.

"I sincerely believe": Brashler, "Hard Fate of a Zealous Man."

"He considered it a slap": Twombly, *Shake Down the Thunder*, 299.

"You never talked that way": Jerry Liska, Associated Press, "Football Fever Hits Notre Dame," *Decatur Daily Review* (IL), Oct. 27, 1964.

"if it's God's last act": Associated Press, "Leahy's Stock Deal Suspect," *St. Joseph Gazette*, July 27, 1961.

Chapter Nineteen: A Great American Family

"the first time in history": Broeg, "Overlooked by Football Hall of Fame?"

"Those virtues I talk about": Twombly, *Shake Down the Thunder*, 11.

the university that he never stopped loving: Krause and Singular, *Notre Dame's Greatest Coaches*, 113.

INDEX